CHALLENGING THE STATE: DEVOLUTION AND THE BATTLE FOR PARTISAN CREDIBILITY

COMPARATIVE POLITICS

Comparative Politics is a series for students, teachers, and researchers of political science that deals with contemporary government and politics. Global in scope, books in the series are characterized by a stress on comparative analysis and strong methodological rigour. The series is published in association with the European Consortium for Political Research. For more information visit www.ecprnet.eu

The Comparative Politics series is edited by Professor David M. Farrell, School of Politics and International Relations, University College Dublin, Kenneth Carty, Professor of Political Science, University of British Columbia, and Professor Dirk Berg-Schlosser, Institute of Political Science, Philipps University, Marburg.

OTHER TITLES IN THIS SERIES

Challenging the State: Devolution and the Battle for Partisan Credibility

A Comparison of Belgium, Italy, Spain, and the United Kingdom

SONIA ALONSO

OXFORD
UNIVERSITY PRESS

OXFORD
UNIVERSITY PRESS

Great Clarendon Street, Oxford, OX2 6DP,
United Kingdom

Oxford University Press is a department of the University of Oxford.
It furthers the University's objective of excellence in research, scholarship,
and education by publishing worldwide. Oxford is a registered trade mark of
Oxford University Press in the UK and in certain other countries

British Library Cataloguing in Publication Data
Data available

Library of Congress Cataloging in Publication Data
Alonso, Sonia.
Challenging the state : devolution and the battle for partisan credibility : a comparison
of Belgium, Italy, Spain and the United Kingdom / Sonia Alonso.
p. cm.
Includes bibliographical references and index.
ISBN 978–0–19–969157–9 (hardback)
1. Decentralization in government–Europe–Case studies.   2. Political parties–Europe–
Case studies.   3. Elections–Europe–Case studies.   4. Electoral geography–Europe–
Case studies.   I. Title.
JN50.A57 2012   320.8094–dc23   2012006934

ISBN 978–0–19–969157–9

Printed in Great Britain
on acid-free paper by
MPG Books Group, Bodmin and King's Lynn

Links to third party websites are provided by Oxford in good faith and
for information only. Oxford disclaims any responsibility for the materials
contained in any third party website referenced in this work.

To my father, Manuel

Contents

Acknowledgements

Despite being a solitary activity, the writing of a book does not happen in a vacuum. There are persons and institutions to which I am gratefully indebted for their support during this time. First of all, I would like to thank the Social Science Research Centre Berlin (WZB) for providing me with an encouraging, resourceful, and supportive work environment. I would like to mention, in particular, the head of my department, Wolfgang Merkel, for his willingness to give me the time, the autonomy, and the confidence that I needed to proceed with my work without distractions from other—more 'worldly'—responsibilities inside the department. My colleagues at the WZB have also been a major source of encouragement and support. Collectively, they have endured with infinite patience the discussion of various versions of the book at least once a year in our research-in-progress seminars, offering me a lot of feedback that contributed to improving the manuscript. Individually, I would like to mention some colleagues to whom I am particularly indebted. Andrea Volkens introduced me to the Comparative Manifestos Project (since 2009 renamed MARPOR—Manifesto Research on Political Representation), a fundamental source of empirical evidence for the book; Heiko Giebler and Dag Tanneberg helped me with the intricacies of statistics and Stata; Katarina Pollner was always there to solve problems with graphs and figures; and Gudrun Mouna was a permanent source of sensible editorial advice and also emotional support. I would also like to thank those WZB colleagues who read parts of the manuscript and from whose detailed comments I have so much benefited: Bernhard Wessels, Ramón Feenstra, and Cristóbal Rovira.

The Center for Advanced Study in the Social Sciences of the Juan March Institute has been a second home in the production of this book. Not only did I receive support in the use of its library and data files (in particular, those dealing with the Spanish and Italian cases), for which I am most grateful to Paz Fernández (library's Director) and Pacho Sánchez-Cuenca (Director of CEACS), but I always found there a community of researchers who encouraged me with ideas, discussions, and comments. I would like to mention Rubén Ruiz-Rufino, from whom I have learned so much about electoral systems and their consequences and who has made so many helpful comments of several draft chapters; Sandra León and Luis de la Calle, who also read some draft chapters and provided me with very helpful feedback; and my colleague and friend Andrew Richards, who has supported me throughout the writing of the book in so many ways, with critical comments, with sources of information and data, with editorial advice, with my English, and above all with his friendship. The Juan March Institute has also been the institutional host of a research project—the Regional Manifestos Project—which emerged as a side-product during the writing of the book in order to fill in a gap in data collection (parties' positions in sub-state electoral arenas). Braulio Gómez and Laura Cabeza started this project with me. Our constant discussions about how to translate the Comparative Manifestos Project's methodology to the analysis of the centre–periphery cleavage in sub-state political arenas has helped me greatly in my understanding of this complex political dimension and in defining ways to tackle it empirically. I am also grateful to Braulio for reading and commenting on draft versions of some chapters.

I am particularly indebted, as ever, to José María Maravall. If there is anything of value in this book I owe it to him, for teaching me that a good social scientist is one who asks the right questions, not one who has—or who thinks he or she has—all the answers. With him I learned (at least I tried to learn) to be a conscientious and honest researcher, not to rush to conclusions, and to take other people's critical comments seriously. He read the whole manuscript at least twice, and made all sorts of comments and criticisms that I was not always happy to hear but which turned out to be absolutely right.

I have left for the end the most personal acknowledgments—those to my family. Alessandro, Marina, and Lucía have endured the process of writing this book with large amounts of patience, tolerance, and also with a lot of humour. They have invented all sorts of names for my constant absent-mindedness, for my changing moods, for my absences from home, and for my apparent schizo-phrenia—one day claiming that the book is going very well while the next day asserting, with equal conviction, that it is a complete disaster. My father, Manuel, has been a constant source of external support, a babysitter of last resort, and always a yes-person, whatever the request. The book has been part of our family agenda for three years. I am profoundly indebted to them for giving me the emotional anchorage to carry it to an end. This book is dedicated to them and, most particularly, to my father.

List of Figures

List of Tables

List of Abbreviations

ACW	Algemeen Christeijk Werkersuerbond (Christian Workers' Movement)
AN	Alleanza Nazionale
ATF	aggregated threshold function
BNG	Bloque Nacionalista Galego
BSP-PSB	Belgische Socialistische Partij-Parti Socialiste Belge
CC	Coalición Canaria
CDH	Center Démocrate Humaniste
CD&V	Christen-Democratisch en Vlaams
CGOS	central-government-office-seeking
CHA	Chunta Aragonesista
CIS	Centro de Investigaciones Sociológicas
CiU	Covergència i Unió
CMP	Comparative Manifestos Project
CVP-PSC	Christeijk Volkspartij-Parti Social Chrétien
DC	Democrazia Cristiana
DS	Democratici di Sinistra
DUP	Democratic Unionist Party
EA	Eusko Alkartasuna
EE	Euskadiko Ezkerra
ERC	Esquerra Republicana de Catalunya
FDF	Front Démocratique des Francophones
FI	Forza Italia
FN	Front National
HB	Herri Batasuna
ICV	Iniciativa per Catalunya Verds
IU	Izquierda Unida
KPB-PCB	Kommistische Partij van België-Parti Communiste de Belgique
LN	Lega Nord
LP-PL	Liberal Party-Parti Libéral
MR	Mouvement Réformateur

MSI	Movimento Sociale Italiano
NILP	Northern Ireland Labour Party
N-VA	Nieu-Vlaamse Alliantie
PA	Partido Andalucista
PAR	Partido Aragonés Regionalista
PC	Plaid Cymru
PCE	Partido Comunista de España
PCI	Partito Comunista Italiano
PDS	Partito Democratico della Sinistra
PNV	Partido Nacionalista Vasco
POS	Position, Ownership, and Saliency model
PP	Partido Popular
PPI	Partito Popolare Italiano
PRC	Partito della Rifondazoine Comunista
PRL	Parti Réformateur Libéral
PSC	Partit des Socialistes de Catalunya
Psd'A	Partito Sardo d'Azione
PSOE	Partido Socialista Obrero Español
PVV	Partij voor Vrijheid en Vooruitgang
RGOS	regional-government-office-seeking
RW	Rassemblement Wallon
SDLP	Social Democratic and Labour Party
SF	Sinn Féin
SNP	Scottish National Party
SP-A Spirit	Socialistische Partij Anders
	Sociaal-Liberale Partij
SVP	Südtiroler Volkspartei
UCD	Unión de Centro Democrático
UPN	Unión del Pueblo Navarro
UUP	Ulster Unionist Party
UV	Union Valdôtaine
VB	Vlaams Berlang (previously Vlaams Blok)
VLD	Open Vlaamse Liberalen en Democraten
VU	Volksunie

1

The Centre–Periphery Conflict
and Two Paradoxes

Peripheral parties defend intrinsically territorial demands: they want political control over the peripheral territory that they claim to represent. According to their view, this territory is, by history and culture, different to the rest of the state territory and, therefore, should be treated as different and should be allowed to remain different. The ideology of peripheral parties, in its most extreme form, defends the secession of the peripheral territory from the state. The tremendous electoral growth of peripheral parties in Europe since the Second World War indicates the receptivity of demands for cultural and political autonomy or independence among the electorate and the increased relevance of territorial conflicts in electoral competition (Amoretti and Bermeo 2004; De Winter, Gómez-Reino, et al. 2006; Tronconi 2006; Brancati 2007; Alonso 2008).

Peripheral diversity, unlike religious, class, or ethnic diversity, poses a threat to the territorial integrity of the state. For this reason, the electoral growth of peripheral parties is often viewed as a challenge for representative democracy. The puzzle to be solved is how to deal democratically with the demands of peripheral parties in such a way that the political and institutional measures taken to appease them—and thereby avoid the secessionist threat—do not, at the same time, strengthen them and help them succeed in their separatist intentions (Kymlicka 1998; Erk and Anderson 2009; Sorens 2009). One measure widely used by governments all over the globe, is regional autonomy or devolution. The paradox of devolution is that, while it is intended to appease the secessionist threat, it also offers peripheral parties the instruments to push it ahead.

This book will be able to add something to this debate although its main objective is not to solve the paradox of devolution but to understand the political rationale behind it. Why do some parties defend it while others fiercely oppose it? Why do some parties defend it in the present when they rejected it in the past or vice versa? What pushes governments to initiate a devolution reform despite its obvious risks? Why does devolution not stop peripheral demands but encourages, instead, new rounds of decentralization? My answer to all these questions is the following: electoral competition between state and peripheral parties pushes some state parties to prefer devolution at some particular point in time. Devolution is an electoral strategy adopted in order to make it more difficult in the long term for peripheral parties to increase their electoral support by claiming the monopoly of representation of the peripheral territory and the people in it. The strategy of devolution is preferred over short-term tactics of convergence towards the peripheral programmatic agenda because the pro-periphery moves of state parties in unitary centralized states are not credible in the eyes of voters. The price that state parties pay for making their electoral moves credible is the 'entrenchment' of the devolution programmatic agenda in the electoral arena.

The final implication of this argument is that in democratic systems, i.e. in countries where parties that want to rule need to establish electoral majorities that will put them in office, devolution is not a decision to protect the state from the secessionist threat. It is, instead, a decision by state parties to protect their needed electoral majorities. Whether devolution endangers or guarantees the territorial integrity of the state is of secondary importance for vote-maximizing state parties. Only when the protection of the state's territorial integrity fully coincides with the aim of achieving an electoral majority do state parties care about protecting the state.

1.1 THE RELEVANCE OF THE CENTRE–PERIPHERY CONFLICT IN EUROPE

Since the origins of the centre–periphery cleavage, which date back to the period of formation of the European nation-states and of the democratic and industrial revolutions of the nineteenth century (Lipset and Rokkan 1967; Rokkan and Urwin 1983), the growth of peripheral parties has happened in waves, with intermittent periods of growth, stagnation, and decline. After the first successful mobilization in the 1880s and 1890s, authors do not agree as to the exact number of subsequent waves of peripheral party growth, although most concede that the 1960s and 1970s was a period of high mobilization (Urwin 1983; Mair 1990; Tiryakian 1994; Newman 2000). Some authors believe that the inter-war period also represents a mobilization peak (Hebbert 1987; Newman 1996) while others argue that the end of the late 1980s and early 1990s are years of 'ethnic revival' (Türsan 1998; De Winter, Gómez-Reino, and Lynch 2006). During these waves of mobilization new peripheral parties have emerged while others have disappeared. Nevertheless, parties of recent creation are as much peripheral parties as those of old historical pedigree (Rokkan and Urwin 1983: 125–7).

The way in which most scholars have dealt empirically with peripheral parties' programmatic issues is to subsume these issues under something else, usually a 'materialist–post-materialist dimension' of party competition (Warwick 2002), also called a 'new politics' dimension (Laver and Budge 1992), considered by some to be the second most relevant after the ideological left–right dimension.

These types of analyses share the perspective of those who associate peripheral parties with new social movements that defend new values and post-materialist issues (Melucci and Diani 1992; Müller-Rommel 1994; Van Atta 2003). Thus, the territorial conflict that is at the heart of the centre–periphery cleavage is interpreted as belonging to another conflict dimension and as not relevant enough to deserve an individual treatment.

This is at best a misrepresentation of the cleavage structure in culturally heterogeneous societies. Peripheral parties certainly use the 'new politics' rhetoric as part of their strategic repertoire. However, this does not mean that their policy programmes are mainly, or even fundamentally, about 'new politics', as contemporary political developments in Europe demonstrate. A few examples will suffice to illustrate this point.

During the 1990s and the 2000s, the centre–periphery conflict has occupied the centre stage of politics in several European countries. In the UK, the Scottish National Party (SNP) was for the first time in 2007 the incumbent party of a devolved, democratically elected, Scottish government while the Irish separatist party Sinn Féin (SF) participated in the coalition government of the devolved Northern Ireland administration. According to a political analyst writing for the British newspaper *The Times*:

> [w]ithin the space of a few weeks this year an administration was formed in Northern Ireland that contains Sinn Féin, a party committed to removing Ulster from the UK and merging it with the Republic of Ireland. Soon afterwards the SNP, a party whose purpose is to release Scotland from the UK, was sworn in to head the executive in Edinburgh. Not long after that Labour was compelled to accept a coalition arrangement in Wales with Plaid Cymru, a party with independence as its ultimate objective. (Tim Hames, *The Times*, 10 September 2007)

In Belgium, the Flemish Christian Democrats won the June 2007 general elections with a campaign based on flirting with separatism. The newly elected prime minister of Belgium, Mr Leterme, while still the prime minister of the Flanders region in 2006 had declared in an interview to the French *Libération* (17 August 2006) that Belgium is 'an accident of history' with 'no intrinsic value'. This blunt declaration made the headlines of the mass media in Europe and across the Atlantic. In Italy, the impressive electoral growth of the *Lega Nord* since the early 1990s, coinciding with the fall of the First Republic, and its participation in successive coalition governments under the presidency of Silvio Berlusconi, put political decentralization and the North–South divide back on the agenda of Italian politics. Spain was intensely debating its constitutional identity between 2004 and 2008, a result of which was the upgrading of the autonomy statutes of all those regions that had been willing to claim for it, with the critical exception of the Basque Country.

1.2 THE PARADOX OF PERIPHERAL PARTY SUCCESS

During the late 1970s and the 1980s many authors explained the electoral decline of peripheral parties during the period—which had followed years of consecutive growth—as the paradoxical result of peripheral parties' policy success (Esman 1977; Rudolf 1977; McAllister 1981; Levi and Hechter 1985; Rudolf and Thompson 1985; Pulzer 1988; Newman 1994).

Rudolf and Thomson argued that the policies of decentralization in Belgium and the United Kingdom paved the way for a closer cooperation between peripheral and state parties which eventually resulted in actual or tacit governing coalitions that included the peripheral parties. Participation in government had, in turn, negative consequences for these parties: 'Inevitably they must compromise ... with system-wide actors, at the cost of ... beginning to appear like "all the other parties" ... [They] may even lose their image as the spokesman for the ethnoterritorial cause' (Rudolf and Thompson 1985: 301). Newman, looking also into the British and Belgian cases in the 1970s and 1980s, showed that once the programme of devolution was voted, regardless of the results, 'the ethnoregional parties' proposals were increasingly ignored ... The decline in salience of independence, sovereignty-association, and federalism led to the public explosion of factional divisions within each party ... Now each faction offered its own proposals for a new party agenda. These new proposals included new policies for regional autonomy and new social and economic policies. The factional divisions were electorally debilitating' (Newman 1994: 46–7). Levi and Hechter (1985), in turn, warned about the negative consequences for the future of peripheral parties if mainstream parties, after granting concessions that promote the peripheral programmatic agenda, were to take over components of the programme previously monopolized by the peripheral party: '[t]he very concessions that promote ethnoregional party support in the short run may undermine the demand for that party in the long run, as stronger, more viable parties take over components of the program previously monopolized by the ethnoregional party' (Levi and Hechter 1985: 141).

According to the paradox-of-success thesis, the policy success of peripheral parties was reflected, above all, in the policies of political decentralization (devolution) initiated by several European governments as a concession to the demands put forward by peripheral parties. Since the Second World War, several European countries have adopted different versions of an asymmetric regionalized constitutional form to accommodate the self-government demands of their respective peripheral minorities: Belgium,[1] Denmark, Finland, France, Italy, Spain, and the United Kingdom. This is a form of political decentralization that differs from other

---

[1] In 1993, Belgium became a federal state.

forms in that it is not, at least not exclusively, inspired by reasons of economic or administrative efficiency but by strictly political reasons, as its asymmetrical form attests.

Policy success, in turn, and always according to the paradox-of-success thesis, is the consequence of state parties' strategic response to the electoral growth of peripheral parties. In order to strip peripheral parties of their programmatic distinctiveness and gain reputation and credibility as defenders of the pro-periphery agenda, some state parties decided to emphasize pro-periphery issues and to implement pro-periphery policies, the most important of which was political decentralization. As a result, the argument goes, the peripheral parties' agenda became increasingly incorporated into mainstream politics rendering peripheral parties' exclusive focus on pro-periphery issues redundant (Olivesi 1998; Tambini 2001; Hooghe 2004; De Winter 2006; Thorlakson 2006; Van Haute and Pilet 2006; Deschower 2009).

According to some authors, the paradox of peripheral party success has been seen most clearly in Belgium (De Winter 2006; Van Haute and Pilet 2006; Deschower 2009). Belgium is the country that has advanced furthest in the political decentralization of the state. Post-war Belgium had strong unitary features until some of its political leaders adopted the programmatic agenda of the peripheral parties and dismantled the centralized state, replacing it with a federal structure that gives considerable powers to regions and language communities (Newman 1994). The process has gone so far that some authors talk about the hollowing-out of the Belgian state (Hooghe 2004). The Belgian peripheral parties, which according to most interpretations were at the origin of the devolution reforms in the first place, have progressively lost their electoral appeal ever since. This process has gone so far that in the 2007 Belgian federal elections no peripheral parties presented lists of themselves; they did so in coalition with other parties (Deschower 2009). Belgian peripheral parties have been unable to capitalize, in terms of their share of votes, on the policy success that the extensive political devolution implemented since the 1970s has represented for their political agendas.

Though theoretically powerful, the paradox-of-success thesis is contradicted by the facts. First, as the literature on federalism and ethnic conflict has demonstrated political decentralization does not always neutralize the threat of separatism. Sometimes, it may even contribute to perpetuate the presence of peripheral parties (Brancati 2009; Erk and Anderson 2009; Roeder 2009). Second, peripheral party growth, no matter how dramatic, does not always lead to policy success (as the failed devolution reform in the UK during the late 1970s indicates). Third, policy success does not inevitably lead to peripheral parties' political irrelevance and electoral decline, as many examples discussed in this book demonstrate. Even in the paradigmatic case of Belgium, two peripheral parties have not only survived but become stronger across time, the (old) Vlaams Blok (later renamed Vlaams Berlang) and the (new) Nieuw-Vlaamse Alliantie. Both parties are splits of the

Flemish peripheral party Volksunie that thrived during the 1960s and 1970s but ceased to exist in 2001.

The paradox of peripheral party success is not so paradoxical, after all. Whether peripheral parties succeed and whether this success leads to political irrelevance depends on the electoral behaviour of parties in competition with one another. Several empirical analyses have demonstrated that a state party losing votes to a peripheral challenger has incentives to be accommodative to the peripheral party's agenda of cultural and/or territorial autonomy in order to stop—and possibly reverse—the defection of voters with pro-periphery sensitivities (Rudolf and Thompson 1985; Harmel and Svasand 1997; Van Houten 2000; Tronconi 2006; Van Biezen and Hopkin 2006; Meguid 2008; Mazzoleni 2009). I argue that peripheral parties are as strategically oriented as state parties are. If state parties strategically adopt the peripheral parties' agenda in an attempt to stop their electoral growth, peripheral parties will, in turn, respond to the 'occupation' of their issue dimension using two main strategies: the development of issue diversification and the radicalization of their programmatic agenda. Should the peripheral parties' strategic response fail, electoral decline will follow; but failure is just one of the two possible consequences of peripheral parties' strategic moves.

Part of the originality of this book rests precisely on studying peripheral parties in all 'the banality of their stretch for political power' (Newman 2000: 28). My argument abandons the whole idea of their uniqueness as defenders of the eternal flame of national liberation and sees them as vote-maximizing actors in competition with mainstream left-wing and right-wing parties. Truly enough, in their origins peripheral parties were clearly differentiated from other party families. Their mission of national liberation set them aside from socialist parties which pursued the liberation of the working class or from Christian Democratic parties which aimed at defending Christian values and the interests of the Church. In their origins, all parties had a constitutive 'mission'. Electoral competition, however, transformed the majority of parties into vote-maximizing organizations, and with good reason, for their constitutive 'mission' would have remained utopian without access to political power. Electoral competition between state and peripheral parties is therefore my point of departure.

In this book, I demonstrate that policy success leads neither to political irrelevance nor to political extinction. The diversity of outcomes among European peripheral parties is proof enough. The paradox-of-success thesis is built on the wrong assumptions about peripheral parties—that they are single-issue parties that cannot strategize outside the centre–periphery dimension. Instead, a closer look at the incentives faced by the competing state and peripheral parties demonstrates, first, that state parties only accommodate peripheral demands—thereby initiating devolution reforms—when they see clear benefits in doing so and, second, that the electoral fortunes of peripheral parties are the result of their own strategic choices in different institutional settings.

1.3 NEUTRALIZING SEPARATISM OR RETAINING ELECTORAL PREDOMINANCE?

Political decentralization (or devolution) is widely seen as a response by state politicians to accommodate political unrest in the periphery. Stepan, for example, argues that federalism—or federal-like institutions—allows peripheral minorities to govern themselves while maintaining the territorial integrity of the state: 'India in late 1948, Belgium in 1969, and Spain in 1975 were countries with strong unitary features *until their political leaders decided that the best way—indeed the only way—to hold their countries together in a democracy would be to devolve power constitutionally and turn their threatened polities into federations*' (Stepan 1999: 21, emphasis added).[2] The attractiveness of this argument lies in its apparent empirical confirmation: a majority of the existing multinational democracies are federations, confederations, or regionalized states (Belgium, Canada, India, South Africa, Switzerland, Spain, Italy, the United Kingdom), or have, at least, federal-like arrangements for their culturally distinct territories (Denmark, Finland).

Political decentralization, however, is not exclusive to countries with a centre–periphery cleavage. The United States and Germany, for example, are two highly decentralized countries with no such cleavage. In fact, countries all over the world have been decentralizing political authority in favour of the sub-state level of government since the early 1970s. The figures in the 'Index of Regional Authority' elaborated by Gary Marks, Liesbet Hooghe, and Arjan H. Schakel (2008) leave no room for doubt. The Index measures the amount of sub-state authority in the hands of sub-state governments for 42 developed countries between 1950 and 2006.[3] The measurements provided by the Index show that 'there has been a marked increase in the level of regional authority over the past half-century' (Marks, Hooghe, et al. 2008: 167). The great leap forward towards increased political decentralization has taken place after 1970, when the number of decentralizing institutional reforms has mushroomed. This tendency has also been detected by other authors. The data collected by Rodden (2004) show an important trend toward decentralization after 1970. This worldwide tendency tells us that state politicians decentralize for reasons that are not necessarily related to a conflict with culturally distinct peripheries.

Therefore, how can we be sure that politicians in culturally heterogeneous states decentralize in response to peripheral unrest and not for alternative reasons, such

---

[2] The accommodation thesis is also part of the *argumentario* of some political parties to justify their decision to decentralize. In its 1997 manifesto, the British Labour Party stated: 'A sovereign Westminster Parliament will devolve power to Scotland and Wales. The Union will be strengthened and *the threat of separatism removed*' (emphasis added).

[3] Regional government is defined as the 'government of a coherent territorial entity situated between local and national levels with a capacity for authoritative decision making' (Marks, Hooghe, et al. 2008: 113).

as economic efficiency or democratic enhancement? We know it by looking at the way they do it: the *timing* of political decentralization (why exactly at one particular time, and neither before nor later, given that the presence of peripheral unrest has been a constant, with intermittent periods of decline, since the late 1890s); the *degree* and *scope* of political decentralization (how much self-government, and how widely applied, is enough to appease peripheral unrest and why politicians choose different degrees of autonomy for different territories both within the same country and across countries); and, finally, the *actors* of decentralization (why politicians within any one country are commonly divided between those who favour decentralization and those who oppose it).

The accommodation thesis, therefore, needs refinement. Apart from the obvious problem that devolution does not put a stop to separatist demands and that, as a result, there must be some other rationale behind state politicians' decision to devolve, this thesis needs to explain two further puzzles: first, why devolution, if only intended to appease peripheral parties, is extended to regions without peripheral mobilization, as in Spain and Italy; and, second, why devolution reforms do not adjust to the electoral growth of peripheral parties in all cases and at all times (Brancati 2007). Devolution failed in the UK in the late 1970s despite a dramatic growth of peripheral parties' vote shares, while it was implemented in Italy in the early 1970s despite the absence of a peripheral threat. Finally, the thesis downplays the fact that devolution is never a unanimous decision by a political leadership convinced of its virtues to manage the peripheral conflict but the decision of some state politicians against the preferences of others.

The accommodation thesis is right to connect political devolution with peripheral unrest, for such a connection exists; however, it wrongly assumes that devolution is implemented *in order to neutralize* the growth of peripheral parties and the risks of separatism. Instead, I contend, in this book, that devolution cannot be explained exclusively as the result of peripheral parties' pressure to decentralize even though they are too willing to take the credit. As others have shown before me, devolution is the rational act of political parties seeking to maximize their electoral possibilities (O'Neill 2003; León 2006; Meguid 2009; Sorens 2009). State parties will not opt for devolution unless they see net electoral gains resulting from such decision. Devolution is intended to save the threatened state party, not the state.

The book, however, does not stop at the moment when the decision to decentralize the state is taken and implemented. The book further explores the aftermath of the first devolution reform, when parties have to adapt to an institutional setting that offers them new opportunities for strategic behaviour and electoral gain.

1.4 THE COMPARISON

The comparative approach is at the heart of the book's argument. The *timing* of devolution, its *actors*, and its *degree* and *scope* are all explained as the result of the (type of) electoral geography[4] faced by the competing state and peripheral parties. State parties are more vulnerable to the growth of peripheral parties in some electoral geographic constellations than in others and this will in great part determine who the actors of devolution are. Similarly, the costs of devolution are different according to the electoral geography in place. Therefore, the timing, and the degree and scope of devolution, which are all the result of a cost–benefit calculation by state parties, will be again influenced to a large degree by the type of electoral geography in which parties compete.

There is no denying that electoral geographies, strictly speaking, are not completely exogenous to the competition between parties. However, for the purposes of this study, they will be assumed as exogenous. The growth of peripheral parties takes place at a time in which a particular electoral geography is in place. The book will analyse how this particular electoral geography influences the electoral competition between state and peripheral parties pushing some state parties to initiate a devolution reform at a concrete point in time and with a concrete degree and scope.

Taking this into account, the criterion for the selection of cases has been twofold: on the one hand, I looked for as much similarity as possible with respect to the emergence and permanence of the centre–periphery cleavage and of peripheral parties; on the other, I aimed at having as much dissimilarity as possible with respect to the electoral geographies in each country. Moreover, all countries have to be unitary centralized states at the time when the peripheral party threat emerged and political decentralization needs to have taken place in all of them. This is so because the variability needed must refer to the timing, the actors, the scope, and the degree of devolution. These are the factors that will be explained as a result of party competition in different electoral geographies, not devolution per se.

Given this, four European countries that are seldom compared in the literature have been selected as cases for the analysis: Belgium, Italy, Spain, and the United Kingdom. This selection provides the necessary cross-country variation in the main independent variable, i.e. electoral geography, as I will show at length in chapter 3. At the same time, there is little cross-country variation with respect to the emergence and persistence of a centre–periphery cleavage: in all four

---

[4] Electoral geography is the combination of two factors: on the one hand, it refers to the geographical distribution of votes that characterizes each of the parties in the party system and, on the other, to the numeric relevance of the country's electoral districts or constituencies in the state parliament. The first factor varies for each party in the polity; the second factor characterizes the polity as a whole.

countries there are long-established peripheral identities among a minority of the population and long-established peripheral parties in the party system. Clearly, there is variation in the intensity of the populations' peripheral identities and in the electoral size of the peripheral parties but this will only contribute to strengthen the argument. Finally, all countries were unitary at the beginning, and decentralized at the end, of the analysed period.

Admittedly, the role of devolution in this analysis may seem ambiguous. This ambiguity comes from the fact that devolution is a both dependent and independent variable, though not simultaneously. There is a sequential logic behind it. When states are fully unitary, as it is at the beginning of the period analysed in the first part of the book (chapters 4, 5, and 6), decentralization is the result of politicians' calculations and decisions, the result of competition between parties, and therefore it constitutes a phenomenon to be explained. Once the first decentralizing reform is implemented, however, as happens with the post-decentralization period analysed in the second part of the book (chapters 7 and 8), the institutions of decentralization become explanatory factors for the politicians' calculations and decisions thereafter, since they frame these decisions within particular sets of incentives, costs, and benefits. Part of the book's originality rests precisely on the analysis of both the pre- and the post-devolution periods to see how actors' political calculations and decisions change in between.

1.5 STRUCTURE OF THE BOOK

The book is divided into nine chapters, including the introduction and the conclusion. Chapters 2 and 3 set the theoretical bases of the discussion and present the main hypotheses to be tested in the subsequent chapters. Chapter 2 presents a series of hypotheses about how centre–periphery party competition occurs based on a combination of the spatial and saliency models of party behaviour. One of the two main theses of the book is introduced, namely that peripheral and state parties compete strategically for votes by partly assimilating each other's programmatic agenda. Therefore, I discuss the conditions under which state parties are likely to engage in the defence of pro-periphery policies and the reaction of peripheral parties to the pro-periphery strategies of state parties. Unlike most authors in the literature, I argue that peripheral parties can and do emphasize issues beyond the centre–periphery conflict in order to compete more effectively against their state adversaries. Chapter 3 presents the second main thesis of the book according to which devolution is the rational response of state parties threatened by the rapid electoral growth of peripheral parties. I argue that a centralized state is an institutional environment that sets insurmountable credibility constraints to threatened state parties that want to assimilate parts of the peripheral parties' programmatic agenda. Devolution is preferred to a centralized state because it gives credibility to the state parties' pro-periphery moves. However, devolution does not make strategic sense in all circumstances; when and how it does is determined by the country's electoral geography.

Chapters 4 to 8 discuss the empirical evidence of the four European cases being compared. Chapter 4 presents an operationalization of the centre–periphery dimension of competition using data from the content-analysis of parties' manifestos. It then proceeds to provide a general description of how parties and voters position themselves along the centre–periphery dimension in the four countries under analysis, highlighting similarities and differences. This chapter is transitional between the presentation of the theoretical model and main hypotheses in chapters 2 and 3 and the empirical testing of the hypotheses in the subsequent chapters.

Chapter 5 characterizes the type of electoral threat to state parties that emerged in Belgium, Italy, Spain, and the UK after the Second World War according to each country's electoral geography. The definition and characterization of the peripheral party threat moves on to an analysis of the strategies followed by state parties to neutralize this threat in chapter 6, concluding with an evaluation of their degree of success. Devolution shall then be explained as the last tool in the hands of state parties when their previous pro-periphery electoral moves did not work as expected.

Chapter 7 discusses the adaptation of state parties' electoral strategies to the new institutional setting of devolution. The chapter shows that state parties' pro-periphery moves are more credible in a decentralized state and that, as a result, pro-periphery strategies become more effective and more widely used. Centre–periphery competition becomes 'entrenched' and new rounds of devolution reforms are implemented. In chapter 8, the strategic reaction of peripheral parties in response to the state parties' pro-periphery moves is analysed. On the one hand, peripheral parties use strategies of pro-periphery issue radicalization, facilitated by the establishment of elected regional assemblies and governments. On the other hand, peripheral parties combine these strategies of radicalization with issue diversification and left–right repositioning, contingent upon political circumstances and past choices. The chapter discusses under what conditions the peripheral parties' strategies are effective, stopping or even reversing their losses to state parties. I argue that radicalization is the rational reaction of vote-maximizing peripheral parties in a decentralized state.

The concluding chapter summarizes the arguments of the book and its main findings. After this, the chapter moves on to discuss the implications of these findings for the electoral fortunes of peripheral parties and for the transformation of state parties in a decentralized state. Finally, the prospects for the territorial integrity of the state under democratic rule are evaluated.

2

Centre–Periphery Party Competition

In this chapter, I present a model of centre–periphery party competition based on a combination of the spatial and saliency theories of party behaviour. I shall argue that peripheral parties are as rationally oriented as any other vote-maximizing party and, therefore, their electoral fortunes depend on how well they strategize against their competitors given the structure of preferences in society. In contrast to a widely held view of peripheral parties as single-issue organizations, this chapter will argue that peripheral parties can and do emphasize issues beyond the centre–periphery conflict in order to compete more effectively against their adversaries.

This chapter first presents a brief summary of the assumptions and predictions behind the theories of voter and party behaviour that will be relevant for understanding centre–periphery party competition. After that, the centre–periphery issue dimension is defined and a classification of parties according to their positions on the centre–periphery dimension is introduced. Finally, the main thesis of the chapter is developed. In it, I argue that peripheral and state parties alike compete for votes by tactically assuming issues of the adversary's programmatic agenda as if these issues were their own. These tactical moves are part of a strategy to maximize the parties' vote shares by appealing *simultaneously* to the voters' preferences in different dimensions of conflict (for example, class and territorial identity).

2.1 MODELS OF PARTY COMPETITION

Parties compete with one another for votes in a political space. The political space represents the preferences of voters and politicians over the problems that need to be dealt with by elected governments. There are, however, different interpretations of what exactly voters perceive and parties convey, on the one hand, and how voters and parties behave about it, on the other.

My point of departure is the spatial theory of voter and party behaviour as developed by Downs (1957). He makes two main assumptions referred to voters and parties that I adopt as assumptions in my own analysis. First, that actors are rational and that they are moved by self-interest; second, that parties are vote-maximizers and, as such, they manipulate policies and actions in whatever way they believe will gain them the most votes (Downs 1957: 31). The voter chooses the party that she believes will provide her with more welfare (highest utility) than any other. Voters' political preferences are treated as fixed in the spatial model, although Downs admits that these preferences change in the long run (Downs 1957: 46).[1] In order to find out which party will bring her the highest utility, the voter uses the information she has about the different parties' platforms and policy records and compares it with her own conception of the 'good society' (i.e. that which would bring the voter the highest utility). When two parties are very similar in the eyes of the voter, she will be indifferent between the two and, as a result, will either abstain or vote attending exclusively to government performance (Downs 1957: 46–50). This is what gives parties incentives to retain the distinctiveness of their own platforms vis-à-vis those of their adversaries. In multiparty systems, a rational voter may at times vote strategically for a party other than the one she most prefers in order to avoid a situation where the party which would bring the voter the least utility is the one that wins the election (Downs 1957: 47).

According to Downs' model, the political space is made up of an unlimited number of issues (problems to be solved by governments) structured in different and often opposing policy alternatives. For each issue, whether it includes two, three, or *n* policy alternatives, there is a distribution of voters' preferences. For all possible distributions the behaviour rule remains the same: the party will offer the policy alternative that attracts the largest number of voters (the median voter).

In Downs' model all the issues that constitute the political space can be reduced to one fundamental dimension that he interprets to be the left–right dimension: 'each party takes stands on many issues and each stand can be assigned a position on our left–right scale' (Downs 1957: 132). The left–right dimension represents aggregate party policy stands or policy packages rather than just one policy alternative: 'the party's net position on this scale is a weighted average of the positions of all the particular policies it upholds' (Downs 1957: 132).

The way the electorate is distributed along the left–right dimension is of great importance to explain party positioning. The vote-maximizing party must find a policy package such that each of the policy alternatives included in the package is preferred by a majority of voters (Downs 1957: 54–5). But this is not always an easy task. A non-consensual distribution of preferences (bi-modal or multi-modal) makes this very difficult and even impossible for it offers the competitor the possibility of strategically using this distribution to defeat the majority-pleasing party. If the voters are normally distributed along the left–right dimension, parties' positions are expected to converge at the point of the median voter. However,

---

[1] At one point in his analysis, Downs recognizes that although parties usually compete by moving ideologically to adjust to the distribution of voters' preferences they will also attempt to move voters towards their own location, thus altering it (Downs 1957: 140).

this uni-modal preference distribution is only to be found in highly consensual societies.

In general, a party will be safer the more it adopts a spread of policies that covers a whole range of the left–right dimension (Downs 1957: 133). The problem of spreading the party's policy stands, however, is that it 'weakens the strength of the appeal to any one viewpoint, because each citizen sees the party upholding policies he does not approve of' (Downs 1957: 133). Therefore, spread of policy appeal comes at the expense of the strength or intensity of the party's position. In some cases, it comes even at the expense of the party's credibility. This dilemma initially defined by Downs has been further explored by the mobilization theory of Przeworski and Sprague (1986).

Downs presents an ideal model of voting behaviour that he immediately corrects to account for the uncertainty and lack of information that characterize the real world. According to Downs, uncertainty and lack of information 'prevent even the most intelligent and well-informed voter from behaving in precisely the fashion we have described' (Downs 1957: 46). Uncertainty transforms the ideal, perfectly informed rational voter into an array of different types of voters, with different levels of certainty about the political world and about their decision on whether to vote or not and for which party (Downs 1957: 84–6). Only a few of these types are voters open to persuasion by political parties.

The development of political ideologies is a means of getting votes in a political world characterized by uncertainty (Downs 1957: 96). Ideologies are useful to voters because they remove the information costs implied in the voting decision and which consist of the necessity to match every issue discussed by each party to the voters' own view of a good society. Ideologies are, in this sense, information short-cuts that simplify the political space defined in terms of all conceivable policy issues (Downs 1957: 98). Ideologies are also information short-cuts for parties. Parties avoid the process of calculating which policies will gain the most votes by designing ideologies that will 'appeal to that combination of social groups which it feels will produce the most support' (Downs 1957: 101).

To be effective as information short-cuts ideologies must be both internally consistent and consistent with the party's concrete policies so as to indicate to voters what each party is likely to do if elected for government. Parties have to be reliable and responsible if ideologies are to serve their purpose (Downs 1957: 105). The need for reliability and responsibility makes ideological immobility a characteristic of political parties. Parties' ideologies react only slowly to changes in society because sudden changes in their policies would make them lose their reputation as reliable and responsible parties. This is also the reason why a party does not make 'ideological leaps over the heads of its neighbours' (Downs 1957: 123). According to the spatial model of party competition, ideological movement is only conceived and conceivable as policy divergence or policy convergence to the nearest competitor on either side, but never beyond it.

Stokes (1963) was the first to notice that often conflicts involve *valence issues*, which are goals generally desired by all voters in the polity—such as high employment and the absence of corruption in administration (Stokes 1963: 373). Where valence issues are at stake, there is no dimension of competition as such but one option preferred by all. Voters will chose those parties that have more competence or credibility in dealing with this generally preferred option.

Parties can either manoeuvre for electoral support on a position dimension or in terms of valence issues. When parties manoeuvre in a position dimension they choose policies from an ordered set of alternatives that deal with the same issue or problem; when they manoeuvre in terms of valence issues, parties 'put together a collection of issues of real or potential public concern whose positive and negative valences' will aid the manoeuvring party and 'embarrass' the competitor (Stokes 1963: 374).

Budge and Farlie (1983) developed a theory of party competition that placed issue saliency at its core. According to them, confrontation around policy alternatives on a common background issue is not the only form of electoral competition. Parties compete *mainly* by selectively emphasizing the importance of different issues. The issues that parties emphasize are those in which they are going to be judged positively by voters. Those issues that will play against the parties will be ignored; if emphasized at all, these will be done by the competitors in order to embarrass the party that has a bad reputation on the issue at stake. Issues that are not emphasized are an indication that parties do not want to convey any position on these issues. As a result, the electorate does not know how to judge the party in connection to such ignored issues.

The reasons why parties are positively judged by voters on some issues and not on others are based on their historically based credibility and reputation. Budge and Farlie's argument at this point resembles closely Downs' arguments about parties' reliability and responsibility. Parties 'own' issues whose saliency in an election will bring these parties net electoral gains (Budge and Farlie 1983: 287). Since parties are differently judged depending on the issues at stake there are some issues that parties will never discuss. This means that the positions in the space of competition are not open for all parties equally. There are parts of the space that are always out of bounds for some parties and 'owned' by others.

The issue saliency model predicts that parties competing in elections will gain electoral support by increasing the saliency of the issues they 'own' during the campaign. This means that parties have good reasons for consistently emphasizing 'their' topics election after election. Implicit is the assumption that the more consistent parties are the more credibility they will gather among the electorate and, therefore, the more those issues will become their own. Parties can of course manoeuvre in the political space by moving along the dimensions of competition. And movement, in turn, is conceived as 'constituted by emphasis or de-emphasis on a party's traditionally favorite issues, along with some adoption of new issues' (Klingemann, Hofferbert, et al. 1994: 24). By shifting the relative emphasis on the issues they own, parties convey to voters a movement towards more extreme or towards more centred positions. But they will usually stick to their own 'side' of the centre and will rarely leapfrog (Budge and Farlie 1983; Klingemann, Hofferbert, et al. 1994). Nothing in Downs' spatial model contradicts the predictions of Budge and Farlie's saliency model. The difference between them is more in emphasis than in content: Budge and Farlie emphasize issue saliency where Downs emphasizes issue position, but both models are talking about the same thing.

The directional theory of Rabinowitz and Macdonald (1989), unlike the spatial and issue saliency theories, explicitly defines the political dimensions of competition in terms of 'sides' and the parties in competition as bound to one of the two sides. The whole notion of 'sides' is based on the directional theory's assumptions about voters' psychology and voters' political choice. Rabinowitz and Macdonald argue that voters perceive political issues in a diffuse fashion rather than in terms of a set of ordered policy alternatives (Rabinowitz and Macdonald 1989: 94). The authors defend this assumption on the basis of its empirical fit; it has been repeatedly shown by mass surveys that a vast majority of voters show low levels of information. The voters' vaguely defined preferences do not go beyond a diffuse sense of direction: how favourable or unfavourable the voter feels about the issue at stake, and how strong are these favourable or unfavourable sentiments (Rabinowitz and Macdonald 1989: 94). Direction and intensity are therefore the two main components of voters' responses to the political issues and cues conveyed by parties.

According to Rabinowitz and Macdonald (1989: 96), a voter's decision is determined by the directional compatibility between the voter and the party ('are they on the same side or opposite sides of the issue?') and by the intensity levels of the voter and of the party ('how strongly does the voter feel about the issue and how intensely does the party stir feelings on the issue?'). The prediction is that a voter will choose the party that is on the same side of the issue as she is and that emphasizes the issue with intensity. And here comes the main difference with Downs' spatial assumption: a voter will prefer a more radical party that is on her side of the issue dimension to a more moderate party that belongs to the other side. Therefore, a party that wants to attract voters on some issue will convey the side it supports with intensity (Rabinowitz and Macdonald 1989: 98). The prediction is that parties competing along one issue dimension will take more extreme positions than their constituencies in order to maximize their electoral support and *irrespective* of the voters' distribution of preferences.

There is, however, a limit to how extreme parties can be. A party must convince voters of the reasonableness of its rhetoric and agenda. Parties that are seen as 'extremists' (too intense to the point of looking 'harsh' and 'strident') will not attract a majority of the voters. There is a 'region of acceptability' outside of which the party loses support (Rabinowitz and Macdonald 1989: 108). Therefore, parties that want to maximize their vote share will position themselves at or near the region of acceptability irrespective of the form that the distribution of voters' preferences takes.[2]

The extension to a multidimensional political space predicts that parties will be 'intense on issues that benefit them and silent on issues that are potentially damaging' (Rabinowitz and Macdonald 1989: 98), which reminds us very much of the issue saliency model's prediction despite their diverse assumptions about voters' electoral behaviour.

The issue ownership model developed by Petrocik (1996) follows from the spatial and issue saliency models, although based on different assumptions about voters' psychology. Petrocik's objective is to explain how voter preferences are affected by parties' electoral campaigns. He assumes that the voters' choice for one party or another is mainly based on socio-tropic calculations and that only a few issues are directly related to the voter's self-interest. Ideological voters may have clear ideas about what policies best deal with a problem but a majority of voters are 'pragmatic and instrumental', interested in 'fixing problems' (Petrocik 1996: 830). For this reason, a party's reputation as a 'fixer' of certain types of problems will attract their vote.

Following Budge and Farlie, Petrocik (1996) argues that those issues in which one party has more credibility or reputation than any other in the system are 'owned' by this party. *Issue ownership* is achieved through a good 'handling' reputation which is, in turn, the ability to resolve a problem of concern to voters (Petrocik 1996: 826). A good 'handling' reputation is achieved through short-term incumbency records and long-term constituency-building (Petrocik 1996: 825–7). This is proximate to Rabinowitz and Macdonald's notion that the more a party shows an intense support for an issue through time, the more committed it looks to work in favour of that issue if elected. Emphasis, repetition, and policy implementation lead voters to believe that the party in question is more sincere and committed to doing something about that issue than any other party.

According to Petrocik, what change between elections are the concerns of voters, while their policy attitudes remain mainly unchanged or, if they change, they do so very slowly. Also constant between elections are the issue-handling reputations of parties, so that the outcome of elections will depend on the advantage that a party receives from the campaign issue agenda. Parties will strive to make owned issues the most salient during the electoral campaign and the criteria by which voters make their choice through strategies of *framing* and *priming*. When the competitor's issues are unavoidable, says Petrocik, 'they can be interpreted in a way to highlight some feature of the issue on which they are likely to be regarded as more competent' (1996: 829). For example, a Conservative Party candidate asked about his plans to deal with unemployment will stress

---

[2] Leaving aside the fact that it is not at all clear how the idea of a region of acceptability follows from the assumptions of the directional model, the implication of this constraint on party extremity is that 'all voters in the policy space agree on the location of the region of acceptability' (Iversen 1994: 162).

the relevance of stimulating business opportunities through less state regulation. By saying so, the candidate is not only truthful to his own beliefs and/or ideology but is also playing his best card if the party is to have credibility towards an issue that it does not own. In this respect, sincerity is an advantageous strategy (Petrocik 1996: 829).

In this book, I shall defend the view that party competition is not a matter of *either* confrontation over different issue positions *or* selective emphasis of some issues over others; one type of competition does not preclude the other, despite Stokes' claim to the contrary (Green-Pedersen and Krogstrup 2008; Maravall 2008; Meguid 2008). A party's strategy is defined by both issue position and issue saliency. Each party will emphasize those issues—valence or positional—in which it has credibility and reputational advantage over its competitors. These issues conform to what I shall call the party's *primary dimension* of competition. In countries characterized by the presence of more than one social cleavage, each party will also face a *secondary dimension* of competition. The secondary dimension structures competition along a set of issues which are not a fundamental part of the party's identity but which may become unavoidable for the party at particular elections or during certain periods. The voter will chose the party that is closer to her preferences, as the spatial theory predicts, but in the issue dimension that is more relevant (salient) for the voter or that the party has led the voter to believe is the most relevant.

What happens when parties want to change their issue profiles in order to adapt to economic, social, and demographic changes? Przeworski and Sprague's mobilization theory abandons the spatial assumption that voters' preferences are exogenous to the competition between parties. According to Przeworski and Sprague, 'the voting behaviour of individuals is an effect of the activities of political parties' (Przeworski and Sprague 1986: 9). In order to demonstrate this, they analyse the evolution of socialist parties in modern societies. Socialist parties emerged as organizations that represented and defended the interests of a well-identified group in society: industrial workers. The problem for socialist parties was that they would never manage to obtain a political mandate exclusively based on an appeal to workers because workers never became a socio-demographic majority (as was originally expected). Therefore, in order to gain electoral influence, working-class parties had to seek support from other people, to enter into alliances, and to make compromises (Przeworski and Sprague 1986: 4). Working-class parties had to broaden their issue profile to include issues that had been ignored until then. Of course, workers' parties had the choice to remain pure class parties and electorally marginal. But those parties that wanted to maximize their vote shares had to face a dilemma, which was described by Downs as the conflict between the maintenance of ideological purity and the winning of elections (Downs 1957: 113). When left parties moved their appeal from the workers to the masses they found it increasingly difficult to recruit and maintain the support of workers. By broadening their appeal, working-class parties diluted the saliency of class issues and, consequently, 'weaken[ed] the motivational force of class among workers' (Przeworski and Sprague 1986: 45). As the saliency of class issues diluted other appeals—religion, ethnicity, territory—were reinforced:

> As individuals [not as part of a class], workers indeed share interests with other citizens, other consumers, taxpayers, parents or renters. As individuals they are concerned about their interests, and when socialist parties offer policies to individuals, workers compare them with policies offered by other parties. (Przeworski and Sprague 1986: 54)

The same dilemma was faced by Christian Democratic parties in Europe, as Kalyvas (1996) beautifully shows in his book:

> despite the benefits it provided, the religious origin and nature of confessional parties limited the parties' electoral appeal . . . How could they deemphasize religion without destroying the confessional character of the parties which guaranteed unity and electoral support? (Kalyvas 1996: 262).

Implicit in these analyses is the recognition that working-class parties and Christian Democratic parties, at the time of their emergence in the electoral arena, were *single-issue parties* that changed their issue profiles only in the medium and long term in order to maximize their vote shares. In doing so, however, they made room for the ascendancy of motivations other than class or religion as determinants of individual voting behaviour. As I shall show below, peripheral parties also followed this type of issue ownership evolution.

Meguid's 'Position, Ownership and Saliency' (POS) model, like that of Przeworski and Sprague (1986): and Kalyvas (1996), is concerned with the emergence of new parties that emphasize issues that have never been discussed before. Her focus, however, is not on the electoral strategies of the new parties (working-class and Christian Democratic parties in the examples mentioned above) but on those of the established mainstream parties that are challenged by the electoral breakthrough of new single-issue parties.

Meguid uses a mixed spatial–saliency approach to study the competition for votes between mainstream and niche parties and, more specifically, the effect of mainstream parties' electoral strategies on the electoral fortunes of niche parties. Niche parties are *new* parties that reject the traditional class-based orientation of politics, prioritizing instead issues that were previously outside the dimensions of party competition (Meguid 2008: 3). These issues are not only new but they cut across the existing left–right lines of political division. Moreover, niche parties limit their issue appeal. Niche party support depends on one single issue and, therefore, 'any tactic that undermines the perceived relevance of that issue or the distinctiveness or credibility of the niche party's position on that dimension will result in niche party vote loss' (Meguid 2008: 29). Although Meguid does not say it explicitly, her model assumes that niche parties are, by their very novel nature, parties without credibility and without reputation or, in Downs' terms, parties that have not had time to build an image of themselves as reliable and responsible parties. They have to generate reputation and credibility from scratch; they need to establish ownership over the new issue with which they have emerged in the electoral arena. Examples of this party family include (always, according to Meguid) green, radical-right, and ethno-territorial parties.

The POS model states that voter support for a party depends on three conditions: '1. The party's issue is considered salient or important; 2. The party's position on a given issue is attractive; 3. The party is perceived to be the rightful "owner" of that policy stance' (Meguid 2008: 24).[3] Parties, consequently, compete in the electoral market by conveying to voters their policy positions in different issue dimensions of competition and by emphasizing those policy positions for which they have an acquired credibility and reputation.

Following Downs' postulates, Meguid defines two main electoral strategies open to parties. The first is a movement along the issue dimension towards the policy position of the competitor, called an *accommodative strategy*. Meguid identifies this strategy with Downs' policy convergence. The second is a movement away from the position of the competitor, referred to by Meguid as an *adversarial strategy*. In spatial terminology, it is equivalent, always according to this author, to policy divergence.[4] There is a third available strategy based on the issue saliency and issue ownership models: the *dismissive strategy*. This implies that the parties ignore certain issue dimensions in which they do not have an acquired advantage or that will not bring the parties any future electoral gains. Ignoring an issue dimension is intended to lead voters to judge parties according to their positions in other dimensions, not in the ignored one (Meguid 2008: 24–8).

Meguid argues that playing with the saliency of different issue dimensions is only possible for parties with a diverse issue portfolio. If the party is known for its stand on only one issue dimension, as niche parties are, a failure to comply with one or more of the three criteria that guarantees the support of voters will bring the party electoral losses (Meguid 2008: 24). This implies that, assuming the electorate's sympathy for the niche party's policy stance, if the niche issue dimension is not salient or if the niche party is not perceived as a credible owner of that positional issue, the niche party will lose voters. What Meguid does not explain is why, with the limitation of the issue appeal being such a suicidal strategy for peripheral parties, they stick to it across time without attending to its negative consequences.

---

[3] Meguid's POS theory seems to assume that an issue and an issue dimension are the same thing. In this sense, her use of the term 'issue' is similar to that of Petrocik's, for whom an issue is equivalent to a problem that needs to be solved by governmental action.

[4] Despite Meguid's assertion to the contrary, the strategies that she defines are not exactly equivalent to Downs' policy convergence and policy divergence. The reason is that in Downs' model the competitor can also move towards or away from the strategizing party whereas in Meguid's model niche parties do not move from their position.

When a niche party successfully enters the electoral arena, mainstream parties must decide whether to recognize and respond to this new issue or not. A mainstream party that ignores the new issue and does not discuss it at all (*dismissive strategy*) is signalling to voters that the issue lacks merit (Meguid 2008: 28) and is encouraging them to ignore the issue when deciding their ballot. Ignoring the issue will reduce the saliency of the issue dimension in the electoral contest and, as a result, the niche party will suffer electoral losses. Alternatively, mainstream parties may decide to take positions on the niche party's issue dimension, thereby rendering the dimension more salient and encouraging voters to decide their ballots attending to their preferences along this dimension. At this point, mainstream parties have two options: they can either engage in an *accommodative strategy*, moving close to the niche party's position along the new issue dimension; or they can opt for an *adversarial strategy*, moving away from the position of the niche party competitor.

An accommodative strategy is expected whenever the mainstream party is directly threatened by the growth of the niche party. This strategy 'is typically employed by parties hoping to draw voters away from a threatening competitor' (Meguid 2008: 24). Why should we expect an accommodative strategy to provoke electoral losses to the niche party? For a niche party it is extremely important that the electorate perceives it as the rightful owner of the issue that it emphasizes (Meguid 2008: 27). This means that the niche party has to convince voters both that it is committed to a given policy stance and that it is the party best able to implement such policy. In a context in which the niche party is new and little known this is hard enough. If, on top of it, a mainstream party decides to emphasize the niche party's issue position, the niche party will be disadvantaged with respect to the established party. Voters that sympathize with the niche issue position will prefer the accommodating mainstream party 'copy' to the niche party 'original'. The reason is that the mainstream party, as an established large party in the system, has more legislative and governmental experience than the niche party and is widely known among the electorate. Since voters are practically minded and what they want is to see their preferred policies implemented they will vote for the established party. They trust this party's capacity to implement the niche party's policy stance more than the capacity of the small and little known niche party (Meguid 2008: 27).

Why would voters believe that, if elected for office, the accommodating mainstream party will de facto implement the niche party policy stance? At first, Meguid claims that voters believe that the mainstream party's adoption of the niche party's policy issue is sincere because 'the adoption of a new policy position is a costly endeavor for a political party, requiring a diversion of its resources away from existing policy commitments' (Meguid 2008: 28) and, therefore, emphasizing a new policy position signals the importance of the issue for the party. Further on, however, Meguid adds two conditions for the accommodative strategy of the mainstream party to be credible: the strategy has to be both consistent and timely.

A party will be more credible the more it sticks to the same issue tactics through time and the earlier it reacts to the new issue introduced by the niche competitor (Meguid 2008: 35–8). Timeliness is relevant because if the newly introduced issue is left in the hands of the niche party for a long time, voters will perceive the niche party as the owner of the issue and, once issue ownership is established, it is difficult to change. This is what Meguid calls the 'lock-in effect' (2008: 37). Accommodative strategies will only be effective if introduced during a 'window of *ownership* opportunity'. Locked-in issue ownerships will not be easily changed.

The problem with Meguid's argument at this point is that the effectiveness of an accommodative strategy is made to depend on an unrecognized trade-off. Consistency needs time to emerge (at least two elections must take place before a consistent pattern of policy positions can emerge, and the larger the number of elections the stronger—or weaker—the level of consistency shown by the party and, therefore, of its image as a responsible party) whereas timeliness requires expediency (the earlier the mainstream party occupies the policy position of the niche party, the more credible it will be and the more effective in preventing the niche party from establishing an exclusive ownership over that issue). More consistency is acquired at the expense of time expediency. Either the mainstream party is timely, but can show no consistency, or it waits to show how consistent its accommodative strategy is, in which case it misses the window of *ownership* opportunity.

The mainstream party only has the chance to harm the electoral prospects of the niche party while it is still novel but, at this early stage, the mainstream party has no way of convincing the electorate that its accommodative move is sincere and not sheer opportunism. The accommodative strategy in these conditions is doomed to fail. Unlike Meguid, I hypothesize that the electoral fortunes of the niche party will not be damaged and that the mainstream party will have to think of alternative ways of making its accommodative move credible.

Meguid's model does not take us any further than the previous theories had already taken us. If the niche party manages to become an established party, with reputation and credibility as the owner of the niche issue, the core assumption of Meguid's model (namely, that voters will prefer the accommodative party 'copy' to the niche party 'original' because the niche party is unknown and has no established issue ownership) disintegrates and the model's predictions with it.

In this book, I shall argue that peripheral parties do not limit their issue appeal to just one issue dimension. This is only applicable to the period in which the peripheral parties are still novel. In the early stages after its emergence a peripheral party has incentives to limit its issue appeal because its entry in the electoral arena is precisely due to the mobilization of a niche issue that was previously ignored by mainstream parties. Later on, however, the incentives to limit the issue appeal will disappear. Eventually the peripheral party's survival will require that the party diversifies its issue portfolio and acquires reputation and credibility beyond the centre–periphery dimension.

2.2 THE CENTRE–PERIPHERY DIMENSION

2.2.1 Centre–periphery issues

For an electoral dimension of competition to emerge, an issue must exist in which the preferences of the electorate are divided. The political status of culturally distinct, geographically concentrated minorities is one such issue.

In their seminal work of 1967, Lipset and Rokkan defined the centre–periphery cleavage as:

> local oppositions to encroachments of the aspiring or the dominant national elites and their bureaucracies: the typical reactions of peripheral regions, linguistic minorities, and culturally threatened populations to the pressures of the centralizing, standardizing, and 'rationalizing' machinery of the nation-state. (Lipset and Rokkan 1967: 14)

Historically, the centre–periphery cleavage emerged when *particular groups* within the distant, distinct, and dependent peripheries of a state opposed the state- and nation-building processes initiated by *central elites* (Lipset and Rokkan 1967). Irrespective of what made the peripheral territory different from the other regions of the state, whether it was language, religion, ancient institutions, a past history of independence, or a combination of some or all of these, the existence of a peripheral identity, however weak or restricted to a small group within the peripheral territory's population, historically provided 'political entrepreneurs' with a common set of aims (a vision of the 'good society', to borrow Downs' expression) around which they could build a political movement.

The term 'periphery' does not mean today what it meant at the time of emergence of the centre–periphery conflict. The 'peripheries' of the centre–periphery cleavage today are not necessarily backward, distant, and dependent territories as they were back then. In fact, there are examples of peripheral territories that constitute the economic vanguard in their respective states. Today the term 'periphery' is used to designate territorial units with a differentiated history within the state, territories that are home to cultural minorities and that at the time of the state- and national-building processes were subject to the homogenization policies of the state's central elites. Thus, the post-Second World War waves of peripheral mobilization are not like those of the late nineteenth century which attacked most forms of modernity for uprooting the features of traditional society. Contemporary peripheral movements are more progressive than their kin movements in the past. And yet they all share, in the present as in the past, the defence of the peripheral territory's differentiation within the state, the right to be and to remain different.

The centre–periphery cleavage is intrinsically territorial; it is about political control over a (peripheral) territory. Political control can, in turn, take several forms: cultural, economic, administrative, institutional, constitutional. For this reason, the centre–periphery cleavage has a complex issue structure and draws together at least three issue dimensions along which are ordered the cultural, the fiscal, and the institutional preferences of the political actors that mobilize this cleavage.

The *institutional dimension* orders the preferences of voters and parties concerning the formal political status of the peripheral territory inside the state. It goes from the preference for the full independence of the peripheral territory to the preference for a centralized unitary state. The *cultural dimension* deals with the means for the protection and preservation of the peripheral group's cultural distinctiveness and identity. It is defined by two extreme preferences: on the one hand, the preservation of the peripheral culture through a complete segregation from the majority cultural community of the state and, on the other hand, the complete assimilation of the peripheral culture in the majority culture of the state. The *fiscal dimension* deals with the way in which the power of revenue and expenditure should be distributed between the central state and peripheral administrations. At one extreme is the alternative of complete fiscal autonomy by which the peripheral territory administers taxes and expenditures and gives a percentage of its total revenues to contribute to general state expenses. At the centralized extreme is a situation where the peripheral and/or local administrations have very few powers of taxation and expenditure, which are decided at the centre.

The three dimensions are closely interconnected. Undoubtedly, a party which proposes a change to the state constitution in order to give the peripheral territory an autonomous political status inside the state is dealing with all three dimensions at the same time. The proposed constitutional change must necessarily include a series of policy choices concerning the institutions of representation that are going to be established in the peripheral territory and the competences that these institutions should be granted to deal with the cultural and economic situation there.

The typical policy issues belonging to the centre–periphery cleavage are well captured by the opposed alternatives 'centralized versus decentralized state' or 'centralization versus decentralization policies'.[5] Following Falleti, decentralization is here defined as 'a process of state reform composed by a set of public

---

[5] Centralization and decentralization are best seen as a process, and not a state of being of the polity (Falleti 2005; León 2006). The countries analysed in this book are *decentralizing* states rather than *decentralized* ones. As the Flemish Christian Democratic leader Jean-Luc Dehaene has put it in connection to the decentralizing reforms in Belgium: 'Each phase of the State reform is fraught with the following one, the next reform exists in the present reform in an embryonic form' (quoted by Martínez de Rituerto in *El País*, 1 August 2008).

policies that transfer responsibilities, resources, or authority from higher to lower levels of government in the context of a specific type of state' (Falleti 2005: 328–9). Because this definition may include different types of devolved authority, with different effects concerning the final degree of autonomous power de facto devolved to the sub-state institutions, Falleti further differentiates between administrative, fiscal, and political decentralization.

Administrative decentralization refers to those policies that transfer 'the administration and delivery of social services' (Falleti 2005: 329). This may entail the devolution of decision-making authority over these policies, but not necessarily. Fiscal decentralization comprises those policies designed to 'increase the revenues or fiscal autonomy of subnational governments'. Finally, political decentralization refers to a set of constitutional amendments and electoral reforms that 'open new spaces for the representation of subnational polities' and thereby devolve 'political authority or electoral capacities to subnational actors' (Falleti 2005: 329). One form of political decentralization is the creation of sub-state legislative assemblies and governments accountable to the sub-state electorate. This form of political decentralization is what is commonly referred to as *political devolution*. The exact powers that the sub-state units of government have vis-à-vis the central state may vary enormously from case to case. Although political devolution is usually accompanied by administrative decentralization, it does not necessarily entail a high degree of fiscal decentralization. The degree of fiscal devolution is usually part of the package of intergovernmental bargaining that is constantly renegotiated once a process of political decentralization has been initiated.

The reader may wonder why, if the issues of the centre–periphery dimension overlap so closely with the centralization–decentralization dimension, I stick to the label *centre–periphery*. The reason is that the centralization–decentralization dimension may, or may not, be connected with a centre–periphery conflict as I have defined here. Many countries enter debates about how much centralization or decentralization is good for a functioning democracy. Not all of them have culturally distinct peripheries organized by peripheral parties that demand decentralization as a way to defend their minority culture and their control over the peripheral territory against the state's policies of nation-building and state-building. Therefore, a peripheral party and a state party may have a similar position about how much decentralization is beneficial for a democracy but they hold this similar position for very different reasons. Moreover, they probably have opposed preferences concerning the degree of asymmetry that decentralization should assume; the peripheral party wants the peripheral territory to be clearly differentiated from the rest of the regions inside the state. The issue overlap exists but there are good reasons to keep the analytical distinction. These reasons will be more evident as the argument unfolds and is tested empirically.

The position that a party or a voter occupies along the centre–periphery dimension is the aggregate of the party's or the voter's policy preferences in each of its component dimensions. Thus, some peripheral parties may emphasize institutional aims over cultural ones while others may do exactly the opposite and yet they are all peripheral parties (Keating and Loughlin 1997; Fabre and Martínez-Herrera 2009). Not all peripheral parties mobilize issues of culture and language (Hepburn 2009). The implication is that the same position along the centre–periphery dimension can be reached through different combinations of cultural, economic, institutional, and constitutional policy preferences.[6] The diversity of 'policy packages' that parties can offer the electorate along the centre–periphery dimension is therefore very large, as is the number of possibilities that this opens to strategizing parties.

2.2.2 Parties along the centre–periphery dimension

Those parties whose agenda is to defend the peripheral territory's distinctiveness and differentiation inside the state constitute the *peripheral* party family and the parties belonging to this category are *peripheral parties* (Rokkan and Urwin 1983). The parties whose agenda is state-wide and whose priority is to defend the interests of the state (i.e., the country as a whole) constitute the *state* party family and the parties belonging to this category are *state parties*. Peripheral parties, by definition, organize exclusively in their peripheral territory and present candidates to elections—state, regional, or local—exclusively within their territory. Peripheral parties aspire to govern their territory but not necessarily the state (unless participation in the state government will bring some tangible benefits for their peripheral territory). Peripheral parties only care about the rest of the state as far as this has an impact on the peripheral territory or on their electoral fortunes. Peripheral parties limit their appeals to the peripheral territory's electorate. State parties, in contrast, organize throughout the geography of the state, presenting candidates in all the country's constituencies—or nearly all. State parties aspire to govern the state (i.e., the whole country), and the problems affecting the totality of the state are their main concern. State parties appeal to the whole state electorate and, when in office, claim to represent all the citizens of the state. State parties may have diverse positions along the centralization–decentralization dimension; peripheral parties' preferences only move in one direction: decentralization. However, within the 'periphery side' of the centre–periphery dimension, peripheral parties vary greatly in their more radical or moderate positions (De Winter 1998; Massetti 2009).

There is another criterion to classify parties along the centre–periphery dimension that often appears in the literature (Pallarés, Montero, et al. 1997). According

---

[6] Despite the spatial reading of the centre–periphery dimension as a set of ordered policy alternatives, the dimension can be easily interpreted in directional terms. One side would represent all those preferences that favour, even if only slightly, the central state over the peripheral territory and the other side would reflect all the preferences, moderate or radical, that favour the periphery over the central state.

to it, parties can be classified attending to their geographical dispersion within the state. Parties that organize exclusively at the local and regional level and that, in state elections, propose candidates exclusively at these sub-state levels are defined as *non-state-wide parties*. Parties that, on the contrary, organize at the state level and that, in state elections, propose candidates in all—or nearly all—the constituencies of the country are denominated *state-wide parties*. The use of this criterion to classify parties along the centre–periphery dimension is based on an implicit assumption according to which the geographical location of a party predetermines its centre–periphery preferences. However, a non-state-wide party may exist that pays no attention whatsoever to centre–periphery issues, something that in terms of the centre–periphery model of party competition would make no sense at all.

PERIPHERAL PARTIES. Once they take the decision to defend their political project through participation in elections, the behaviour of peripheral parties is driven in no small part by their need to gain votes.

Peripheral parties give priority to centre–periphery issues in their agendas. Their positions along the centre–periphery dimension will always be on the periphery side. However, within the periphery side, their positions may vary according to the radicalism of their objectives and the intensity of their pro-periphery preferences relative to other issues outside the centre–periphery dimension. With respect to the former, peripheral parties may support secession from the state, which would be the most radical policy alternative belonging to the periphery side, or other forms of self-government that fall short or very short of complete independence. They may also be radical in other respects. For example, they may aspire to a culturally homogeneous peripheral territory where only the minority language is recognized as the official language. Peripheral parties may also combine radical issues with moderate ones. The structure of the centre–periphery issue dimension offers peripheral parties wide room for manoeuvre to design the 'issue package' that will best maximize the party's vote share. Following Downs' terminology, peripheral parties can 'spread' their appeal by mixing in their electoral package issues that attract partisan/ideological voters (such as, for example, a renegotiation of the peripheral territory's constitutional status that will enhance its degree of self-government) and issues that attract more pragmatic/non-ideological voters (such as, for example, more fiscal powers to be devolved to the peripheral territory so that the money collected in the territory is not used by the state to pay for the economic development of other regions). This example shows that the issue structure of the centre–periphery dimension is such that, unlike parties along the left–right dimension, peripheral parties may spread their appeal without necessarily reducing the intensity of their pro-periphery position.

With respect to the relative intensity of their pro-periphery preferences, peripheral parties will vary according to the relevance they give to issues outside the centre–periphery dimension. Vote-maximizing peripheral parties will not limit their appeals to centre–periphery issues. Peripheral parties have incentives to convey to the electorate their preferences with respect to other societal problems as well because as parties that aspire to govern one day their respective peripheral territories they need to show that they are able to address all the problems that worry voters. The decision to emphasize or downplay centre–periphery issues with respect to other types of issues, such as socio-economic, religious, or left-libertarian issues, is a strategic one and depends on the structure of party competition in each particular context.

In the real world, many peripheral parties convey a clear and salient position along the left–right dimension of competition (Mair and Mudde 1998; Erk 2005; De Winter, Gómez-Reino, et al. 2006; Lynch 2009; Maddens and Libbrecht 2009; Massetti 2009). The Catalan peripheral party Convergència i Unió is a good example of the combination of two identities belonging to two issue dimensions: a strong pro-periphery identity and a strong Christian Democratic identity. It is not an isolated case. Many peripheral parties have a clear left-wing, right-wing, or even extreme-right identity that they combine with a strong pro-periphery stance. On the other hand, there are peripheral parties which change left–right positioning across time, such as the Welsh Plaid Cymru in Great Britain, which initiated a turn to the left as a response to the competition for votes with Labour, while others defend less extreme left–right positions with time, such as the Galician Nationalist Bloc (Elias 2009). Peripheral parties, as rational actors, will try to use to their advantage the existence of two or more relevant dimensions of electoral competition in their country.

This goes against the interpretation of peripheral parties as single-issue organizations (Müller-Rommel and Pridham 1991; Smith 1991; Adams, Clarke, et al. 2006; Meguid 2008; Brancati 2009; Meguid 2009) which are 'out of competition' because their support is based on identified, as opposed to volatile, voters (Sartori 1976). This interpretation assumes that voters who cast their ballot for a peripheral party are *ethnic voters* that only take into account their membership of the cultural-ethnic group represented by peripheral parties when casting their vote.[7] However,

---

[7] Even in the case of ethnic parties that defend the protection of their minority cultures without seeking territorial self-government, the Sartorian 'out of competition' interpretation is unconvincing. Let us take the example of the Swedish People's Party in Finland, which represents, according to Sartori (1976), an ethnic out-group that neither loses nor gains votes in a competitive space. In theory, it is possible to conceive the Swedish People's Party in competition with parties on the left–right dimension. Even if we assume that the Swedish People's Party is a catch-all party that ignores socio-economic issues and focuses exclusively on ethnic membership, it may still be worth for the Finnish left-wing and right-wing parties to poach on that segment of the Swedish pool of voters that, on socio-economic issues, is expected to defend a left-wing or a right-wing position. In heterogeneous electorates, the same voters may be addressed attending to one or more of the multiple characteristics that they embody: in the example that we are discussing, voters can be addressed attending to their belonging to the Swedish minority culture and to their belonging to a social class. We can conceive a scenario in which a left-wing Finnish party tries to attract the votes of the Swedish workers. In such case, the party would be in

which types of voters choose peripheral parties is an empirical question to be tested rather than a theoretical a priori because the degree to which voters are identified with their cultural group is partly a result of the activities of peripheral parties themselves and, as such, changes across time and place.

Peripheral parties only share with niche parties the fact that, at least at the state level, they are minority or small parties. Therefore, they have in common with niche parties some of the limitations of being small. Unlike state niche parties, these limitations are compensated by one clear advantage: geographical concentration favours peripheral parties with a larger share of seats in the state parliament than they would have if they were geographically dispersed, particularly if the electoral system is highly disproportional.

STATE PARTIES. State parties have little in common other than being state-wide parties and, therefore, filling candidates throughout the state geography, aspiring to govern the state, and appealing to all the citizens of the state. State parties prioritize all kinds of issues in their agendas depending on which is their primary dimension of competition. Socialist parties emphasize left socio-economic issues and green parties make salient ecological and left-libertarian issues, and so on. State parties also differ according to their centre–periphery positions. Some state parties have a reputation as defenders of a centralized unitary state or as supporters of a culturally homogeneous state that assimilates all minority cultures into the majority one. They 'own' these issues in the eyes of the electorate and of their adversaries. Other state parties have acquired a reputation as defenders of decentralization, be it administrative, economic, or political. Still others have no issue profile around centre–periphery issues.

The spatial models that extend Downs' theory to a scenario with two or more relevant dimensions of competition assume that these dimensions are independent from one another. In other words, they assume that the position of the party in one of the dimensions has nothing to do with its position in another (Hinich and Munger 1997). This assumption, however, is contradicted by empirical facts. There are countries in which a left-wing party is more likely to be close to its peripheral competitor along the centre–periphery dimension than a right-wing party, or vice versa, as the presentation of the cases will show. This is what

competition with the Swedish People's Party. The strategy of the Finnish left-wing party would of course fail if the Swedish minority voted exclusively according to its ethnic identity and not its social class. But this cannot be established a priori. In fact, the Swedish People's Party was internally heterogeneous, in terms of class, although a majority of the Swedish minority worked in manual and agricultural occupations. The Swedish People's Party was unable to establish an overriding common identity cutting across class differences based solely on language identity (as was also the case of the Flemish party Volksunie and of the Front Démoratique des Francophones, as we will see in subsequent chapters). What helped the Swedish People's Party to cement a common group identity were the Finnicization attempts by the central government (Rokkan and Urwin 1983: 139). The strategies of state parties in their competition with peripheral parties played a central role.

explains the fact that not all state parties are equally threatened by the peripheral party's electoral growth. Historical trajectories of proximity to peripheral parties' positions set some state parties in the path of electoral vulnerability in the event of a sudden growth of their peripheral competitor but not others. Therefore, I shall make no assumption about the type of connection that exists between the centre–periphery dimension and other dimensions of competition. This connection is the result of long historical developments and will therefore vary across countries and time (Coakley 1992; Erk 2005; Massetti 2009). It will, however, be determinant in understanding—and predicting—the strategies of competition used by state parties.

State parties also vary according to size and relevance in the party system. I shall analyse here large mainstream state parties to the left and to the right of the political left–right spectrum, ignoring small and niche state parties. The reason is twofold: on the one hand, competition between peripheral and small state parties has little impact on the structure of party competition in the country; on the other, competition for votes along the centre–periphery dimension usually takes two forms: competition between peripheral parties, when more than one exists, and competition between peripheral parties and large mainstream state parties.

2.3. A MIXED MODEL OF CENTRE–PERIPHERY PARTY COMPETITION

Downs' assumption that all policy issues can be ultimately reduced to one left–right dimension has proved to be unrealistic. The policy issues that constitute the political space of any one country are generally structured in more than one dimension of competition. Empirically, the number of dimensions varies with each historical period and with each country. For the model presented here, the political space is assumed to be structured along two relevant dimensions, the centre–periphery and the left–right,[8] which cross-cut one another.[9] The electoral support of the parties is therefore defined in terms of two dimensions *at once*, so that electoral majorities are based either on 'joint distributions or marginal distributions' (Stokes 1963: 377).

---

[8] The same postulates should work for three or more dimensions.

[9] If the dimensions overlap, and this overlapping is large, then we are back to the scenario of Downs' uni-dimensional model.

2.3.1 Voters and parties in two dimensions

Let us begin the discussion with an illustration taken from a historical example: the electoral competition that during the 1940s and 1950s emerged between the Ulster Unionist Party (UUP) and the Northern Ireland Labour Party (NILP). The UUP and the NILP were positioned in two different dimensions, the former in the centre–periphery dimension and the latter in the socio-economic left–right dimension. The UUP represented the Protestant minority in Northern Ireland and defended an inter-class political agenda that nevertheless included at times a strong emphasis on social issues in order to keep the loyalty of Protestant workers (Smith 2006). The NILP originally competed on an exclusively socio-economic dimension, catering for a mixed Catholic–Protestant pool of voters (Edwards 2007). In theory, each party was talking to different voters: the UUP to Protestants along the centre–periphery dimension of competition; the NILP to workers along the left–right dimension. In reality, however, they were talking to a segment of each other's electorate precisely because there was a sizeable proportion of voters who were both Protestant and working class. The NILP caused the UUP some difficulties during this period, by attracting a segment of the UUP's Protestant voters and thus challenging the hegemony of the UUP over the Protestant workers (Smith 2006). There was competition between the two parties and it was because of this competition that the UUP, paradoxically, maintained at times an easier relationship with the Labour governments in London, defenders of a social welfare agenda, than with the Conservative ones. As Edwards puts it: 'The hegemony established by the Unionist Party over the Protestant working class since state formation in the early 1920s was crucial to the state's very existence and would not be sacrificed lightly, even if this necessitated embracing British "socialist" measures' (2007: 599).

Although the NILP initially ignored the centre–periphery cleavage between Protestants and Catholics and focused on a working-class clientele, it was eventually forced by the increasing sectarianism of Northern Irish Protestant and Catholic parties to position itself clearly on the constitutional status of Northern Ireland. It was precisely the invasion of the NILP's 'electoral hunting grounds' by the UUP during the 1930s and 1940s that forced the NILP to vote, in the 1949 party conference, in favour of the Union between Northern Ireland and Great Britain. This decision not only split the party but also changed its sociological basis of support, since Catholic workers began to abandon it. Although throughout the 1950s the NILP 'sought to present itself as a real alternative to the tribal politics practised by unionism and nationalism . . . *only by giving equal weight to socio-economic policies and constitutional priorities could the NILP manoeuvre itself back onto the political radar screen*' (Edwards 2007: 560–1, emphasis added). The ultimate consequence was that the saliency of the centre–periphery dimension increased even more and contributed to the disappearance of cross-community parties in Northern Ireland.

As the example above has shown, when two or more dimensions of competition are relevant in a polity, parties will consider the distribution of voters' preferences along the two dimensions simultaneously when deciding which move to make. The dilemmas of electoral socialism have largely been conceived in terms of class—that is, the need for left-wing parties to gain middle-class votes in order to win elections involves, at the same time, a dilution of socialist commitments and the possible alienation of their traditional working-class constituency (Przeworski and Sprague 1986). However, in countries with peripheral minorities these historical dilemmas may be even more acute. Where a centre–periphery cleavage cuts across the class cleavage, class parties and peripheral parties may well compete for the loyalty of the same voters. In a context where peripheral and class allegiances are simultaneous, what requires explanation is how this is manifested in terms of voting choice. Although such explanation goes beyond the objective of the present book, we need to reconsider, if only briefly, some of the spatial assumptions about voters' behaviour in order to adapt them to a bi-dimensional political space.

In a one-dimensional world, the result of elections generally depends on a small proportion of the electorate, those voters who are uncertain about which party to vote for and who therefore are 'open to persuasion' (Downs 1957: 85). Partisan and ideological voters are certain about their vote and unless the party of their choice has been lacking in integrity or responsibility they will not see the need to change it. In our bi-dimensional political space things are a bit more complicated. Voters have at least two main identities, determined by their social class (working or middle class, for the sake of simplicity) and by their territorial identity (state majority or peripheral minority). An ideological voter selects the party that best defends the interests of the social categories to which the voter belongs. If the voter belongs simultaneously to two social categories that cross-cut each other, as is the case of social class and territorial identity, she has to decide which of the two categories is more relevant for her welfare before choosing her ballot.

Three alternatives are possible: (1) social class is more relevant or more intensely felt by the voter than territorial identity; (2) territorial identity takes precedence over social class in the mind of the voter; (3) both social class and territorial identity are equally important or intense. When one of the two identities—class or territory—is more intensely felt by the voter, it is reasonable to expect that the voter will be better informed and will have more clearly defined preferences about issues that concern her most important identity while she will show lower levels of information and more vaguely defined preferences concerning issues of the less important identity. As a result, the voter will be more open to cues coming from political parties on her secondary, less important, identity. It could even be hypothesized that the voter behaves spatially in her primary identity and directionally in her secondary one though I am not going to test these ideas here.

What impact does this have over parties' expected strategies? Assuming that parties only convey positions in their primary dimension of competition while using a catch-all strategy on the secondary dimension, the parties' fortunes will depend on the relative relevance of the class versus the territorial identities for the electorate as a whole. If the median voter gives more relevance to class than to territory, she will choose the class party that is closest to her preferences and, therefore, class parties will get more support than centre–periphery parties. If the median voter considers territorial identity as the more fundamental of the two identities, she will choose the centre–periphery party that best represents her territorial preferences and, therefore, centre–periphery parties will have an advantage over class parties. If the median voter feels equally intense about her class and territorial identities and given that we have assumed that parties convey positions only in their primary dimension of competition, she will be unable to prioritize one identity over the other and will decide her ballot attending to cues other than the ideological and identity ones. It could also happen that the distribution of preferences in society has a bi-modal structure by which half of the voters give more relevance to territorial identity and the other half considers class identity as the most important factor, in which case no one party would get the majority of the votes.

This assumption about parties' behaviour, however, needs revision. Parties do not take positions only in their primary dimension of competition while using a catch-all strategy on the secondary dimension. This will make sense some of the time in some places but not all of the time everywhere. If they are vote-maximizing parties, which I have assumed them to be, parties will adopt positions in both dimensions whenever the situation of competition so requires it. Parties will abandon the catch-all strategy in their secondary dimension in order to persuade the electorate that they can take care of the voters' multiple identities *simultaneously*. This will make parties more attractive for voters for whom their class and territorial identities are equally important, but not only for them. Parties can make good use of *priming* and *framing* in order to change the relative weight of the voter's class and territorial identity to their advantage.

The historical example discussed above shows this very clearly. Initially, each party had a position in its primary dimension of competition (the centre–periphery dimension, in the case of the UUP, and the left–right dimension, in the case of the NILP) and tried a catch-all strategy in the secondary dimension.[10] Because of the cross-cutting nature of the cleavages, with Protestants and Catholics each divided into working and middle class, the catch-all strategy in the secondary dimension brought the parties into each other's 'hunting grounds'. The increasing polarization of the Northern Irish parties along the centre–periphery dimension, with the split between Protestants and Catholics becoming increasingly sectarian, gave an advantage to the UUP with respect to the NILP. The relevance of the

---

[10] Examples of the opposite also exist. For example, the peripheral Walloon party Rassemblement Wallon was initially conveying its separatist message mainly to a working-class constituency but soon changed this strategy for a more catch-all one in the left–right dimension (Kelly 1969: 361). After this strategy also failed, the party moved back to its Socialist origins.

centre–periphery cleavage made it impossible for the NILP to maintain its catch-all strategy in this dimension while it allowed the UUP to take a pro-workers position along the left–right dimension without losing its middle-class Protestant supporters, who were loyal to the UUP for its Protestant stance against Catholics. Eventually the NILP had to take a position on the centre–periphery conflict, characterized by a bi-modal distribution of preferences in society, Protestant and Catholic. Whatever position the NLIP would have chosen it would have lost a large chunk of its working-class electorate, either the Catholic workers or the Protestant workers.

A simultaneous position along the two relevant dimensions of competition has proved a successful strategy on many occasions, as will be shown in the discussion of the cases.[11] The presence of two dimensions allows parties to define electoral strategies not just on their primary dimension, by converging towards the competitor's position, but by using strategic repositioning on the secondary dimension as well. For example, a socialist party that wants to converge towards the centre of the left–right dimension can move towards a pro-periphery position in the secondary dimension as a way to maintain the party's distinctiveness vis-à-vis its centre-right competitor in the primary dimension. This is in fact what the Labour Party did during the 1990s in order to take power after years in opposition. Therefore, the secondary dimension is used as a complement to the first. All that is necessary for this complementation to succeed is that the strategizing party is credible in its moves.

2.3.2 Party strategies along the centre–periphery dimension

An electoral strategy is a set of simultaneous tactics or moves along two or more relevant dimensions of competition with the aim to achieve a positive electoral result for the strategizing party or a negative one for its adversary. An electoral move is a change in the relative emphasis of different issues of the 'package' that represents the party's ideology.

When two dimensions coexist in a polity they need not be equally salient all of the time. There will be periods when one dimension occupies the centre stage while the other remains dormant until some domestic or external event brings it back in. The centre–periphery dimension in Europe has been such a periodically dormant conflict that always comes back. For this reason, an analysis of centre–periphery party competition requires the specification of the period or periods that will enter the analysis and the recognition that many state parties do not face the

---

[11] Esquerra Republicana de Catalunya (ERC), a left-wing secessionist party of Catalonia, has made significant electoral advances in its condition as both a left-wing and a peripheral party at the expense of both the mainstream peripheral party Covergència i Unió (CiU), and the main Socialist party in Catalonia, the Partit des Socialistes de Catalunya (PSC-PSOE).

peripheral challenge for the first time. This means that state parties may already have an acquired profile concerning centre–periphery issues.

The period of interest for us starts after the Second World War, a time when the left–right dimension was the most relevant cleavage line in Europe and when a majority of European countries were centralized unitary states (Marks, Hooghe, et al. 2008). After years of class issues dominance in the 1950s and early 1960s, peripheral parties—old and new—began to make inroads into the electoral arena with demands of political devolution for their territories. Eventually, their growth was large enough to threaten the electoral fortunes of state parties and this is when our story begins.

In their origins, peripheral parties—as any other new party—usually dedicate themselves to one issue only and have no built credibility and reputation; they have everything to prove ahead of them. They are better characterized as protest parties than parties with government aspirations (Elias 2009). This also applies to peripheral parties that return to the political stage after a long period of electoral irrelevance or after a period of democratic breakdown. In order to grow enough to become a threat to mainstream parties and force them to react, peripheral parties need to go beyond the niche of voters with strong pro-periphery preferences that is their initial target. The electoral ceiling that peripheral parties can aspire to is the totality of the peripheral territory's electorate.[12] By definition, peripheral parties cannot and will not go beyond that. The problem is that in polities where other dimensions of competition are also relevant determinants of voting behaviour peripheral parties rarely control more than half the electorate of the peripheral territory and very often much less than half. Therefore, to gain electoral relevance, they need to credibly cater to the voters' multiple territorial and class identities.

Sooner or later vote-maximizing peripheral parties will diversify their issue portfolio. In this respect the peripheral party has several options. One is to emphasize left–right issues, thus getting closer to the issue profile of its immediate state competitor. This would be a strategy of convergence towards the state party's adversary in the left–right dimension. Another option is to emphasize new non-mainstream issues such as the environment or immigration. The incursion into new issues still ignored by the mainstream state competitors is a way of strengthening the peripheral party's reputation as an alternative to mainstream politics. Finally, a third option is to emphasize valence issues such as government efficiency, political corruption, etc. The peripheral party will use these diverse tactics depending on the structure of competition at each particular time and place. *Issue*

---

[12] Most analyses use the size of the minority group as a proxy of the electoral strength that a peripheral party can achieve. This proxy, however, rests on the assumption that *all* the members of the minority and *only* the members of the minority will vote for the peripheral party. In contrast, I use the peripheral territory's population size as the electoral ceiling that a peripheral party can achieve. I do not take identity voting for granted. All the citizens of the peripheral territory are potential voters of the peripheral party and of any other party that competes in that territory.

diversification plays a crucial role in the initial electoral breakthroughs of peripheral parties (Rudolf and Thompson 1985). And, once the breakthroughs are consolidated, state parties cannot ignore peripheral parties and their agendas any longer.

State parties have two main movements along the centre–periphery dimension. They can either converge towards the issue position of their peripheral party competitor (*pro-periphery convergence*) or move away from it and closer to the centralist pole of the dimension (*anti-periphery polarization*). Pro-periphery convergence is an attempt to take voters away from the peripheral party by challenging the exclusivity of the peripheral party's programmatic stance. Only state parties directly threatened by peripheral parties will attempt a pro-periphery move (Harmel and Svasand 1997) for the risks are high that the strategy may backfire, as I will soon explain. Anti-periphery polarization, in turn, aims to attract those voters whose preferences go against the proposals of peripheral parties and who give more relevance to centre–periphery issues than to left–right issues when deciding their vote. Both strategies signal to the electorate that the state party cares about the voters' territorial identities as well as about their social class.

Let us suppose there are two large state parties, A and B, who compete against each other along the left–right dimension. Faced with a peripheral party growth, state party A will continue to ignore centre–periphery issues in its statements if (1) the peripheral party does not directly threaten its capacity to form governing majorities or if (2) state party B is also ignoring centre–periphery issues. There are times, however, when one or both of these possibilities are present. First, it is possible that the electoral growth of the peripheral party makes it a credible electoral threat to state party A (not to party B). In this case, avoiding the issue will signal to party A's voters, who are obviously inclined towards pro-periphery issues and are defecting to the peripheral party, that party A does not care or does not dare to face the demands put forward by the peripheral party. Second, it is possible that state party B, with a reputation as a state nationalist party with centralization preferences, decides to emphasize anti-periphery issues in an attempt to attract voters with anti-periphery preferences who would not otherwise vote for party B but for party A. Third, it is possible that scenarios (1) and (2) occur simultaneously. In any of the three scenarios, the centre–periphery dimension becomes more salient in the electoral arena. The best strategy for state party A is, at this point, to position itself along this dimension. Otherwise, the increasing saliency of the centre–periphery dimension will lead voters to cast their ballot according to their territorial identity and state party A will lose votes to the peripheral party and to state party B.

The strategy of anti-periphery polarization can be used as a reaction to a threatened state party that has taken a pro-periphery move in order to benefit from the difficult position in which the converging state party finds itself (Meguid 2008). The direct benefits of party B's strategy of polarization would come from those voters who are against the agenda of peripheral parties and for whom the centre–periphery dimension is more important than the left–right one when deciding their ballot. The indirect benefits would come from the electoral harm that the polarization strategy may inflict upon the converging state party A (Meguid 2008). Party B presents itself as the only one committed to save the nation-state from the peripheral attacks. This polarization will give state party B an electoral advantage vis-à-vis its opponent, state party A, because now the two camps ('the centre' and 'the periphery') are well defined and very salient. The periphery camp is owned by the peripheral party and the centre camp by polarizing state party B. Under these circumstances, converging state party A would risk losing its anti-periphery voters to party B. The Belgian Liberal Party, for example, benefited from the growth of peripheral parties by adopting an anti-periphery strategy, defending anti-periphery issues, because this provoked the desertion of the 'most moderate and unitarist clienteles' of the Christian Democrats and the Socialists to the Liberals and this 'made them vulnerable to federalist pressure at their fringes' (Kelly 1969: 354).

The strategy of anti-periphery polarization may be *primed* and *framed* in such a way as to transform a position issue (i.e., defending the centralized state) into a valence issue (defending the territorial integrity of the state). Maravall (2008) has been the first author to describe and explain the electoral strategy of conversion of a position issue into a valence issue by way of issue framing and issue saliency.[13] This extreme polarization is intended to attract the vote of the majority of voters outside—and even inside—the peripheral territory that do not want to see the territorial integrity of the state at risk.

As state parties, peripheral parties also have two main movements along the centre–periphery dimension which I prefer to name differently. On the one hand, the peripheral party can radicalize its pro-periphery agenda, increasing the saliency of pro-periphery issues and moving further towards the pro-periphery extreme (*pro-periphery radicalization*). On the other hand, the peripheral party can take a more moderate pro-periphery stance, moving away from the pro-periphery extreme, although staying within the periphery side of the dimension (*pro-periphery moderation*). Alternatively, the peripheral party can strategize outside its primary dimension of competition, by moving along the left–right dimension towards the left or the right side of it (and so mirroring the state parties' 'occupation' of the centre–periphery dimension). This would imply diversifying its issue appeal (*issue diversification*). The strategy of pro-periphery radicalization can be framed in such a way as to transform an issue position (i.e., demand for political decentralization) into a valence issue (i.e., the survival of the peripheral territory

---

[13] He has described this strategy as part of the repertoire of state parties in the United States and Spain: 'It is true that the policy of decentralization does not constitute a valence issue: voters can have diverse preferences. But the Popular Party's strategy dramatized this dimension, transforming it into a threat for the territorial integrity of the Spanish state and polarizing the electorate extremely' (Maravall 2008: 104).

as a differentiated community within the state). The peripheral party can artificially dramatize the situation of danger or neglect of the peripheral territory inside the state in order to convince voters that the only sensible choice for everyone is to defend the interests of the territory against the threat from the central state. By framing pro-periphery issues as if they were valence issues the party aims to change the perceptions of the peripheral electorate about the priority that pro-periphery issues should be given in their voting decision. If successful, this strategy will result in the weakening of the left–right ideological vote in favour of the peripheral identity vote and will provide the peripheral party with the necessary votes to compensate its losses to the pro-periphery state competitor.

To sum up, state parties can converge towards the pro-periphery positions of their peripheral adversaries or move away from these positions and polarize their programmatic agenda. They can also ignore centre–periphery issues completely and intensify their ideological left-wing or right-wing profile. Peripheral parties can radicalize or moderate their pro-periphery profile. Alternatively, they can diversify into other—non-centre–periphery—issues, for example intensifying their left–right message or changing their left–right positions. For peripheral parties diversification makes sense while state parties ignore centre–periphery issues and polarization is more adequate when state parties converge. For state parties, pro-periphery convergence is to be expected when they are directly threatened by the growth of peripheral parties and anti-periphery polarization is most likely when the state party expects that this will damage its left–right adversary.

2.4 CONCLUDING REMARKS

This chapter has presented a model of centre–periphery party competition based on the following assumptions and premises:

1. Voters and parties are rational actors moved by self-interest.

2. Voters have at least two identities, a territorial and a class identity, one of which usually takes precedence over the other.

3. The voter will choose the party that is closest to her policy preferences in the issue dimension that is closest to the voters' main identity; alternatively, the voter will choose the party that is on the same side as the voter in the issue dimension that belongs to the voter's less relevant identity. Normally, the voter will vote attending to its main identity but strategies of *priming* and *framing* during the electoral campaign may change this by giving relevance to issues related to the voter's less relevant identity.

4. Parties are vote-maximizers; they manipulate policies and actions in whatever way they believe will gain them the most votes.

5. Parties use ideologies as information short-cuts; in order to avoid the process of calculating what policy packages will gain the most votes they design ideologies that will appeal to the combination of social groups that are expected to produce the most support.

6. In a two-dimensional policy space, there is more than one combination of social groups that parties can target simultaneously in order to maximize their vote.

7. Parties have to show responsibility and reliability in their programmatic positions if they want to be credible in their promises and thereby keep the loyalty of voters.

According to this, in a country where the policy space is made up of two main dimensions of competition—the centre–periphery and the left–right dimensions—parties will appeal to voters by using saliency and position in both dimensions *simultaneously*. However, the behaviour of parties in the primary dimension of competition (i.e. the dimension in which the party has an acquired reputation and credibility) will differ from those in the secondary dimension. This is so because parties 'own' the issues of the primary dimension whereas the credibility of parties is always at stake on issues of the secondary dimension. This limitation is compensated by the fact that parties have more room for manoeuvre in their secondary dimension of competition than in their primary one. In the latter, lack of integrity or responsibility could be severely punished. In the former, by contrast, parties can more flexibly adapt to the circumstances, moving from a catch-all to a positional tactic and even leapfrogging between positions.

Parties do not aim at *issue ownership* along their secondary dimension of competition. Thus, state parties that adopt a pro-periphery position do not intend to become the 'true proponents' of the issue, as Meguid (2008) claims. For strategizing parties, it is enough that they have credibility in their tactical adoption of the pro-periphery programmatic agenda and that, by gaining this credibility, they deprive peripheral parties of their monopoly over the issue. How effective these strategies are in achieving their goal partly depends on the institutional setting in which they take place. This is the object of analysis of the next chapter.

3

Political Devolution and Credibility Constraints

Political devolution is not intended to accommodate and neutralize the peripheral parties' agenda of decentralization within the state or independence from the state. It would be a futile attempt, since devolved institutions strengthen peripheral parties and encourage their drive to demand further decentralization, as real-life examples continually show (Lustick, Miodownik, et al. 2004; Brancati 2009; Erk and Anderson 2009; Meadwell 2009; Roeder 2009). State politicians know this, if only because they have seen it happen before, so there must be some other reason that encourages them to support devolution regardless. Political devolution is, instead, an electoral strategy that allows state parties to compete effectively with peripheral parties and cause them electoral losses without losing face in front of the electorate and without raising suspicions of opportunism.

This chapter introduces one of the central theses of this book, namely that political devolution reduces the credibility constraints that otherwise limit the state parties' room to manoeuvre and, consequently, their ability to converge towards the positions of peripheral parties' electoral 'hunting grounds'. When threatened by the growth of a peripheral party, a state party cannot permanently ignore centre–periphery issues if it is to retain its electoral plurality or majority. The rational response in this situation is to move closer to the peripheral party's position along the centre–periphery dimension of competition, as we saw in the previous chapter. The problem becomes that in centralized states the state party's pro-periphery moves are so hindered by credibility constraints that convergence will not be effective as a way to stop the defection of voters to the periphery competitor or to attract back the voters already lost to such a competitor.

3.1 THE CREDIBILITY CONSTRAINTS
OF ELECTORAL MOVES

Electoral strategies are not without limits. A party is not free to move anywhere it wants in the political space if it cares about its impact on the voters' opinion; and it does care. Parties must show integrity and responsibility: they must be credible in their statements and promises.

Voters believe that parties will implement their promises if selected for office (Downs 1957; Klingemann, Hofferbert, et al. 1994; Hinich and Munger 1997). Otherwise, they would not vote for the party of their choice or, in some cases, they would not vote at all. The voters' belief that parties will abide by their promises is based on the observation of the parties' past actions. For this reason, the ideology of a party is consistent with its actions in prior election periods, with its statements in the preceding campaign, or with both (Downs 1957: 103). This means that the party is *responsible* (i.e., its statements during the campaign can be projected from its past actions) and *reliable* (i.e., its future actions can be accurately predicted from its statements). A party that changes position, moving far from its established ideological identity, may damage its reputation and lose credibility among its voters and support among its members.

Institutional structures impose certain credibility constraints on the strategic moves of state and peripheral parties along the centre–periphery dimension. In centralized states, state parties' moves are limited by their state-wide constituency: they are parties that organize and mobilize throughout the state, that aim to govern the state and that address the whole state electorate. Consequently, they cannot convincingly defend particularistic sub-state territorial interests (Van Biezen and Hopkin 2006). If a state party defends a pro-periphery agenda[1] and voters believe that the state party's convergent move is truthful, it would be seen as an irresponsible and an unreliable state party and, therefore, its reputation would be damaged. As Heller has put it: 'Any concern about treating all citizens equally conflicts with the kind of locally differentiated policy making that allows local credit claiming' (Heller 2002: 658). If, on the contrary, the state party's pro-periphery move is not credible it would be seen as the opportunistic behaviour of a party willing to pay any price to get to—or stay in—office. In turn this would also damage the party's reputation. As long as state parties remain state-wide they will have difficulties when trying to counteract their peripheral competitors by partly assuming their pro-periphery agendas. Unless state parties justify their move as being positive for all citizens of the state equally, and for all the territories of the state equally, the credibility of the party will be questioned. As a consequence, their reputation will suffer. This often collides with what peripheral parties most want, i.e., recognition of their territories' particularities and differences or, in other words, differential treatment inside the state.

Peripheral parties also face credibility constraints on their strategic moves, but these are less acute than those faced by state parties. The main credibility constraint appears when there is more than one peripheral party competing for votes in the same peripheral territory. Competition between peripheral parties forces them

---

[1] Let us remember that a pro-periphery agenda is not equivalent to a preference for a decentralized state. A pro-periphery agenda implies making concessions to peripheral parties' demands for territorial differentiation and self-government for the geographically concentrated cultural minorities that are commonly—although not necessarily—self-defined as nations with the right to self-determination.

to occupy diverse positions along the pro-periphery side of the dimension with one party always being more extreme or radical (nearer the periphery extreme) than the other. Thus, a moderate peripheral party competing with a state party has to pay attention to what its radical peripheral adversary is doing. Pro-periphery radicalization will be difficult for the moderate peripheral party because the more radical position is already occupied. This is precisely what happened to the Flemish peripheral party Volksunie. Forced out of its moderate pro-periphery position by the regionalized Christian Democratic competitor (Flemish split of the Belgian Christian Democratic party), Volksunie tried to radicalize its pro-periphery stance to no avail, since this position was already 'owned' by the secessionist Vlaams Blok. When only one peripheral party exists, it faces no credibility constraints along the pro-periphery side of the centre–periphery dimension.

The issue diversification strategy may also impose credibility constraints on peripheral parties because it may make them lose their credibility as owners of the pro-periphery agenda. However, this is unlikely to happen since the issue structure of the centre–periphery dimension offers peripheral parties wide room to manoeuvre. This, in turn, allows the party to present to the electorate an 'issue package' that combines radical pro-periphery propositions with issues that will attract less identified voters. Peripheral parties can combine constitutional issues (for example a demand for a directly elected parliament) that would satisfy their intensely pro-periphery voters with economic and social propositions for their respective peripheral territories thereby attracting voters worried by the economic and social situation of the territory in which they live. The latter issues would belong to the left–right dimension and emphasizing them would be part of an issue diversification strategy. Contrary to what happens when state parties want to converge towards pro-periphery positions the issue diversification strategy of peripheral parties allows them to spread their appeal without damaging their reputation and credibility.

Credibility constraints are further enhanced or reduced according to the incumbency status of the party. Incumbent parties show responsibility and reliability both through their statements and their actions. Opposition parties, however, cannot take action (Downs 1957: 104). They rely on their statements to show responsibility and reliability. Peripheral parties in centralized states are most of the time opposition parties.[2] At the state level they are too small to become governing parties and it is generally against their interests to participate as the small partner in coalition governments with state parties. Therefore, they cannot show responsibility and reliability through their government actions but only through the consistency of their statements internally (in relation to their ideology) and externally (across time). This inability to show responsibility and reliability is

---

[2] In decentralized states, peripheral parties may be incumbent parties at the sub-state level of government.

not necessarily a disadvantage for peripheral parties. Voters know that peripheral parties do not aspire to govern the state and therefore, in state elections, they cannot be judged according to their incumbency record. This allows peripheral parties to avoid some of the dilemmas that come with office (i.e., when government parties are forced by external circumstances to do something different from what they had promised) thereby risking the punishment of voters for their unreliability or their opportunism. The status of peripheral parties as opposition parties is, therefore, something that they can use to their advantage while the state is centralized. The few times that peripheral parties have participated in state governments they have paid for it with vote losses in the following election and their credibility as owners of the pro-periphery agenda has been damaged (Rudolf and Thompson 1985; Pulzer 1988).

The incumbent state party at election time will try to replicate the same majority that put the party in office in the previous election since this majority was proven a winning combination. Therefore, the incumbent state party will repeat whatever centre–periphery position and saliency it had in the previous election and will focus the campaign on its incumbency record and on the issues it owns. Thus, the party will show responsibility and reliability in the eyes of the voters. Incumbent state parties which are directly threatened by peripheral parties do not strategize along the centre–periphery dimension between two consecutive elections (the election that put the party in office and the election in which its continuity in office is decided). Instead, they stay put. When governing state parties implement periphery-friendly policies it is because these policies were part of their promises as opposition parties and not because the parties' leaders have changed their minds while in office. This move would show irresponsibility and unreliability; it would be criticized by the adversaries and punished by voters for its opportunism.

The incentives for opposition state parties are completely the opposite to those of parties in office, regardless of whether they are directly threatened by a growing peripheral party or not. They need to find an alternative majority that will throw the incumbent out. As Klingemann, Hofferbert, et al. have put it, '[o]pposition parties, in particular, have a *strong incentive for innovative framing of alternatives to current policy*' (1994: 24, emphasis added). As opposition parties, they have strong incentives to use the centre–periphery dimension to prevent the incumbent party's electoral victory if they think that a left–right move alone will not do it. Therefore, the opposition state party will move strategically between two consecutive elections (the election that put—or kept—the party in the opposition and the election that will decide whether it remains in the opposition) by changing its centre–periphery saliency and/or position.[3]

---

[3] The limiting effect of past trajectories on future strategies is not deterministic; state parties can try to make their 'leapfrogs' look like reasonable moves, but only if they are restricted to positions along the centralization-decentralization scale. No leapfrog along the centre–periphery dimension can pass as anything but sheer opportunism in the eyes of the voters. There are empirical examples of parties that

To sum up, state and peripheral parties strategizing along the two dimensions must be credible in their moves and not look opportunistic. The question is whether they can manage this or not. In this respect, peripheral parties have an advantage over state parties. Peripheral parties can strategize along the two dimensions—centre–periphery and left–right—without raising suspicions of opportunism, unreliability, and/or irresponsibility, whereas state parties have to be careful as to how they justify their pro-periphery moves if their electoral strategy of convergence is to be successful. Without such care, and against the original intention of causing the peripheral party electoral losses, the state party could end up losing even more votes to its peripheral and state adversaries.

One of the central theses of this book claims that a *centralized state is an institutional environment that sets insurmountable credibility constraints for threatened state parties that want to converge towards pro-periphery positions in order to stop the defection of voters with intense pro-periphery preferences from their ranks.* The pro-periphery convergence strategy of threatened state parties will be ineffective and will not put a stop to the growth of peripheral parties because of the credibility constraints attached to it in a centralized institutional setting. These constraints are further strengthened by a likely move of anti-periphery polarization of the adversary. The only way that threatened state parties can effectively compete with peripheral parties along the centre–periphery dimension is if the threatened state party reduces the credibility constraints that accompany a pro-periphery convergence move. In order to reduce these credibility constraints, a politically decentralized institutional setting is necessary. Therefore, *political devolution is an electoral strategy intended to make the state parties' pro-periphery tactics credible and consequently effective to retain voters with pro-periphery preferences who are defecting to the peripheral adversary.*

3.2 DEVOLUTION AND THE WEAKENING OF CREDIBILITY CONSTRAINTS

A state party that is threatened by the growth of a peripheral party faces a double challenge. On the one hand, it needs to move closer to the peripheral party's

---

have made successful shifts from a position against decentralization to a position in favour of it, being rewarded with more votes at election time. Among them are the British Conservative Party, the Belgian Liberal Party, the Spanish Popular Party and the Italian Communist Party and Christian Democracy. However, these repositionings along the centralization–decentralization scale were presented to the electorate with arguments that emphasized aspects of decentralization in which these parties had more credibility and better reputation than their Socialist and Social Democratic competitors. Subsequent chapters will deal with these cases in detail.

agenda with credibility (that is, without the move seeming like sheer political opportunism). On the other hand, credibility cannot come at the expense of responsibility and integrity. The state party has to be credible without looking irresponsible or unreliable and thereby losing face in the eyes of its voters. A centralized unitary state makes this double challenge insurmountable. In the absence of sub-state electoral arenas, it is difficult for a state party to convince voters that the party's leaders really care about what happens in one or two regions of the country[4] for the simple reason that the electoral arena is exclusively state-wide and the party will be rendered accountable at the state level. Therefore, the incentives to care about regional particularities, which are at the core of the centre–periphery conflict, are low.

The presence of regional electoral arenas changes the incentives. When regional parliaments and governments exist state party elites will have to be responsive and accountable to regional electorates as well as to the state-wide one. Regional elections deal with regional issues, even more so the higher the level of competences placed in the hands of the regional administration. León (2006) has demonstrated that as decentralization increases electoral externalities become weaker. The main reason behind this is that the existence of regional governments and legislatures eventually leads to the development of differentiated constituencies that vote differently depending on the level of government (León 2006: 75). Regional institutions become a ubiquitous reality. They have their own symbols and their own particular names. People are born into these political communities; they become familiarized with them and grow an identity with them. Differentiated regional constituencies are formed who, through time, develop a taste for decentralization or at least grow accustomed to it. State parties develop institutional interests at the regional level (Van Houten 2000). According to Martínez-Herrera, 'it is not rare for incumbents to try to gain support for their structures, and for their management of them, by appealing to identification with the regional community' (Martínez-Herrera 2002: 429). Regional governments actively try to produce regional identities and the incumbents of regional governments engaged in this process of regional *nation-building* are not only, or not exclusively peripheral parties (Beramendi 1995; Núñez-Seixas 2005; Brancati 2009).

As a result of all this state parties can adopt pro-periphery positions more freely or, put it differently, state parties are less likely to raise suspicions about their credibility, their consistency, or their opportunism if they defend regional interests at state elections. Decentralization makes it easier for state parties to

---

[4] I use the term 'region' to refer to a geographically defined area within the state that can serve as the basis for a self-governing administrative unit in between the state and the local levels, with an elected parliament and a government accountable to it. A peripheral territory is a special type of region, in the sense of being the homeland of a minority culture which, through social movements and political parties, claims the right of the peripheral territory to self-government or to national self-determination.

successfully compete against peripheral parties on their own terms: those of the centre–periphery dimension.

Credibility constraints do not disappear fully in a politically decentralized state. The conflict is no longer exclusively between 'centralizers' and 'decentralizers' but also between different types of political decentralization. State parties in favour of decentralization are still constrained to defend a symmetrical type of devolution that guarantees the equality of state citizens throughout the state territory irrespective of where they live. Clearly, this is difficult to reconcile with the asymmetric type of devolution that protects territorial particularities which is defended by peripheral parties. Yet a decentralized state allows state parties to adapt their electoral offer to the level on which they are competing and to their interests at each particular level. This means that, in regional elections, state parties can compete against peripheral parties emphasizing exclusively regional issues and defending regional particular interests vis-à-vis the state as convincingly as peripheral parties can. Moreover, state parties can simultaneously play the 'regional card' in regional elections and the 'national card' in state elections without necessarily incurring a contradiction.

The problem for state parties in a decentralized state is no longer how to make a pro-periphery move with credibility but how to avoid that credibility comes at the expense of the state party's unity and the state party's territorial cohesion and consistency. Intergovernmental relations are now a fundamental feature of the system (see Table 3.1). The same party may be in government at the state and regional level simultaneously and have contradicting interests and aspirations on each level. Alternatively, the incumbent state party at the state level may find itself in need of parliamentary support from peripheral parties and peripheral parties may condition this support to their own interests at the regional level. These interests, in turn, may contradict with the interests of the regional branch of the incumbent state party.

The multi-level institutional structure of electoral competition introduces centrifugal pressures within the structure of state parties (Roller and Van Houten 2003: 3; Hough and Jeffery 2006; León 2006; Van Biezen and Hopkin 2006). Regional elections give the regional branches of state parties an independent source of representative legitimacy and a power stronghold. The prestige of a regional political career increases and making a state career relies more strongly on making a regional one. The central party elite has to take into account the regional *barons* because, among other things, if disagreements go utterly wrong it is credible for the regional party elite to split up from the state party. And this is less costly than before devolution. The aftermath of decentralization will empower the regional branches of the state party and will set the respective regional and state-wide strategies apart. Those state parties that are directly threatened by peripheral parties will have incentives to get ever closer to the positions of peripheral parties in regional elections irrespective of the consequences that

TABLE 3.1. *The institutional setting of political devolution*

Institutions		Processes
Regional arena of democratic representation	‣ Regional legislature ‣ Regional executive ‣ Regional party system ‣ Regional electoral system ‣ Regional policy competences constitutionally defined	*Multi-level governance* ‣ State government-state opposition relationship ‣ Regional government– regional opposition relationship ‣ State government– regional government relationship *Multi-level party competition* ‣ State party competition ‣ Regional party competition ‣ Intra-party competition (central leadership versus regional branches) *Multi-level constituencies* ‣ Differential voting

these converging moves may have for the state party's central leadership at the state level (Alonso and Gómez Fortes 2011).

The centre–periphery conflict is entrenched as a result of political devolution. Issues that set the centre against the regions, or some regions against other regions, will be part of daily politics in a decentralized state. Therefore, the relevance of the dimension is, in a way, guaranteed. Its relative saliency with respect to other lines of conflict will, of course, vary from one election to the next but this saliency will never disappear completely.

The establishment of elected regional assemblies and governments, and the subsequent entrenched saliency of the centre–periphery conflict, allow peripheral parties to trade '(national) policy for (regional) authority' (Heller 2002: 658). The peripheral party is in an advantageous position to press for further decentralization whenever the state party at the central government does not have a sufficient majority to govern (Field 2009). Thus, the peripheral party will offer its parliamentary support to the state party so that the latter can see its policies implemented at the state level. The peripheral party will do this in exchange for further authority devolved to the regional institutions. Decentralization offers incentives to parties for this type of exchange and, as a result, a built-in tendency towards the radicalization of the peripheral agenda is created.

Radicalization also serves to artificially create a climate of emergency for the peripheral cause which contributes to make the centre–periphery dimension the most salient in voters' minds when they cast their vote. The more demands granted to peripheral parties the more peripheral parties can present them as achievements to their constituencies and get rewarded with votes in return. The claim that the assimilation of the pro-periphery agenda by state parties would eventually lead to the neutralization of the centre–periphery conflict is unwarranted since such neutralization would require a degree of consensus among state parties that the dynamic of electoral competition disincentives. There will always be electoral benefits to reap from manipulating the centre–periphery conflict in the state party's own benefit.

Devolution also facilitates radicalization in an indirect way. In a decentralized state it is more likely for peripheral parties to become government parties. Being a governmental party at the regional level strengthens the position of the peripheral party vis-à-vis its competitors and enhances its credibility as a party with policy experience and governmental aspirations. Incumbency also offers the peripheral party the opportunity to influence voters' preferences on the centre–periphery dimension through the implementation of *nation-building* public policies. In this manner, the peripheral party is better situated to initiate a radicalization of its pro-periphery agenda, since it has the institutional instruments and the credibility to push it ahead.

This is, very likely, the most enduring and deep effect of political devolution: it changes the distribution of centre–periphery preferences in the electorate. As the literature on policy feedback and political behaviour shows, the implementation of particular policies has direct effects on two fundamental aspects of political behaviour: defining membership and forging a political community or delineating groups (Mettler and Soss 2004). A policy of decentralization may have the unanticipated side-effect of making the electorate in general more receptive to pro-periphery issue positions.

Political devolution seems, therefore, a costly electoral strategy best summarized in one main result: the centre–periphery dimension is made a permanent line of conflict. Why would state parties support devolution if it is so costly? The answer is that state parties discount the costs of devolution when these are not assumed individually by the party that implements devolution but collectively by all the parties in the political system while the benefits are expected to benefit the devolutionist party more than any other party in the system. In the post-devolution era, all state parties will be subject to the same kind of strategic trade-offs and will have to deal with the same divisive pressures that were described in the previous paragraphs. However, only the devolutionist state party will be able to compete credibly and effectively against peripheral parties using strategies of pro-periphery convergence.

3.3 WHEN DEVOLUTION MAKES STRATEGIC SENSE

For this part of my argument, I rely on Meguid's (2009) explanation of devolution, according to which a state party supports devolution when faced with a peripheral party taking votes from the party in state elections in regions in which the party is electorally vulnerable (i.e., upon whose seats the party depends for legislative success). However, my argument moves away from Meguid's in two main respects. First, we have a different understanding of the costs of devolution that brings us to different predictions about state parties' behaviour. Second, I provide an explanation for all-round devolution whereas Meguid's model does not account for this outcome. These differences between Meguid's explanation and that which I present here will become more obvious as I unfold the argument.

When can a threatened state party expect that the costs of devolution will be assumed collectively and the benefits individually by the devolutionist party? I argue that this depends on the country's electoral geography. Electoral geography (i.e., the geographical distribution of parties' votes and the diverse electoral relevance of a country's constituencies) partly determines the incentives for parties to support devolution and the institutional resources available to push it ahead. In this respect, I shall present two main theses, the first of which is taken from Meguid (2009). First, the capacity of a peripheral party to threaten a state party in state elections is determined by the electoral geography of the country. Second, devolution will be supported by threatened state parties with a double, simultaneous, electoral aim: as a means to stop and reverse their state-level electoral losses *and* as a way to secure regional-level electoral majorities.

Explanations of political decentralization in terms of functionalist pressures and administrative efficiency (Sharpe 1993; Marks, Hooghe, et al. 2008), democracy enhancement (Bird 1993; Aja 2003), or state break-up prevention (Stepan 1999) systematically fail to account for the diversity of *actors*, *timing*, *scope* and *degrees* of political decentralization in the world. These analyses describe the outcomes of decentralization but do not explain the political process leading to those outcomes. A more accurate way of explaining the process of political decentralization is by looking at it as the rational act of political parties seeking to achieve certain electoral goals. For some authors, this goal is vote-maximization (O'Neill 2003; León 2006); for others, it is the retention of electoral majorities (Meguid 2009; Sorens 2009).

O'Neill (2003) was among the first to connect political decentralization to parties' electoral calculations. She analyses five presidential systems of Latin America in order to explain their respective processes of political and fiscal decentralization. The trigger of a process of decentralization is a situation in which national parties are nationally weak but sub-nationally strong (I am using O'Neill's terminology here). This happens when national parties have strong pockets of support throughout the country but low expectations about their abilities to remain in the national government (O'Neill 2003: 1069). O'Neill demonstrates that governing parties devolve fiscal and political power to those sub-national arenas in which they are most likely to gain control of it (O'Neill 2003: 1087). Her conclusion is that decentralization is a strategy of power-seeking at the sub-national level intended to compensate for the weakness of the governing party at the national level.[5]

Meguid (2009) extends O'Neill's model to the European context. She also assumes that devolution is the result of a rational political calculation. The trigger of devolution in Europe, as in Latin America, is a situation in which a party is becoming weaker at the state level. However, in contrast to Latin America, the cause of this weakness is the electoral threat coming from peripheral parties with a devolutionist agenda. In Meguid's model, devolution is a strategy of electoral competition aimed at reversing the state party's growing weakness at the state level.

Thus, we arrive at the reverse logic of O'Neill's analysis: parties seek power at the state level and are willing to trade it for less power at the regional level (Meguid 2009). Meguid sees no advantage for the state party at the regional level and, therefore, concludes that devolution will be implemented only when the threatened state party prioritizes state-level power over regional control (Meguid 2009).

Sorens (2009) compares the two rationales for devolution to see which of them can better account for parties' support of decentralization in five European countries (Belgium, France, Italy, Spain, and the United Kingdom). He refers to them as the regional-government-office-seeking motivation (RGOS), which would roughly correspond to O'Neill's model of political and fiscal decentralization, and central-government-office-seeking motivation (CGOS), which would more or less fit Meguid's model of devolution.

According to Sorens' argument, the RGOS motivation is present when the state party expects to join at least one regional government if devolution were to be implemented but does not expect to either join or remain in government at the state level (2009: 257). The implication is, Sorens claims, that opposition parties are more likely to support decentralization than parties in central government, the more so, the more regionally concentrated is the opposition's support. If we are to believe Sorens then government parties would seldom be moved by an RGOS motivation.

The CGOS motivation is present when the state party is convinced that supporting devolution will maximize its countrywide electoral support. This will depend on the electoral system in which the party operates. Always according to Sorens (2009), the more proportional—and multiparty—the electoral system, the more

[5] Although O'Neill's model says nothing about opposition parties' support for decentralization, the motivations that her model attributes to governing parties would explain equally well—or even better— the opposition parties' support for decentralization, particularly when opposition parties have been out of power for a long time.

diverse will be the positions of state parties on the issue of devolution, since different parties will cater to voters with different preferences. The author concludes that in proportional systems the CGOS motivation does not yield strong predictions as to which parties will support devolution (Sorens 2009: 258). In less proportional systems with fewer parties the positions towards devolution will tend to converge towards the median voter. Therefore, says Sorens, support for devolution will only occur when significant majorities in the periphery support it and voters in the core of the country are not significantly opposed (2009: 258).

Sorens concludes that state parties' support for devolution follows more closely the RGOS logic (2009: 269). He finds little evidence of CGOS motivations, a result that he explains because 'the votes won in the periphery can be cancelled out by votes lost in the core' (Sorens 2009: 269) and, therefore, supporting devolution is hardly ever a net vote-winning strategy. Paradoxically, while Meguid's model, based on the state-level logic, satisfactorily explains the British case, Sorens claims that this logic (CGOS) leaves the British case unexplained (2009: 261).

Meguid's and Sorens' models exclude a priori the possibility that state parties' motivations to support and/or to implement a devolution reform simultaneously combine a state-wide *and* a regional logic. And yet it is evident that, in the European cases under analysis here, both logics are simultaneously at play, because state parties need to gain credibility as both state-wide parties and parties with a regional agenda.

3.3.1 How electoral geography matters for the emergence of a peripheral party threat

Peripheral parties are, by definition, geographically concentrated. This implies that their electoral ceiling and, consequently, their threat capacity, is demographically and institutionally determined. Demographically, their electoral ceiling depends on the size of the peripheral territory's population. Institutionally, this population size has a reflection in the electoral system. A peripheral territory (i.e., the territory that is home to a cultural minority within a country) is assigned a number of seats in the state parliament that is more or less proportional to its population size according to the country's electoral rules. How these seats are won is also determined by the electoral system but this is less relevant for the argument at this point so I will return to it at the end of this section. What matters now is the way in which the population size of the peripheral territory translates into the number of seats that the peripheral territory contributes to the state parliament. The larger the number of seats it contributes the larger the electoral relevance of the peripheral territory for state parties with government aspirations. The threat capacity of a peripheral party is therefore defined by the peripheral territory's population size and, through the electoral system, by the number of seats that this territory contributes to the state parliament. Its maximal threat capacity equals the peripheral territory's population size and/or number of seats.

Like Meguid (2009), my first thesis claims that a peripheral party is an electoral threat to a state party when the peripheral party takes votes away from the state party in state elections *(1) in an electorally relevant region in which (2) the threatened state party has a high concentration of its total state-wide vote.* In these circumstances the challenged state party must develop strategies to counteract the peripheral threat if it wants to obtain or retain a parliamentary majority. These strategies are divided into two kinds: those aimed at stopping the defection of voters to the peripheral competitor in the peripheral territory and those aimed at compensating the electoral losses in the peripheral territory by increment-ing electoral support in other regions of the state.

The state parties whose support is geographically concentrated in one or more electorally relevant regions where they are losing votes to growing peripheral parties are more likely to support devolution than those state parties who have either an even distribution of support throughout the country—making them less dependent on the votes coming from particular constituencies—or who do not have to compete with peripheral parties in the electorally relevant constituencies in which they are the strongest party (Meguid 2009).

The electoral system is, of course, a relevant intermediating factor between electoral geography and the emergence of an electoral threat (Meguid 2009). The electoral system establishes the threshold that a party must cross in order to win at least 50 per cent of the seats in parliament and this is a fundamental piece of information for a vote-maximizing party. Additionally, this information is open for all to see and, therefore, available to all the competing parties in the system.

An electoral system is perfectly proportional when a party needs 50 per cent of the votes to obtain 50 per cent of the seats in parliament. This threshold of the necessary number of votes to gain 50 per cent of the seats has a double reading. On the one hand, the lower the threshold, the more beneficial for large parties and the more likely it is for a large party to achieve governmental office. On the other hand, this threshold informs us as to how large a peripheral party needs to be in order to jeopardize the status of a state party as the largest party in the country. Iain McLean has described this very accurately for the Scottish National Party (SNP) in Scotland: 'On a vote share of somewhere between 30 and 35%, the SNP would flip from victim of the electoral system to its beneficiary. With an evenly distributed 35% of the vote, it could win more than half of the seats in Scotland (Labour had just won forty out of seventy-one seats—that is, 56%—in Scotland on 37% of the vote)' (2004: 151). This is why, in general, the lower the minimum percentage of votes necessary to obtain a majority of the seats the more relevant is the threat of peripheral party growth to the threatened state party.

In the case of *winner-takes-all* systems, the value of this threshold depends exclusively on the number of parties. The larger the number of parties, the lower the minimum proportion of votes required to win a majority of seats in parliament[6] (Ruiz-Rufino 2007). In the case of list proportional representation systems, this threshold depends on the assembly size, the number of districts and their sizes, and also on the number of parties (Ruiz-Rufino 2007). In any electoral system that is highly disproportional, the larger the number of parties the larger the possibility of displacement of the majoritarian party by another party.[7] Large state parties will feel more threatened in a highly disproportional system than in a highly proportional one because the number of votes that a peripheral party needs to obtain in order to gain 50 per cent of the seats in parliament is smaller.

Of course, peripheral parties are in general much smaller than state parties. However, within their regions, they can be relatively large, and even the largest. They can be the ones obtaining a majority of the region's seats, particularly in disproportional electoral systems when the vote share necessary is relatively low. For this reason, the threat for state parties at the state level is not a threat of displacement of the state party by the peripheral party. Rather, the threat is that of displacement of the state party as the largest party in the country and as the party of government. Put differently, it is the threat of displacement of the state party by another state party competitor. To sum up, the expectation is that the lower the necessary number of votes to win 50 per cent of the seats, the higher the threat to state parties in the event of a peripheral party growth.

3.3.2 How electoral geography provides incentives to transit the devolutionist path

Meguid (2009) sees devolution as very costly for state parties for two main reasons: first, because it strengthens peripheral parties at the regional level (see also Brancati 2009) and, second, because the powers of the central government are reduced to the benefit of the regional administrations.

In contrast, I argue that *the costs of devolution are not the same across countries but vary with the electoral geography of each country*. On the one hand, the electoral dominance of peripheral parties in regional elections should not be taken for granted, as Meguid does. If the state party is strongly supported in the

---

[6] Let us see it with an example. Let us assume a winner-takes-all electoral system in which there are only two parties. If one of the two parties obtains 50% of the votes in 50% of the districts it can win the elections, i.e., it can gather 50% of the seats in parliament. This the party could achieve with just 25% of the state-wide vote. Now let us increase the number of parties in this fictitious electoral system to four, instead of just two. Now if a party obtains 25% of the votes in 50% of the districts, it can gather 50% of the seats and win the election. This the party could manage with a mere 12.5% of the vote.

[7] Politicians are only too aware of these facts. Meguid (2009: 16) quotes a Labour MP from Scotland, John P. Mackintosh, who remarked: 'If there was a 3% swing from Labour to the SNP, it would give the party a popular majority in Scotland and with each percentage point a number of the 36 seats held by Labour in which the SNP is now running second, would change hands.'

peripheral territory in which it competes with a peripheral challenger, the newly acquired reputation as 'decentralizer' will also help the threatened state party retain and/or regain its support in regional elections as opposed to only in state elections, as Meguid defends. In this case, devolution will actually increase, rather than decrease, the competition between state and peripheral parties in regional elections. On the other hand, the weakening of the central government is not necessarily mirrored by an equal weakening of the state parties' power as Meguid seems to assume. Governing state parties will certainly have fewer competences than before devolution but, in exchange, they will have a chunk of the regional power cake. Besides, the multi-level structure of government offers governing state parties enhanced opportunities for establishing alternative and ad hoc parliamentary majorities at the centre by giving support of regional legislation in exchange for support of state legislation. These processes contribute to enhance the governability of the country in polities with two very large parties highly polarized (Field 2009). Therefore, state parties' net control over political power and economic resources in the country as a whole will be increased. Moreover, it is bound to happen that sooner or later a state party will go to the opposition. When this happens, it is no small consolation if it is still in office in one or more self-governing regions, particularly if they include a wide array of competences and resources.

Different types of electoral geography will therefore render devolution more or less costly to the state parties that face a peripheral threat. Table 3.2 shows the predicted support of state parties for different types of devolution according to the type of electoral geography present in each election and the incumbency status of the party.

When the threatened state party has concentrated support *only* in regions in which it faces a peripheral challenger, its prospects in a decentralized state are uncertain. I argued before that the state party's reputation as a 'decentralizer' will help reverse its losses to the peripheral challenger in regional elections. The party's regional electoral fortunes, therefore, need not be negative. But there is no guarantee. It may well happen that the state party finds itself in the opposition at both the state and the regional level, a most undesired outcome. The electoral prospects of the state party at the regional level will depend on its relative strength with respect to the other parties in the region—peripheral and state parties alike—as well as on the electoral system. The more the uncertainty about the party's electoral prospects in the peripheral region the more the support for decentralization inside the party will depend on other factors.

Meguid, with the British case in mind, advanced two of these factors: the level of party centralization and the state party's leadership's prioritization of state-level power over regional control (2009). I argue, instead, that the most determinant factor is whether the state party is in government or in opposition and, if in opposition, for how long it has been out of office. After all, power abstinence has

TABLE 3.2. *Threatened state parties' predicted support for devolution according to the type of electoral geography*

Type of Electoral Geography	State Party's Incumbency Status	Support for Devolution Inside the State Party	Implemented (If Incumbent) or Promised (If Opposition) Reform
State party has concentrated support *only* in region(s) in which it faces a peripheral party threat	In government	Ambivalent/divided support	No devolution or partial devolution
	In opposition	Unanimous support	All-round devolution
State party has concentrated support not only in region/s with a peripheral party but also, *simultaneously*, in at least one region without peripheral party threat	In government	Unanimous support	All-round devolution
	In opposition	Unanimous support	All-round devolution

Notes: Let us remember that for a threat to exist three conditions must be present: the state party has (1) concentrated electoral support in regions (2) that are electorally relevant and (3) in which state parties face a peripheral challenger.

a direct fundamental impact on a party's leadership and priorities. As Mazzoleni has put it:

> [T]here are instances of opposition parties that supported devolution in order to establish new institutional arenas in which they could exercise political power: this was the case for the various left parties in Italy in the 1960s, in France in the 1970s and in Britain in the 1980s–90s. (2009: 214)

If the party has been in opposition for a long period of time, the benefits of devolution will be strongly appreciated by many inside the state party. When long in opposition, devolution becomes, in the eyes of both the party's members and leadership, equivalent to more democracy and more accountability. Therefore, state parties in the opposition for a long time and with a geographical concentration of support in regions in which they face a peripheral challenger grow dear to the idea of devolution more easily than state parties in government. If instead the state party is in government when the peripheral threat arises then devolution will be seen by many inside the party as an unacceptable price to be paid for peripheral acquiescence and as detrimental to staying in office. Devolution is, under these conditions, unlikely to be supported inside the party for fear that the party would seem irresponsible and unreliable in the eyes of the voters. If the party's leadership decides to implement devolution regardless by giving in to the peripheral party's pressure out of sheer political opportunism then partial devolution (i.e. devolution of power only to the region or regions in which there is a relevant peripheral challenger) will be chosen.

When the threatened state party has concentrated support not only in regions where there is a peripheral party but also, and *simultaneously*, in regions where it does not face a peripheral challenger then the party will opt for all-round devolution. By extending devolution to all the regions of the state, a state party will actually enhance—rather than undermine—its future prospects in those regions where there are no strong peripheral parties and where the state party benefits from a high concentration of support. In this case, all-round devolution is a means to increase the threatened party's power regionally while at the same timing stopping or reversing its losses to the peripheral competitor at state elections. The state-wide and regional logics are therefore simultaneously at play.

All-round devolution has one further advantage: it is easier to 'sell' to the electorate than partial devolution. All-round devolution allows framing decentralization as a good in itself, beneficial for all the citizens and all the regions of the state, beneficial to the quality of the democratic system, and not as the price to pay for peripheral unrest. This is particularly important when the state party is vulnerable to accusations by its state adversaries of 'selling the country off' to the separatists. Therefore, all-round devolution allows a state party to defend political decentralization without looking unreliable and irresponsible *as* a state-wide party. Under these conditions, the threatened state party will support all-round devolution irrespective of whether it is in office or in opposition.

Meguid's model is, in fact, ill prepared to explain all-round devolution due to its assumptions about the costs of devolution. Being so costly, Meguid (2009) argues, state politicians will decentralize just enough to appease peripheral parties and their voters. The implication is that in those regions where there are no voters and parties with a pro-periphery agenda there will be no devolution of powers—a prediction that is empirically wrong.

All-round devolution is not equivalent to symmetrical devolution. The competences that are devolved to the regions need not be exactly the same for all. As a matter of fact, in the presence of a peripheral threat, state parties will choose *all-round asymmetrical devolution*. The reasons have to do with the contradictory demands that state parties are trying to satisfy simultaneously. On the one hand, all-round devolution offers them a credible 'justification' to their pro-periphery strategic move and the opportunity to establish regional electoral strongholds. However, all-round devolution will be opposed by peripheral parties because it does not allow for the differentiation inside the state that they want for their peripheral territories. The solution is to offer peripheral territories more powers than those that will be enjoyed by ordinary (non-peripheral) regions. The problem with this solution is that it is intrinsically unstable. If presented to the electorate as a definitive solution, the electoral selling force of all-round devolution will be lost. This is why it will be put forward as a temporary arrangement until competency symmetry is finally achieved.

Before concluding this section, a word is necessary concerning state parties unthreatened by peripheral parties: Do they have incentives to support devolution? They do, when they are threatened by a state adversary that has concentrated support in electorally relevant regions and defends a decentralization agenda. This is the 'functional equivalent' of a peripheral party. However, this is not a centre–periphery conflict but the centralization–decentralization dimension of competition of which I talked in chapter 2. In this case, the threatened state party will support *all-round symmetrical devolution* given that the pro-decentralization state adversary has no exigency for territorially differentiated decentralization.

3.4 CONCLUDING REMARKS

In a nutshell, the argument presented in this chapter runs as follows. State parties directly threatened by the electoral growth of peripheral parties need to react in order to retain their electoral majorities or pluralities. An immediately available response to the peripheral party growth is to tactically defend some of the least costly policies that are at the core of the peripheral challenger's programmatic agenda. This is expected to allow the threatened state party to retain those voters that are close to it along the left–right dimension but who have strong peripheral identities and, therefore, intense pro-periphery preferences. The problem of this response is that tactical moves in the short-term have to be credible for the success of the strategy in the long-term. Given that state parties' tactical moves are taking place in a unitary centralized state the credibility constraints of a pro-periphery move are very strong indeed. Voters with pro-periphery preferences will not believe that the state party's pro-periphery turn is a truthful one and will not vote for it. Voters with anti-periphery preferences will interpret the state party's move as opportunistic and will punish it by not giving it their vote.

Political devolution is the institutional device to transform the tactical pro-periphery moves of state parties into a credible long-term electoral strategy. The fact that devolution has costs for the strategizing parties will be no constraint as far as the costs are shared equally among all the state parties in the system and the benefits concentrate on the state party that initiates the devolution reform. And this will depend on the electoral geography in place.

Electoral geography refers, on the one hand, to the geographical distribution of votes that characterizes each of the parties in the party system and, on the other hand, to the numeric relevance of the country's electoral constituencies in the state parliament. Electoral geography determines in the first place whether a direct electoral threat emerges or not but, moreover, it also contributes to determine the costs and benefits of devolution. If the threatened state party has concentrated support exclusively in regions in which it faces a peripheral adversary, devolution will only be the best option while the party is in opposition. If the threatened state party has concentrated support in several regions of the state, some of which do not have peripheral parties, the party's best choice is to support devolution irrespective of the party's incumbency status, although being in opposition will urge the party towards devolution to a greater extent.

4

Parties and Voters in Two Dimensions: A First Examination of the Landscape

The aim of this chapter is to provide a first empirical examination of the behaviour of parties and voters in a set of countries in which two dimensions of competition—the centre–periphery and the left–right—have been historically relevant, even though the relative saliency of each dimension has varied across periods and elections within each country. In order to empirically measure the behaviour of parties along the two political dimensions I rely on data from the Comparative Manifestos Project (Volkens, McDonald, et al. 2007), which measures the positions of parties in the political space based on the content-analysis of their electoral programmes or manifestos. The preferences of voters will be measured using respondents' self-placement along the two dimensions as declared in electoral surveys. I then use the empirical indicators of parties' positions and voters' preferences for two main purposes. The first purpose is, as already stated, to offer a general description of the centre–periphery conflict dimension relative to the left–right dimension in Belgium, Italy, Spain, and the UK. The second purpose is to test the assumptions about party behaviour and about the connection between the two dimensions introduced in the previous chapters. Let me repeat them here.

The first assumption is that parties are vote-maximizers and, therefore, they will not limit their issue appeal to just one dimension of competition when the saliency of the other dimension is damaging their electoral prospects. The literature accepts this assumption unproblematically when it refers to mainstream parties (the state parties of this analysis). Peripheral parties are instead characterized as single-issue or niche parties. Contrary to this view, I assume that peripheral parties are also vote-maximizers and will not limit their issue appeal to the centre–periphery dimension but will instead assume positions along other relevant dimensions as well. The second assumption is that the parties' ideologies determine their primary and secondary dimensions of competition. I expect parties to give more saliency to their primary dimension of competition and to assume clearer (i.e. away from the neutral centre) and more consistent positions along their primary dimension of competition relative to the secondary one. I also expect parties to ignore issues only if they belong to the secondary dimension; issues of the primary dimension will always be discussed and highlighted. With respect to the connection between the two dimensions, I test whether they are independent from one another or whether, on the contrary, the parties' and the voters' position in one dimension is related to the position in the other.

4.1 THE NON-EXISTENT CENTRE–PERIPHERY EMPIRICAL SCALE

The centre–periphery dimension is strikingly absent from scholarly attempts to produce comparative empirical models of the space of political competition. During the last 30 years, an impressive amount of research efforts have been dedicated to characterizing, empirically, the policy spaces of Western democracies in terms of the left–right dimension. The same is not true of the centre–periphery cleavage. A clear indicator of this neglect is the absence of a centre–periphery scale of measurement for common use among scholars. Only since 2008 have a few isolated efforts been dedicated to developing an empirical scale of the centre–periphery dimension (Fabre and Martínez-Herrera 2009; Maddens and Libbrecht 2009). The absence of a centre–periphery scale is, in turn, the result of the scarcity of comparative data available to estimate the policy positions of political parties along a centre–periphery dimension—a stark contrast to the relative abundance of comparative data on the left–right dimension.

There are three main sources of data on left–right party positions: expert surveys, mass surveys, and parties' electoral manifestos. The expert surveys consist of asking experts to provide estimates of parties' left–right positions on specific party systems (Castles and Mair 1984; Laver and Hunt 1992; Huber and Inglehart 1995; Laver, Benoit, et al. 2003; Benoit and Laver 2006). The mass surveys, such as the World Values Survey, provide information on the self-reported left–right position of party supporters and have also been used to estimate parties' policy positions (Inglehart and Klingemann 1976; Huber 1989). Finally, the content-analysis of parties' electoral manifestos can, in turn, be divided between those who use human coders for the content-analysis of texts (the Comparative Manifestos Project: Budge, Robertson, et al. 1987; Klingemann, Hofferbert, et al. 1994; Budge, Klingemann, et al. 2001; Klingemann, Volkens, et al. 2006) and those who rely on computerized techniques (Laver and Garry 2000; Laver, Benoit, et al. 2003; Slapin and Proksch 2008).

In theory, the same sources of data could be used to analyse the centre–periphery dimension given that the policy categories for which data are collected do not limit themselves to left–right issues. In practice, however, this is not quite so easy for two main reasons. First, because the existing categorizations of issues in either expert surveys or manifestos' content-analyses do not provide all the information necessary for distilling general centre–periphery positions from policy specific information. The centre–periphery dimension is usually captured by just one or two categories, usually 'centralization–decentralization' and 'nationalism' (Laver and Hunt 1992; Huber and Inglehart 1995; Laver, Benoit, et al. 2003; Benoit and Laver 2006).

In the expert surveys of Laver and Hunt (1992) and Benoit and Laver (2006) the centre–periphery dimension is further captured, somehow arbitrarily, by country-specific categories: the 'Quebec question' is used as a category or policy issue in Canada and the 'Northern Ireland' question is used as a category in the United Kingdom. Following their logic, Benoit and Laver should justify why the 'Basque and Catalan questions' are not considered for Spain, the 'Federation versus Confederation' question is not taken into account for Belgium, and the 'North versus South' question is ignored for Italy.

Decentralization is a basic component of the centre–periphery dimension and, in a sense, this category can be profitable for analysing the policy positions of parties along this issue dimension. However, the centre–periphery dimension does not end with the question of political decentralization, as was explained in chapter 2. In addition, there is a cultural dimension that is at least as important but that is rarely measured.[1] Also, there is an insistence on differential treatment inside the state, or a preference for secession, that cannot be captured either by the centralization–decentralization categories. The Comparative Manifestos Project (CMP) data-set is, in this respect, a bit more generous than the existing expert surveys. At least six positional issues, among a total of 56, are related to the institutional and the cultural aspects of the centre–periphery dimension: centralization–decentralization,[2] national way of life[3] (positive and negative), and multiculturalism[4] (positive and negative). In sum, the existing data-sets dedicate much more space in their operationalization of policy issues to economic, social welfare, and external relations categories. Territorial claims—be they institutional, cultural, or economic—are relegated to one or two categories which do not reflect all the aspects of the centre–periphery dimension.

---

[1] The only two exceptions known to the author are the works by Fabre and Martínez-Herrera (2009) and of Maddens and Libbrecht (2009), who measure the two components—institutional and cultural—of the centre–periphery dimension when analysing the party manifestos of British and Spanish state parties, respectively, in regional elections.

[2] *Centralization*: 'Opposition to political decision-making at lower political levels; support for more centralisation in political and administrative procedures; otherwise as 301, but negative' (Volkens 2001: 31). *Decentralization*: 'Support for federalism or devolution; more regional autonomy for policy or economy; support for keeping up local and regional customs and symbols; favourable mentions of special consideration for local areas; deference to local expertise' (Volkens 2001: 31).

[3] *National way of life, positive*: 'Appeals to patriotism and/or nationalism; suspension of some freedoms in order to protect the state against subversion; support for established national ideas' (Volkens 2001: 34). *National way of life, negative*: 'Against patriotism and/or nationalism; opposition to the existing national state; otherwise as 601, but negative' (Volkens 2001: 34).

[4] *Multiculturalism, positive*: 'Favourable mentions of cultural diversity, communalism, cultural plurality and pillarization; preservation of autonomy of religious, linguistic heritages within the country including special educational provisions'. *Multiculturalism, negative*: 'Enforcement or encouragement of cultural integration; otherwise as 607 but negative' (Volkens 2001: 35).

The second reason why existing data-sets cannot be used to satisfactorily estimate policy positions of parties along a centre–periphery dimension is because all of the existing data have a clear nation-state bias. No comparative data-set of the policy positions of parties exists for the sub-state level. Therefore, existing categorizations do not distinguish between the levels of government to which the policy issues refer (Agasoster 2001). Some initial steps are being taken in this direction, but they are either one-case studies (Agasoster 2001; Pogorelis, Maddens, et al. 2005; Fabre and Martínez-Herrera 2009; Libbrecht, Maddens, et al. 2009), or they are still research in progress.[5]

A partial exception to the absence of available data needed to estimate the policy positions of parties along a centre–periphery dimension are country-specific mass surveys. Although comparative survey data such as the Eurobarometer, the European Social Survey or the World Value Survey do not include questions about the respondent's national/regional identity or the respondent's preferred form of state that could be used for constructing a centre–periphery scale, these questions (and their corresponding scales) do exist in individual country surveys. Unfortunately, they are not comparable because they take different forms and phrasing in different countries. Thus, we are left with scattered data from which to extract party positions that have only limited comparative value.

There is a pressing need to develop a comparative data-set of party policy positions along a centre–periphery dimension of political competition. This need is even more pressing given the multitude of scholarly articles and books being written about multi-level governance within states and the consequences for party competition and for state and sub-state party systems (Deschower 2003; Roller and Van Houten 2003; Amoretti and Bermeo 2004; Hough and Jeffery 2006; Thorlakson 2006; Van Biezen and Hopkin 2006; Hopkin and Van Houten 2009).

With these constraints in mind, the data for this book will come from the best available option: the Comparative Manifestos Project data-set. The CMP data-set has three major advantages with respect to the other data sources. First, it was conceived to test the saliency theory of electoral competition (already discussed in chapter 2) which is one of the basis of my model of competition between parties. Second, it has produced scores over time since 1945 for 54 countries, among them the countries of interest for this analysis. Last, but not least, it includes several issue categories that belong to the centre–periphery dimension of competition as explained above.

---

[5] Marc Debus (Mannheim Centre for European Social Research, MZES) is heading a project entitled 'Party competition, government formation and policy outcomes in West European multi-level systems', for which he is doing content-analysis of party manifestos in sub-state elections. Sonia Alonso (Social Science Research Centre Berlin) and Braulio Gómez (University of Edinburgh) are working on the project 'Regional Manifestos Project. Extending the Manifesto Dataset to Sub-state Elections', with the first phase of the project dedicated to the party manifestos of regional elections in Spain.

Nevertheless, there is one relevant limitation of the CMP data which it shares with expert surveys: it does not distinguish between the levels of government to which the policy issues refer. This limitation has two consequences. First, I will not be able to test any hypothesis involving a comparison between the regional and the state levels of electoral competition; all scores refer to party manifestos written for state elections. Second, the condition for the inclusion of parties in the CMP data-set is that they receive at least 5 per cent of the total vote share in state elections. Exceptionally, some parties under the 5 per cent threshold are included if they are particularly relevant in terms of government formation or of political impact. This threshold leaves out of the CMP data-set many peripheral parties that are electorally significant only at the regional level. The consequence is that only one Italian peripheral party is included in the data-set, Lega Nord, despite the regional relevance of parties such as Südtiroler Volkspartei and Union Valdôtaine. Therefore, the reader should take into account that Italian peripheral parties, being reduced to the Lega Nord, are clearly under-represented in the results. Similarly, the Welsh nationalist party Plaid Cymru is not part of the data-set.

4.2 MEASURING CENTRE–PERIPHERY SALIENCY AND POSITION

The text unit of analysis of the CMP coding procedure is the quasi-sentence, defined as an argument. An argument is the verbal expression of one political idea or issue.[6] All the sentences of parties' electoral programmes are coded into fifty-six issue categories which refer to a wide variety of questions including external relations, democracy and the political system, the economy, welfare and quality of life, the fabric of society and social groups. The CMP registers the number of sentences that a party manifesto dedicates to each category and calculates this number as a percentage over the total number of sentences in the manifesto. The saliency score of each category is, therefore, the rate of mentions that this category receives in a given party manifesto. Most categories of the CMP data-set allow, more or less clearly, for a positional interpretation, despite the emphasis of the data-set on issue saliency.

Table 4.1 shows the categories of the CMP data-set that belong to the centre–periphery dimension and those that belong to the left–right dimension, according to the left–right variable elaborated by Laver and Budge in *Party Policy and Government Coalitions* (1992) and incorporated as such by the CMP data-set (*rile*). The left–right dimension here defined is not exclusively socio-economic.

---

[6] For simplicity I will refer to it as sentence. For an explanation, see Volkens (2001).

The CMP uses a broad operationalization of this dimension by including issues that, strictly speaking, are outside the socio-economic cleavage. For example, some of the issues could well be applied to a progressive–conservative dimension of competition. The advantage of using this broadly conceived left–right dimension is that it subsumes issues that, even if not socio-economic in nature, are still very relevant in the party systems of the countries under analysis.

Concerning the centre–periphery dimension, there are six CMP categories that capture, in part, the issues of the centre–periphery dimension as were defined in chapter 2. These categories are structured in three policy alternatives:

TABLE 4.1. *The CMP categories of centre–periphery and left–right dimensions*

Centre—Per Dimension	CMP Category	CMP Data-set ID number
Centre	Centralization	Per302
	National way of life: positive	Per601
	Multiculturalism: negative	Per608
Periphery	Decentralization	Per301
	National way of life: negative	Per602
	Multiculturalism: positive	Per607

Left–Right Dimension	CMP Category	CMP Data-set ID number
Left	Anti-imperialism	Per103
	Military: negative	Per105
	Peace	Per106
	Internationalism: positive	Per107
	Democracy	Per202
	Market regulation	Per403
	Economic planning	Per404
	Protectionism: positive	Per406
	Controlled economy	Per412
	Nationalization	Per413
	Welfare state expansion	Per504
	Education expansion	Per506
	Labour groups: positive	Per701
Right	Military: positive	Per104
	Freedom and human rights	Per201
	Constitutionalism: positive	Per203
	Political authority	Per305
	Free enterprise	Per401
	Incentives	Per402
	Protectionism: negative	Per407
	Economic orthodoxy	Per414
	Welfare state limitation	Per505
	National way of life: positive	Per601
	Traditional morality: positive	Per603
	Law and order	Per605
	Social harmony	Per606

1. State nationalism versus anti-state nationalism ('national way of life negative and positive').
2. Multiculturalism versus cultural homogeneity ('multiculturalism positive and negative').
3. Centralization versus decentralization.

Saliency scores have both an absolute and a relative meaning. Concerning the former, we need to know what the saliency scores mean in terms of the absolute degree of attention that parties' manifestos give to pro-periphery and pro-centre issues; in other words, we need some yardstick defining what a high- and a low-saliency score are. For this purpose, I have calculated the mean saliency score of the fifty-six categories in our four countries under study. This value is 1.6, with a standard deviation of 1.54. Only a minority of the categories (16 per cent) have an average saliency score above 2 per cent of mentions. Among them, there is one category that belongs to the centre–periphery dimension, 'decentralization', which is the fourth most mentioned category (4.9 average per cent of mentions).[7] Percentages above four are already quite large, and rare, if we look at the totality of manifestos in our sample of countries.

The calculation of the saliency indicator for the centre–periphery dimension is straightforward, i.e. the percentage of sentences that the party manifesto dedicates to the six categories that belong to the centre–periphery dimension:

Centre–periphery saliency = 'decentralization' + 'multiculturalism: positive' + 'national way of life: negative' + 'centralization' + 'national way of life: positive' + 'multiculturalism: negative'.

Pro-periphery saliency = 'decentralization' + 'multiculturalism: positive' + 'national way of life: negative'.

Pro-centre saliency = 'centralization' + 'national way of life: positive' + 'multiculturalism: negative'.

When the saliency score of the pro-periphery issues or that of the pro-centre issues is below 1.6 per cent of mentions in the party manifesto, we can say that the manifesto is ignoring pro-periphery and/or pro-centre issues.

The formula for calculating the saliency of the left–right dimension follows the same logic, but uses, instead, the twenty-six categories identified as belonging to the left–right dimension (Laver and Budge 1992).

In theory, the saliency of the centre–periphery dimension ranges from 0 to 100 per cent. Empirically, however, it ranges from 0 to 46 per cent. This means that there is no party manifesto that has dedicated more than 46 per cent of all its

---

[7] 'Non-economic Demographic Groups' and 'Welfare state expansion' are the two categories with the largest mean rate of mentions, 6.5% and 6% respectively, and the largest empirical range, from 0% to 57% and from 0% to 43%, respectively.

sentences to centre–periphery issues. In turn, the left–right dimension goes from 4 to 59 per cent.

Let us now turn to the relative meaning of the saliency scores. The way in which the dimensions of competition have been constructed poses a problem. Out of fifty-six categories in total in the CMP data-set the left–right dimension is made up of twenty-six categories whereas the centre–periphery dimension only includes six categories. This means that, assuming that both dimensions have the same relevance in any given manifesto, a sentence randomly picked is roughly four times more likely to belong to the left–right dimension than to the centre–periphery one (probability = 0.25). For this reason, when comparing the centre–periphery and the left–right dimensions, I am not interested in the absolute differences between the saliency scores of the two dimensions but in the relative ones. I need to compare the saliency scores of the centre–periphery dimension relative to the saliency scores of the left–right one. The way to compare them is by using a ratio in which our value of interest (the saliency score of the centre–periphery dimension) is divided by our reference value (the saliency score of the left–right dimension). I can then multiply the result by one hundred in order to provide the percentage difference.

In order to create a centre–periphery scale along which parties' preferences as reflected in their manifestos can be placed, I have to derive an indicator of position from the saliency scores that the data-set provides. There are two ways to do this. The first way is to subtract the percentage of pro-centre sentences from the percentage of pro-periphery ones (Budge, Klingemann, et al. 2001):

$$\textit{Centre–periphery position} = \text{Pro-periphery} - \text{Pro-centre}$$

Theoretically, this variable ranges from -100 for a manifesto exclusively dedicated to pro-centre categories to 100 for a manifesto totally devoted to pro-periphery issues. Empirically, however, the variable ranges from -10 to 38. The left–right dimension, on the other hand, ranges from -50 to 59.

Calculated in this way, the position scores obtained do not simply reflect the relative weight of pro-periphery categories with respect to pro-centre ones but are also influenced by the total content of the manifesto (i.e., its size). In other words, two manifestos may share the same number of pro-periphery versus pro-centre sentences and still obtain different position scores if one of the manifestos is much longer in its total number of sentences than the other. This would make the percentages of the larger manifesto different to those of the smaller one, influencing the final score.[8]

---

[8] Let us see it with an example. Let us suppose a manifesto A of 400 sentences that dedicates 200 sentences to pro-periphery categories (50%) and 120 sentences to pro-centre categories (30%). The position score of this manifesto would be: 50 - 30 = 20. Let us suppose that we have another manifesto B which also dedicates 200 sentences to pro-periphery categories and 120 sentences to pro-centre ones. However, this manifesto is 1000 sentences long, which translated into percentages makes the saliency of pro-periphery and pro-centre categories 20% and 12% respectively. This means that the position

Those who defend a confrontational approach to party competition, by contrast, would claim that it is necessary to make the calculation of the position score independent from the size of the manifesto. One such way was defined by Laver and Garry as the 'relative balance of pro and con text units, taken as a proportion of all text units conveying information on this matter' (2000: 628). This is an attempt to separate position from saliency and create a 'pure position' score:

$$Centre–periphery\ pure\ position = (\text{pro-periphery - pro-centre})/$$
$$(\text{pro-periphery + pro-centre})$$

The position variable, so calculated, ranges from -1 for those manifestos that dedicate all the sentences to pro-centre categories to 1 for those manifestos that dedicate all the sentences to pro-periphery categories.[9]

The weakness of this formula is that it assumes that one policy area has nothing to do with the others. This assumption, however, seems unrealistic. Here I follow the Manifesto group when they argue that '[s]ubstantively, this implies that the authors of a programme present policy in one area totally separately from policy in another area, never reviewing the balance of the document as a whole. This seems unrealistic from what we know of the writing of programmes, which are finely tuned and revised as a whole not once but many times' (Budge, Klingemann, et al. 2001: 89). For this reason, the Manifesto group's formula for calculating a party's position along a policy scale is used here.

The centre–periphery scale presented above cannot, strictly speaking, measure extremist policy preferences. For example, the pro-periphery side of the dimension is not measured through categories that differentiate the secessionist territorial preference from territorial preferences that fall short of secession and that would go from a very wide self-government inside the state to a more limited one. At the risk of being repetitive, I insist that the categories available to us through the CMP data-set reflect three dichotomous preferences: decentralization versus centralization; respect and defence of minority cultures versus cultural integration/assimilation inside the majority culture; and state patriotism/nationalism versus opposition to the existing national

---

score would then be: 20 - 12 = 8. If we were to decide which manifesto is more pro-periphery, we would say that on the basis of their position scores manifesto A is more pro-periphery than manifesto B. Let us further suppose that these two manifestos belong to the same party at two different elections and that making its second manifesto much longer, the party has now more space to discuss issues that before were left outside the manifesto. The defenders of the saliency theory would argue that this is the result of a conscious strategy on the part of the party to dilute its pro-periphery profile by dedicating more space to the discussion of other issues that were not dwelled upon in detail on the first manifesto (Budge, Klingemann, et al. 2001: 24). One reason to do so could be that the party leadership does not want the party to be seen by voters as a single-issue party.

[9] If we apply this new formula to the manifestos A and B of the example in the previous footnote, we would obtain the same position score: 0.25.

state. A pro-periphery position indicates the degree of intensity with which the party defends decentralization and minority cultures and opposes the existing national state; it does not tell us whether the peripheral party is or is not a secessionist party. And yet a very intense preference for the defence of minority cultures or against the existing national state would be expected from the more radical peripheral parties, not from the moderate ones. Therefore very high pro-periphery scores do represent, even if only indirectly, more radical positions.

4.3 THE CENTRE–PERIPHERY DIMENSION IN BELGIUM, ITALY, SPAIN, AND THE UK[10]

This section provides an overview of the emphasis that parties give in their manifestos to centre–periphery issues in comparison to left–right ones and of the positions that parties occupy along both dimensions of competition. Data are presented disaggregated by country in order to allow for the identification of commonalities and differences.

The time span for which data exist differs for each country. In Belgium, party manifestos between the years 1946 and 2003 are coded. In Italy, the time span goes from 1946 to 2001; in Spain, from 1977 to 2008; and, finally, in Great Britain from 1945 to 2005. The data-set for this subset of countries has a total of 446 observations or party manifestos. For each party manifesto in the data-set, every quasi-sentence is coded according to the 56 category scheme already discussed in the previous sections. The average length of party manifestos is 700 sentences although there are some manifestos that include as many as 6,000 sentences. The number of sentences dedicated by the party manifesto to each category is calculated as a percentage over the total number of sentences. This is the saliency score of each category. The list of peripheral parties included in the Manifesto Project is provided in Table 4.2.

Table 4.3 shows the mean saliency percentages dedicated by party manifestos to the centre–periphery dimension relative to the left–right dimension for all parties in our four countries. Results are also presented for state and peripheral parties separately. The saliency of the left–right dimension is nearly five times that of the centre–periphery dimension. The ratio means that the centre–periphery categories are only

---

[10] Unfortunately, the CMP data-set does not include the parties of Northern Ireland that participated in British general elections before the devolution of 1998. (For this reason, the CMP refers to 'Great Britain' instead of 'the United Kingdom'. This is, however, inexact, since the parties from Northern Ireland that participated in the British general elections after 1998 are included for analysis.)

TABLE 4.2. *Peripheral parties in Belgium, Italy, Spain, and UK included in the CMP data-set*

Name of Party	Region/s	Country
Volksunie	Flanders	Belgium
De Volksunie-Ideen voor de 21ste eeuw	Flanders	Belgium
Nieuw-Vlaamse Alliantie	Flanders	Belgium
Vlaams Blok	Flanders	Belgium
Front Démocratique des Francophones	Brussels	Belgium
Rassemblement Wallon	Wallonia	Belgium
Lega Nord	North Italy	Italy
Convergència i Unió	Catalonia	Spain
Esquerra Republicana de Catalunya	Catalonia	Spain
Partido Nacionalista Vasco	Basque Country	Spain
Euzkadiko Ezkerra	Basque Country	Spain
Eusko Alkartasuna	Basque Country	Spain
Partido Aragonés Regionalista	Aragon	Spain
Chunta Aragonesista	Aragon	Spain
Coalición Canaria	Canary Islands	Spain
Bloque Nacionalista Galego	Galicia	Spain
Unión del Pueblo Navarro	Navarre	Spain
Scottish National Party	Scotland	United Kingdom
Sinn Féin	Northern Ireland	United Kingdom
Ulster Unionist Party	Northern Ireland	United Kingdom
Democratic Unionist Party	Northern Ireland	United Kingdom

Notes: In 1982–9, the Union of Navarrese People (UPN) joined the PP's parliamentary group in the upper and lower houses although, regionally, they stood as separate parties. From 1991 to 2008 was UPN, part of the PP's parliamentary group, while the PP was represented by UPN in Navarre's regional elections in a relationship that could be considered quasi-federal (Verge and Barberà 2009). This organic relationship prevents us from analysing UPN as an independent peripheral party. The same applies to the peripheral party Initiative for Catalonia Greens (ICV) with respect to the Spanish left-wing party United Left (IU) and, to an extent, the Socialist Party of Catalonia (PSC) with respect to the Spanish Socialist Party (PSOE).

TABLE 4.3. *Mean saliency of the centre–periphery dimension in party manifestos according to party type (Belgium, Italy, Spain, and UK, 1945–2008)*

ALL PARTIES	Mean	S.D.	Min	Max	N
Left–right saliency	38.3	12.8	6.3	86.7	446
Centre–periphery saliency	7.5	7.3	0	38	446
Ratio LR–CP	**0.20**				
ONLY PERIPHERAL PARTIES					
Left–right saliency	31.4	10.5	6.5	55.5	112
Centre–periphery saliency	15.6	8.2	0.7	38	112
Ratio LR–CP	**0.63**				
ONLY STATE PARTIES					
Left–right saliency	40.6	12.7	6.3	86.7	325
Centre–periphery saliency	4.8	4.4	0	29.5	325
Ratio LR–CP	**0.18**				

20 per cent as likely to appear in party manifestos as the left–right categories. We know that, as a result of the embedded inequality in the number of categories that constitute each dimension, the ratio in a manifesto that dedicates the same number of sentences to the centre–periphery and the left–right dimensions should be 0.25 (the left–right dimension has four times more issue categories than the centre–periphery). Therefore, the 0.20 ratio means that political parties give more relevance to the left–right dimension in their manifestos, after controlling for the number of categories that belong to each dimension.

Looking only at peripheral parties, we see that the centre–periphery categories are 63 per cent as likely to appear in party manifestos as left–right categories. By contrast, if we look exclusively at state parties, we see that centre–periphery categories are a mere 18 per cent as likely to appear in party manifestos as left–right categories. The difference between the ratios is very large. This indicates that the centre–periphery dimension is more important for peripheral parties than for state parties, as is to be expected.

Let us now compare the two dimensions of political competition across countries (Table 4.4). In all countries, the difference that sets peripheral parties apart from state parties is large. Peripheral parties everywhere give considerably more emphasis to the centre–periphery dimension relative to the left–right one.

The country where the weight of the centre–periphery dimension relative to the left–right dimension sets the peripheral and the state party families furthest apart is Spain. While the LR–CP ratio among peripheral parties is 0.59 (well above the 0.25 ratio attributable to the unequal number of categories that belong to each dimension), this ratio among state parties is 0.09. Comparatively, state parties in Spain dedicate the least number of sentences to the centre–periphery dimension of competition. In Belgium, Italy, and the United Kingdom the distance between the two party families is similar and half as large as that in Spain. State parties in Belgium, on the other hand, give the largest relevance to the centre–periphery dimension in comparison to the state parties elsewhere. This result is to be expected if we think that state parties in Belgium have not existed since the mid-1970s—having split into francophone and Flemish parties precisely due to the importance that they attributed to the centre–periphery cleavage. At the same time, however, a ratio of 0.17 is a strikingly low figure, considering that the result of this process was the complete territorial division of the party system.

I turn now to a discussion of the parties' positions along the centre–periphery and the left–right dimensions. I expect peripheral parties to always take positions along the centre–periphery dimension and to always be located on the periphery side, although showing a relatively large positional diversity within it. State parties, by contrast, are expected to occupy the pro-centre (pro-state) side of the dimension and to do so also with a relatively large variance. I also expect to see a large number of state parties who avoid taking a position along the centre–periphery dimension of competition. This expectation arises as this dimension is not their primary dimension: the one which they own and in which they have good handling reputations.

TABLE 4.4. *Mean saliency scores of the centre–periphery and left–right dimensions in the party manifestos of Belgium, Italy, Spain, and UK, according to party family*

BELGIUM				
ALL PARTIES	Mean	S.D.	Min	Max
Left–right saliency	36.6	12.3	6.3	66.8
Centre–periphery saliency	8	6.6	0	29.5
Ratio LR–CP	**0.22**			
ONLY PERIPHERAL PARTIES				
Left–right saliency	29.9	13.1	6.5	55.5
Centre–periphery saliency	11.9	7.1	0.7	26.2
Ratio LR–CP	**0.40**			
ONLY STATE PARTIES				
Left–right saliency	39.1	10.9	6.3	66.8
Centre–periphery saliency	6.5	5.7	0	29.5
Ratio LR–CP	**0.17**			
ITALY				
ALL PARTIES	Mean	S.D.	Min	Max
Left–right saliency	38.6	15.5	7.7	86.7
Centre–periphery saliency	3.9	4	0	25.9
Ratio LR–CP	**0.10**			
ONLY PERIPHERAL PARTIES				
Left–right saliency	37.7	4.6	30.9	40.7
Centre–periphery saliency	11.7	4.9	4.3	14.7
Ratio LR–CP	**0.31**			
ONLY STATE PARTIES				
Left–right saliency	38.6	15.8	7.7	86.7
Centre–periphery saliency	3.6	3.7	0	25.9
Ratio LR–CP	**0.10**			
SPAIN				
ALL PARTIES	Mean	S.D.	Min	Max
Left–right saliency	36.5	10.6	16.6	67.2
Centre–periphery saliency	12.7	9.7	1.6	38
Ratio LR–CP	**0.35**			
ONLY PERIPHERAL PARTIES				
Left–right saliency	31.7	8.7	16.6	46.3
Centre–periphery saliency	19.1	7.9	6.7	38
Ratio LR–CP	**0.60**			
ONLY STATE PARTIES				
Left–right saliency	43.1	9.3	22.6	67.2
Centre–periphery saliency	3.8	1.6	1.6	9
Ratio LR–CP	**0.09**			

(Continued)

TABLE 4.4. *Continued*

UNITED KINGDOM				
ALL PARTIES	Mean	S.D.	Min	Max
Left–right saliency	44.9	8	21.7	61.1
Centre–periphery saliency	5.7	3.7	0	15.7
Ratio LR–CP	**0.13**			
ONLY PERIPHERAL PARTIES				
Left–right saliency	42.4	5.0	32	48.3
Centre–periphery saliency	12.4	4.5	7.4	15.7
Ratio LR–CP	**0.29**			
ONLY STATE PARTIES				
Left–right saliency	45.4	8.5	21.7	61.1
Centre–periphery saliency	4.8	3.1	0	15.7
Ratio LR–CP	**0.10**			

TABLE 4.5. *Parties' mean positions along the left–right and the centre–periphery dimensions (Belgium, Italy, Spain, and, UK 1945–2008)*

ALL PARTIES	Mean	S.D.	Min	Max	N
Left–right position	−4.3	17	−50	59	364
No LR position[*]					**0**
Centre–periphery position	6.3	8	−9.6	37.8	364
No CP position					**82 (18%)**
ONLY PERIPHERAL PARTIES					
Left–right position	−8.2	9.6	−28.3	18.7	108
No LR position					**0**
Centre–periphery position	14.8	8.7	−0.29	37.8	108
No CP position					**2 (1.8%)**
ONLY STATE PARTIES					
Left–right position	−3.2	18.7	−50	59	248
No LR position					**0**
Centre–periphery position	2.9	4.1	−9.6	23.1	248
No CP position					**79 (24%)**

[*] Some readers may think that given that the left–right dimension is made up of 26 categories, it comes as no surprise that parties' manifestos do not ignore this dimension. However, the same figures of Table 4.5 are obtained if the left–right dimension is defined exclusively in socio-economic terms (this would reduce the number of LR categories from 26 to 15).

The data in Table 4.5 largely confirm these expectations.[11] Peripheral parties always take position in their primary dimension; the opposite would not make

[11] Let us remember that the position indicator is calculated only if the saliency scores are larger than 1.6. Otherwise, it is assumed that the party shows no position on the scale. On the other hand, a position

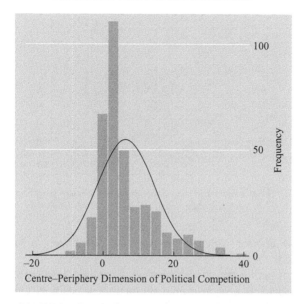

FIGURE 4.1. *The distribution of party positions along the centre–periphery scale (Belgium, Italy, Spain, and the UK, 1945–2008).*

sense. Only 1.8 per cent of the observations correspond to parties that did not take position along the centre–periphery dimension in some election. State parties, in contrast, ignore centre–periphery issues in 25 per cent of all observations. When state parties do take a stand, however, it is a mild pro-periphery one (state parties' mean centre–periphery position is 2.9). State parties are unwilling to take a clear pro-centre (or anti-periphery) stand; only a few do it. There is a major behavioural division between state parties adopting a mild pro-periphery position and those ignoring the centre–periphery dimension altogether. Despite the mild pro-periphery mean score of state parties, the difference with the mean position of peripheral parties is very large and statistically significant. This means that peripheral parties show a considerably more intense pro-periphery stand than state parties do. Table 4.5 further confirms that peripheral parties are highly heterogeneous with respect to their left–right positions and that, on average, they are more to the left than state parties. No party ignores the left–right dimension of political competition.

In Figure 4.1, we can see the empirical distribution of party positions along the centre–periphery dimension. The distribution is skewed to the periphery side of the dimension, as was already insinuated by the data in Table 4.5. This means that the pro-periphery side of the dimension is more densely populated than the pro-centre side. The distribution mean, 6.3, and the median, 3.7, are quite some way

of value '0' means that the pro- and anti- sentences in the manifesto cancel each other out, therefore conveying a neutral (neither nor) or an inconsistent position.

Challenging the State

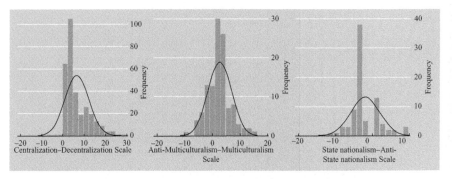

FIGURE 4.2. *The distributions of party positions along the centre–periphery sub-scales*
(Belgium, Italy, Spain, and the UK, 1948–2008)

apart from one another which means that the distribution is far from being normally shaped.

A majority of parties are divided between those in a position of neutrality or ambivalence (score '0'), or in a mild pro-periphery position. Only a minority defend positions clearly in favour of the centre (state), and the few who do it are located in moderate pro-centre positions, mainly supporting state nationalism ('national way of life: positive') and against multiculturalism ('multiculturalism: negative'), as Figure 4.2 shows. This is consistent with other existing research on the subject (Mazzoleni 2009). No party defends political centralization in a consistent and non-ambivalent way, as can be seen if we disaggregate the centre–periphery dimension into its three oppositional categories and look separately at their respective distributions (Figure 4.2). The zero position along the centralization–decentralization scale is favoured by many parties. This means that they are either neutral or inconsistent in their defence of decentralization (i.e., the positive references to centralization and to decentralization cancel each other out). On the decentralization side of the scale, there is variance between those parties that take mild positions in favour of decentralization (a large majority of the cases) and those which take very intense pro-decentralization positions. Curiously though, there are few parties that show ambivalence or inconsistency along the multiculturalism or the state nationalism scales. The zero positions are in both these scales under-populated. A majority of parties are mild state nationalists, mild multiculturalists, and mild or ambivalent decentralizers, as would be expected from vote-maximizing parties.

In the presence of a bi-dimensional political space, the spatial theory of party competition assumes the independence of the dimensions. Two dimensions are independent when the positions of parties in one dimension have no connection with those in the other. This assumption, however, is unrealistic. A connection between the two dimensions has already been empirically demonstrated by some comparative analyses (De Winter 1998; Massetti 2009). The root of this connection is to be found in history.

We know from dozens of historical analyses that the electoral trajectories of socialist and peripheral parties in Spain and the UK have been interwoven from very early on, with socialists and minority nationalists engaged in a direct competition for votes due to the high concentration of working-class voters in their culturally distinct regions, and with the Labour Party and the Socialist Party of Spain hosting among their ranks pro-devolution and pro-federalist pockets of support.[12] Labour's long-term domination of Welsh and Scottish politics has reflected the party's ability to combine both class-based and territorially based sources of electoral support (Keating and Bleiman 1980; Balsom 1983). In fact, a purely class-based explanation of Labour voting in Wales and Scotland has never been able to account for the consistent differences in the size of the Labour vote in these regions compared to Britain as a whole. In the contemporary period, since the early 1970s, direct competition between Labour and the peripheral parties for the working-class vote has become increasingly accentuated.

In Spain socialist and peripheral parties began to emerge simultaneously in the Basque Country and Catalonia during the last decade of the nineteenth century. Neither the Spanish left nor the peripheral parties were electorally strong in the Basque Country or Catalonia until the Second Republic (1931–6). It was then when the Basque Nationalist Party achieved its best electoral results so far in a general election and when the left-wing nationalist party, Esquerra Republicana de Catalunya, became the incumbent party in the Catalan autonomous government, the Generalitat, with votes from both the middle- and the working class. Also during the Second Republic, the Spanish left started to be increasingly sympathetic to the decentralization programme defended by the moderate peripheral parties in the Basque Country and Catalonia. It was precisely due to the dual threat of socialism and separatism (the *rojoseparatista* alliance) that Franco initiated his coup against the Republican government. During the transition to democracy the alliance between socialism, communism, and minority nationalism continued to work through the negotiations of a new Constitution that would re-establish for Basques and Catalans the status of autonomous regions that they had enjoyed, however briefly, during the Second Republic.

In Belgium, Walloon nationalism has historically been associated with left politics while Flemish nationalism has been ideologically Christian Democrat (Erk 2005). In Wallonia, there has been a direct competition for votes between the Rassemblement Wallon and the Walloon branch of the Belgian Socialist Party. Moreover, the Belgian Socialist Party in Wallonia has always hosted a strong pro-devolutionist wing, to the point that the Rassemblement Wallon had its origins in a Walloon separatist movement, the Mouvement Populaire Wallon, established in 1960 by a socialist trade-union leader, André Renard, who, at a Walloon

---

[12] As early in the history of the Labour Party as 1888; Ramsay MacDonald, a Scot and co-founder of the Labour Party, thought that the cause of Labour and the cause of Scottish nationalism were one and the same thing (quotation in McLean 2004: 146).

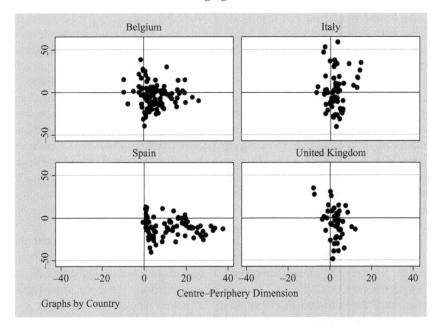

FIGURE 4.3. *The parties' positions along the left–right and the centre–periphery dimensions, by country*

nationalist meeting in that year declared: 'I am a socialist and a Walloon at the same time and I stand for Walloon positions because they are socialist' (Erk 2005: 564). In sum, during the initial years of the Walloon nationalist movement, in the 1950s, the pressure for Walloon devolution came almost exclusively from elements inside the Socialist Party (Kelly 1969: 360; Verleden 2009). The Belgian right represented by the Liberal Party was, by contrast, strongly unitarist or pro-centre (Kelly 1969). On the other hand, in Flanders '[i]n the course of the process towards mass politics, Catholicism and Flemish nationalism became intertwined' (Erk 2005: 560).

These historical trajectories lead us to expect the existence of a relationship between the left–right and the centre–periphery dimensions of competition. Figure 4.3 plots the positions of party manifestos in the two dimensions by country, with the centre–periphery scale occupying the x axis and the left–right scale occupying the y axis. The lower right quadrant of the graph gathers the manifestos that are left and pro-periphery. This lower right quadrant is most populated in the Spanish case, followed by the UK and Belgium. In Italy, there seems to be no relation between ideology and centre–periphery position.

The analysis of the Pearson correlations in Table 4.6 introduces some qualifications to the information provided by the scatter plots. First, in Belgium there seems to be no relevant and statistically significant relationship. Second, in Italy the relationship seems to be the inverse to that found in Spain and the UK:

TABLE 4.6. *Correlations between the party positions on the left–right and the centre–periphery dimensions*

Pearson R	All Countries	Belgium	Italy	Spain	UK
LR * CP	−0.19**	−0.04	0.15	−0.21*	−0.36*

* significant at 5%; ** significant at 1%.

pro-periphery positions are a thing of the right, not of the left. However, the relationship is not relevant and is statistically insignificant.

In those cases in which a significant correlation is found, the correlations are not so high that one can claim that the two dimensions of competition are measuring a single underlying one. Thus, while I can confidently conclude that the assumption of independent dimensions is not a valid one, I cannot confidently conclude that the two dimensions can be 'squeezed' together (Sartori 1976).

To sum up the analysis to this point, I have shown that my main assumptions about the two dimensions of competition are empirically sound. First, the centre–periphery cleavage is a relevant dimension of political competition in the group of countries under analysis. Second, all the parties in these polities convey to the electorate their positions in all the dimensions of competition. The difference between the state and the peripheral party families lies in the saliency that the parties from each family give to each dimension and in the positions that each party family occupy in each dimension. Third, the assumption about the independent relationship between the two dimensions does not hold empirically. In two out of our four countries, being more pro-periphery is associated with being more left-wing.

4.4 THE DIVERSITY OF ISSUES INSIDE PERIPHERAL PARTIES' MANIFESTOS

In chapter 2, I argued that peripheral parties do not limit their issue appeal to the centre–periphery dimension, as is widely assumed in the literature. Once they take the decision to defend their political project through participation in elections, peripheral parties, as any other vote-maximizing party, are driven by their need to gain votes. The decision to emphasize or downplay centre–periphery issues with respect to other types of issues is a strategic one and depends on the structure of party competition in each particular context. For example, many peripheral parties convey a clear and salient position along the left–right dimension of competition (Lynch 2009).

As we also saw in chapter 2, peripheral parties can 'spread' their appeal beyond voters with intense pro-periphery preferences by mixing into their electoral package those issues that attract pro-periphery voters (for example, enhancing the peripheral territory's degree of self-government) and issues that attract more pragmatic voters with no preferences on the centre–periphery cleavage (for example, more fiscal transfers to the peripheral territory that will serve to improve the economic situation there). The implication is that although peripheral parties' positions along the centre–periphery dimension are always on the periphery side, these positions will still vary strategically according to the radicalism of their objectives and the intensity of their pro-periphery preferences relative to other issues outside the centre–periphery dimension.

From these assumptions (namely, that peripheral parties are vote-maximizers and, as such, strategize using saliency and position both within and beyond the centre–periphery dimension) it follows that peripheral parties' electoral fortunes will not automatically suffer whenever state parties assume pro-periphery positions or whenever the centre–periphery dimension is less salient at election time.

It is, therefore, fundamental to test whether these assumptions about the behaviour of peripheral parties are empirically sustained. This section will provide evidence that confirms that peripheral parties constantly change the saliency and position along the centre–periphery and the left–right dimensions of competition in order to maximize their vote shares.

I shall first measure the movements of peripheral parties along the centre–periphery and the left–right dimensions of competition across time. If it is true, as many in the literature claim, that peripheral parties attend exclusively to centre–periphery issues in their agendas, and that they do not strategize outside the centre–periphery dimension, I should find that peripheral parties move little—or not at all—along the left–right scale. Instead, these parties should position themselves at—or near—the centre of the dimension (which shows, as was already explained in the previous section, that the pro-right and pro-left statements in the peripheral parties' manifestos cancel each other out). At the same time, I should also see that peripheral parties move little along the centre–periphery dimension, keeping their positions in the pro-periphery side and at a distance from the neutral centre of the dimension.

Figure 4.4 shows the mean positions of peripheral parties along the centre–periphery and the left–right dimensions across time, disaggregated by country.[13] Peripheral parties change their centre–periphery and left–right positions considerably between elections, particularly their left–right positions. Against the expectation of the niche party thesis, peripheral parties take clear left-wing or right-wing positions along the left–right dimension and only seldom do they position themselves at the centre of the scale. At the same time, peripheral parties take clear

---

[13] Unfortunately, as I have explained earlier, the CMP data-set does not provide data for the peripheral parties of the United Kingdom before the mid-1990s or for the Italian peripheral parties other than the Lega Nord. For this reason, we have few data points for peripheral parties in these two countries.

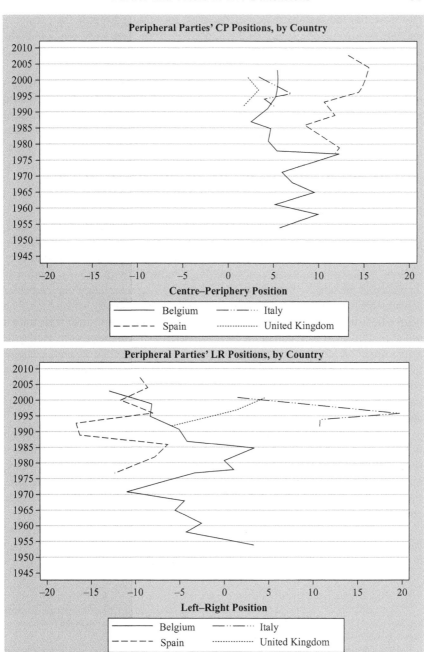

FIGURE 4.4. *The evolution of peripheral parties' mean positions along the centre–periphery and the left–right scales, by country*

moves within the periphery side of the scale by turning towards the periphery extreme or towards the centre of the dimension from election to election as the context of competition requires. Therefore, they tactically move between elections as a result of their electoral strategies of competition.

Next, I look at three main indicators concerning the composition of the peripheral parties' 'issue packages'. *Issue diversity* is the degree to which electoral manifestos have diversified contents, i.e., dedicating attention to a wide range of issues. Peripheral parties are expected to have less diversified manifestos than state parties. In terms of the fifty-six CMP categories into which the manifestos' contents are classified, I define a fully diversified manifesto as the one which gives the same saliency to all fifty-six issue categories or, in other words, a manifesto in which the standard deviation of the saliency scores is 0. Therefore, the larger the standard deviation is the lower the diversity of the manifesto.

Issue consistency is related to reputation. As was already explained in chapter 2, parties 'own' those issues for which they have acquired good 'handling' reputations. In turn, these good reputations emerge as a result of short-term incumbency records and long-term constituency-building (Petrocik 1996: 825–7). I am only interested in the latter, which depends on the party's representation of a particular constituency, and thus of a particular set of issues, consistently across time. The degree of issue consistency conveyed by a party on a particular issue is measured as the coefficient of variation of the issue's saliency score in the party's manifestos across time.[14] A large coefficient of variation would indicate that the party changes its emphasis on an issue greatly from manifesto to manifesto. By contrast, when a party 'owns' an issue, it makes it salient consistently in all of its manifestos (i.e., the coefficient of variation is small). A coefficient of variation below 0.25 reflects a very strong degree of issue consistency.

Finally, the relative saliency of the centre–periphery dimension with respect to the left–right dimension is measured by calculating the left–right/centre–periphery (LR–CP) ratio. Single-issue peripheral parties are assumed to give, proportionally, more relevance in their manifestos to centre–periphery issues relative to the left–right issues. This would be indicated by a ratio above 1 or a percentage change above 100 per cent.

Table 4.7 shows the mean scores of issue consistency, issue diversity, and LR–CP ratio of peripheral parties' manifestos between 1945 and 2008.[15] As the data show, peripheral parties do not restrict their programmatic agendas to

[14] The coefficient of variation is the standard deviation divided by the mean and generally ranges between 0 and 1 (unless the standard deviation is larger than the mean, in which case the coefficient of variation may be larger than 1).

[15] Unfortunately, the degree of issue consistency cannot be calculated for those peripheral parties for which there is a single observation (only one codified manifesto). This happens for all the peripheral parties in the United Kingdom, for which only the 2001 manifestos are codified, and for some Spanish peripheral parties.

TABLE 4.7. *Issue consistency and issue diversification of peripheral parties' manifestos (mean values, 1945–2008)*

Party Name	Issue Diversity	LR/CP Ratio	Consistency 'Decentralization'	Consistency 'National way life: -'	Consistency 'Multiculturalism: +'	Consistency CP Dimension
Convergence and Unity (CiU)	2.83	0.43	0.19	3	0.71	0.21
Catalonian Repub. Left (ERC)	3.15	1	0.26	0.47	0.43	0.24
Basque Solidarity (EA)	2.79	0.37	0.32	0.91	0.64	0.25
Basque Nationalist Party (PNV)	3.22	0.74	0.21	1	0.72	0.18
Galician Nationalist Bloc (BNG)	3.94	1.42	0.35	2	0.33	0.12
Canarian Coalition (CC)	3.24	0.78	0.23	0	0.97	0.22
Andalusian Party (PA)	2.77	0.42	0.05	0	0.39	0.11
Aragonese Union (CHA)	3.20	0.66	0.26	0	0.17	0.23
Walloon Rally (RW)	4.30	0.63	0.67	2.44	0.88	0.66
Francoph. Dem. Front (FDF)	3.90	0.69	0.54	0	0.68	0.51
People's Union (VU)	2.84	0.96	0.60	1.73	0.90	0.44
Flemish Bloc (VB)	2.71	0.18	0.97	1.38	0.51	0.59
Northern League (LN)	2.88	0.30	0.40	0	2	0.42
Scottish National Party (SNP)	2.66	0.37	–	–	–	–
Sinn Féin (SF)	3.29	0.23	–	–	–	–
Ulster Unionist Party (UUP)	2.77	0.18	–	–	–	–
Democratic Unionist P. (DUP)	2.92	0.13	–	–	–	–

centre–periphery issues. On the contrary, they also dedicate a great deal of space to left–right issues, although there is large variation between peripheral parties. Some, such as the Galician Nationalist Bloc, give more relevance to centre–periphery issues relative to left–right issues. Others, such as the Northern Irish parties and the extreme-right peripheral parties Vlaams Berlang and Lega Nord, give more relevance to the left–right issues relative to the centre–periphery ones. Even large governmental parties, such as the Catalan nationalist Convergència i Unió and the Basque Nationalist Party, vary greatly in their relative emphasis to centre–periphery issues. The former is less centre–periphery focused than the latter.

Some small peripheral parties, such as Coalición Canaria (CC), Chunta Aragonesista (CHA), or Partido Andalucista (PA), all three in Spain, give more relative weight to centre–periphery issues with respect to left–right ones than large peripheral parties of long 'pedigree', such as Convergència i Unió (CiU) or the Scottish National Party (SNP). This may be an indication that new peripheral parties have the need to gain credibility and reputation as 'owners' of the pro-periphery agenda to a greater extent than large and consolidated peripheral parties do.

The issue diversity scores further confirm the results of the LR–CP ratio. Peripheral parties are not single-issue parties. Some peripheral manifestos (Rassemblement Wallon, 4.3; Front Démocratique des Francophones, 3.9; Bloque Nacionalista Galego, 3.9), tend to concentrate their attention on a small set of issues and are, therefore, a good approximation to the single-issue depiction of peripheral parties. By contrast, other peripheral parties (Convergència i Unió, 2.8; Scottish National Party, 2.6) show a high degree of issue diversity, close to the diversity levels of state left and right parties (the mean diversity score of the Spanish Socialist and Conservative parties is 2.56 and 2.64 respectively; that of Labour and the Conservatives in the UK is 2.23 and 2.21 respectively). Even within the same country we find variation among parties which is an indication that country factors, though important, are not alone in explaining the degree of issue diversity of peripheral parties' manifestos. The within-country variation is widest in Belgium and narrowest in the UK. Concerning the cross-country differences, peripheral parties in Belgium are those with the least diversified manifestos (mean value is 3.14) whereas peripheral parties in the UK are slightly more diversified (mean value is 2.91).

The issue consistency scores further reveal country-specific patterns. Centre–periphery issues are a *must* of Spanish peripheral manifestos whereas Belgian peripheral parties are not constant in the defence of centre–periphery interests. There is a high variability across manifestos in the degree of attention that Belgian peripheral parties dedicate to the issues of decentralization, multiculturalism, and nationalism. No such variability is to be found among Spanish peripheral parties. They all show a high level of consistency of centre–periphery issues (i.e. low coefficients of variation), particularly of political decentralization. At the same time, the saliency of negative references to Spanish nationalism ('national way of life: negative') varies a lot from election to election for all peripheral parties in

Spain. This shows that Spanish peripheral parties do not frame their manifestos in terms of opposing the Spanish national idea but, instead, in terms of institutional claims for more political autonomy. Again we find empirical confirmation of the saliency theory of electoral party competition.

To sum up, peripheral parties are a heterogeneous group. There is great variation: across place and time, in the degree of attention that peripheral parties dedicate to the centre–periphery dimension relative to the left–right one, and in the positions occupied along these dimensions. It would be a mistake to consider peripheral parties as single-issue actors that cannot strategize outside their issue dimension. The saliency and position of centre–periphery and left–right issues in peripheral parties' manifestos is as much a result of electoral calculation as it is for state parties. We should therefore expect that the variation found can be partly explained by the dynamic of competition between state and peripheral parties.

4.5 VOTERS' PREFERENCES ALONG THE CENTRE–PERIPHERY DIMENSION

Until now, I have looked exclusively at the positions of political parties along the centre–periphery dimension. I shall end this presentation of the centre–periphery cleavage by looking into the distribution of preferences in society.[16] What is the position of the mass publics concerning the centre–periphery dimension? Are parties faithfully representing the opinions of their mass electorates?

It is difficult to estimate the electorate's positions along the centre–periphery dimension using comparative data. Questions concerning the respondent's national/regional identity or the respondent's preferred form of state, which could be used to create a centre–periphery scale, are not included in comparative European and international surveys. These questions and scales do exist in individual country surveys but their formulation is country-specific in that they are adapted to the historical and political circumstances in each country. The way surveys formulate their items is a reflection of the society in which they are embedded. In Italy, for example, election studies do not include any question about national/regional identity or concerning the respondent's preferred form of state or territorial distribution of state power.[17] Clearly, the centre–periphery dimension is not considered to be of relevance for the study of public opinion although, as we know, political decentralization has moved up in the agenda of political parties

---

[16] All the descriptive statistics presented in this section, and based on survey data, have been calculated applying the population weights indicated by the respective surveys' documentation.

[17] Italian election studies realized by Doxa (Istituto per le Ricerche Statistiche e l'Analisi dell'Opinione Pubblica) for the Cattaneo Institute (1968–2006).

during the last decade—particularly since 2001. I am, therefore, unable to use Italian survey data in order to measure the position of the Italian public on centre–periphery issues.

In Great Britain, it is only recently (after 1997) that the election studies include questions on identity in all three British regions, England, Scotland, and Wales.[18] The 1992 general election study includes the Moreno question[19] only for the Scottish sample. Before that, there were no questions concerning the centre–periphery cleavage, again showing a clear disregard for the issues of the centre–periphery dimension while these issues were upfront in the agenda of political parties, at least in the elections of 1974 and 1994. For the analysis of the data, I use the 2005 British Election Study which includes the Moreno question, and I assume that it approximates the centre–periphery dimension in the following manner: those who feel exclusively or mainly from a sub-state nation (i.e., English, Scots, Welsh) are assumed to represent the periphery side of the dimension while those who feel exclusively or mainly from the state nation (i.e., British) are assumed to represent the centre side.

Spanish electoral surveys[20] have included, since 1980, a 'nationalism scale' for the surveys in the Basque Country, Catalonia, and Galicia and, during the last years, a 'regionalism scale' for the surveys in the rest of the Autonomous Communities, indicating a growing relevance of the centre–periphery dimension in regions of no distinctive cultural background. The formulation of the nationalism scale included in Spanish surveys changed in 1988. Before 1988, the scale was similar to the centre–periphery scale that I am proposing here: it went from 1 (maximum minority nationalism) to 10 (maximum centralism). After 1988, however, the scale was changed to range from 1 (minimum minority nationalism) to 10 (maximum minority nationalism). Thus, the scale after 1988 does not include the two possible extremes of the dimension but only the periphery extreme. This change is a completely different way of understanding the dimension of competition. Those respondents who would like to position themselves as Spanish nationalists cannot do so. Respondents are either minority nationalists or non-minority nationalists which is a one-sided understanding of nationalism indeed. For the present analysis, two surveys by the Centro de Investigaciones Sociológicas from 1992 (CIS 2025–2041) and 1998 (CIS 2286) are used. These two surveys use the same questionnaire in all the Autonomous Communities (regions) of Spain with large samples in each. Both include the nationalism scale. The 1992 survey uses a nationalism scale in the historical Autonomous Communities (Basque Country, Catalonia, and Galicia) and a regionalism scale in the rest of regions. The 1998 survey,

[18] British General Election Studies (1974–2005).

[19] The Moreno question is formulated as follows: 'Do you feel only Scot/Eng/Welsh, more Scot/Eng/Welsh than British, equally Scot/Eng/Welsh and British, more British than Scot/Eng/Welsh or only British?'

[20] CIS (Centro de Investigaciones Sociológicas) surveys (1980–2007).

by contrast, applies both scales to all the Autonomous Communities. Thus, each regional questionnaire asks respondents to place themselves both on a regionalism scale and a nationalism scale. It is difficult to understand the rationale behind this proceeding. Moreover, it is not clear to what extent respondents were able to understand the full implications of the distinction between regionalism and nationalism. The two scales have a Pearson correlation of 1, indicating that they are measuring the same thing. The difference between them is that only 21 per cent of respondents answered the nationalism scale whereas 79 per cent answered the regionalism one. In all the Autonomous Communities except in the Basque Country, a great majority of respondents answered the regionalism scale as opposed to the nationalism one. I discuss the results from both scales.

Belgian election studies include a centre–periphery scale, but the formulation is different to the Spanish one.[21] The Belgian scale asks respondents to position themselves in a continuum that ranges from 0 (if respondents think that Flanders/Wallonia/Brussels must be able to decide everything by themselves), to 10 (if respondents think that Belgium must be the one able to decide everything). In contrast with the Spanish nationalism and regionalism scales, which present before respondents ideological labels, the Belgian scale explicitly refers to one feature of the centre–periphery issue: which territorial level should have the power and authority to make all political decisions. For the present analysis I shall use the Belgium Election Studies of 1991 and 2005.

In the cases of Spain and Belgium, I present the results for two different years in order to test the assumption that the distribution of preferences in society does not change very much across time. Testing this assumption is important because the electoral strategies of parties are either constrained or enhanced by the distribution of voters' preferences. When this distribution changes so do the choices available to political parties. The selection of years is dependent upon the availability of data. The time gap between the two Belgian surveys used is fourteen years. In Spain it is a mere five-year gap but there is no previous survey that includes the required question for all the Autonomous Communities in a large sample.

The distribution of preferences in society is, in most cases, uni-modal (Belgium in 1991 would be the exception) with the majority of observations positioned at the centre of the scale similar to the distribution of parties' positions (see Figure 4.5). This means that the majority of mass publics in our sample of countries defend a moderate centrist position. In some distributions, however, the ends of the scale are also largely populated. In particular, this is seen on the periphery end (see, for example, Belgium and Spain).

[21] Belgium General Election Studies (1991–2003), ISPO and PIOP—Inter-university Centres for Political Opinion Research.

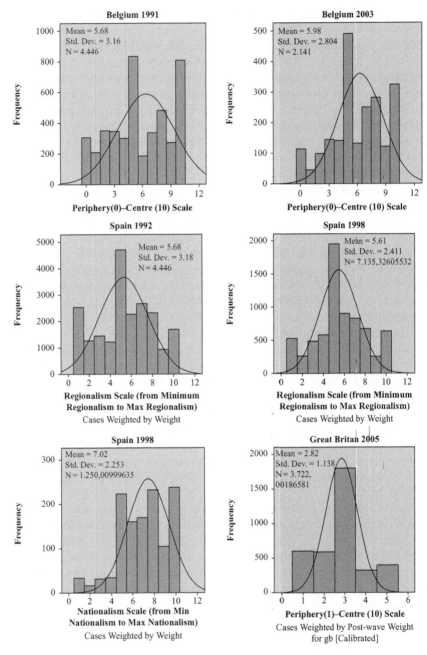

FIGURE 4.5. *Distributions of preferences of survey respondents along the centre–periphery dimension*

TABLE 4.8. *Contingency tables of respondents' left–right self-placement as depending on the centre–periphery self-placement in Belgium, Great Britain, and Spain*

Spain 1992			
	Left	Right	Total
Non pro-periphery	6662	2066	8729
	76.32	23.68	100.00
Pro-periphery	5885	1984	7869
	74.79	25.21	100.00
Spain 1998			
	Left	Right	Total
Non pro-periphery	2335	899	3234
	72.19	27.81	100.00
Pro-periphery	2242	1010	3252
	68.94	31.06	100.00
Belgium 1991			
	Left	Right	Total
Pro-centre	1648	895	2543
	64.81	35.19	100.00
Pro-periphery	876	510	1386
	63.20	36.80	100.00
Belgium 2003			
	Left	Right	Total
Pro-centre	1040	409	1449
	71.77	28.23	100.00
Pro-periphery	324	180	504
	64.29	35.71	100.00
Great Britain 2005			
	Left	Right	Total
Pro-periphery	557	493	1050
	53.07	46.93	100.00
Centre of scale	913	616	1529
	59.73	40.27	100.00
Pro-centre	382	256	638
	59.82	40.18	100.00

Figure 4.5 shows that the distribution of preferences in society does change across time, even if not greatly. In Belgium, the two extremes of the scale are less densely populated in 2003 with respect to 1991, while the centre of the scale accommodates a larger number of observations. The median of the distribution has moved from 5 to 6 and the standard deviation has decreased. This is an indication of increased moderation in society. In Spain, the extremes of the scale are less

densely populated in 1998 than in 1992, particularly the pro-centre or state centralist extreme. The median of the distribution has moved from 7 to 6 and the standard deviation is smaller. This indicates, as in Belgium, a movement towards more centred positions among the mass public.

I finish this section by testing the assumption of independence between the dimensions. Are the left–right and the centre–periphery scales independent from one another from the point of view of the voters? In order to answer this question, I have transformed the diverse centre–periphery scales into a two-category variable by country as follows: In Belgium the new categories are: pro-periphery and pro-centre or state centralist; in Spain: pro-periphery and non pro-periphery; and, finally, in Great Britain, given that the centre–periphery scale is based on the Moreno question and thus it cannot be sensibly reduced into a two-category variable, I have transformed it into three categories: pro-periphery, centre of the scale, pro-centre or state centralist. The left–right scale has also been recoded into a two-category variable: left and right. Table 4.8 shows the contingency tables of the centre–periphery scale as the independent variable (rows) and the left–right scale as the response variable (column) by country. The assumption of independence between the centre–periphery and the left–right dimensions has to be rejected.[22] The results show that the respondents' preferred position in the left–right dimension partly depends on their position on the centre–periphery dimension. The only exception is Belgium in 1991, where the two dimensions are independent.

Everywhere the pro-periphery position is more likely to be right-wing than the pro-centre (or non pro-periphery) position. The relationship between the two dimensions at the level of mass publics is the opposite of the one found in the party manifestos of two of our countries under analysis. In other words, the results indicate that left parties, but right voters, are the most likely pro-periphery defenders. However, given our knowledge of the particular cases, this seems an inaccurate description of the electorate of some regions in Spain and Great Britain in which the association between minority nationalism and the left is very strong. I am referring to the Basque Country, Scotland, and Wales. If I replicate the contingency tables disaggregated for these regions, I find that among the Scottish and Welsh mass publics the two dimensions of competition are actually independent from one another. In the Basque Country the assumption of independence varies across time. In 1992, a pro-periphery voter in the Basque Country was more likely to be left-wing than a non-pro-periphery voter. In 1998, by contrast, the voters' position on the centre–periphery dimension was independent from the left–right position.

---

[22] The Pearson Chi square test finds a significant relationship in all cases at the 0.05 level except in Belgium 1991, where the null hypothesis of independence cannot be rejected.

4.6 CONCLUDING REMARKS

The main objective of this chapter has been to test the assumptions about party behaviour on which the hypotheses about centre–periphery party competition are based. I have proposed an empirical scale with which to measure the centre–periphery dimension of electoral competition. The scale is based on data that come from the content analysis of parties' electoral manifestos (the Comparative Manifestos Project data-set).

Descriptive statistics have been used subsequently to present a general picture of the centre–periphery and the left–right dimensions of competition in the four countries under analysis. The peripheral and the state party families have been compared attending to their saliency and position on the two dimensions of competition. It has been shown that state parties' manifestos give comparatively more saliency to left–right issues than to centre–periphery ones, and that their positions are comparatively less pro-periphery than those of peripheral parties. Moreover, a considerable amount of state parties prefer to completely ignore centre–periphery issues in their manifestos rather than adopting an anti-periphery position. It has also been demonstrated that peripheral parties are not single-issue organizations, even if their manifestos dedicate much more space to emphasize centre–periphery issues than state parties do. Peripheral parties are a heterogeneous group whose manifestos present a large variance in the levels of saliency, position, and consistency of the pro-periphery issues.

Finally, I have shown that the voters' preferences along the centre–periphery dimension concentrate on the middle of the scale and that there has been a process of increased moderation across time. The voters' distributions of preferences are consistent with the average positions adopted by political parties—which tend to be mildly pro-periphery—as is to be expected from vote-maximizing parties. It will be the task of the following chapters to analyse the dynamic of centre–periphery competition between state and peripheral parties and to explain the differences found among the four countries under analysis.

5

The Emergence of a Peripheral Party Threat

In chapter 3, I argued that the perception of an electoral threat coming from a challenger with a devolutionist agenda is the trigger that unleashes a dynamic of political decentralization. Faced with a direct electoral threat, a state party has to react and stop the defection of voters to the devolutionist competitor or regain voters who already defected. This usually takes the form of a convergent move towards the devolutionist agenda of the challenging party, as will be shown in chapter 6.

For a threat to exist, however, it is not enough that the state party loses voters to the devolutionist challenger. At the same time these votes must be relevant or indispensable for the state party to achieve a plurality or a majority of the seats in parliament. A threat exists only when the electoral losses have weakening effects for the state party at the state level.

The aim of this chapter is to test the arguments, put forward in chapter 3, which explain the emergence of an electoral threat. According to these arguments, the capacity of a peripheral party to threaten a state party in a state election is determined by the country's electoral geography, being the electoral system an important intermediating factor. Concerning electoral geography the thesis is as follows: a peripheral party is an unavoidable electoral threat to a state party when (a) the peripheral party takes votes away from the state party in state elections (b) and this happens in an electorally relevant region in which (c) the state party has a high concentration of its total state-wide vote. Concerning the electoral system, this thesis establishes that the lower the necessary number of votes to win 50 per cent of the parliamentary seats is the larger the vulnerability of the state party to the peripheral challenger will be.

The chapter proceeds as follows. First, I will present data that demonstrate the electoral growth of peripheral parties in the four countries under study. Second, I will show which state party or parties are losing most voters to the peripheral challenger. Third, I will describe the electoral geography of each country with respect to three indicators: electoral relevance, electoral vulnerability, and concentration of electoral support. Next, I will discuss the electoral systems of each country in terms of their respective thresholds of vulnerability for state parties. Finally, I will identify those parties whose losses to peripheral parties had become a liability for their aspirations to achieve parliamentary majorities.

5.1 THE ELECTORAL GROWTH OF PERIPHERAL PARTIES

The presence of peripheral parties and peripheral mobilization in Belgium, Italy, Spain, and the UK precedes, by several decades, the devolution reforms initiated during the post-Second World War period. Self-proclaimed 'national minorities' had been pushing for cultural and/or territorial recognition since the early 1900s when the first regionalist and nationalist movements began to organize politically and to present candidates in—mainly local—elections. All four countries experienced peripheral mobilization by regionalist and nationalist movements during the beginning of the 1900s, albeit with different degrees of success.

Figure 5.1 shows the trajectories of peripheral party formation in our sample of countries. The data-set on which Figure 5.1 is based includes all the peripheral parties founded during this period, irrespective of whether they have had electoral success or not, and including those that have already been dissolved or merged into other parties. It is, therefore, a measure of party formation but not of party strength or party stability. As one goes back in time, the difficulty of finding appropriate data increases. Because of this, the figures for the first two decades of the 1900s probably underestimate the actual number of peripheral parties that were being established during that period, particularly if they did not survive for more than one electoral cycle.

If we look at the period before 1960 we see that, with the exception of war periods, peripheral parties were being created everywhere and at all times. In Spain during the 1920s and 1930s the formation of peripheral parties showed a peak of intensity that was then stopped by the outbreak of the Civil War. In Italy, peripheral party formation increased in intensity during the late 1940s when the country embarked on the design and approval of a new Constitution. In Belgium, peripheral party formation took place during the 1920s and 1930s and again after the Second World War. Finally, in the UK the formation of peripheral parties increased, in particular, during the first decades of the 1900s at the height of the Irish conflict and when nationalists in Wales and Scotland were starting to organize themselves.

The number of peripheral parties being created, however, tells us nothing about their strength or, as Brancati (2007) would put it, about their capacity to force state parties into institutional policies of decentralization. If it did, we should have seen devolution taking place earlier in all four countries. And yet there are only two episodes of devolution prior to the Second World War: the granting of political autonomy to Catalonia and the Basque Country during the Spanish Second Republic (1930–6) and to Northern Ireland in 1921. The latter case was the last episode in a decades-long process of Irish Home Rule that ended with the north–south division of Ireland and the independence of its Southern part from the United Kingdom. These three episodes of devolution are beyond the scope of analysis of this book. Yet, all three are susceptible to the same explanation as the most recent ones. In a nutshell, peripheral parties in Catalonia and the Basque Country during the 1930s and in Ireland during the 1910s and the 1920s were

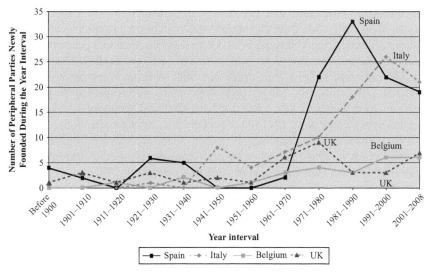

FIGURE 5.1. *Number of new peripheral parties established per decade since 1900 in Belgium, Italy, Spain, and the UK*

growing enough as to represent a direct electoral threat for the Spanish and British state parties (Tussell 1982; Preston 1984; McLean 2001; Jackson 2003).

Let us now turn back to the post-Second World War devolution episodes. Peripheral parties in Belgium, Italy, and the UK began to grow electorally in the 1960s: the Volksunie in Flanders and the Brabant province (where Brussels was situated); the Rassemblement Wallon in Wallonia; the Front Démocratique des Francophones in Brussels; the Scottish National Party in Scotland; Plaid Cymru in Wales; the Südtiroler Volkspartei in South Tyrol; and the Union Valdôtaine in Valle d'Aosta. Since they are, by definition, exclusively active in one or two regions their electoral impact in state elections is better analysed at the regional level at which they compete. All the electoral data discussed in this section are presented in the Appendix to this chapter.

The Flemish peripheral party Volksunie, a successor to the Christian Flemish People's Union founded by an alliance of Flemish nationalists, competed for the first time in state elections in 1954 and obtained 4 per cent of the vote (Table 5.3 in Appendix). The Christian Democrats (CVP-PSC) fell from nearly 61 per cent of the Flemish vote in 1950—its maximum ever in the region of Flanders (and the country as a whole)—to 52.8 per cent. Part of this vote may have gone to the Liberals and Socialists, which increased their Flemish vote share by 2 per cent and 3 per cent respectively, but this still leaves a part of the Christian Democratic electoral loss unaccounted for. In this respect, it is very likely that the great bulk of the Volksunie's vote share came from Christian Democratic voters. Unfortunately, I know of no survey data from that period which can be used to confirm this. In the following election, the Volksunie's (VU) vote share declined to 3 per cent, only to double in the next one: from 3 per cent in 1958 to 6 per cent in 1961. The results of the 1961 election suggest that, again, the bulk of these votes came from the Christian Democrats, who lost six percentage points with respect to the previous election. As a matter of fact, since 1958 the CVP-PSC continuously lost votes election after election until 1971 (6 per cent in 1961, 7 per cent in 1965, 5 per cent in 1968) while the VU continuously gained them, multiplying by five its first electoral result in 1954. The VU also grew considerably in the Brabant region, from slightly more than 1 per cent in 1958 to 8 per cent in 1971.

Rassemblement Wallon (RW) was a relatively short-lived party, representing the French-speaking community of the Walloon region. However, in the decade between 1968 and 1978 (Table 5.3 in Appendix) it became the fourth electoral force in the region. Its peak vote share of 20 per cent came in 1971, when it displaced the Liberals as the third largest party (after the Socialists and the Christian Democrats). Its electoral growth started four electoral periods after the Volksunie and was clearly a reaction to the success of the Flemish peripheral party and to the impact that this success was having in the policy agenda of the state parties in Flanders. The Socialists maintained their vote share in Wallonia between 1965 and 1971. The CVP-PSC—concretely its Walloon wing—was the one party to lose heavily to RW (Coombes and Norton-Taylor 1968). The Walloon peripheral party did not manage to harm the Socialists in their electoral stronghold despite the proximity of the two parties in the left–right dimension. The fact that the Christian Democrats were the ones to lose voters to RW despite the larger distance separating them in the left–right dimension is an indicator that the centre–periphery dimension was for some voters more important than the left–right one when deciding their vote.

The Front Démocratique des Francophones (FDF) represented the French-speaking community of Brussels, situated in the province of Brabant. It contested elections for the first time in 1965, obtaining 6 per cent of the province's vote. In the following election it doubled its vote share to 13 per cent, and in the next one it joined forces with its sister party in Wallonia, the RW, to obtain 24 per cent of votes in the province (28 per cent in the Bruxelles-Hal-Vilvorde electoral district). The most affected by the growth of the FDF were the Liberals who were slightly stronger in Brussels than in the rest of the country. The Liberal Party's percentage of the vote fell from 30 per cent in the province in 1965 to 16 per cent in 1971.[1] Meanwhile, the vote shares for the Socialists and the Christian Democrats in Brabant remained more or less the same.

---

[1] This is the vote share that results from adding together the votes of the Liberal Party and of its split, the Liberal Party of Brussels.

Peripheral parties had only two seats in the Belgian state parliament which resulted from the 1954 election. By the 1968 election, by contrast, they had already gathered 37 seats, out of a total of 212 (see Table 5.8 in Appendix). As I will soon demonstrate, such a dramatic growth of peripheral representation had a considerable impact on the state parties' strategies.

Though Plaid Cymru (PC) was founded in 1925, and the Scottish National Party (SNP) in 1928, it was not until after the Second World War that they began to achieve a measure of electoral success. The 1966–70 period was one of take-off for both peripheral parties, starting with various by-election victories. In the 1966 British general election, the SNP achieved notable advances in the industrial Labour-held seats of central Scotland (see Table 5.9 in Appendix). A near-victory in the Glasgow Pollok by-election in 1967, with the SNP gaining 28 per cent of the vote, was followed by its sensational by-election victory later the same year in Hamilton. Hamilton was, at the time, Labour's second-safest seat in Scotland. The SNP had yet another strong showing in Glasgow Gorbals, in 1969, winning 25 per cent of the vote (Butler and Pinto-Duschinsky 1971: 111–12). In Wales, too, PC had a dramatic victory with 40 per cent of the vote in the March 1967 by-election in Rhondda West. This constituency was a mining electoral district which epitomized a declining working-class community in which unemployment was double the average rate for Britain as a whole. The significance of this victory was that it took place in a bedrock district of the Labour movement. PC went on to almost snatch Caerphilly—another old mining stronghold—from Labour in a by-election the following year, again with 40 per cent of the vote (Butler and Pinto-Duschinsky 1971; Cook 1978: 149). The by-election victories were followed by the impressive increase in the 1970 British general election, in which PC gained 11 per cent of the vote in Wales (compared to 4 per cent in the previous election) and the SNP gained also 11 per cent of the vote in Scotland (compared to 5 per cent in the previous election) and won its first parliamentary seat in a state election (Table 5.4 in Appendix).

The state party most impacted by the growth of the British peripheral parties was the Labour Party. In Wales, Labour's average vote share in state elections dropped by over ten points from an average of 58 per cent in 1950–66 to 52 per cent in 1970 and 7 per cent in February 1974. Meanwhile, PC's average vote share more than tripled. In Scotland, Labour's average vote share declined from an average of nearly 48 per cent in 1950–66 to 44 per cent in 1970 and 37 per cent in February 1974, while the SNP's average vote share increased *twelve-fold* from 1.6 per cent in 1950–66 to 22 per cent in February 1974. The SNP gained its peak 30 per cent of the vote in the October 1974 state election, trailing Labour's vote share by a mere 6 per cent and coming second in thirty-five of the forty-one electoral districts won by Labour.

Survey data from the time confirm this direct competition between Labour and the peripheral parties. According to the 1974 British Electoral Study (no. 359), 22 per cent of those who voted for the SNP in the February 1974 election had voted for Labour in 1970, followed by 16 per cent coming from the Conservatives and 5 per cent from the Liberal Democrats. Even more clearly in the case of Wales, 33 per cent of those who voted for PC in February 1974 had voted for Labour in the previous state election. The rest were coming either from PC itself or from abstention.

The particularity of the Spanish and Italian cases, in comparison to Belgium and the UK, is that the devolution of power to sub-state territories was part of a wider process of transition to democracy. Therefore, there is not a period of peripheral party growth during which there were free and fair elections and the state was centralized. This, of course, poses a problem for my argument, since the factors leading to a decentralized state combine electoral calculations derived from the expected—not yet fully realized—electoral threat coming from peripheral parties with other factors related to the historical centre–periphery conflict in these polities. I will refer to these factors in the following chapter. Here, I will present the data that explain the Spanish and Italian state parties' *expected* electoral threat based on the results of peripheral parties at the first two democratic elections.

Two peripheral parties emerged as potential threats for state parties in Italy during the first democratic elections, corresponding to two of the five culturally distinct and politically mobilized Italian peripheries between 1944 and 1948: the Partito Sardo d'Azione in Sardinia (Psd'A) and the Movimento Indipendentista Siciliano (MSI) in Sicily (MSI). The Psd'A obtained 15 per cent of the region's vote and the MSI 8 percent (see Table 5.5 in Appendix). Other two territories where peripheral parties had been established, namely South Tyrol and Venezia Giulia, could not participate in the 1946 elections. The former was under an allied administration and the latter under a mixed Allied–Yugoslav administration. Therefore, the Südtiroler Volkspartei in South Tyrol (SVP), formed in 1945 to represent the German-speakers and Ladins of South Tyrol, would only show its threat potential in the 1948 elections, when it gathered an impressive 30.7 per cent of the region's vote. A fifth peripheral party that was established before the 1946 constitutional elections was Union Valdôtaine in Valle d'Aosta (UV). UV was during these early democratic years a very close ally of the Italian Christian Democrats (DC), with whom they entered into pre-electoral coalitions in regional and local elections.

Catalonia and the Basque Country were the two regions with the strongest peripheral parties in Spain at the time of the first democratic elections. In the Basque Country, there were several peripheral parties competing in state elections, the most relevant of which were the Basque Nationalist Party (PNV), Euskadiko Ezkerra (EE), and Herri Batasuna (HB). The Basque Nationalist Party (PNV) initiated its post-Franco electoral trajectory with a large share of the region's vote in state elections. In the first democratic elections of 1977 the PNV obtained nearly 30 per cent of the vote while the second largest Basque party, EE, obtained 6 per cent, far away from the PNV's level (Table 5.6 in Appendix). This result made the PNV the largest party in the Basque Country, above the Socialist Party (PSOE) who obtained

26 per cent of the votes. It would remain so for three decades. In the 1979 elections, HB, the party close to the terrorist Basque organization ETA, participated in the Spanish state elections for the first time—obtaining a relevant 15 per cent of the vote in the Basque Country. The PNV was again the first party in the region, with nearly 28 per cent, and the third was EE, which increased its vote share to 8 per cent. In the 1982 state elections the PNV increased its vote share to nearly 32 per cent of the Basque vote, followed by HB, with nearly 15 per cent, and EE, with nearly 8 per cent. If we consider all the Basque peripheral parties' vote shares together, by 1982 it represented a majority of 54 per cent in the Basque Country.

In Catalonia there were two main peripheral parties competing for votes, Convergència i Unió (CiU) and Esquerra Republicana de Catalunya (ERC). CiU emerged as the largest peripheral party in Catalonia. In the 1977 state elections it obtained 17 per cent of the vote in Catalonia, far from the 4 per cent of ERC (Table 5.6 in Appendix). The 1979 national elections, in general, left things unchanged for CiU and ERC. In the elections of 1982 CiU increased its vote share by six points, reaching nearly 23 per cent of the votes. ERC seemed to have reached its electoral ceiling as it had only moved between 4 and nearly 5 per cent during the period (1977–82). The Socialist Party, however, was not negatively affected by the growth of the Catalan peripheral parties. In 1977 and 1979 it obtained nearly 29 and 30 per cent of the vote respectively, while in 1982 its results increased to 46 per cent, making it the largest party in Catalonia. Its growth was at the expense of state parties to its right (Unión de Centro Democrático, UCD—Suárez's party) and to its left (Partido Comunista de España, PCE).

Survey data show that there were transfers of votes from the main state parties (PSOE, UCD, and Alianza Popular) to the main Catalan and Basque peripheral parties (PNV and CiU) between the 1977, 1979, and 1982 state elections and that these transfers of votes increased with each election. Between 1977 and 1979 there were no transfers of votes from the state parties to the Basque and Catalan peripheral parties that were above 3 per cent (Maravall 1981: 65). Between 1979 and 1982, 3 per cent of PNV voters in 1982 had voted for the UCD and none had voted for either the PSOE or AP in 1979.[2] Ten per cent of CiU voters in 1982 had voted for the UCD and 4 per cent for the PSOE in 1979.

5.2 ELECTORAL GEOGRAPHIES

As has just been shown, peripheral parties increased their vote shares continuously during the 1950s and 1960s (in Spain, the 1970s). In Belgium and the UK, the

---

[2] CIS survey no. 1327 'Post-Electoral 1982'.

growth was quite dramatic; in Spain and Italy, peripheral parties had a high level of electoral support to begin with (i.e., since the first democratic elections, in 1946 and 1977 respectively). This electoral growth, however, was not necessarily a threat for state parties. What matters most for the state parties' perception of threat is the relevance that these votes in the peripheral territories have for the parties' future electoral prospects as well as for their capacity to obtain electoral pluralities and parliamentary majorities at the state level. And this, in turn, depends on the specific combination of electoral geography and electoral system in each country. As Kim and Ohn have put it, '[i]t is not the size [of districts] alone but the particular distribution pattern that matters' (Kim and Ohn 1992: 581). They continue: 'In general, the greater the regional concentration of potential supporters of minor parties, the smaller the conversion bias against minor parties' (Kim and Ohn 1992: 588).

Concerning electoral geography, I defend that a peripheral party becomes an electoral threat to a state party when the latter's electoral losses to the former take place in an electorally relevant region in which the state party has a concentration of its total state-wide vote.[3] In order to test this hypothesis, I use three indicators (Table 5.1). The first is the *electoral relevance* of a country's region, which is calculated as the percentage of seats that come from the region over the total number of seats that constitute the state parliament. The second indicator is the *electoral vulnerability* of a state party in a particular region and is calculated as the percentage of seats that the party has obtained in that region over the party's total number of seats in the state parliament. The third indicator is the state party's *concentration of electoral support*. It is calculated by subtracting the region's seat share in the state parliament to the electoral weight of the region's seats on the party's total number of seats (columns 5 and 7 in Table 5.1). A positive figure indicates that the region is over-represented in the party's total state-wide support; alternatively, a negative figure indicates that the region is under-represented. The last two indicators take different values for each state party.

There were large differences in the electoral relevance of regions at the time of the first devolution reform in each country. In 1977 Spain, some regions contributed to the state parliament with just a few seats while others were represented by a large number of seats such as Andalusia, with 17 per cent, or Catalonia, with 13 per cent. In 1946 Italy, Lombardia was the most relevant region, followed by Sicilia, Emilia-Romagna, Veneto, and Campania; meanwhile, regions such as Val d'Aosta or South Tyrol had little or no electoral relevance. In the UK, Scotland had

---

[3] The electoral relevance of the region together with the geographical concentration of voters' support will also have intra-party consequences. The internal distribution of power within the party depends on the electoral relevance of each region and the party's level of support in it. Thus, the Catalan and Andalusian groups are very strong within the Spanish Socialist Party's organization, the same as the Walloon group is stronger than the Flemish one inside the Belgian Socialist Party or that the Flemish group is very strong inside the Belgian Christian Democrats. Therefore, these groups may successfully push the state party into using a pro-periphery electoral strategy.

TABLE 5.1. *The electoral geography of Belgium, Italy, Spain, and Great Britain in the last elections before the first devolution reform*

Country	Year	Region	Region's Electoral Relevance	Electoral Vulnerability of Main Left Party*	Concentration of Support of Main Left Party	Electoral Vulnerability of Main Right Party**	Concentration of Support of Main Right Party
Spain	1977	Andalucía	17.1	22.9	**5.8**	15.7	−1.4
Spain	1977	Aragón	3.7	4.2	**0.5**	4.2	**0.5**
Spain	1977	Asturias	2.6	3.4	**0.8**	2.4	−0.2
Spain	1977	Baleares	2.0	1.7	−0.3	2.4	**0.4**
Spain	1977	Canarias	4.0	2.5	−1.5	6.1	**2.1**
Spain	1977	Cantabria	1.4	0.8	−0.6	1.8	**0.4**
Spain	1977	Castilla-León	9.7	6.8	−2.9	15.1	**5.4**
Spain	1977	Castilla-LM.	5.7	6.8	**1.1**	7.2	**1.5**
Spain	1977	Cataluña	13.4	12.7	−0.7	5.4	−8.0
Spain	1977	C.Valenciana	8.9	11.1	**2.2**	6.7	−2.2
Spain	1977	Extremadura	3.1	3.4	**0.3**	4.8	**1.7**
Spain	1977	Galicia	7.4	2.5	−4.9	12.1	**4.7**
Spain	1977	La Rioja	1.1	0.8	−0.3	1.2	**0.1**
Spain	1977	Madrid	9.4	9.3	−0.1	7.2	−2.2
Spain	1977	Navarra	1.4	1.7	**0.3**	1.8	**0.4**
Spain	1977	País Vasco	5.7	5.9	**0.2**	2.4	−3.3
Spain	1977	R. de Murcia	2.6	3.4	**0.8**	2.4	−0.2
Italy	1946	Piemonte	11.7	9.6	−1.7	7.7	−4.0
Italy	1946	Liguria	4.6	4.8	**0.4**	2.9	−1.7
Italy	1946	Lombardia	19.7	13.5	−5.7	14.5	−5.2
Italy	1946	Trentino-AA.	1.1	0.0	−1.1	1.4	0.3
Italy	1946	Veneto	11.4	5.8	−5.4	10.6	−0.8
Italy	1946	Val d'Aosta	0.3	0.0	−0.3	0.0	−0.3

TABLE 5.1. *Continued*

Country	Year	Region	Region's Electoral Relevance	Electoral Vulnerability of Main Left Party*	Concentration of Support of Main Left Party	Electoral Vulnerability of Main Right Party**	Concentration of Support of Main Right Party
Italy	1946	*Friuli-VG.*	3.1	1.0	-2.1	2.9	-0.2
Italy	1946	*Emilia-Romagna*	11.7	15.4	**4.3**	4.8	-6.9
Italy	1946	*Toscana*	9.4	12.5	**3.6**	5.3	-4.1
Italy	1946	*Marche*	3.7	2.9	-0.7	2.4	-1.3
Italy	1946	*Umbria*	2.6	2.9	**0.4**	1.4	-1.1
Italy	1946	*Lazio*	8.3	3.8	-4.3	5.3	-3.0
Italy	1946	*Abruzzo*	3.4	1.0	-2.4	3.4	0.0
Italy	1946	*Molise*	2.0	0.0	-2.0	1.9	-0.1
Italy	1946	*Campania*	11.1	2.9	-8.1	7.2	-3.9
Italy	1946	*Puglia*	8.6	4.8	-3.6	5.8	-2.8
Italy	1946	*Basilicata*	1.4	1.0	-0.4	1.0	-0.5
Italy	1946	*Calabria*	6.0	2.9	-3.0	3.9	-2.1
Italy	1946	*Sicilia*	12.6	2.9	-9.6	8.7	-3.9
Italy	1946	*Sardegna*	3.1	1.0	-2.1	2.9	-0.2
Belgium	1968	*Wallonie*	30.3	42.1	**11.8**	20.3	-10.0
Belgium	1968	*Vlaanderen*	46.9	43.9	-3.0	60.9	**14.0**
Belgium	1968	*Brabant*	22.7	14.0	-8.7	18.8	-3.9
G.Britain	1997	*Scotland*	10.9	13.4	**2.5**	0.0	-10.9
G.Britain	1997	*Wales*	6.1	8.1	**2.0**	0.0	-6.1
G.Britain	1997	*North-East Region*	4.7	5.3	**0.6**	1.2	-3.5
G.Britain	1997	*North-West Region*	13.8	14.4	**0.5**	5.5	-8.4
G.Britain	1997	*Yorkshire & the H.*	10.1	11.5	**1.3**	2.4	-7.7
G.Britain	1997	*East Midlands*	9.0	7.2	-1.8	7.9	-1.1
G.Britain	1997	*West Midlands*	11.5	10.3	-1.2	7.9	-3.6
G.Britain	1997	*East Anglia*	11.3	5.3	-6.0	20.0	**8.7**
G.Britain	1997	*South-East*	16.4	5.5	-10.9	31.5	**15.1**
G.Britain	1997	*South-West*	9.0	3.3	-5.6	11.5	**2.5**
G.Britain	1997	*Greater London*	14.2	13.6	-0.6	6.7	-7.6
G.Britain	1997	*England total*	80.3	78.5	-1.8	100.0	**19.7**

* The main left parties are: the Belgian Socialist Party, the Italian Communist Party, the Spanish Socialist Party, and the British Labour Party.

** The main right parties are: the Belgian Christian Democratic Party, the Italian Christian Democratic Party, the Union of the Democratic Centre in Spain, and the British Conservative Party.

Source: Own calculation based on official electoral results.

11 per cent of the parliament's total number of seats in 1997, followed by Wales (6 per cent).[4] A very large majority of the parliament's total seat number belonged to England, with 529 constituencies representing 80 per cent of the national seats and almost 85 per cent of the UK's population.[5] This made England disproportionately larger than the other three regions. For this reason, another way to look at England is to disaggregate it into its eight administrative regions, a method discussed by successive Labour governments as the possible units of future devolution reforms. The South-East and the Greater London regions were the most relevant in electoral terms in 1997, with 16 and 14 per cent of the total number of state seats respectively. The least relevant was the North-East region, with 5 per cent. In Belgium, Flanders was the most relevant region with 47 per cent of all the state seats in 1968, followed by Wallonia (30 per cent) and Brabant (23 per cent). However, the differences in this country were comparatively smaller.

The electoral growth of a peripheral party is most threatening to a state party if this growth happens in an electorally relevant region and if the state party has its support concentrated therein. Table 5.1 shows that the state parties' geographical concentration of electoral support was a widespread phenomenon before the first devolution reforms but it did not always coincide with the presence of a peripheral party or with a region that was electorally relevant.

In the UK, the Labour Party was proportionally stronger in the Northern regions of England (North-East, North-West, and Yorkshire & Humber), Scotland, and Wales. In both Scotland and Wales, peripheral parties were challenging the Labour party's electoral hegemony. The Scottish National Party (SNP) in Scotland and Plaid Cymru (PC) in Wales initiated a period of considerable electoral growth during the 1960s that continued well into the 1990s—mainly at the expense of Labour votes. The Conservative Party, on the other hand, was stronger in Southern England in regions that were electorally very relevant but where there was no peripheral party threat (East Anglia, South-East, and South-West). The Conservative Party's concentration in southern England was so overwhelming that 'the prospects of the party winning control of the government were relatively immune to the loss of votes in Scotland and Wales' (Meguid 2009: 15). Although Scotland and Wales were not the most relevant regions in the country, together they represented 17 per cent of all Westminster seats which is more than the 16 per cent dominated by the Conservatives in the South-East region. Therefore, being vulnerable to electoral losses in both regions simultaneously was a direct threat for the Labour Party. Had it been only one of them, the electoral threat would have been less severe.

---

[4] In Northern Ireland there are no UK-wide parties. For this reason, I have not included it in Table 5.1. Its electoral relevance is, nevertheless, negligible (2% of the total number of Westminster seats).

[5] There was a previous failed attempt to decentralize the British state devolving power to Scotland and Wales in 1974. It will be discussed in detail in subsequent chapters. However, at this point it is necessary to make clear that the electoral geography of Great Britain in 1974 was very similar to that in 1997. The corresponding figures were 11% (Scotland), 6% (Wales), and 81% (England).

In Belgium, Flanders was a region of concentrated Christian Democratic vote in which a new peripheral party at the time, VU, experienced a period of dramatic electoral growth during the 1960s, as was shown in the previous section. The growth of this peripheral party took place at the expense of the Belgian Christian Democratic Party (CVP-PSC). Moreover, Flanders was a region that contributed the largest number of seats to the Belgian parliament. According to my hypothesis, therefore, the Christian Democrats would be the first to support devolution. Unlike the other three countries, however, the structure of incentives in Belgium was centrifugal. The Belgian Socialists received more support in Wallonia, where they were electorally threatened by the growth of RW. The Liberal Party, the third largest party in the country, had a high concentration of votes in Brussels— although it was equally distribute between Flanders and Wallonia—where it was threatened by the FDF. Therefore, there were three regions and three state parties each one of which was dominant in one of the three regions and each one of which was losing votes to a peripheral challenger. It was a zero-sum game: whatever the state party lost in one region could not be compensated by electoral gains in another. Each state party was forced to stop the defection of its voters to the peripheral challenger if it wanted to maintain its electoral strength in the country.

In Spain, the first democratic elections showed the Socialist Party to be strongest in Andalusia and Catalonia, the two most relevant regions of Spain. The centre-right UCD was particularly strong in Castilla-León and Galicia, which although also relevant had no peripheral parties with parliamentary representation at this early stage. The Socialist Party in Catalonia had to compete with the Catalan peripheral party CiU and with the PNV in the Basque Country. Catalonia and the Basque Country, the two regions of strongest peripheral party support, represented 19 per cent of the total parliamentary seats in Spain and were, therefore, an important prize for state parties with government aspirations. The Spanish Socialist Party, while not yet over-represented in these two regions, had a large electoral presence in both of them, being the first party in Catalonia and the second in the Basque Country. The Socialist Party was therefore the most vulnerable to the growth of peripheral parties in Spain.

In Italy, the Communist Party (PCI) had its electoral strongholds in the regions of Toscana and Emilia-Romagna. At the time of the first constituent elections in 1946 the Christian Democrats (DC) had no concentration of votes anywhere in the country. The DC was the party with the most votes in all regions except Toscana, Emilia-Romagna, and Valle d'Aosta, having a relatively equal distribution of votes in the rest of the Italian regions. With the exception of the MSI in Sicily, an electorally relevant region, the rest of the peripheral parties with a potential for growth in Italy belonged to regions that were electorally irrelevant. This was particularly the case in South Tyrol and Valle d'Aosta, two regions that contributed very few seats in the state parliament. The main peripheral party in Sardinia, the Psd'A, obtained 15 per cent of the region's state votes in 1946, but the region was also quite irrelevant electorally for Italian state parties (see Tables 5.5 and 5.10 in Appendix). Besides, the Christian

Democrats were the largest party in Sardinia, with 40 per cent of the state vote and, therefore, the Partito Sardo d'Azione was no real threat for them. Only in Sicily did the MSI have a potential for threat to Italian state parties.

5.3 THE ELECTORAL SYSTEM AND THE VULNERABILITY OF STATE PARTIES

The electoral system is a relevant factor in a state party's perception of electoral threat. The electoral system transforms political preferences into political representation, thereby determining the relative significance of each ballot.

One way of characterizing electoral systems, the most relevant for our discussion, is their distance from the yardstick of perfect proportionality. An electoral system is perfectly proportional when a party needs 50 per cent of the votes to obtain 50 per cent of the seats in parliament. Most of the available empirical measures of an electoral system's degree of proportionality, such as the disproportionality index (Loosemore and Hanby 1971; Rae 1971) or the effective threshold (Taagepera and Shugart 1989), rely on the electoral results that are generated by the very electoral system that is being characterized. There is one measure, however, that is calculated independently of electoral results. Ruiz-Rufino's *aggregated threshold functions* (2007) calculate the necessary and sufficient share of the total vote to win a given number of seats in parliament, given any electoral formula, any number of districts, any legislative size, and any given number of parties.[6]

I shall characterize the electoral systems of our four countries under analysis using the aggregated threshold function (ATF) of the *necessary votes* to obtain 50 per cent of the seats in parliament.[7] For example, an ATF value of 0.25 is telling us that, without taking into account the voters' preferences and strategic calculations, a party can win 50 per cent of the seats in parliament with 25 per cent of the total vote. Considering that the value of perfect proportionality is 0.50, this would be an example of a highly disproportional electoral system.

---

[6] The aggregated threshold functions (ATFs) are, therefore, general and quasi-universal. General, because they can characterize a complete electoral system taking into account all districts, and not just one, in contrast to the other existing measures. Quasi-universal because these functions can be applied to the great majority of existing electoral systems, except to those that use single transferable vote or alternative vote.

[7] A note of caution is at this point necessary. ATFs are simulations. They tell us the necessary or sufficient share of the total vote to achieve any number of seats given the electoral mechanism of a particular system, irrespective of the existing distribution of votes in the country. Therefore, they do not anticipate the performance of any political party because this depends not only on the mechanical effects of the electoral system but also on the distribution of voters' preferences.

As was explained in chapter 3, I assume that the lower the necessary number of votes to win 50 per cent of the seats is the higher the vulnerability of state parties in the event of a peripheral party growth will be. This is why I shall refer to the ATF values as the threshold of vulnerability for state parties. The average ATF values of our group of countries in the years before the first decentralizing reform were the following:[8] 35.8 in Belgium (1946–71), 31.3 in Spain (1977–82), and 20.7 in the UK (1945–74). Unsurprisingly, the UK is the country that is furthest away from perfect proportionality and, therefore, the country in which a state party that is losing votes to a peripheral party would be most vulnerable.

According to this, the party that was most vulnerable to the growth of peripheral challengers was the Labour Party. This party was being challenged in two regions in which, theoretically, a peripheral party that gathers approximately 21 per cent of the regional votes in state elections is already in a position to win a majority of the region's seats in the state parliament. The SNP in Scotland had already passed that electoral threshold in 1970, which accounts for the first—and eventually failed—attempt at devolution in the UK in 1974–5.

The vulnerability of the Belgian Christian Democrats in Belgium and the Socialists in Spain was not as high as that for Labour in the UK though given the dramatic increase of the peripheral vote in Belgium and the high levels of peripheral party vote in Spain they were also likely to feel considerably vulnerable.

The Belgian Christian Democrats were losing votes to the VU in Flanders quite dramatically. This peripheral party was approaching 20 per cent of the regional vote in state elections at the end of the 1960s. We know that, according to the ATF score of Belgium, 35 per cent of the vote at the state level could give a party a majority of the seats in the state parliament. A 20 per cent vote share by a peripheral party in one region did not leave the Belgian Christian Democrats as close to the threshold of vulnerability as Labour was in the UK. The protective effects of a more proportional electoral system were further shown in the fact that the main Belgian parties in general, and the Christian Democrats in particular, were used to sharing executive power in coalition governments with their main adversaries. This 'protected' Belgian major state parties against the blackmail potential of smaller parties such as the peripherals, in contrast to the situation in the UK and in Spain. In these two countries, state parties were likely to perceive the peripheral threat in terms of their capacity to form parliamentary majorities and the blackmail power that this gives the growing peripheral parties. British state parties at the time of the failed devolution reform of 1974–5 had already an abundant historical experience of such a scenario (Jackson 2003).[9] Thus from

---

[8] The ATF value cannot be calculated for Italy because it used the limited vote system.

[9] The willingness of successive Liberal governments between the late 1890s and the early 1920s to initiate a process of Home Rule for Ireland was always stimulated by the need of the Liberal Party to get the support of the Irish Nationalist Party's votes in order to achieve a parliamentary majority in the House of Commons (Jackson 2003). Of course, this can also play against peripheral parties. For

the point of view of the vulnerability threshold, the Christian Democrats were in a better position than Labour in the UK and the Socialists in Spain. However, and in contrast to the former two countries, the electoral geography of Belgium set the stakes very high indeed for state parties. If the Belgian Christian Democrats were to lose their electoral stronghold in Flanders they would be unable to compensate their losses by growing elsewhere in the country since the other two regions were the hunting grounds of the Christian Democrats' adversaries—the Socialist and Liberal parties. For this reason, even if the proportionality of the electoral system made the Christian Democratic Party less vulnerable to the peripheral party growth relative to state parties in other countries the structure of electoral geography did away with this relative advantage.

The Socialists in Spain were not as vulnerable as Labour in the UK but the potential for a high vulnerability was clear. The Catalan nationalist CiU was increasing its vote share, reaching 23 per cent by the beginning of the 1980s. Together with the other nationalist party, ERC, they gathered at the 1982 election 27 per cent of the vote in a region, when for the country as a whole a 31 per cent share could give a party a majority of the seats in parliament (as we know from the AFT value of Spain). This means that the Catalan peripheral parties were very close to the threshold above which they would be able to obtain 50 per cent of the Catalan seats in the Spanish parliament.

Since the AFT values cannot be calculated for Italy, I have also looked at other indices of disproportionality in order to compare the relative vulnerability of Italian state parties and those of Belgium, Spain, and the UK. According to the results shown in Table 5.2, Spain and the UK had the most disproportional systems, as the AFT values have already shown. Moreover, according to the Loosemore-Hanby index, Spain was on average even more disproportional than the UK.

Italy had at the time (1946–8) the most proportional electoral system of all the countries under analysis (after 1993, however, it became much less proportional). It was therefore the country where state parties were comparatively less vulnerable to the growth of peripheral parties in the regions.

example, during the inter-war period in the UK, the solid Conservative majorities obtained in 1922, 1924, 1931, and 1935 limited the parliamentary value of the Ulster Unionist Party to the Tories (Smith 2006). Some decades later, the Unionist Party's commitment to follow the Conservative whip in Westminster was so harmful for the Labour Party in the aftermath of Harold Wilson's narrow victory at the 1964 national election (which gave him a majority of just five) that the Labour Party, in response, initiated a policy of hostility towards the Unionists' position in Northern Ireland, pressing on a reform agenda for the region that harmed the Unionists' hegemonic power (Smith 2006). The Unionist Party learnt its lesson. After the Conservative Party opposed the Sunningdale Agreement, when the opportunity of another state party's narrow victory arrived, in October 1974, the UUP used its modest number of seats to impede the Conservatives to form a parliamentary majority, giving the government to the Labour Party.

Challenging the State

TABLE 5.2. *The average degree of disproportionality of the electoral systems in Belgium, Italy, Spain, and UK according to different indices*

Country	Years	Rae[*]	Loosemore/Hanby[**]	Gallagher[***]
Belgium	1945–70	1.45	5.32	3.47
Italy	1946–8	0.67	4.24	2.81
Spain	1977–9	1.69	17.28	10.6
UK	1945–97	2.49	13.82	10.76

[*] Rae's (1967) is the oldest proposed measure of proportionality. It sums the absolute differences between vote percentages and seat percentages and the outcome is divided by the number of the political parties. The problem of this index is its sensitivity to the presence of small parties, in which case it underestimates the degree of disproportionality in a system

[**] In trying to solve the sensitivity of Rae's index to the presence of small parties, Loosemore and Hanby's index of disproportionality (1971) also sums the absolute differences between vote percentages and seat percentages but this time the outcome is divided by 2. Thus, it generally gives higher values than the Rae's index.

[***] Gallagher's least squares measure (1991) gives an index which theoretically runs from 0 to 100. In the presence of just two parties, Gallagher's index produces the same values as Rae's and Loosemore and Hanby's. For multiparty systems, it generally produces a value that is between that of the other two indices.

Source: Database 'Elections, Parties, Governments' of the Research Unit *Democracy* at the Social Science Research Center Berlin (WZB).

5.4 CONCLUDING REMARKS

The aim of this chapter has been to explain the vulnerability of state parties when peripheral parties' vote shares grow. I have argued that the vulnerability of state parties depends on the country's electoral geography and on the degree of proportionality of its electoral system. The most vulnerable state party is the one which (a) loses votes to a peripheral adversary (b) in an electorally relevant region (c) in which the state party has a concentrated electoral support and (d) under a disproportional electoral system in which the necessary number of votes to win 50 per cent of the seats is relatively low.

At the country level, I have shown that in the post-Second World War period that I am analysing state parties in Belgium were the most vulnerable to the peripheral party growth according to electoral geography but, according to the proportionality of the electoral system, state parties in the UK were the most at risk. The country level, however, hides a lot of variability inside each country. Thus, in Belgium it was the Christian Democratic Party that was most vulnerable to the growth of the Volksunie in Flanders while in Spain the Socialist Party was the most at risk from the growth of Catalan peripheral parties. Finally, in the UK, it was the Labour Party that was the most sensitive to the growth of peripheral parties in Scotland and Wales.

Italy's electoral geography and its relatively proportional electoral system explain why the main Italian state parties were not directly threatened by the growth of peripheral parties during the constitutional period (1946–8) although there was a potential for threat evolving in Sicily. Therefore, it is not possible to explain the partial devolution opted for by the Italian Constitution between 1946 and 1948 as a response to the *electoral* threat coming from peripheral parties. The peripheral threat in Italy was not based so much on the electoral strength of its parties, since no matter how large it was it would always have a small impact for state parties in state elections, but on other factors, as I will show in the following chapter.

APPENDIX

TABLE 5.3. *Vote shares of Belgian parties in state elections (1946–2003), disaggregated by region (percentage over valid vote)*

	1946*	1949	1950	1954	1958	1961	1965	1968	1971	1974	1977	1978	1981	1985	1987	1991	1995	1999	2003
Wallonia																			
BSP/PSB	37.3	30.2	45.8	49.1	43.8	46.3	35.5	35	35.1	37.4									
PSB (PS)											38.2	35.6	35.2	40	45	40.6	33.7	29.2	36.4
CVP/PSC	27.2	40	34	30.9	33.8	31.2	24.8	21.5											
PSC (CDH)									20.9	22.8	25.8	24.2	17.8	23	23.5	22.9	22.5	16.8	15.4
LP/PL	10.2	14.8	12.2	12.6	13.1	11.7	24.9	26.2	17.6	15.1									
PRLW											23.5	14.6							
PRL													19	23.3	21	18.8			
FDF-PRL (MR)																	23.9	24.7	28.4
KPB/PCB	21.4	12.1	7.9	6.9	4.4	6.4	5.3	7.1	6	1.9									
PCB											2.3	5.8	4.2	2.6	1.7	0	0	1	0
RW							**1.5**	**9.8**	**19.6**	**17.6**	**6.1**	**6**	**5**	**0**	**0.6**	**0.2**	**0**	**0**	**0**
Ecolo											1.12	1.08	5.8	6.2	6.3	13.4	10.3	18.3	7.5
Others	3.9	2.9	0.1	0.5	4.9	4.4	8	0.4	0.8	5.2	2.98	12.72	13	4.9	1.9	4.1	9.6	10	12.3
Total %	100	100	100	100	100	100	100	100	100	100	100	100	100	100	100	100	100	100	100
Flanders																			
BSP/PSB	28.1	24.3	26.7	29.5	27.5	29.7	24.6	26.2	24.7	22.7									
BSP (SP)											23	21.3	21	24	24.3	14.7	20.7	15.7	
SP-A Spirit																			24.3
CVP/PSC	56.8	55	60.9	52.8	57.2	51.7	44.7	39.5	38.3	40.3	44.3								
CVP												44.3	32.5	34.9	31.7	27.3	27.6	22.6	
CD&V																			21.4
N-VA																			4.9
LP/PL	8.2	12.6	9.8	11.3	9.1	10.8	15.5	15.2	15.5	16.7	14								
PVV (VLD)												16.9	18.3	17.2	13.9	18.8	20.9	22.7	24.4
KPB/PCB	5.3	3.5	2.5	1.6	0	1	1.7	1.4	0	1.6	1.2								
KPB												1.9	1.3	0.5	0.4	0	0	0	0
VU				**4**	**3.5**	**6.2**	**13.2**	**17.5**	**19.4**	**17**	**16.2**	**11.6**	**16.1**	**12.9**	**13.1**	**9.5**	**7.3**	**8.8**	
VB												**2**	**1.9**	**2.2**	**3.1**	**10.5**	**12.3**	**15.4**	**18.1**
Agalev											0.1	0.3	4	6.2	7.4	7.9	7.2	11.3	4

Others	1.6	4.6	0.1	0.8	2.7	0.6	0.3	0.2	2.1	1.7	1.2	1.7	4.9	2.1	6.1	11.3	4	3.5	2.9
Total %	100	100	100	100	100	100	100	100	100	100	100	100	100	100	100	100	100	100	100
Brabant																			
BSP/PSB	34.02	28.67	38.07	42.02	39.16	38.59	26.37	13.73											
PSB									13.6	14	11.8	10.6	10	11.8	14.8	11.2	11.49	9.97	15.3
BSP										7.4	7.6	8.3	8.6	11	11.6	9.4	6.73	4.84	
Sp,a-Spirit																			8.5
CVP/PSC	36.7	36.89	41	31.82	39.53	33.89	25.91		24.5										
CVP								19.9		16.7	20	19.1	14.4	16.6	15.4	12.9	12.45	9.63	
PSC (CDH)								9.2		10.9	10.8	11.1	6.7	7.27	6.9	7	6.01	5.9	6.3
CD&V																			8.7
N-VA																			2.2
LP/PL	11.8	22.1	16.36	17.41	16.64	16.56	30.08	25.61	9.02	10.4									
PLP (Brux)									7.5										
PVV (VLD)											7.3	9	11.6	9.3	10.7	10.9	10.5	11.2	11.5
PRLW												2.2							
PRL												3.4	11.9	17.6	16.9	14.3			
KPB/PCB	14.4	8	4.57	2.92	2.16	2.91	3.55	2.23	2.4	3.2	2.3	1.9	1.9	1	0.6	0			
VU					**1.42**	**2.39**	**3.66**	**6.69**	**8.2**	**8.8**	**9.2**	**5.8**	**7.9**	**6.3**	**6.5**	**4.8**	4.3	4.3	
FDF							**5.91**	**13.03**	**24**	**21.2*****	**25.6****	**21.1**	**12.9****	**5.6**	**5.5**	**6.1**			
MR																	**23**	**20.7**	**21.6**
VB												**1.6**	**0.8**	**1.3**	**1.4**	**5.4**	**7.2**	**8.7**	**10.3**
FN																	4.7	1.6	2.2
Ecolo													2.6	3.7	3.8	6.6	6.5	14.3	6.2
Agalev													1.4	2.7	0.3	3.8	2.9	4.6	1.6
Others	3.08	4.34	0	5.83	1.09	5.66	4.52	9.61	10.78	28.6	31	5.9	22.2	5.83	5.6	7.6	4.22	4.26	5.6
Total %	100	100	100	100	100	100	100	100	100	100	100	100	100	100	100	100	100	100	100

* In the years 1946, 1950, and 1954 the Socialist and Liberal parties presented joint lists in two electoral constituencies, Limbourg (Flanders) and Luxembourg (Wallonia). The electoral results are given only for the joint list, not for each party individually. In order to be able to calculate the aggregated electoral results at the regional (not the constituency) level, I have used the separate results of each party in these constituencies at the 1949 elections to estimate their respective results in the years in which they presented joint lists.

** with Rassemblement Wallon; *** with PLDP.

Source: Author's own elaboration based on electoral data of the Gouvernement du Belgique (site officiel des résultats électoraux belges).

TABLE 5.4. *Vote shares of British parties in state elections (1945–2005), disaggregated by region (percentage over valid vote)*

	1945	1950	1951	1955	1959	1964	1966	1970	1974f	1974o	1979	1983	1987	1992	1997	2001	2005
England																	
Conservative	36.9	41.1	45.6	47.8	47.9	43	42.1	48.3	40.1	38.8	47.2	46	46.1	45.5	33.7	35.2	35.7
Labour	48.6	46.1	48.8	46.8	43.6	43.5	47.7	43.2	37.6	40.1	36.7	26.9	29.5	33.9	43.5	41.4	35.5
Liberal	9.32	9.4	2.3	2.6	6.3	12.1	9.1	7.9	21.3	20.2	14.9	14.5	13.6	19.2	17.9	19.4	22.9
Others	5.18	3.4	3.3	2.8	2.2	1.4	1.1	0.6	1	0.9	1.2	12.6	10.8	1.4	4.9	4	5.9
Total %	100	100	100	100	100	100	100	100	100	100	100	100	100	100	100	100	100
Wales																	
Conservative	16.6	21	27.6	26.7	30.8		27	27.7	25.9	23.9	32.1	31	29.5	28.6	19.6	21	21.4
Labour	58.52	58.1	60.5	57.6	56.4		60.7	51.6	46.8	49.5	46.9	37.5	45.1	49.5	54.7	48.6	42.7
Liberal	14.9	12.6	7.6	7.3	5.3		6.3	6.8	16	15.5	10.6	12.1	10.7	12.4	12.3	13.8	18.4
PC	**1.1**	**1.2**	**0.7**	**3.1**	**5.2**	**4.8**	**4.3**	**11.5**	**10.7**	**10.8**	**8.1**	**7.8**	**7.3**	**8.8**	**9.9**	**14.3**	**12.5**
Others	8.88	7.1	3.6	5.3	2.3	95.2	1.7	2.4	0.6	0.3	2.3	11.6	7.4	0.7	3.5	2.3	5
Total %	100	100	100	100	100	100	100	100	100	100	100	100	100	100	100	100	100
Scotland																	
Conservative	36.7	37.7	40.7	41.5	40.7	37.7	37.3	38	32.9	24.7	31.4	28.4	24	25.6	17.5	15.6	15.8
Labour	47.9	46.2	47.9	46.7	46.7	48.7	49.9	44.5	36.7	36.3	41.5	35.1	42.4	39	45.6	43.3	38.9
Liberal	5.6	6.6	2.7	1.9	4.1	7.6	6.8	5.5	7.9	8.3	9	12.8	10.3	13.1	13	16.3	23.1
SNP	**1.28**	**0.4**	**0.3**	**0.5**	**0.5**	**2.4**	**5**	**11.4**	**21.91**	**30.4**	**17.3**	**11.7**	**14**	**21.5**	**22.1**	**20.1**	**17.7**
Others	8.52	9.1	8.4	9.4	8	3.6	1	0.6	0.59	0.3	0.8	12	9.3	0.8	1.8	4.7	4.5
Total %	100	100	100	100	100	100	100	100	100	100	100	100	100	100	100	100	100
Northern Ireland																	
UUP[19]	54.5	62.8	59.3	68.5	71.5	63	61.8	54.2	41.5	58	36.6	34.4	37.8	34.5	32.6	26.8	17.76
DUP									5.7		3.22	19.92	11.73	13.1	13.6	22.5	33.7
Irish Nationalist	20.57	11.6															
NLP		12.1	13.5														
Sinn Féin			13	23.5								13.6	11.4		16	21.7	24.32
SDLP									22.4	22	19.7	18.1	21.1	23.5	24.1	21	17.51
Others	24.93	13.5	14.2	8	28.5	37	38.2	45.8	30.4	20	40.48	13.98	17.97	28.9	13.7	8	6.71
Total %	100	100	100	100	100	100	100	100	100	100	100	100	100	100	100	100	100

Source: University of Keele, database UK General Election Results (regional distribution of seats and percentage vote).

TABLE 5.5. *Vote shares of Italian parties in state elections (1946–2006), disaggregated by region (percentage over valid vote)*

	1946	1948	1953	1958	1963	1968	1972	1976	1979	1983	1987	1992	1994	1996	2001	2006
PIEMONTE																
DC	33.2	47.9	39.6	40.6	36	36.7	36.7	35.7	33.9	27.6	28.2	21	11.9			
PCI (PDS)	19.6	32	21.4	19	23.2	26.1	26.2	35.4	30.6	30.1	25.2	12.7	16.7			
PSI	26.3	11.5	13.4	14.6	14.3	16.5	11.1	10	10.3	10.5	13.2	13.4	1.7			
FI													26.5			
PRC												6.5	5.8	10.4	5.9	5.9
Polo/Casa Libertà														47.1	50.2	23.5
L'Ulivo														33.2	67.1	31.4
Lega Nord												16.3	**15.7**	**19.1**		**6.3**
Others	20.9	8.6	25.6	25.8	26.5	20.7	26	18.9	25.2	31.8	33.4	30.1	21.7	-9.8	-23.2	32.9
Total %	100	100	100	100	100	100	100	100	100	100	100	100	100	100	100	100
LIGURIA																
DC	32.5	45.9	38.6	39.8	32.2	33.3	35	34.4	32.2	27.3	28.4	21.8	8			
PCI (PDS)	28.5	39.1	25.7	24.6	28.4	30.9	31.6	39.1	35.5	35.7	32.3	18.7	22.2			
PSI	25.9	9.8	16.2	17.2	15.5	15.8	11.2	10.9	11.5	10.1	13.9	11	1.7			
FI													22.6			
PRC												7.4	8.1	10.2	6	6.8
Polo/Casa Libertà														37.6	44.3	23.5
L'Ulivo														39.8	44.8	34.8
Lega Nord												14.3	**11.4**	**11**		**3.7**
Others	13.1	5.2	19.5	18.4	23.9	20	22.2	15.6	20.8	26.9	25.4	26.8	26	1.4	4.9	31.2
Total %	100	100	100	100	100	100	100	100	100	100	100	100	100	100	100	100
LOMBARDIA																
DC	36.3	52.5	45.9	44.9	39.8	41.8	41.1	41.1	39.4	33.4	33.5	24.1	11.2			
PCI (PDS)	18.9	33.3	17.8	18.6	20.1	22.9	23.8	31.6	28.4	28	23.5	12.1	13			
PSI	28.7	9.5	18.2	18.4	18.2	16.9	12.1	11.7	11.3	12	16.9	12.6	1.4			
FI													26			
PRC												4.9	5.1	6.8	5	5.5

(Continued)

TABLE 5.5. *Continued*

	1946	1948	1953	1958	1963	1968	1972	1976	1979	1983	1987	1992	1994	1996	2001	2006
Polo/Casa Libertà														36.9	53.9	27.1
L'Ulivo														29.7	33.8	26.7
Lega Nord												**23**	**22.1**	**26.4**		**11.7**
Others	16.1	4.7	18.1	18.1	21.9	18.4	23	15.6	20.9	26.6	26.1	23.3	21.2	0.2	7.3	29
Total %	100	100	100	100	100	100	100	100	100	100	100	100	100	100	100	100
TRENTINO-ALTO ADIGE*																
DC	57.4	50.5	45.1	43.2	39.5	38	39.2	32.8	31	27.5	26	21.5	11.6			
PCI (PDS)	8.1		5.2	5.2	5.8	30	7.62	13.2	11.1	11.1	8.1	5.1	6.6			
PSI	27.7		6.9	8.1	12	12.9	7	7.9	6.6	6.8	9.6	6.9	0.9			
FDP**		9.6														
FI													15.6			
PRC												1.7	2.3	3.6		3
Polo/Casa Libertà														27.6	31.4	16.6
L'Ulivo														29.8	26.1	20.7
SVP		**30.7**	**28.3**	**29.3**	**27.8**	**30**	**30.1**	**32.5**	**35.8**	**32.4**	**33**	**31.1**	**36.8**	**25.8*****	**30.7**	**28.5**
Lega Nord														**11.3**		
Others	6.8	9.2	14.5	14.2	14.9	-10.9	16.08	13.6	15.5	22.2	23.3	33.7	26.2	27.7	11.8	31.2
Total %	100	100	100	100	100	100	100	100	100	100	100	100	100	100	100	100
VENETO																
DC	46	60.5	53.4	55.5	52.8	53.1	53.4	51.8	50.4	42.8	43.9	31.7	15.6			
PCI (PDS)	12.9	24.5	14.4	13.5	15	16.9	17.5	23.8	21.8	20.9	18.3	10	12.2			
PSI	24.7	9.8	14.9	16.3	15.6	14.7	9.5	10.3	4.4	10.5	14	10.5	1.7			
FI													23.6			
PRC												3.6	4.4	5.3	4	3.9
Polo/Casa Libertà														33.3	50.6	24.5
L'Ulivo														27.1	32.1	26.6
Lega Nord													**21.6**	**31**	**4**	**11.1**
Liga Fronte Veneto												**17.3**				
Others	16.4	5.2	17.3	14.7	16.6	15.3	19.6	14.1	23.4	25.8	23.8	26.9	20.9	3.3	9.3	33.9
Total %	100	100	100	100	100	100	100	100	100	100	100	100	100	100	100	100
FRIULI-VENEZIA GIULIA†																
DC	47.7	57.8	50.8	47.1	43.8	43.6	43.7	42.7	37.8	34.9	33.6	28	15.6			

PSI	31	14.1	12.7	13.5	13.6	19.4	11.3	11.6	8	11.1	18.5	15.5	1.8			
FI													24.3			
PRC												4.6	6	7.4	4.5	4.9
Polo/Casa Libertà														39.6	49.6	23.4
L'Ulivo														27	32.2	29.1
Lega Nord												**17.1**	**16.9**	**23.9**		**7.2**
Others	8.8	7.1	22	24	25.3	18.3	25.7	19.6	30.9	32.4	28.7	24.3	23.4	2.1	13.7	35.4
Total %	100	100	100	100	100	100	100	100	100	100	100	100	100	100	100	100
EMILIA-ROMAGNA																
DC	22.2	33	30.5	30.6	26	26.7	26.8	28.4	27.3	22.7	24.1	19.5	8.3			
PCI (PDS)	35.8	51.3	36.7	36.7	40.7	43.3	43.9	48.5	47.3	47.5	44.1	32.5	36.5			
PSI	26.7	4.6	14.4	16.4	14.2	14.4	8.2	8.9	8.6	9.8	12.4	10.6	1.7			
FI													16.5			
PRC												7.1	6.6	8.3	5.5	5.6
Polo/Casa Libertà														32.5	37.7	18.6
L'Ulivo														50.1	51.9	44.8
Lega Nord												**9.6**	**6.4**	**7**		**3.9**
Others	15.3	11.1	18.4	16.3	19.1	15.6	21.1	14.2	16.8	20	19.4	20.7	24	2.1	4.9	27.1
Total %	100	100	100	100	100	100	100	100	100	100	100	100	100	100	100	100
TOSCANA																
DC	26.7	39	34.3	35.2	30.5	30.8	31	31.4	30.1	25.3	25.8	22.1	8.3			
PCI (PDS)	31.8	48.1	35.1	34.4	38.5	41	42.1	47.5	45.8	46.4	43.4	29.7	33.6			
PSI	20.7	5.7	15.4	16.8	14.7	13.7	8.9	9.8	9.8	11	12.9	12.8	2.5			
FI													16.4			
PRC												9.6	10.1	12.4	6.9	8.2
Polo/Casa Libertà														35.6	37.1	16.9
L'Ulivo														47.2	52.5	43.3
Lega Nord												**3.1**	**2.1**	**2**		**1.1**
Others	20.8	7.2	15.2	13.6	16.3	14.5	18	11.3	14.3	17.3	17.9	22.7	27	2.8	3.5	30.5
Total %	100	100	100	100	100	100	100	100	100	100	100	100	100	100	100	100
MARCHE																
DC	30.6	46.7	41.6	43.5	38.3	39.4	39.5	39	37.9	33.4	34.5	31.5	17.2			
PCI (PDS)	21.8	34.2	23.1	25.7	30	32.3	32.8	39.9	38.1	37.7	34.7	23	28.9			

(Continued)

Table 5.5. Continued

	1946	1948	1953	1958	1963	1968	1972	1976	1979	1983	1987	1992	1994	1996	2001	2006
PSI	18.8	6.2	16.5	15.4	14.2	12.9	7.9	8.3	7.9	9.8	12.1	12.6	2.4			
FI													19.7			
PRC												8.3	8.7	10.4	5.7	6.6
Polo/Casa Libertà														41.3	41	19
L'Ulivo														39.6	45.9	39.1
Lega Nord												1.3	**0**	**1.5**		**1**
Others	28.8	12.9	18.8	15.4	17.5	15.4	19.8	12.8	16.1	19.1	18.7	23.3	23.1	7.2	7.4	34.3
Total %	100	100	100	100	100	100	100	100	100	100	100	100	100	100	100	100
UMBRIA																
DC	28.5	39	32	34.3	31.9	39.2	32.2	32	31.1	27.8	29.2	26.2	9.9			
PCI (PDS)	25.5	43.9	26.2	28.8	36	31.6	39.1	45.1	43	42.6	40.2	28.1	35.7			
PSI	21	5.4	22.2	20.5	15.8	12.7	9.7	11.1	11.2	12.5	14.3	15	2.7			
FI													15.3			
PRC												10.1	8.9	12.3	7.7	7.9
Polo/Casa Libertà														41.3	41.2	17.8
L'Ulivo														43.7	48.1	39.2
Lega Nord														1.3		**0.8**
Others	25	11.7	19.6	16.4	16.3	16.5	19	11.8	14.7	17.1	16.3	20.6	27.5	1.4	3	34.3
Total %	100	100	100	100	100	100	100	100	100	100	100	100	100	100	100	100
LAZIO																
DC	32.4	51.9	36.9	37.6	33.2	34.4	34.4	35.7	36.5	30.9	34.4	30.9	8.4			
PCI (PDS)	14.2	27.2	23.4	22.9	25.6	27.6	27.2	36	30.2	29.6	25.9	17.8	23.3			
PSI	10.7	4	8.7	12.4	11.9	12.9	7.6	7.6	8.6	9.9	12.9	12.4	1.7			
FI													20.5			
PRC												5.9	6.6	10.4	5.5	7.4
Polo/Casa Libertà														47.7	48.8	21.4
L'Ulivo														37.6	40.4	31.1
Others	42.7	16.9	31	27.1	29.3	25.1	30.8	20.7	24.7	29.6	26.8	33	39.5	−6.1	5.3	40.1
Total %	100	100	100	100	100	100	100	100	100	100	100	100	100	100	100	100
ABRUZZI																
DC	43.3	53.7	41.5	46.6	45.4	48.7	48.2	44.2	45.7	42.1	42.2	40.4	15.4			
PCI (PDS)	11.5	26.8	22	20.9	24.4	25.4	27	34.9	31.1	29.4	27.4	17.5	20.2			

FI													17.8			
PRC												5.1	7.4	11	5.5	6.5
Polo/Casa Libertà														46.3	47.3	22.8
L'Ulivo														37.7	37.7	32.4
Others	31.9	14.1	26.6	20.2	18.7	14.4	17.9	13.1	15.7	18.8	18.4	23.9	35.8	5	9.5	38.3
Total %	100	100	100	100	100	100	100	100	100	100	100	100	100	100	100	100
MOLISE																
DC	41.1	56.1	46	55.1	51.4	49.9	55.1	50.7	54.7	55.5	57.2	51.8	15.8			
PCI (PDS)	4.4	13	13.8	17.5	16.5	18.1	17.3	26	21.5	19.7	20.1	13.5	17.5			
PSI	7.5	2.7	5.2	5.1	8.9	15.7	5.1	6.7	7.4	7.9	8.3	14.6	2.6			
FI													15.4			
PRC												3.4	5.5	8.8	3.8	4.9
Polo/Casa Libertà														47.3	39.4	26.6
L'Ulivo														34.7	33	29.7
Others	47	28.2	35	22.3	23.2	16.3	22.5	16.6	16.4	16.9	14.4	16.7	43.2	9.2	23.8	38.8
Total %	100	100	100	100	100	100	100	100	100	100	100	100	100	100	100	100
CAMPANIA																
DC	28.4	50.5	36.1	42.3	39.7	39.4	39.2	39.5	42.2	36.2	42	41.1	9.6			
PCI (PDS)	6.7	18.8	19.3	21.8	22.3	23.3	22.7	32.3	24.9	24.3	21	12.3	19.7			
PSI	5.9	2.9	6.8	8.5	11.1	13.2	8.1	7.8	9.4	12.9	14.9	19.6	3			
FI													19.8			
PRC												4	6.9	9.1	4.8	6.1
Polo/Casa Libertà														47.6	45.6	27.2
L'Ulivo														37.3	35	28.5
Others	59	27.8	37.8	27.4	26.9	24.1	30	20.4	23.5	26.6	22.1	23	41	6	14.6	38.2
Total %	100	100	100	100	100	100	100	100	100	100	100	100	100	100	100	100
PUGLIA																
DC	29.8	48.6	38.5	44.1	43.2	44.2	41.6	41.7	42.8	36.3	37.9	35.8	13.8			
PCI (PDS)	8	26.6	23.7	24	26.2	27.2	25.7	31.7	26.7	25.4	23.1	13.8	19.9	22.1		
PSI	7.4	3.5	9	11.4	10.7	12.9	10	9.2	10.2	14.3	15.3	17.8	2.8			
FI																
PRC												5.2	7	7.5		5.7
Polo/Casa Libertà														47.8	47.3	27.3
L'Ulivo														37.6	35.8	29.1
Lega d'Az. Merid.														**11.1**	**0.9**	

(*Continued*)

TABLE 5.5. *Continued*

	1946	1948	1953	1958	1963	1968	1972	1976	1979	1983	1987	1992	1994	1996	2001	2006
Others	54.8	21.3	28.8	20.5	19.9	15.7	22.7	17.4	20.3	24	23.7	27.4	56.5	−26.1	16	37.9
Total %	100	100	100	100	100	100	100	100	100	100	100	100	100	100	100	100
BASILICATA																
DC	31.3	48.4	41.3	46.7	42.5	48.8	49.2	44.5	43.6	46	46.1	44.4	19.6			
PCI (PDS)	13	25.6	25.9	25.9	28.9	26.1	24.9	33.3	28.9	27.9	25.5	16.8	23.2			
PSI	16.2	8.3	6.8	9.5	10.3	14.2	9.8	10.3	10.9	10.9	13.5	14.7	8.6			
FI													11.6			
PRC												5.5	7.5	9.9	4.5	5.6
Polo/Casa Libertà														42.1	35.6	19.8
L'Ulivo														40.7	44	35.3
Others	39.5	17.7	26	17.9	18.3	10.9	16.1	11.9	16.6	15.2	14.9	18.6	29.5	7.3	15.9	39.3
Total %	100	100	100	100	100	100	100	100	100	100	100	100	100	100	100	100
CALABRIA																
DC	34.3	48.8	40.6	47.3	43.9	41.9	39.1	39.3	42.8	36.8	37	36.6	11.9			
PCI (PDS)	12.1	29.5	20.9	23	26.3	23.8	25.9	33	26.7	26.2	25.3	14.7	22.2			
PSI	11.1	2.1	11.2	13.2	13	17.8	12.4	11.5	12.8	16.2	16.9	17.2	3.9			
FI													19			
PRC												6.6	9.3	10		6
Polo/Casa Libertà														48.4	42.5	20.7
L'Ulivo														37.5	35.7	26.3
Others	42.5	19.6	27.3	16.5	16.8	16.5	22.6	16.2	17.7	20.8	20.8	24.9	33.7	4.1	21.8	47
Total %	100	100	100	100	100	100	100	100	100	100	100	100	100	100	100	100
SICILIA																
DC	30	47.9	36.4	43	38.8	40.4	39.8	42.2	43.7	37.9	38.8	41.2	8.3			
PCI (PDS)	7.1	20.9	21.8	21.9	23.7	22.5	21.3	27.5	21.1	21.6	19.8	10.1	16.5			
PSI	10.9	4.9	7.5	10.8	10.9	11.5	8.6	9	10	13.3	14.9	14	2.8			
MSI	**8**	**3.2**														
FI													33.6			
PRC												3.2		7	3.2	4.1
Polo/Casa Libertà														54.8	53.2	29.2
L'Ulivo														33.2	30.8	25.3
Others	44	23.1	34.3	24.3	26.6	25.6	30.3	21.3	25.2	27.2	26.5	31.5	38.8	5	12.8	41.4
Total %	100	100	100	100	100	100	100	100	100	100	100	100	100	100	100	100
SARDEGNA																
DC	41.1	49.3	41.7	47.1	42.5	42.9	40.9	39.8	38.1	31.7	34.2	33.6	9.9			

	C1	C2	C3	C4	C5	C6	C7	C8	C9	C10	C11	C12	C13	C14	C15	C16
PCI (PDS)	12.5	19.1	21.2	19.8	22.5	23.7	25.3	35.5	31.7	28.8	25.3	14.3	19.7			
PSI	8.8	6.6	9	12.3	11	10.7	8.1	9.3	8.9	10.1	11.4	15.4	3.2			
FI													21.2			
PRC												6.6	6.1	8.4	4.7	6.7
Polo/Casa Libertà														46.7	47.3	22.5
L'Ulivo														25.5	38.4	33.3
Psd'A	14.9	10.3	3.9			3.6			1.9	9.4	12			3.8‡		3.7
Lega Sarda	2															
Others	20.7	14.7	24.2	20.8	24	19.1	25.7	15.4	19.4	20	17.1	30.1	19.4	5.9		37.5
Total %	100	100	100	100	100	100	100	100	100	100	100	100	100	100	100	100

VALLE D'AOSTA

	C1	C2	C3	C4	C5	C6	C7	C8	C9	C10	C11	C12	C13	C14
DC	48.2	58.9	53.3	46.4	48	52.1	49.5	32	18.3	39.6				
FDPR§	51.8													
PCI (PDS)		29.7					22.2	35.5		28				
PSI		5.4						7.3						
Polo per la Libertà													20.5	
L'Ulivo												15	21.9	
PRC											3.7		7.3	
Progressisti											22.2			
Gruppo Dolchi-Fosson											36.8			
UV				50.9	49.8	47.9	45.2	38.9	55.1					
L. Valle d'Aosta											**49.6**	**54.1**	**48.6**	**35**
Lega Nord												**17.2**		**8.1**
Others	0	6	46.7	2.7	2.2	0	50.5	32.5	36.5	31.6	5.3	9.9	0.5	15.1
Total %	100	100	100	100	100	100	100	100	100	100	100	100	100	100

Note: I only present the electoral results of the most relevant parties given the high fragmentation of the Italian system and the fact that my interest is only on the three main state parties. At the first democratic elections of 1946, there were two parties that were very successful (Fronte dell'Uomo Qualunque and Unione Democratica Nazionale) but whose success was short-lived. They soon became marginal and for this reason I have ignored their results even for the 1946 election.

Source: Author's own elaboration based on electoral data of the Ministero dello Interno.

* In 1946 the elections took place only at the province of Trento; in 1948 it was already Trento and Bolzano.

** Frente Democratico Popolare: PCI + PSI.

*** In proportional lists, in coalition with POP, PRI, UD and Prodi (together, 17.7% vote share).

† In 1946, without Trieste.

‡ Psd'Az result in proportional lists; in uni-nominal circumscriptions it went in coalition with L'Ulivo.

§ PCI, PSIUP, Pd'A, PRI.

Challenging the State

TABLE 5.6. *Vote shares of Spanish parties in state elections (1977–2008), disaggregated by region (percentage over valid vote)*

	1977	1979	1982	1986	1989	1993	1996	2000	2004	2008
ANDALUCÍA										
UCD	36.2	33.5	5.9	–	–	–	–	–	–	–
CDS	–	–	1.3	5.6	4.7					
PSOE	34.4	31.8	60.4	57.07	52.5	51.4	46.7	43.9	52.9	51.9
AP (PP)	7.1	4.3	22.2	22.7	20.2	29.8	35.3	40.6	33.7	38.2
PCE (IU)	11.3	13.3	6.2	8.1	12	12.1	13.5	7.8	6.4	5.1
PA	**4.7**	**11.1**	**2.3**	**2.8**	**6.2**	**2.4**	**3.1**	**5.1**	**4**	**1.5**
Others	6.3	6	1.7	3.73	4.4	4.3	1.4	2.6	3	3.3
Total %	100	100	100	100	100	100	100	100	100	100
ARAGÓN										
UCD	37	40.9	9.5	–	–	–	–	–	–	–
CDS	–	–	4.2	11.2	7.6	1.3				
PSOE	24.7	28.3	49.4	43.4	38.7	34.3	47.9	31.1	41.3	46.2
AP (PP)	8.8	5.6	30.8	26.1	27.8	32.9	34.6	47.2	36.5	37.1
PCE (IU)	4.9	7.1	2.9	3.4	9.7	9.7	9.1	3.5	2.8	2.8
PAR		6.1		11	10.9	19		5.4	4.7	5.2
CHA						0.83	6.4	10.4	12.1	5
Others	24.6	12	3.2	4.9	5.3	1.97	2	2.4	2.6	3.7
Total %	100	100	100	100	100	100	100	100	100	100
ASTURIAS										
UCD	30.9	33	4.9	–	–	–	–	–	–	–
CDS	–	–	4.3	13.2	12.5	3.7				
PSOE	31.7	37.3	52.1	46	40.6	39.3	39.8	46.3	43.4	46.2
AP (PP)	13.5	8.6	27.9	27.2	26.5	37.4	41	37	43.8	42.1
PCE (IU)	10.5	13.7	8.1	9.2	15.6	15.4	15.5	10.3	8.4	7.3
URAS	**1.9**							**2**		
CNA		**0.57**								
PAS					**0.58**	**1.6**	**1.7**		**0.61**	
UNA					**0.53**			**0.9**		
Others	11.5	6.83	2.7	4.4	3.69	2.6	2	3.5	3.79	4.4
Total %	100	100	100	100	100	100	100	100	100	100
BALEARES										
UCD	51.9	48.9	10.4	–	–	–	–	–	–	–
CDS	–	–	5.2	11.2	9.2	1.8				
PSOE	23.3	29.4	40.4	40.3	34.5	34	35.9	29.3	39.5	40.3
AP (PP)	9	9.2	37.7	34.3	40.7	46.4	45.1	53.9	45.9	34.3
PCE (IU)	4.5	4.9	1.7	2.3	5.1	6	7.7	4		2.8
UAM	**3.8**									
SMIM		**3.3**								
PSM/ENTSA			**2.4**	**2.2**	**2.3**	**4.9**	**5.7**	**5.9**	**8.6**	
UNITAT										**5.4**
Others	7.5	4.3	2.2	9.7	8.2	6.9	5.6	6.9	6	17.2
Total %	100	100	100	100	100	100	100	100	100	100

CANARIAS

UCD	59.8	58.4	16.4	–	–	–	–	–	–	–
CDS	–	–	4.9	16.9	17.6	1.2				
PSOE	16.5	17.8	36.6	36.1	36.1	29.8	30	29.6	34.4	39.6
AP (PP)	8	3.7	26.9	23.3	19.4	33.9	37.6	41.8	35.4	35.5
PCE (IU)	3.3	3.7	0.22	4.31	8	5	5.5	2.4	1.9	1.3
PCU	**3.2**									
UPC		**11**								
CC			**3.9**							
AC-CC			**2.9**							
AIC				**9.8**	**9.7**					
CC						**25.6**	**25.1**	**22.2**	**24.3**	**16.8**
Others	9.2	5.4	8.18	9.59	9.2	4.5	1.8	4	4	6.8
Total %	100	100	100	100	100	100	100	100	100	100

CANTABRIA

UCD	40.1	41.9	5.4	–	–	–	–	–	–	–
CDS	–	–	5.1	13	9.7	1.5				
PSOE	26.4	30.3	45	44.3	40.1	37.2	35.6	33.5	40.9	43.4
AP (PP)	14.3	10.3	38.9	34.1	38.4	37	50.5	56.8	51.9	50.2
PCE	5.4	6.6	3.1	3.1	6.4	7.4	11.4	5	3.3	2.3
Others	13.8	10.9	2.5	5.5	5.4	16.9	2.5	4.7	3.9	4.1
Total %	100	100	100	100	100	100	100	100	100	100

CASTILLA-LEÓN

UCD	51.4	51	12.3	–	–	–	–	–	–	–
CDS	–	–	5.5	17.5	12.7	4.1				
PSOE	23.6	25.6	42.4	38.8	35.5	36.7	35	32.2	41.9	42.8
AP (PP)	11.7	9.4	34.6	35.8	40.2	47.4	52.2	55.7	50.3	50
PCE (IU)	3.7	4.9	2	2.5	6.6	7.7	9.1	4.4	2.8	2.5
Others	9.6	9.1	3.2	5.4	5	4.1	3.7	7.7	5	4.7
Total %	100	100	100	100	100	100	100	100	100	100

CASTILLA-LA MANCHA

UCD	42.5	43	10.8	–	–	–	–	–	–	–
CDS	–	–	2	17.5	7.7	2				
PSOE	29.8	34.5	49.2	38.8	48	45.3	42.6	40.8	46.5	44.5
AP (PP)	12.9	5.8	31.2	35.8	33.8	43	47.2	52.3	47.4	49.4
PCE (IU)	7.2	9.8	3.7	2.5	7	7.6	8.4	4.3	3.4	2.9
Others	7.6	6.9	3.1	5.4	3.5	2.1	1.8	2.6	2.7	3.2
Total %	100	100	100	100	100	100	100	100	100	100

CATALUÑA

UCD	16.91	19.35	2.04	–	–	–	–	–	–	–
CDS	–	–	2	4.12	4.32	0.75				
PSOE	28.56	29.67	45.8	41	35.59	34.87	39.36	34.13	39.47	45.33
AP (PP)	3.55	3.6	14.6	11.4	10.64	17.04	17.96	22.79	15.58	16.39
PSUC	**18.3**	**17.4**	**4.6**	**3.9**						
CiU	**16.9**	**16.4**	**22.8**	**32**	**32.7**	**31.8**	**29.6**	**28.8**	**20.8**	**21**
ERC	**4.7**	**4.2**	**4**	**2.7**	**2.7**	**5.1**	**4.2**	**5.6**	**15.9**	**7.9**
IC (IC-V)					**7.3**	**7.5**	**7.6**	**3.5**	**5.8**	**4.9**
Others	11.08	9.38	4.16	4.88	6.75	2.94	1.28	5.18	2.45	4.48
Total %	100	100	100	100	100	100	100	100	100	100

(*Continued*)

TABLE 5.6. *Continued*

	1977	1979	1982	1986	1989	1993	1996	2000	2004	2008
COM, VALENCIANA										
UCD	33	36.5	6.3	–	–	–	–	–	–	–
CDS	–		2.5	8.8	7.8					
PSOE	36.3	37.3	53.1	47.5	41.5	38.3	38.3	34	42.4	41
AP (PP)	5.9	4.5	29.1	28.8	27	40.5	43.7	52.1	46.8	51.6
PCE (IU)	9.1	12	4.6	4.7	9.1	10.5	11.1	5.8	4.6	2.7
PSPV	**1.7**									
UV				**3.1**	**6.8**	**4.6**	**3.5**	**2.4**		
UPV-BN			**0.9**	**1.9**	**1.9**	**1.7**	**1**	**2.4**	**1.5**	**1.1**
Others	14	9.7	3.5	5.2	5.9	4.4	2.4	3.3	4.7	3.6
Total %	100	100	100	100	100	100	100	100	100	100
EXTREMADURA										
UCD	50	45.6	10.1	–	–	–	–	–	–	–
CDS	–	–	1.6	8	9.5	2				
PSOE	30.8	37.6	55.4	55.9	53.9	51.5	48.4	44.7	51.2	52.3
AP (PP)	7.8	3.7	23.8	26.7	25	35.8	40.3	47.3	42.4	41.8
PCE (IU)	5.4	7.8	3.2	3.9	6.9	7.8	8.9	4.7	3.5	2.9
EU			**4.3**	**4.3**	**2.7**	**1.8**	**1**	**1**	**0.7**	**0.6**
Others	6	5.3	1.6	1.2	2	1.1	1.4	2.3	2.2	2.4
Total %	100	100	100	100	100	100	100	100	100	100
GALICIA										
UCD	53.8	48.2	17.7	–	–	–	–	–	–	–
CDS	–	–	2.6	8.6	7.8	1.5				
PSOE	15.5	17.3	32.8	35.8	34.6	35.9	33.5	23.7	37.2	39.5
AP (PP)	13.1	14.2	37.6	39.2	39	47.1	48.3	54	47.1	44.5
PCE (IU)	3	4.2	1.5	1.1	3.2	4.7	3.6	1.3	1.7	1.4
BNG	**2**	**5.9**		**2.1**	**3.6**	**8**	**12.8**	**18.6**	**11.4**	**12.1**
PG-POG-PSG		**5.4**	**3**							
PSG	**2.4**									
CG				**6.2**	**3.4**					
Others	10.2	4.8	4.8	7	8.4	2.8	1.8	2.4	2.6	2.5
Total %	100	100	100	100	100	100	100	100	100	100
LA RIOJA										
UCD	41.3	48	7.4	–	–	–	–	–	–	–
CDS	–	–	3.7	10.1	7.2	2.1				
PSOE	26.3	29.1	43.4	39.2	39.7	37.6	36.6	34.9	44	43.6
AP (PP)	14.5	13.9	41.5	43.9	41.1	46.6	49.4	54.1	49.9	49.5
PCE (IU)	2.8	3.6	1.6	2	6.4	7	8.7	4	2.8	1.9
PR						**4.4**	**3.4**	**3.6**		**1.5**
Others	15.1	5.4	2.4	4.8	5.6	2.3	1.9	3.4	3.3	3.5
Total %	100	100	100	100	100	100	100	100	100	100
MADRID										
UCD	31.9	33.1	3.3	–	–	–	–	–	–	–
CDS	–	–	4.1	13.9	11	3				
PSOE	31.7	33.3	52.1	40.8	33.5	35	31.42	33.1	44.1	39.7
AP (PP)	10.5	8.6	32.2	32	34.2	43.9	49.3	52.5	45	49.2
PCE (IU)	10.7	13.5	5	6	15.4	14.6	16.4	9.1	6.4	4.7
Others	15.2	11.5	3.3	7.3	5.9	3.5	2.88	5.3	4.5	6.4
Total %	100	100	100	100	100	100	100	100	100	100

NAVARRA									
UCD	29	32.9	10.5	–	–	–	–	–	–	–
CDS	–	–	4.1	9.6	7	1.7				
PSOE	21.2	21.9	37.6	35.5	31.2	34.9	30.3	27.3	33.5	34.6
AP(PP)-UPN			25.6	29.6	33.2	36.1	37.12	49.9	37.6	39.3
UPN		**11.2**								
PCE (IU)	**2.4**	**2.2**	**0.7**	**1.5**	**5.7**	**8.7**	**12.4**	**7.6**	**5.9**	**3.3**
UNAI	**9.5**	**4.3**								
HB		**8.7**	**11.7**	**13.9**	**11**	**10.4**	**8.2**			
EE			**2.8**	**2.8**	**2.9**	–	–	–	–	–
EA					**4.8**	**3.7**	**3.8**	**4.7**		
NABAI									18	18.5
Others	37.9	18.8	7	7.1	4.2	4.5	8.18	10.5	5	4.3
Total %	100	100	100	100	100	100	100	100	100	100
PAÍS VASCO									
UCD	12.8	16.9		–	–	–	–	–	–	–
CDS	–	–	1.8	5	3.46	0.76				
PSOE	26.5	19.1	29.2	26.3	21.1	24.5	23.7	23.3	27.2	38.1
AP (PP)	7.11		11.64	11.64	10.05	9.37	14.68	18.34	18.9	18.5
PCE (IU)	4.54	4.59	1.75	1.25	3.01	6.31	9.21	5.45	8.2	4.49
PNV	**29.3**	**27.6**	**31.7**	**27.8**	**22.8**	**24.1**	**25**	**30.4**	**33.7**	**27.1**
EA					**11.2**	**9.8**	**8.2**	**7.6**	**6.5**	**4.5**
EE	**6.1**	**8**	**7.7**	**8.9**	**8.8**	–	–	–	–	–
HB		**15**	**14.7**	**17.7**	**16.9**	**14.5**	**12.3**			
Aralar									3.1	2.7
Others	13.65	8.81	1.51	1.41	2.68	10.66	6.91	14.91	2.4	4.61
Total %	100	100	100	100	100	100	100	100	100	100
REGIÓN DE MURCIA									
UCD	40.7	39.1	6.4	–	–	–	–	–	–	–
CDS	–	–	1.9	8.3	10.4	2.2				
PSOE	34.9	39.1	50.8	48.8	46.1	38.6	38	32.4	35	32.8
AP (PP)	6.8	5.7	35.6	34.3	30	47.3	49.9	58.1	57.4	61.2
PCE (IU)	6.7	7.9	3.8	4.5	9.2	9.7	10.5	6.2	4.3	2.9
Others	10.9	8.2	1.5	4.1	4.3	2.2	1.6	3.3	3.3	3.1
Total %	100	100	100	100	100	100	100	100	100	100

Source: Author's own elaboration based on electoral data of the Ministerio del Interior.

Table 5.7. *Number of seats of the major state parties in the Spanish parliament, by region (1977–2008)*

	1977		1979		1982		1986		1989		1993		1996		2000		2004		2008	
	Psoe	PP	Psoe	PP	Psoe	PP	Psoe	PP	Psoe	PP	Psoe	PP	Psoe	PP	Psoe	PP	Psoe	PP	Psoe	PP
Andalucía (60)	27	0	24	0	43	15	42	15	42	12	37	20	32	24	30	28	38	23	36	25
Aragón (13)	5	0	5	0	9	5	8	5	7	4	7	4	8	5	4	8	7	5	8	5
Asturias (9)	4	1	4	1	6	3	5	3	4	3	4	4	4	4	3	5	4	4	4	4
Baleares (7)	2	0	2	0	3	3	3	3	3	3	3	4	3	4	2	5	4	4	4	4
Canarias (14)	3	0	3	0	7	4	6	4	7	3	5	5	5	5	3	7	6	6	7	6
Cantabria (5)	1	1	2	1	3	2	3	2	3	2	3	2	2	3	2	3	2	3	2	3
Castilla-León (34)	8	2	10	2	18	13	16	14	14	18	13	20	11	22	11	22	14	19	14	18
Castilla-LM (20)	8	1	8	1	13	8	16	8	12	8	10	10	9	11	8	12	9	11	9	12
Cataluña (47)	15	0	17	1	25	8	21	6	20	4	18	8	19	8	17	12	21	6	25	7
C. Valenciana (31)	13	1	13	0	19	10	18	10	16	9	12	15	13	15	12	19	14	17	14	19
Extremadura (11)	4	0	5	0	9	3	7	4	7	4	7	4	6	5	5	6	5	5	5	5
Galicia (26)	3	4	6	4	9	13	11	13	12	14	11	15	9	14	6	16	10	12	10	11
La Rioja (4)	1	1	1	1	2	2	2	2	2	2	2	2	2	2	1	3	2	2	2	2
Madrid (33)	11	3	12	3	18	11	15	11	12	12	13	16	11	17	12	19	16	17	15	18
Navarra (5)	2	0	1	0	3	2	2	2	2	3	2	3	2	3	2	3	2	2	2	2
País Vasco (20)	7	1	5	1	8	2	7	2	6	2	7	4	5	5	4	7	7	4	9	3
R. de Murcia (9)	4	0	4	0	5	3	5	3	5	3	4	4	3	5	6	3	6	3	7	3

Note: The number of seats of 'other parties' has not been calculated given that it is numerically irrelevant.
Source: Author's own elaboration based on electoral data of the Ministerio del Interior.

TABLE 5.8. *Number of seats of the major state parties in the Belgian parliament, by region (1946–2003)*

	1946	1949	1950	1954	1958	1961	1965	1968	1971	1974	1977	1978	1981	1985	1987	1991	1995	1999	2003
Wallonia	71	71	71	71	67	71	67	64	67	60	65	65	65	63	63	63	48	48	49
BSP/PSB	29	28	33	37	35	36	26	24	25	26	–	–	–	–	–	–	–	–	–
PSB (PS)	–	–	–	–	–	–	–	–	–	–	29	27	30	29	32	39	19	17	21
CVP/PSC	22	27	26	24	27	24	17	14	–	–	–	–	–	–	–	–	–	–	–
PSC (CDH)	–	–	–	–	–	–	–	–	15	16	19	19	15	15	14	12	11	9	7
LP/PL	6	8	7	8	5	6	17	19	11	9	–	–	–	–	–	–	–	–	–
PRLW	–	–	–	–	–	–	–	–	–	–	8	11	–	–	–	–	–	–	–
PRL	–	–	–	–	–	–	–	–	–	–	–	–	17	15	14	12	13	13	18
Flanders	89	97	97	97	97	97	99	99	99	99	99	99	99	101	101	101	80	80	76
BSP/PSB	26	26	25	30	27	30	25	25	25	23	–	–	–	–	–	–	–	–	–
BSP (SP)	–	–	–	–	–	–	–	–	–	–	23	22	22	26	26	23	18	13	–
Sp.a-Spirit	–	–	–	–	–	–	–	–	–	–	–	–	–	–	–	–	–	–	21
CVP/PSC	54	60	64	56	53	56	47	42	–	–	–	–	–	–	–	–	–	–	–
CVP	–	–	–	–	–	–	–	–	40	42	46	47	36	40	35	32	26	19	–
CD&V	–	–	–	–	–	–	–	–	–	–	–	–	–	–	–	–	–	–	19
PL	7	11	8	10	8	7	16	15	16	16	–	–	–	–	–	–	–	–	–
PVV (VLD)	–	–	–	–	–	–	–	–	–	–	14	18	22	17	20	23	19	20	22
Brabant (Brussels)	42	44	44	44	44	44	46	48	46	48	48	48	48	48	48	48	22	22	22
BSP/PSB	14	13	17	19	18	18	13	8	7	7	–	–	–	–	–	–	–	–	–
PSB (PS)	–	–	–	–	–	–	–	–	–	–	0	5	5	5	8	6	2	2	4
BSP (SP)	–	–	–	–	–	–	–	–	–	–	6	4	4	4	6	5	2	1	–
Sp.a-Spirit	–	–	–	–	–	–	–	–	–	–	–	–	–	–	–	–	–	–	2
PSC/CVP	16	18	18	15	16	16	13	13	–	–	–	–	–	–	–	–	–	–	–
CVP	–	–	–	–	–	–	–	–	12	8	10	10	9	8	8	7	7	3	–
CD&V	–	–	–	–	–	–	–	–	–	–	–	–	–	–	–	–	–	–	2
PSC (CDH)	–	–	–	–	–	–	–	–	4	5	5	6	3	4	3	3	1	1	2
LP/PL	5	10	7	8	7	7	15	13	4	–	–	–	–	–	–	–	–	–	–
PVV	–	–	–	–	–	–	–	–	–	–	3	4	6	5	5	8	5	3	3
PRL	–	–	–	–	–	–	–	–	–	–	–	–	7	9	9	8	5	5	6

Note: The number of seats of 'other parties' has not been calculated given that it is numerically irrelevant.

Source: Author's own elaboration based on electoral data of the Gouvernement du Belgique (site officiel des résultats électoraux belges).

TABLE 5.9. *Number of seats of the major state parties in the British parliament, by region (1945–2005)*

	1945	1950	1951	1955	1959	1964	1966	1970	1974 F	1974 O	1979	1983	1987	1992	1997	2001	2005
England	510	506	506	511	511	511	511	511	516	516	516	523	523	524	529	529	529
Labour	331	251	233	216	193	246	285	216	237	255	203	148	155	195	328	323	286
Conserv.	159	242	259	279	302	255	216	292	267	252	306	362	357	319	165	165	194
Liberal	5	2	2	2	3	3	6	2	9	8	7	10	7	10	34	40	47
Wales	35	36	36	36	36	36	36	36	36	36	36	38	38	38	40	40	40
Labour	25	27	27	27	27	28	32	27	24	23	21	20	24	27	34	34	29
Conserv.	3	3	5	5	7	6	3	7	8	8	11	14	8	6	0	0	3
Liberal	6	5	3	3	2	2	1	1	2	2	1	2	3	1	2	2	4
Scotland	71	71	71	71	71	71	71	71	71	71	71	72	72	72	72	72	59
Labour	37	37	35	30	38	43	46	44	40	41	44	41	50	49	56	55	40
Conserv.	24	26	29	34	25	24	20	23	21	16	22	21	10	11	0	1	1
Liberal	0	2	1	1	1	4	5	3	3	3	3	5	7	9	10	10	11
N. I.	12	12	12	12	12	12	12	12	12	12	12	17	17	17	18	18	18
UUP*	8	10	9	10	11	12	11	8	9	10	5	11	9	9	10	6	1

Note: The number of seats of 'other parties' has not been calculated given that it is numerically irrelevant.

* The Ulster Unionist Party of Northern Ireland followed the Conservative whip in the British parliament. This is the reason why it appears in this table as part of the seats of British state parties.

Source: University of Keele, database UK General Election Results (regional distribution of seats and percentage vote).

Table 5.10. *Number of seats of the major state parties in the Italian parliament, by region (1946–2006)*

	1946	1948	1953	1958	1963	1968	1972	1976	1979	1983	1987	1992	1994		1996	2001	2006
Piemonte	41	36	42	40	47	47	48	54	54	50	48	47	12		49	49	46
DC (later PPI)	16	21	19	20	18	18	18	20	19	16	15	11	2	L'Ulivo	25	19	
PCI (later PDS)	9	14	10	8	12	13	13	20	17	15	13	6	3	Polo Liberta	16		
PSI	13	5	6	6	7	8	6	5	5	5	7	7	0	Casa Liberta		28	
UDN	2													Lista Prodi			25
Rif. Com.												4	1	Lta. Berlusconi			21
FI													2				
Liguria	16	19	17	21	23	22	22	22	23	20	21	19	6		19	19	17
DC (later PPI)	6	9	8	9	8	8	8	8	8	6	6	5	1	L'Ulivo	10	11	
PCI (later PDS)	5	8	5	5	7	7	7	9	8	8	7	4	2	Polo Liberta	6		
PSI	5	2	3	4	3	4	3	2	3	2	3	2	0	Casa libertà		8	
Rif. Com.												1	0	Lista Prodi			10
FI													1	Lta. Berlusconi			7
Lombardia	69	79	80	82	90	92	90	100	104	101	96	97	25		97	98	98
DC (later PPI)	30	46	43	40	40	42	41	44	43	35	34	25	4	L'Ulivo	18	13	
PCI (later PDS)	14	27	14	16	18	22	22	32	30	29	24	13	6	Polo Liberta	35		
PSI	24	6	16	15	18	16	11	11	11	11	17	13	0	Casa Liberta		83	
FUQ	1													Lista Prodi			48
Rif. Com.												6	2	Lta. Berlusconi			50
FI													5				
Trentino-AA	4	9	8	10	10	9	10	9	10	8	10	10	2		10	10	11
DC (later PPI)	3	5	5	5	5	4	5	4	4	3	3	3	1	L'Ulivo	4	6	
PCI (later PDS)	0	0	0	0	0	1	1	1	1	1	1	0	0	Polo Liberta	2		
PSI	1	1	0	1	1	1	1	0	1	1	1	1	0	Casa Liberta		1	
Rif. Com.														Lista Prodi			8
FI													1	Lta. Berlusconi			3

(*Continued*)

Table 5.10. Continued

	1946	1948	1953	1958	1963	1968	1972	1976	1979	1983	1987	1992	1994		1996	2001	2006
Veneto	40	44	44	45	46	46	46	46	46	36	46	44	13		50	50	49
DC (later PPI)	22	29	27	27	26	26	26	24	24	21	21	15	3	L'Ulivo	16	12	
PCI (later PDS)	6	11	6	7	7	8	9	11	11	10	9	3	2	Polo Liberta	12		
PSI	12	4	7	7	7	7	4	5	4	5	7	3	0	Casa Liberta		37	
Rif. Com.													1	Lista Prodi			23
FI													2	Lta. Berlusconi			26
Friuli-VG	11	15	15	18	17	16	15	16	11	14	13	12	3		13	13	13
DC (later PPI)	6	9	9	10	9	9	9	8	7	7	6	5	1	L'Ulivo	3	2	
PCI (later PDS)	1	3	2	3	3	4	4	5	4	4	4	2	1	Polo Liberta	6		
PSI	4	2	2	2	2	3	2	2	1	2	4	3	0	Casa Liberta		10	
Rif. Com.													0	Lista Prodi			6
FI													0	Lta. Berlusconi			7
E. Romagna	41	42	42	46	46	45	47	46	36	46	46	46	9		42	42	43
DC (later PPI)	10	14	14	14	12	12	13	13	13	10	12	9	1	L'Ulivo	31	34	
PCI (later PDS)	16	23	18	17	20	21	18	24	23	23	21	15	3	Polo Liberta	6		
PSI	13	4	6	7	7	7	4	4	4	4	6	5	0	Casa Liberta		6	
PRI	2													Lista Prodi			28
Rif. Com.												3	1	Lta. Berlusconi			15
FI													2				
Toscana	33	36	37	37	41	40	41	38	42	40	37	40	11		39	39	38
DC (later PPI)	11	16	15	14	13	13	16	14	13	11	12	10	1	L'Ulivo	26	31	
PCI (later PDS)	13	20	16	15	17	19	19	21	21	21	20	13	3	Polo Liberta	7		
PSI	8	0	6	7	7	5	3	3	4	5	5	5	0	Casa Liberta		7	
PRI	1													Lista Prodi			25
Rif. Com.												4	1	Lta. Berlusconi			13
FI													3				

Marche																		
	13	17	15	19	19	17	17	16	17	17	16	17	16	16	16	4	16	16
DC (later PPI)	5	9	8	7	7	7	6	7	6	6	6					1		
PCI (later PDS)	3	6	4	6	6	7	7	6	7	4	4					1		
PSI	3	1	3	2	2	1	2	2	2	2	2					0		
PRI	2																	
Rif. Com.											1					0		
FI																1		
L'Ulivo																	10	12
Polo Liberta																	4	4
Casa Liberta																		
Lista Prodi																	10	
Lta. Berlusconi																	6	

Umbria																		
	9	11	11	13	13	13	11	10	11	12	11	9	9			2	9	9
DC (later PPI)	3	5	4	5	5	4	4	3	5	4	3					0		
PCI (later PDS)	3	6	3	4	5	5	5	5	4	5	4					0		
PSI	2	0	3	3	3	2	2	1	1	2	2					0		
PRI	1																	
Rif. Com.											1					0		
FI																1		
L'Ulivo																	6	8
Polo Liberta																	7	
Casa Liberta																		1
Lista Prodi																	6	
Lta. Berlusconi																	3	

Lazio																		
	29	34	38	39	48	47	48	54	55	54	53	54	54			13	57	57	56
DC (later PPI)	11	20	15	16	16	17	17	20	19	17	17	19	17			2		
PCI (later PDS)	4	10	10	9	12	13	13	16	20	16	14	10				5		
PSI	3	1	3	5	6	6	7	5	4	5	5	7				0		
PRI	5																	
UDN	5																	
FUQ	2																	
BNL	2																	
Rif. Com.	2												3			2		
FI																1		
L'Ulivo																	29	24
Polo Liberta																	25	
Casa Liberta																		32
Lista Prodi																	30	
Lta. Berlusconi																	26	

Abruzzi																		
	12	16	14	17	16	15	15	14	14	14	15	17				3	14	14	14
DC (later PPI)	7	10	7	8	8	8	8	7	7	7	7	6				1		
PCI (later PDS)	1	5	4	4	4	4	4	5	5	5	4	3				1		
PSI	2	1	1	2	2	4	4	1	1	1	2	2				0		
PRI	1																	
UDN	1																	
Rif. Com.												1				0		
L'Ulivo																	7	7
Polo Liberta																	6	
Casa Liberta																		7
Lista Prodi																	8	
Lta. Berlusconi																	6	

(Continued)

Table 5.10. Continued

	1946	1948	1953	1958	1963	1968	1972	1976	1979	1983	1987	1992	1994		1996	2001	2006
Molise	7	4	5	6	4	5	4	4	4	4	4	5	1		4	4	2
DC (later PPI)	4	3	3	4	3	3	3	3	3	3	3	3	1	L'Ulivo	3	1	
PCI (later PDS)	0	1	1	1	1	1	1	1	1	0	0	1	0	Polo Liberta	1		
PSI	0	0	0	1	0	1	0	0	0	0	0	1	0	Casa Liberta		3	
UDN	2													Lista Prodi			1
FUQ	1													Lta. Berlusconi			1
Rif. Com.													0				
FI													0				
Campania	39	49	51	54	59	59	61	57	56	60	61	63	15		62	63	62
DC (later PPI)	15	28	20	24	25	25	24	24	26	23	26	27	2	L'Ulivo	26	23	
PCI (later PDS)	3	10	11	12	14	14	14	20	15	15	14	8	3	Polo Liberta	30		
PSI	3	0	3	5	6	8	5	4	5	8	9	13	0	Casa Liberta		38	
UDN	9													Lista Prodi			35
FUQ	5													Lta. Berlusconi			27
BNL	3																
Rif. Com.												2	0				
FI													4				
Puglia	30	38	40	40	41	42	42	41	41	45	45	43	10		44	44	44
DC (later PPI)	12	21	17	19	19	20	19	18	19	17	18	17	3	L'Ulivo	18	15	
PCI (later PDS)	5	11	10	11	11	12	12	14	12	11	11	6	3	Polo Liberta	24		
PSI	3	0	3	5	5	5	5	4	4	7	7	8	0	Casa Liberta		28	
FUQ	4													Lista Prodi			23
UDN	3													Lta. Berlusconi			21
Rif. Com.												2	2				
Basilicata	5	6	7	8	8	8	8	8	7	7	7	6	2		7	7	6
DC (later PPI)	2	4	4	4	4	5	5	3	4	4	4	4	1	L'Ulivo	5	6	
PCI (later PDS)	1	2	2	2	3	2	2	3	2	2	2	1	0	Polo Liberta	2		
PSI	1	0	0	1	1	1	1	1	1	1	1	1	0	Casa Liberta		1	
UDN	1													Lista Prodi			4
Rif. Com.												0	0	Lta. Berlusconi			2
FI													0				

Calabria

	21	24	25	25	26	26	24	23	23	22	24	6		23	23	22
DC (later PPI)	8	13	11	13	12	11	10	10	9	9	9	1	L'Ulivo	11	9	
PCI (later PDS)	3	8	6	6	7	6	7	8	6	6	6	1	Polo Liberta	10		
PSI	2	0	3	3	3	5	3	3	4	4	4	0	Casa Liberta			
UDN	3												Lista Prodi			14
FUQ	2												Lta. Berlusconi			8
PRI	1															
Rif. Com.												2				
FI												1				

Sicilia

	44	51	50	50	58	59	60	44	52	52	56	56	14		55	55	54
DC (later PPI)	18	28	21	26	24	25	24	24	22	22	24	24	2	L'Ulivo	14	5	
PCI (later PDS)	3	11	12	12	14	14	15	11	12	12	11	11	4	Polo Liberta	38	50	
PSI	6	2	4	6	6	6	4	6	6	7	8	8	0	Casa Liberta			
UDN	7													Lista Prodi			26
FUQ	4													Lta. Berlusconi			28
MIS	4																
PRI	1																
BNL	1																
Rif. Com.													2				
FI													4				

Sardegna

	11	14	15	18	19	17	16	17	18	19	4		17	18	18
DC (later PPI)	6	9	8	8	8	8	7	7	6	7	1	L'Ulivo	8	7	
PCI (later PDS)	1	3	3	4	5	5	6	6	6	5	1	Polo Liberta	8		
PSI	1	0	2	2	2	1	2	2	2	3	0	Casa Libertà		11	
FUQ	1											Lista Prodi			10
PSd'Az	2											Lta. Berlusconi			8
Rif. Com.											0				
FI											1				

(Continued)

TABLE 5.10. *Continued*

	1946	1948	1953	1958	1963	1968	1972	1976	1979	1983	1987	1992	1994		1996	2001	2006
V. d'Aosta	1	1	1	1	1	1	1	1	1	1	1	1	1				
DC (later PPI)	0	1	1	0	0	1	1	1	0	0	0	0	0	L'Ulivo	0	0	
FDPR	1													Polo Libertà	0		
PCI (later PDS)		0	0	0	0	0	0	1	0	0	0	0	0	Casa Libertà		0	
PSI		0	0	0	0	0	0	0	0	0	0	0	0	Lista Prodi			0
Rif. Com.												0	0	Lta. Berlusconi			0
FI													0				0

Note: The number of seats of 'other parties' has not been calculated for the sake of simplicity.
Source: Author's own elaboration based on electoral data of the Ministero dello Interno.

6

Devolution: Making Electoral Moves Credible

When directly threatened by the growth of a peripheral party, state parties cannot ignore centre–periphery issues if they are to maintain their electoral pluralities or majorities. The rational response in this situation is to move closer to the peripheral party's position along the centre–periphery dimension in an attempt to get back those voters with pro-periphery preferences who are being lost to the peripheral challenger. The hypothesis most widely shared in the literature is that the accommodation of the peripheral challenger's demands by the threatened state party will cause the challenger electoral losses. The assumption behind this is: if the strategy is credible, and voters are convinced that the state party sincerely cares about pro-periphery issues, at least some of the voters will return to the state party.

According to the argument that I present in this book, the pro-periphery convergence of threatened state parties will not cause the peripheral challengers electoral losses because the strategy is unlikely to be credible. This lack of credibility is not only related to the inter-temporal inconsistencies of the state parties' pro-periphery strategies (Meguid 2008). Such inter-temporal inconsistencies are to be expected when competition is taking place along the *secondary* issue dimension, as is the case of state parties and the centre–periphery conflict. The lack of credibility is, above all, the result of the unitary centralized structure of the state.

In the previous chapter, I explained the emergence of the peripheral electoral threat in the countries under analysis. I have shown that the peripheral threat was not ubiquitous and was not equally threatening for all the state parties. This chapter looks into the electoral moves of the main left-wing and right-wing state parties during the period of emergence and growth of peripheral party challengers, before the first devolution reform had taken place. First, I show how widespread the pro-periphery convergence was among threatened state parties; and how effective this strategy was in bringing down the vote shares of peripheral parties. Second, I explain the first devolution reform as an attempt to make pro-periphery convergence more credible and, therefore, more effective in making life difficult for peripheral parties.

6.1 STATE PARTIES' MOVES ALONG THE CENTRE–PERIPHERY DIMENSION

6.1.1 Pro-periphery convergence and its impact on peripheral parties' growth

In this section, I will discuss three main indicators: first, what type of electoral moves were used by state parties during the period of emergence and growth of peripheral parties; second, how widespread were pro-periphery converging moves by threatened state parties; and, finally, to what extent pro-periphery converging positions led peripheral parties to electoral stagnation or to vote losses.

In order to measure the electoral moves used by state parties, I look at the saliency scores of pro-periphery and anti-periphery issues in party manifestos, as described in chapter 4. I will use the mean saliency score for the fifty-six CMP categories, whose value is 1.6, as the threshold defining the line that separates the strategy of centre–periphery avoidance from the strategies that emphasize centre–periphery issues (pro-periphery convergence and anti-periphery polarization). Thus, a pro-periphery move takes place when the saliency score of the pro-periphery issues is above 1.6 and the same applies to an anti-periphery (i.e. pro-centre) move when the score of anti-periphery issues is above 1.6. However, it may also be the case that a party mentions both pro-periphery and anti-periphery issues in the same manifesto. In such cases, a pro-periphery move takes place when the saliency score of the pro-periphery issues is above 1.6 and larger than that of the anti-periphery issues. An anti-periphery move takes place when the saliency score of the anti-periphery issues is above 1.6 per cent and larger than that of the pro-periphery issues. When the pro-periphery and the anti-periphery saliency scores are the same they cancel each other out. This means that the party manifesto does not follow a consistent position or that it is neutral between the two. Finally, a centre–periphery avoidant position is that in which the saliency scores of the pro-periphery and the anti-periphery issues is equal to, or smaller than, 1.6.

Table 6.1 shows the centre–periphery moves of each of the main state parties across time until the election after which the first devolutionary reform was implemented: 1970 in Belgium and 1998 in the UK. In Italy and Spain, first-time devolution coincided with the constitutional process and the re-establishment of democracy. For this reason, only the first two democratic elections (the one that elected the constitutional assembly and the one that ratified the new democratic Constitution) are considered. The last rows of Table 6.1 present the vote shares that the peripheral parties obtained in their respective regions at state elections.

A word of caution is, at this point, necessary. The CMP categories 'centralization' and 'decentralization' are not subtle enough to differentiate general manifestations in favour of decentralization from statements in favour of either local or regional decentralization and, most importantly for us, from an explicit support/

TABLE 6.1. *Centre–periphery moves of state parties and peripheral party growth before the first devolution reform*

Belgium

	1946	1949	1950	1954	1958	1961	1965	1968
CVP-PSC	P	P	P	P	P	P	P	P
PSB-SPB	C	AV	C	P = C	AV	P	AV	C
PL-LP	C	AV	C	C	C	C	AV	P = C
VU				4	3.5	6.2	13.2	17.5
RW							1.5	9.8
FDF							8.3	15.4

Italy

	1946	1948
DC	AV	AV
PCI	AV	AV
PSI	AV	AV
SVP		30.7
UV*		
MSI	8	3.2
PSd'A	15	10.3

Spain

	1977	1979
UCD	AV	P
PSOE	P	P
CiU	16.9	16.4
ERC	4.7	4.2
PNV	29.3	27.6
HB		15

*In coalition with DC.

Great Britain

	1945	1950	1951	1955	1959	1964	1966	1970	1974f	1974o	1979	1983	1987	1992	1997
Con	C	C	C	P	AV	P	AV	P	C	P	AV	AV	AV	C	C
Lab	AV	AV	AV	P	AV	P	C	P	AV	AV	AV	P	P	P	P
SNP	1.3	0.4	0.3	0.5	0.5	2.4	5	11.4	21.9	30.4	17.3	11.7	14	21.5	22.1
PC	1.1	1.2	0.7	3.1	5.2	4.8	4.3	11.5	10.7	10.8	8.1	7.8	7.3	8.8	9.9

Legend: P – Pro-periphery; AV – Centre–periphery avoidance; C – Pro-centre (Anti-periphery).

rejection of regional devolution. Similarly, the category 'multiculturalism: positive' is not subtle enough to differentiate between a defence of the autochthonous cultural minorities, at the origin of peripheral political mobilization, and a defence of the cultural minorities coming from abroad (i.e. immigrants). Therefore, the definition of the parties' strategies based on the manifesto data will be combined with a qualitative revision of the manifestos themselves, whenever in doubt, in order to confirm the positions of each party derived from the CMP data or to correct them whenever necessary.

Table 6.1 summarizes information for a total of twenty-seven state elections. Of these, five elections have taken place with no peripheral party threat at all (between

1946 and 1950 in Belgium and the 1946 and 1948 elections in Italy[1]). Of the remaining twenty-two elections, I eliminate from consideration the first election in which a peripheral party has obtained votes, since there is no previous election with which to compare the peripheral party's evolution. This leaves us with nineteen elections with which to test if a pro-periphery move by the threatened state party is putting a stop to the electoral growth of the peripheral party.

The first observation is that, out of a total of nineteen elections, the threatened state parties (the Christian Democratic Party in Belgium, the Socialist Party in Spain, and Labour in the UK) adopted a pro-periphery position in twelve. Of these twelve, peripheral parties suffered electoral losses on just three occasions (25 per cent of the time). For another seven elections, peripheral parties gained votes (58 per cent of the time) and, for two elections, the evidence is mixed (i.e. one peripheral party increased its vote share while the other experienced electoral losses).

Some authors may object, saying that I should not compare the effect of the threatened state party's move considered individually but should instead compare the combined tactics of the two or three most relevant state parties (Meguid 2008). When I do such a comparison, the results do not change much. According to Meguid's POS theory, the combined accommodative and dismissive tactics, on the one hand, and dismissive tactics by both mainstream parties, on the other, are the most likely to put a stop to the growth of niche parties. Translating this to the centre–periphery conflict, it means that if both state parties avoid centre–periphery issues or if one of them avoids centre–periphery issues while the other adopts a pro-periphery position, the peripheral party is likely to suffer at elections day. Of the twenty-two elections in Table 6.1, Meguid's prediction occurs on six occasions (i.e. 27 per cent of the time).[2]

---

[1] As was explained in the previous chapter, the large vote shares of peripheral parties in Italy did not yet represent a direct threat to any of the main state parties.

[2] Meguid's statistical model uses the peripheral party/year as the unit of analysis. This means that the state party's strategies are defined individually for each peripheral party and not collectively for the country as a whole. The data of the Comparative Manifestos Project only allow us to look at the general position of the state parties with respect to the centre–periphery dimension and not at their position/ reaction to one peripheral party in particular. Meguid justifies the need to define the state party's reaction towards each individual peripheral party on the basis that a state party reacts differently to different peripheral parties. While this is generally true at the sub-state level of electoral competition, it is not less true that a state party, in state elections, has to convey a *state-wide* position on the centre–periphery dimension of competition and it is this state-wide position that is of interest here. A large divergence of responses to different peripheral parties is not to be expected from a state party precisely because the state party would lose credibility. By large divergence I mean the use of antagonist strategies vis-à-vis two different peripheral parties. This kind of divergence is to be expected only when different electoral arenas exist (i.e., regional elections) and the state party diversifies its position according to the electoral arena. Only under very particular circumstances, such as the existence of links between the peripheral party and a terrorist organization (as is the case in Spain or in the UK) will a state party use two divergent strategies at the state level, one for the particular case and another one for the rest of peripheral parties in the country.

Figure 6.1 provides the same basic information as Table 6.1 but it is displayed in the form of a graph and it includes more detail. It shows the evolution of the main state parties' centre–periphery position scores[3] in Belgium and the UK before the first devolution reform. Horizontal lines have been included to represent elections at which peripheral parties had a particularly good result in comparison with their past electoral showings (following my argument about the regional basis of an electoral threat presented in Chapter 3, vote shares refer to results obtained at the state election in the region that corresponds to each peripheral party). This is a way of making the connection—or lack thereof—of the state parties' moves with the peripheral parties' growth visible. Italy and Spain are not graphed because there is no real trend to be shown with just two observations (the 1946 and 1948 elections in Italy and the 1977 and 1979 elections in Spain).

The graphs shown in Figure 6.1 provide important information for the argument defended here. First, it is evident that there is no widespread strategy of pro-periphery convergence adopted as a response to the peripheral party growth. There are tactical moves that turn towards more pro-periphery positions but many of these are later reversed. The Belgian Christian Democratic Party, the most pro-periphery state party in our sample, makes more pro-centre turns than pro-periphery ones during this period. The Labour Party ends the period at approximately the same moderate pro-periphery position at which it started, after making pro-centre and pro-periphery turns. There is something common in the behaviour of the Labour Party and the Belgian Christian Democratic Party. At one point both make a dramatic pro-periphery turn: at the 1970 election in the case of Labour, in 1958 in the case of the CVP-PSC. In both cases, this tactical move was the ad hoc reaction to the growth of one or more peripheral competitors to which Labour and the CVP-PSC were losing votes.

The second observation is that state parties are scarcely consistent across time in their centre–periphery positions. Some state parties move between the pro-periphery and the pro-centre sides of the dimension quite easily, as is the case of the British Conservative Party. The Belgian Socialists stay mostly on the pro-centre side of the dimension, but also change to the other side at least once. The Labour Party stays mostly on the pro-periphery side but at one point it moves to the pro-centre side. Inter-temporal consistency is to be found only in Spain and Italy, where state parties stick to ignoring centre–periphery issues in their manifestos, with the exception of the Spanish Socialists, which remain pro-periphery (see Table 6.1). However, there are only two observations for these countries and therefore, as I will soon show when discussing the cases, this apparent consistency should not be taken too far. Moreover, the Italian and Spanish observations correspond to their first democratic elections—a special and trying period for any polity and one which, therefore, is not strictly comparable to a period of 'politics as usual'.

---

[3] See Chapter 4 for an explanation about how they are measured.

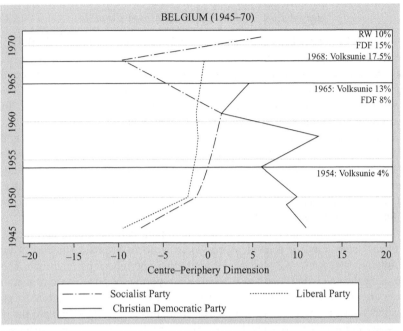

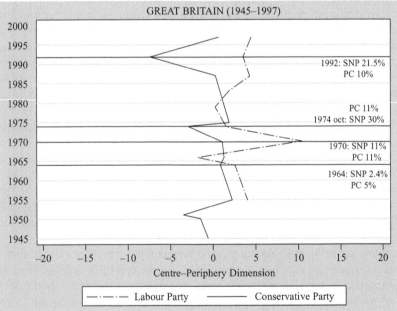

Notes: Avoidant positions in the graphs are filled in, for the sake of graph clarity and given that they are already described in Table 6.1. The lines in the graphs go straight from a non-avoidant position (be it pro- or anti-periphery) to another non-avoidant position even if in between there is an avoidant position. When several avoidant positions are placed consecutively (as for example in the Labour Party between 1945 and 1951), no line is shown. This empty space is therefore indicative of consecutively ignoring centre–periphery issues.

Figure 6.1. *Evolution of state parties' centre–periphery positions in Belgium and Great Britain during the period before the first devolution reform*[4]

The final observation concerning Figure 6.1 is that there is no connection between pro-periphery moves and peripheral parties' electoral losses, as was already clear from the data in Table 6.1. During the whole period between the early 1950s and the first devolution reforms, peripheral parties grew continuously in Belgium and, except for a temporary setback during the 1980s, also in the UK. Their agenda for devolution seemed unstoppable.

6.1.2 The comparative intensity of pro-periphery moves

I have defined a pro-periphery position by looking at the minimum degree of saliency of an issue in a party manifesto in order to be considered as a non-neglected issue. However, this tells us nothing about the intensity (degree of saliency) with which the issue or group of issues appears in the manifesto. Two pro-periphery positions are different if their respective saliency scores diverge. For example, party A dedicates 10 per cent of mentions to the 'decentralization' issue category and party B 35 per cent. It is clear that party B's pro-periphery position is more intense (its saliency is higher) than party A's.

As was already argued in Chapter 3, a state party that adopts a pro-periphery position may be unconvincing if the intensity is too low compared to that of the peripheral party competitor. When the intensity of the state party's pro-periphery position is low, the peripheral party will still keep intact its reputation as the 'owner' of the pro-periphery position.

Table 6.2 shows the saliency of the state parties' pro-periphery statements and the total percentage that a party manifesto dedicates to centre–periphery issues relative to the total percentage dedicated to left–right issues (see Chapter 3).[4] When this ratio is below one, it means that the party manifesto is giving more relevance to the left–right dimension than to the centre–periphery one. When the ratio is above one, it means the opposite. Unfortunately, due to lack of data on peripheral parties for this period in Italy and the UK, I can only compare peripheral parties and state parties in Belgium and Spain.

State parties that conveyed pro-periphery positions on the centre–periphery dimension did so with relative low intensity in comparison to peripheral parties, and necessarily so, since they had to divide their attention between the centre–periphery issues and those of their primary dimension of competition, the left–right conflict. As it was their secondary dimension of competition, state parties could never match the level of attention and of radicalism of peripheral parties along the centre–periphery dimension. Consequently, peripheral parties remained the indisputable 'owners' of the pro-periphery agenda.

---

[4] It is calculated as follows: ((% centre-periphery issues)/(% left-right issues)) × 100. For example, the PSOE's ratio of 0.11 is telling us that the centre–periphery issues are only 11% as likely to appear in party manifestos as the left–right issues.

TABLE 6.2. *The saliency of pro-periphery issues and the relative saliency of the centre–periphery dimension in party manifestos before the first devolution reform*

Belgium			Italy			Spain			UK		
(mean 1946–70)			(mean 1946–8)			(mean 1977–9)			(mean 1945–97)		
Party	pro-per	lrcp	Party	pro-per	lrcp	Party	pro-per	lrcp	Party	pro-per	lrcp
	saliency	_ratio		saliency	_ratio		saliency	_ratio		saliency	_ratio
CVP-PSC	9.7	0.34	**PCI**	2.0	0.13	**PSOE**	4.5	0.11	**CP**	2.4	0.13
VU	13.9	1.68	**PSI**	2.3	0.14	**PP**	1.7	0.02	**LP**	2.7	0.09
PSB-BSP	2.8	0.18	**DC**	0	0	**UCD**	1.9	0.05	**SNP**	NA	NA
RW	18.8	0.72	**UV**	NA	NA	CiU	13.1	0.39	**PC**	NA	NA
PL-LP	2.0	0.16	**SVP**	NA	NA	**ERC**	13.6	0.56			
FDF	18.4	1.32	**PSd'Az**	NA	NA	**PNV**	18.5	0.75			

Both in Belgium and in Spain peripheral parties defended pro-periphery positions with much more intensity than state parties did; with the difference in Spain being even larger than in Belgium. Let us focus on the two most pro-periphery state parties at that time, the CVP-PSC and the PSOE. The Spanish Socialists dedicated an average of nearly 5 per cent of its manifestos to pro-periphery issues, while the average for the Catalan CiU and ERC was nearly double, and that of the Basque PNV was nearly three times higher. The Belgian Christian Democrats dedicated the largest amount of sentences to pro-periphery issues among state parties, nearly 10 per cent. However, it was still short of its peripheral competitor, Volksunie, which dedicated an average of 14 per cent of its sentences to pro-periphery issues.

This picture is incomplete unless I also examine the relative saliency of the centre–periphery dimension with respect to the left–right dimension. As is shown in Table 6.2, peripheral parties dedicated more space in their manifestos to the centre–periphery dimension relative to the left–right dimension than state parties did. This is particularly the case in Belgium. In Volksunie's manifestos, for example, centre–periphery issues were 168 per cent as likely to be mentioned as left–right issues. This means that for Volksunie, as for the Front Démocratique des Francophones, the centre–periphery dimension was the main focus of attention of the electoral manifesto and the left–right dimension was very secondary to it. The 'ownership' of the pro-periphery issues lay clearly with the peripheral parties. It would have been very difficult for a Belgian state party to reach the levels of intensity with which peripheral parties defended pro-periphery issues. At the time, Belgian peripheral parties were the most single-issue oriented among all the peripheral parties under analysis, as was already discussed in Chapter 3. This had obviously an effect on the effectiveness of the pro-periphery moves adopted by state parties.

I turn next to a brief discussion of the country cases in order to see in more detail the general trends that have been described in the previous two sections.

6.1.3 Belgium

Language disputes were at the origin of the relatively high saliency of the centre–periphery dimension in post-war Belgian politics. At the time, 55.4 per cent of the population of Belgium lived in the five Northern provinces. These provinces were (and remain) predominantly Flemish-speaking and, as a whole, constitute the region of Flanders. Another 32.6 per cent of the Belgians lived in the four Southern provinces which are predominantly French-speaking. Finally, 11.4 per cent lived in Brussels, where both languages were spoken (Coombes and Norton Taylor 1968). The assertiveness of the Flemish grew along with their economic and cultural development while simultaneously Wallonia, once a prosperous economy based on coal-mining and steel-production, underwent a process of economic depression. To make things worse for Wallonia, the Walloon population was ageing and, therefore, growing at a much slower rate than that of Flanders. As a result of these processes, '[t]he Flemings wanted political power to match their new economic power; the Walloons wanted political power to counter their economic decline' (Saey, Kesteloot, et al. 1998: 175). The Brussels question intensified the conflicts between the two communities because the city is situated in the Flemish region but is overwhelmingly French-speaking.

In the first three post-war elections, the CVP-PSC suffered no electoral threat from a peripheral party. At the time, Flemish nationalism was still tainted and discredited by its collaboration with the Nazis during the war (Gerard 1998) and so it was negligible in terms of votes and popular support. Therefore, the pro-periphery positions of the Christian Democrats were not an electoral strategy of adaptation to a situation of threat but instead comprised part of the party's identity. The core of the CVP-PSC party was constituted by the Christian Workers' Movement (Algemeen Christelijk Werkersverbond, ACW) which, since the late 1880s, had been engaged in the defence of Flemish interests inside Belgium.[5] In the aftermath of the Second World War, despite the 'constructive *Belgian* stance' adopted by the CVP-PSC, the attitude of the Christian Workers' Movement towards Flemish emancipation remained a positive one. As Gerard has put it: 'The demand for sound linguistic and cultural relations in the country remained topical and again burst into the open after the parliamentary elections of February 1946' (1998: 135). In these years, the CVP-PSC was dedicating an average of 11 per cent of its electoral manifestos to pro-periphery issues, while the Socialists and Liberals were ignoring them. The

---

[5] According to Gerard, 'the pro-Flemish petty bourgeoisie took control of the workers' and farmers' organizations so as to strengthen its position vis-à-vis the conservative and pro-French dignitaries in the Catholic Party' (1998: 129).

emergence of Volksunie in 1954 and its subsequent steady growth caused unrest among the Flemish wing within the CVP-PSC. Years later, the division between the two linguistic groups inside the party would prove impossible to appease.

The Liberal Party, on the other hand, mostly adopted anti-periphery positions which it combined with some avoidance of centre–periphery issues.[6] The advantage of the Liberal Party was its 'great strength in Brussels and evenly balanced support in Wallonia and Flanders, making it more representatively "national"' (Kelly 1969: 354). The Liberal Party in the 1960s took a clear anti-periphery stance, in defence of Belgian unity and against proposals for devolution or federalism. During the 1961–5 legislative session, new language laws were being discussed and negotiated in parliament. The Liberal Party refused to support the government's proposals to change the Constitution in order to avoid internal dissension over the matter. The opposite would have been damaging for its electoral strategy in favour of national unity (Verleden 2009). The Liberals did really well at the 1965 elections, doubling their vote share with respect to the previous election. However, by 1968, the defence of national unity proved to be the wrong strategy and electoral success was not repeated.

By contrast with the Christian Democrats, the Flemish Socialists remained fairly indifferent to the Flemish nationalist movement until the Second World War (Gerard 1998: 133). Despite the fact that there had always been Socialists among the Walloon nationalist movement, 'there were no mediators to defend the Walloon cause among the [Socialist] party leadership' (Kesteloot 1998: 151). In the early post-war years, the Socialist Party used anti-periphery and avoidance tactics. In this period, Flemish nationalism had not yet materialized and the majority of Walloons considered that a federal solution to tackle the communal conflicts in the country was a danger to national unity (Van der Bruggen 1950: 342). A pro-periphery strategy during these years would have been extremely hazardous for the Belgian Socialist Party. Inside the party, the Walloon Socialists were already supporting the emergence of a 'leftist' Walloon Movement that openly favoured federalism but, at this early stage, 'the Socialist national party structure was not really questioned' (Verleden 2009: 154).

By 1961, however, Flemish nationalism was already strong and this strength, together with the economic and demographic growth of the Flemish provinces, helped to create Walloon unrest. A Walloon peripheral party demanding federalism finally emerged. These Walloon nationalists had their origins in the Mouvement Populaire Wallon founded by the socialist trade unionist André Renard (Verleden 2009). Therefore, inside the Walloon branch of the Belgian Socialist Party, a strong pro-federalist minority was forming which pressed to move towards a pro-periphery electoral strategy. As a result of this pressure, the Belgian Socialist Party adopted

---

[6] Only once, the pro-centre tactic came with a pro-periphery tactic of equal weight and thus they cancelled each other out.

for the first time a clear pro-periphery position at the 1961 elections. The party improved its electoral results, winning three percentage points in Wallonia with respect to the previous elections. In 1964, the overt defenders of Walloon national-ism were excluded from the Belgian Socialist Party and at the 1965 elections the party ignored centre–periphery issues. The electoral results were bad, suffering severe losses, particularly in Wallonia. After that, the party moved to an anti-periphery position at the 1968 elections, and it even leapfrogged from an anti-periphery to a pro-periphery position at the next election in 1971.

Belgian state parties reacted to the peripheral party threat not just by emphasiz-ing pro-periphery or anti-periphery issues but also by proposing or opposing periphery-friendly policies, according to the pledges of their manifestos. At the 1961 elections the Belgian Socialists and Christian Democrats, both pressed by increasing social unrest between the linguistic communities and by the continuous growth of the peripheral parties, assumed pro-periphery programmatic positions in the campaign. After the elections, the two parties formed a coalition government that chose to pursue a series of linguistic laws in the hope of diffusing the danger of linguistic polarization. One of these laws permanently fixed the territorial borders of the linguistic communities—an issue which had already been tackled tentatively by the 1932 law, but which was then left in a state of provisionality. With this new law, a few districts were shifted from one linguistic region to another in order to make each region as linguistically homogeneous as possible. Another law provided better education and cultural facilities in Flemish for the Brussels Flemings. Yet another law strengthened the position of the Flemish language in the local administration of the Brussels region and established lin-guistic facilities in French for those French-speakers that lived in Flemish com-munes on the outskirts of Brussels (Dunn 1974: 148).

Therefore, Belgian state parties had promised in their manifestos to accommo-date some of the peripheral parties' demands and, once in government, they had transformed their promises into policies. They were thus showing reliability and responsibility. In this way, they had hoped to settle the problem 'for a generation' (Dunn 1974: 148). Instead of solving the linguistic issues, however, these laws exacerbated the problem. They were not to the complete satisfaction of anybody and they served to contribute to the increased saliency of the regional and linguistic conflicts. According to Verleden, it was precisely due to the renewed attention to the language issue that peripheral parties grew in elections on both sides of the 'linguistic frontier' (Verleden 2009: 150–1). The following elections in 1965 saw the continuous electoral growth of Flemish and Walloon peripheral parties, while the Belgian Socialists and Liberals decided to ignore centre–periphery issues.

During the 1965–8 legislative period, a linguistic crisis at the University of Louvain broke out. This crisis, initiated by a demand from Flemish leaders, with wide support among the Flemish community, that the French section of the University of Louvain be moved to a French-speaking area, split the governing Christian Democratic Party and the government itself into its two linguistic groups and brought about the resignation of the prime minister and his cabinet. At the next elections of 1968, the two linguistic-territorial wings of the CVP-PSC presented independent lists and diverse electoral strategies. For their part, the Belgian Socialists and Liberals also began to suffer internal divisions along linguistic lines. The Belgian Socialist manifesto assumed an anti-periphery position at the 1968 election. As a result, in the Brussels constituency the Flemish Socialists presented an independent list, called the 'Red Lions', in disagreement with the increasingly pro-Walloon positions that the state party central leadership was adopting (anti-periphery, during this period, was equivalent to pro-Walloon). Peripheral parties continued their dramatic growth.

To summarize, Belgian state parties reacted to the peripheral party growth of the 1960s in a similar manner to the way they had reacted in the 1930s (Verleden 2009). First, they set up 'checks and balances between French- and Dutch-speaking politicians within the central party structures, so that no language community would be capable of unilaterally dominating policy-framing'. Second, they created 'two "party wings" within the state party, each with some degree of autonomy and *the ability to present the party to the Flemish or francophone electorate with a more outspoken Flemish or francophone profile*' (Verleden 2009: 152, emphasis added). With the number of votes lost to the peripheral parties growing, the linguistic wings inside each state party took increasingly separate, and at times even divergent, positions on centre–periphery issues. It was obvious that Belgian state parties were having extreme difficulties in reconciling a *state-wide* point of view with one which defended the linguistic communities. With peripheral parties playing the card of defending exclusively one or the other community, the simultaneous defence of both communities by state parties in a credible way turned to be an impossible task. Verleden's analysis of the Belgian state parties' split concludes that '[f]ormally severing ties with the national party structure was *a strategy to regain some of the electorate lost to the autonomist parties*' (2009: 160, emphasis added).

6.1.4 United Kingdom

In a period of nearly thirty years, between 1945 and 1974, the British state parties adopted all possible positions along the centre–periphery dimension, assuming avoidance, pro-periphery, and anti-periphery tactics and leapfrogging between the pro-periphery and the anti-periphery sides of the conflict. As in Belgium, this was in part a reflection of the state parties' internal divisions between those in favour of devolution and those against it. This is particularly true of the internal workings of the Labour Party. As Iain McLean has put it, they were divided into 'hedgers and ditchers':

> The hedgers, led by Harold Wilson, believed that making some gestures to devolution would head off the Scottish Nationalist threat. . . . The ditchers, led by Labour's once

and future Scottish Secretary Willie Ross and (in a quite different mode) by the MP for West Lothian Tam Dalyell, believed that any concession to the SNP was dangerous. (Iain McLean 2004: 151)

The Conservative Party moved historically between the anti-periphery and the centre–periphery avoidance strategies. Until 1921, it showed a firm, straightforward commitment to the preservation of the Union (United Kingdom of Great Britain and Ireland). After the establishment of devolved government in Northern Ireland, in 1921, the Conservative Party's leader, Bonar Law, pledged to 'safeguard the freedom of choice and security of the Parliament and Government of Northern Ireland' (as quoted in Smith 2006: 75). Between 1923 and 1935 the issue of Northern Ireland was not mentioned in the Conservative Party's manifestos and eventually the Conservatives showed a 'more measured support for a bipartisan approach in handling the region' (Smith 2006: 85). With respect to Scotland and Wales, however, they opposed devolution, although they often played the Scottish card during the 1950s in Scotland, when they were still called the Scottish Unionists (McLean 2004).

Although early in its history the Labour Party was sympathetic to the demands of the Irish nationalists for Irish Home Rule,[7] and during the early 1920s Home Rule was 'part and parcel of the Labour staple', the deteriorating economic situation of the 1930s led the party to focus on socio-economic issues. As Finlay has put it: 'as the economic reality bit in, the party moved away from the idea as it was believed that it was no longer feasible because the resources for social reconstruction would have to be utilized at a British level' (2004: 29). Therefore, by choosing an anti-periphery and an avoiding strategy respectively, the Conservatives and the Labour Party were just being congruent with their historical positions.

In the aftermath of the Second World War, successive Labour governments 'demonstrated the ability of the British state to deliver for Scotland' (McLean 2004: 36). The Scottish Labour Party grew satisfied with the degree of administrative decentralization and fixed on the delivery of housing, local government, and the local party organization. Home rule was not a priority (Finlay 2004: 32). At the 1956 Conference of the Scottish Council of the Labour Party Hugh Gaitskell (Attlee's successor) stated that the notion of home rule for Scotland was dead because Labour's achievements in government and the development of national planning 'had rendered the old policy obsolete' (McLean 2004: 38). In September 1958, Labour formalized its opposition to Scottish home rule.

Peripheral parties in Scotland and Wales started their electoral growth in the 1950s. Initially, their vote shares were not alarming for British state parties.

---

[7] The third Irish Home Rule Act was passed by the Commons in 1912 at the initiative of the Liberal government and with the support of the Irish Nationalist Party and the Labour Party. It was, however, rejected by the House of Lords.

Labour had firm majoritarian support in Wales and the as-of-yet small vote share of the SNP in Scotland did not lead British state politicians to foresee its dramatic growth during the following years. Therefore, ignoring centre–periphery issues did not seem risky at the time. As the peripheral party's vote shares increased, however, ignoring pro-periphery issues made no sense anymore, particularly since it seemed to have a receptive public in the electorate. Above all, the threat coming from the SNP forced Labour to reconsider its position. Between 1968 and 1974 the Labour central leadership, led by Wilson, moved towards a pro-periphery strategy, 'best illustrated by the BLP's preoccupation with developing the UK peripheries in its election manifesto *The New Britain* (1964). Northern Ireland was allotted its own distinct regional identity on an equal par with those of Scotland and Wales' (Edwards 2007: 608). In 1970, the party's manifesto dedicated an unusually large space to the discussion of pro-periphery issues: 13 per cent of all its sentences. This coincided with a 6 per cent increase in the SNP' vote share, which gave it one seat in parliament.

The first post-war attempt to initiate a devolution reform occurred in 1974. Events were precipitated by the February 1974 election results. For the first time in the post-war period no party obtained an overall majority in Westminster. Labour needed the support of the peripheral parties in order to control a parliamentary majority and these parties took the opportunity to pressure in favour of devolution. New elections were called in October 1974. The SNP grew from 22 per cent to 30 per cent in Scotland and agreed to support from outside a Labour government. In exchange for this, Labour published, in November 1975, its devolution proposals.

This was the beginning of a 'legislative marathon' (McLean 2004: 41) along which several manoeuvres inside the Labour party by those factions opposing devolution managed to undermine the process. Labour's anti-devolutionist faction imposed a condition on Welsh and Scottish devolution: it should be subject to a referendum and accepted by at least 40 per cent of the registered electorate. The anti-devolutionist faction also organized as *Labour Vote No* during the 1979 referendum campaigns. As a result, the assemblies for Scotland and Wales failed to pass. Labour's central leadership never penalized those who led the *Labour Vote No* campaign for their defiance of party policy, a fact that some analysts interpret as an indicator of the little importance that the issue of devolution had for the Labour Party at the time (McLean 2004: 42).

The devolution attempt of the late 1970s failed because it was the result of crude political expediency by a Labour government that was weak and that needed the support of the peripheral parties in order to survive. In this context, the central leadership forced its regional branches to support an agenda of devolution that they were not prepared to accept. During the 1974–9 Labour government, it was obvious that the government's devolution agenda was exclusively intended to pacify the Scottish and Welsh peripheries. Labour's leadership was unable to convince the public, on the one hand, and its own party, on the other, of the benefits of devolution. Eighteen years in opposition would change the scenario and would give, to devolution's supporters, arguments capable of convincing both the public and the party that devolution was the right thing to do.

6.1.5 The peripheral party threat during the transition to democracy: Spain and Italy

As was already advanced in chapter 5, in Spain and Italy the devolution of power to sub-state territories was part of a wider process of transition to democracy. As a result, it is difficult to extricate the political calculation involved in the decision to decentralize the state from the general political calculation involved in the democratization of the polity. Nevertheless, I shall try to keep them analytically separate.

Regionalism was part of the Christian Democratic tradition in Italy. As Kogan reminds us, '[i]n the early twentieth century, the Catholic political movement made decentralization a cardinal principle' (Kogan 1975: 384). During the constitutional process, the DC was an advocate of a wide regional autonomy for all regions, in part as a result of this historical identity, but also as a way of breaking with the immediate past of extreme centralization under the regime of Mussolini (Groppi 2007), particularly in the face of intense separatist mobilization in the peripheral regions during the pre-constitutional years (Spotts and Wieser 1986). In Sicily the pre-constitutional Italian parliament declared the island semi-autonomous in May 1945. In Val d'Aosta, a regional council was independently established in 1946. South Tyrol wanted to secede and join Austria (it had been won by Italy as a result of the First World War). The Austrian government supported this move and only the compromise between Italy and Austria by which Italy conceded special autonomy status to South Tyrol saved the territory for Italy. Therefore, 'by the time the constitution came to be written, regional autonomy was already an established fact in certain areas' (Spotts and Wieser 1986: 223).

The reluctance to devolve came from the parties of the left, Communists and Socialists, worried that the fragmentation of state power implicit in a decentralized state form would limit, or even undermine, the implementation of the necessary socio-economic reforms, and would increase inequalities between persons and territories. Their arguments against political devolution were no different from those offered by the Labour Party in the 1950s and 1960s.

In Spain, the Socialist Party between 1977 and 1979 conveyed clear pro-periphery positions. As with the Belgian CVP-PSC, it was not so much an adaptation to a situation of threat but a consubstantial part of the party's identity. The Spanish Socialist and Communist parties at the time of Franco's death defended intense and far-reaching pro-periphery positions that Blas Guerrero has described as 'quasi-nationalist' (Blas Guerrero 1988: 72). At the 1974 party congress, the PSOE defended in one of its documents the right of the national minorities within

Spain to territorial self-determination and stated as the party's preferred solution for Spain a federal republic of all the nationalities within the state (Blas Guerrero 1988: 72). The Spanish left and the peripheral nationalists had shared underground political activity and exile, as well as the objective of bringing down the Francoist regime, and had collaborated in the mobilization and organization against the regime. Peripheral nationalists in the Basque Country and Catalonia had been among the most active organizations in the fight against the dictatorship. This created a link between Basque and Catalan nationalists and the Spanish left, both at the level of parties and of voters. When the first democratic elections were called for, in 1977 to approve the Constitution and in 1979 as the first democratic elections of the post-Franco era in Spain, the Socialists and Communists were still under the influence of this recent past (Aja 2003: 65).

There are relevant parallelisms between Spain and Italy. Spanish politicians at the constituent Assembly (1977–9) agreed that the state should avoid the extreme centralization of the Franco regime. As in Italy, extreme centralization and dictatorship were linked is such a way that the establishment of a democratic state implied the establishment of a decentralized state, as a form of break with the past. As Aja has put it: 'autonomy [for the regions] appeared as an essential requirement of democracy in Spain' (Aja 2003: 60). Continuing with the Italian parallel concerning separatist unrest in the periphery, the high level of mobilization of the Catalan and Basque nationalisms in favour of re-establishing the regional autonomies that they had enjoyed at the end of the Second Republic, and whose demands were actively supported by the Spanish Socialists and Communists, was a further indication that the design of the form of state would have to somehow incorporate the demands for self-government coming from the culturally and territorially distinct peripheries (Aja 2003). In contrast to Italy, however, the Spanish left was vigorously in favour of decentralization and it was the Spanish right that displayed more reluctance to the idea.

Nevertheless, despite the relevance of these factors directly connected to the process of transition, this is not the whole story. In both Italy and Spain the decision to give a decentralized structure to the new state involved certain political calculations whose electoral nature was very much the same as the one that moved Belgian and British parties to initiate a process of devolution, a point that will be further developed later.

To sum up what has been said until here, state parties' pro-periphery moves along the centre–periphery dimension happened on an ad hoc basis and not as part of a well-defined converging strategy. State parties were trying different responses in different elections and according to a short-sighted attention to their immediate needs. This is especially the case when state parties did not have a parliamentary majority and had to rely on the votes of peripheral parties to achieve one. In such a situation, state parties were pressed to make more pro-periphery concessions than they would otherwise have wished for.

Given the—at times blunt—opportunism of state parties' pro-periphery moves in Belgium and the UK, it is little wonder that their tactics did not stop the growth of peripheral parties. Even if, at particular elections, playing the pro-periphery card would yield temporary electoral benefits to state parties, the overall trend was not favourable. As Meguid's theory predicts, inconsistency leads convergence to fail (Meguid 2008). Why were state parties so inconsistent in their centre–periphery moves? The main reason had to do with the divisions inside each party. Engaging in a pro-periphery strategy was something that not everybody inside state parties agreed with. So much so that in Belgium these divisions eventually led to the split of the state parties into the French and the Flemish linguistic groups, in order to be able to cater exclusively to their respective Walloon and Flemish constituencies. The split left no state party to defend a state-wide point of view. It gave Belgian state parties almost unlimited room for manoeuvre to compete credibly against their peripheral competitors by assuming their role as defenders of the Flemish or the Walloon communities. They had to face no further credibility constraints.

Even those state parties whose pro-periphery positions were part of the party's true preferences at the time, as in the case of the Spanish Socialists during the transition to democracy, or part of the party's historical identity, as in the case of the Belgian Christian Democrats, their relatively consistent pro-periphery stance did not limit the growth of their peripheral competitors either. This means that consistency is only part of the explanation. The other fundamental part is that of reconciling a *state-wide* point of view with a *regional* or *community* one.

State parties, by definition, represent the whole state population and not a particular territory within it, even if historical circumstances may make state parties temporarily more sympathetic to the demands coming from particular territories within the country. Peripheral parties, in contrast, represent only one part of the country's territory and population. They can freely engage in territorial zero-sum games because this is precisely their *raison d'être*: whatever they claim for their territory and its population has to be done at the expense of some other territory. State parties that attempt to imitate peripheral parties enter into a deadly contradiction and can hardly be credible. The only institutional context that allows a state party to defend a regional agenda with credibility is that of regional-level electoral competition and this can only happen in a decentralized state.

During the period leading to the first devolution reform state parties played the pro-periphery card only half-heartedly; as state parties, they could do no better than that. They could neither reach the levels of saliency that pro-periphery issues had in peripheral parties' manifestos nor match the depth of their proposals for devolution. Pro-periphery issues remained firmly in the hands of peripheral parties with the involuntary help of state parties, which contributed to make the centre–periphery conflict a salient one in the electoral arena.

6.2 ENHANCING CREDIBILITY THROUGH DEVOLUTION

Political devolution entails costs. The distribution of power between the central government and the regional administrations not only leaves fewer competences in the hands of the former, but also institutionalizes territorial issues as a permanent feature of the electoral competition between parties. These costs, however, are not assumed individually by the state party that implements devolution but by all the state parties in the polity collectively. Therefore, the decision to decentralize will depend on the selective benefits expected by the state party that decentralizes and not on the collective costs equally borne by all state parties. In this section I show that the benefits accompanying a devolution reform are dictated by the country's electoral geography. This means that the degree (symmetrical or asymmetrical devolution) and scope (partial or all-round devolution) that the decentralizing reform will take is explained by the different distribution of costs and benefits particular to each electoral geography and each party within it.

When the threatened state party has concentrated geographical support *only* in regions in which the threatened state party has to compete with peripheral parties, the benefits of devolution are uncertain. On the one hand, the reputation of the state party as a 'decentralizer' may increase the support of the party among regional voters with pro-periphery preferences. On the other hand, the region's voters may decide to split their vote according to the electoral level, voting for the state party at the state level and for the peripheral party at the regional level. The net effect of these processes on the state party's aggregate electoral strength is difficult to foresee. This will bring about divisions inside the party between those who see the benefits of devolution clearly and those who see devolution only as an unacceptable price to pay for peripheral acquiescence (see Table 6.3). The threatened state party's support for devolution will therefore not be unanimous inside the party.

At this point, the incumbency status of the state party becomes a relevant factor pushing the party towards or away from the decision to devolve. If the party is in government, the internal divisions will make it very difficult to implement a devolution reform. If the party is in opposition, particularly if it has been in opposition for a long time, the benefits of devolution will be strongly appreciated by most inside the party: it would offer the possibility of enjoying the perks of office at the region in which the party has concentrated support while the party is kept in the opposition at the state level (see Table 6.3).

When the threatened state party enjoys concentrated support not only in regions in which it faces a growing peripheral party but *also* in regions free of peripheral parties, the advantages of all-round devolution are immediately perceived (see Table 6.3) irrespective of whether the threatened state party is in government or in opposition. Needless to say, when *all* regions of the state have a strong peripheral party threatening a state party, all-round devolution is inevitable.

TABLE 6.3. *Threatened state parties' support for devolution reform according to the type of electoral geography*

Type of Electoral Geography	State Party's Incumbency Status	Support for Devolution Inside the State Party	Type of Reform Implemented (If Incumbent) or Promised (If in Opposition)	Support for Devolution by Threatened Parties in Belgium, Italy, Spain, and the UK
State party has concentrated support *only* in region/s in which it faces a peripheral party threat	In government	Ambivalent/divided support	Partial devolution	Labour (1974–9), failed BSP-PSB (1968–71) CVP-PSC (1968–71)
State party has concentrated support not only in region/s with a peripheral party but also, *simultaneously*, in at least one region without peripheral party threat	In opposition	Nearly unanimous support	All-round devolution	Labour (1983–97)
	In government	Nearly unanimous support	All-round devolution	DC (1963–8)
	In opposition	Nearly unanimous support	All-round devolution	PSOE (1977–82)

Notes: Let us remember that for a threat to exist three conditions must be present: the state party has (1) concentrated electoral support in regions (2) that are electorally relevant and (3) in which state parties face a peripheral challenger. The Italian state parties between 1948 and 1963 were not threatened by the growth of peripheral parties.

All-round devolution can, in turn, take two forms: symmetrical or asymmetrical. Symmetrical devolution means that all the regions have been devolved the same competences and to the same degree. By contrast, asymmetrical devolution implies that some regions will be devolved more competences or the same competences to a larger degree (for example, some regions will have exclusive competences over some areas while other regions have to share those competences with the state). In the presence of a direct peripheral threat to state parties' electoral majorities, asymmetrical devolution is the only way to attend to two conflicting objectives simultaneously. On the one hand, give pro-periphery voters what they are claiming for: a differentiated status inside the state. On the other hand, obtain electoral benefits from the devolution reform, by preferring all-round devolution—with its opportunities for building regional electoral strongholds—over partial devolution.

6.2.1 Belgium

The 1968 elections brought into government a coalition of Socialists (PSB-BSP) and Christian Democrats (CVP-PSC). This coalition initiated a devolution reform under the leadership of the Prime Minister, the Flemish Christian Democrat Gaston Eyskens. The two parties alone did not gather the necessary two-thirds majority to change the Constitution and, therefore, they needed the support of either the Liberals or the peripheral parties in order to go ahead with the changes as planned. Only the Flemish branch of the Liberal Party supported the reform; the francophone Liberals were against it.

A parliamentary commission with the participation of all represented parties was constituted. This commission reached an agreement on many issues but the borders and the status of Brussels could not be part of the agreement. Eyskens took a pragmatic approach. On the one hand, 'he pushed through as many proposals as he could, while sometimes changing the partners he needed for support'; on the other hand, '[t]he problems for which he could not find a two-third majority he left unsolved' (Falter 1998: 181). The need to circumvent the insoluble Brussels problem led to a peculiar form of simultaneous cultural and territorial devolution: linguistic communities were created side by side territorial ones, called regions.

The communities were conceived as federated institutions to which cultural competences from the central state (including education) were transferred (Falter 1998). Their creation responded to the Flemish demand for greater cultural autonomy. The regions were geographic entities with decentralized economic powers (Falter 1998) whose establishment was largely the result of Walloon demands for greater regional economic power (Verleden, 2009). The communities were endowed with their own parliament which was formed by state deputies from the community concerned, and with their own government, whose few ministers remained within the Belgian state government and had a state budget at their disposal (Falter 1998). With respect to the regions, the Constitution merely sanctioned their existence. This was similar to what the 1948 Constitution had done in Italy. This meant it was left to future governments to decide how they were to operate (Falter 1998). However, without an agreement on Brussels the establishment of the regions could not be completed. As a result, an autonomous political arena of party competition at the regional level would not emerge in Belgium until the 1993 reform.

And yet, the most important effect of the Belgian first devolution reform was to provoke the split of the state parties. Each state party was threatened by a peripheral party in its respective regional stronghold. If the peripheral parties were to grow as much as to risk the state party's status as the largest party in its regional stronghold, the state party had little hope of finding compensation by growing electorally in another region, as was the case in Italy, Spain, and the UK. The Belgian Christian Democratic Party was the first to break into two separate, and linguistically homogeneous, parties presenting separate lists at the 1968 early-called state elections. The devolution proposal produced an enormous pressure on the Liberals, and the Socialists followed suit: the Liberals split during the devolution negotiations; the Socialists resisted united a bit longer, until 1974.

6.2.2 Italy

In Italy, as in Spain, the first steps towards devolution were taken as part of the political process to establish a new democratic constitution. During the constitutional process, the DC was an advocate of a wide regional autonomy for all regions in Italy (all-round devolution), and not just for the peripheral territories (Sardinia, Sicily, South Tyrol, Friuli-Venezia Giulia, and Val d'Aosta), because of the belief that the left would shortly take over the state parliament, a belief based on the combined results of the Communist and the Socialist parties in the 1946 elections. In such a case, regional parliaments could prevent the control of the country by Communism (Amoretti 2002; Mazzoleni, 2009). At the 1946 elections, the DC obtained 35 per cent of the vote, the Socialists nearly 21 per cent, and the Communists 19 per cent. The parties of the left had together more votes and seats than the DC at these foundational elections. The DC's fear that the Italian left could one day control the state government was not unfounded.

Despite its regionalist stance at the constitutional assembly, however, the DC stuck to ignoring centre–periphery issues between 1946 and 1958. This had a lot to do with the results of the following elections, in 1948. The DC obtained nearly 50 per cent of the vote and its seat share was quite evenly distributed among all Italian regions, with the exception of Tuscany and Emilia-Romagna where the Christian Democrats were behind the Communists. These results turned the DC's preferences against all-round decentralization. The fear of Communist domination had disappeared and the growth of peripheral parties in Val d'Aosta, Sardinia, and

South Tyrol entailed no risks for the Italian state parties since, as we have seen already, these regions were electorally irrelevant.[8] On the other hand, the MSI had sunk from its 8 per cent of Sicily's total vote in 1946 to 3 per cent in 1948. At the same time, the left–right conflict increasingly monopolized the political debate, pushing the centre–periphery issues to a very marginal corner: '[t]he stark division between pro-Western and pro-Soviet forces that dominated Italian politics in the years after World War II' inhibited the salience of 'any parties or movements that might otherwise have wanted to organize political competition along regional or territorial lines' (Amoretti 2002: 131).

The DC, however, could not defend a centralized state in 1948 when it had been such a clear supporter of regionalism in 1946. To avoid such flagrant inconsisten-cy, the result was the support of a partial devolution reform: keeping the politically noisy but electorally harmless peripheries happy with some degree of regional autonomy while maintaining centralized control of the rest of the country. The 1948 Italian Constitution established four special-statute regions with their own elected legislatures which roughly corresponded to the culturally distinct and politically mobilized Italian peripheries: Trentino-Alto Adige (South Tyrol), Val d'Aosta, Sardinia, and Sicily. To this, a new special-statute region was added in 1964, Friuli-Venezia Giulia, after post-war controversies with Yugoslavia were settled. The Italian Constitution left open the possibility of extending regionaliza-tion to the whole country, much in the same way as Belgium left to the future the establishment of the regional territorial assemblies. In Italy, the devolution to the ordinary status regions would not occur until 1970.

Although reluctant to the idea of a decentralized state during the constitutional process, the PCI and the PSI soon understood that they had much to gain by pressing for the extension of autonomy to all the regions of Italy (all-round devolution). This understanding was the result of their high concentration of the vote in a few regions whose representative weight in parliament was quite large (see chapter 5). All-round devolution would mean the possibility of obtaining, at least, some regional power strongholds—in regions without a peripheral challenger—as opposed to having nothing at all. At the state level, the PCI was kept out of government by a tacit agreement between the Italian parties to exclude the Communists (and, until 1963, also the Socialist Party).

With clientelism and patronage creeping in the Communists and Socialists, who were permanently out of office, saw an opportunity to criticize the hegemonic

---

[8] In the 1953 state elections, the SVP obtained 28% of the South Tyrol votes, which by the 1968 elections had become already 30%. The UV, representing the French-speaking community in Val d'Aosta, was at the time the largest peripheral party in Italy, ahead even of SVP. Although initially a very close ally of the Christian Democrats, by 1954 the alliance was broken. In its first participation on its own in state elections, in 1958, UV obtained an impressive 51% of the vote, which in successive elections slightly declined to 50% in 1963 and to 48% in 1968. No other peripheral party in our sample of countries has ever managed to obtain such large vote shares in a state election.

system being created by the DC and to defend the need for less concentration of power and more democracy at all levels (these were the exact same arguments used by the Labour Party to support all-round devolution during their long period in opposition between 1979 and 1997). Therefore, during the 1960s, the Italian left in opposition pressed ahead with an agenda for decentralization (Tarrow 1974; Kogan 1975). This pressure worried the Christian Democratic governments due to the electoral growth of the PCI and the PSI at the time. Leaving aside those regions in which they were strongest, Emilia-Romagna and Tuscany, the votes of the PCI and the PSI together surpassed those of the DC by 1963 in Marche, Umbria, and Lazio, while in Campania, Piedmont, and Calabria—all three very relevant electorally—they were very close to doing so.

At the 1963 elections, the PCI obtained 25 per cent of the vote and the PSI 14 per cent. Together they gathered 39 per cent of the Italian vote, one percentage point above the DC. The Italian left was only seven seats behind the DC in parliament (253 and 260 seats respectively). In order to form a majority, the DC needed 55 seats from outside the party. The only parties large enough to provide, by themselves, the required 55 seats were the Socialists and Communists. The DC leader Aldo Moro, following a strategy of approximation to the left (*apertura a sinistra*), invited for the first time the Socialists to participate in government. The Socialists conditioned their participation on the continuation of the process of decentralization that had been initiated by the 1948 Constitution and put on standby ever since. The condition was granted and the PSI entered an Italian government for the first time. On 17 February 1968, the law for the elections of the regional parliaments, the law that framed the second decentralizing reform in Italy, was passed by parliament. The first regional elections took place in June 1970 and the first regional constitutions were approved in 1972. All-round devolution had been established.

All-round devolution put a stop to the growth of the Italian left in the electorally relevant regions of Lombardy and Piedmont, which is what the DC wanted in the first place. Paradoxically, however, during the late 1980s it set the stage for the growth of the first peripheral party in Italy with a great threat potential: the Lega Nord. The decentralizing reforms of the 1990s and 2000s would be precipitated by the electoral threat that the Lega Nord represented for the Christian Democrats, before 1993, and for Forza Italia, afterwards, to be discussed in subsequent chapters.

6.2.3 Spain

The 1978 Constitution opted for all-round devolution, albeit asymmetrical. It established two main types of regional autonomy. The highest level of autonomy was granted to the Basque Country, Catalonia, and Galicia, while the rest of the regions would have a comparatively lower level of autonomy. At the time of the constitutional debates, Galicians were not mobilized in favour of autonomy with the intensity of Basques and Catalans, as shown by the absence of Galician peripheral parties in the constitutional assembly. Why, then, was Galicia granted a high level of autonomy? *Allegedly* because Galicia was, together with the Basque Country and Catalonia, a 'historical nationality' or, in other words, one of the only three regions that had held a referendum on autonomy during the Second Republic. This justification, however, seems ad hoc. At the time when the Civil War broke out, there were other Statutes of Autonomy at different stages of preparation (some of them waiting to be discussed in the Spanish parliament). Among them were those from Andalusia, Valencia, Balearic Islands, Canary Islands, Aragon, and Asturias. Therefore, by the same rule, these regions should have been defined too as 'historical nationalities' and granted higher levels of autonomy in 1978. The reason why Galicia was included among the 'historical nationalities' had more to do with the fact that the Spanish right was, by far, the largest political force in Galicia and, therefore, the region was a potential stronghold of regional power in the hands of right-wing parties. This could compensate for the Socialists' electoral strength in Catalonia and, to a lesser degree, in the Basque Country.

History, in fact, would repeat itself. Between 1978 and 1980, regions such as Andalusia, Valencia, and the Canary Islands mobilized to obtain high-level autonomy. The UCD government, however, wanted lower-level autonomy for Andalusia. Let us remember that Andalusia, the most relevant Spanish region in electoral terms (see Table 5.1 in chapter 5), was the dominion of the Socialist Party. It was in the interest of the Spanish right to make Andalusian regional institutions less powerful than those in the Basque and Catalan regions which were already dominated by left and peripheral forces. However, the results of the 1980 referendum over the Andalusian statute of autonomy left no doubt as to the preferences of the electorate: a majority voted in favour of the maximum level of autonomy. The result was a clear defeat for the UCD government's policy for decentralizing from above and a victory for the Spanish Socialists. Valencia, the Canary Islands, and Navarre would eventually follow the steps of Andalusia. By 1983, the statutes of autonomy of all the Spanish regions were approved and the landscape of territorial decentralization in Spain looked like this: seven regions achieved the maximum level of competences (Basque Country, Catalonia, Galicia, Navarre, Andalusia, Valencia, and the Canary Islands) and the other ten would have a lower level of autonomy with the possibility of moving up to the higher level after five years had passed and the necessary majorities were in favour of it (Aja 2003). As was the case of Italy and Belgium, the first devolution reform in Spain left many issues open, to be dealt with in future rounds of negotiation.

6.2.4 *Great Britain*

Between 1979 and 1990, the years of Conservative hegemony, the commitment of the Labour Party to devolution returned. Scottish and Welsh Labour voters were behind this resurgence, continuously increasing through the eighteen years of Conservative dominance and making these regions a safe haven of votes for Labour. At the 1987 general elections, this safe haven was seriously threatened when the SNP jumped to 14 per cent of the region's vote (Cozens and Swaddle 1987: 266). In 1989, Labour responded to the renewed threat of a rising SNP by developing the all-party Scottish Constitutional Convention to develop a compromise plan for Scottish self-government. In Wales, no such open developments occurred, probably because PC represented less of a threat to Labour's predominance in Wales than the SNP did in Scotland.

The longer Labour remained in opposition, the stronger became its commitment to devolution (Bradbury, Lynch, et al. 1996: 607). Labour supporters of devolution to Scotland and Wales convincingly argued about the existing democratic deficit in these regions. Scottish and Welsh Labour realized that despite the continued rejection of the Conservatives by Scottish and Welsh voters in Westminster elections, the Labour Party was 'doomed to be governed by them without any effective power to resist' (Bradbury, Lynch, et al. 1996: 692). Labour's willingness to give relevance to the issue of devolution, particularly in Scotland, was crucial for maintaining its levels of electoral support. Support for devolution enabled Labour to compete with the SNP with greater credibility (Bradbury, Lynch, et al. 1996: 602). At the same time, this strategy exacerbated the perception that the Conservatives were anti-Scottish and more concerned with Southern England (Bradbury, Lynch, et al. 1996: 602).

The 1992 Labour manifesto expressed a firm commitment to an extensive programme of devolution to Scotland, Wales, and *the English regions*. This programme appeared explicitly in Labour's 1995 detailed proposals for all-round devolution.[9] Unlike the 1970s, Labour's devolution proposals in opposition were presented as a package of reforms intended to benefit the whole country (Bradbury, Deacon, et al. 1996; Bradbury, Lynch, et al. 1996) and not as the price to pay to the peripheries for their support at Westminster. All-round devolution is the only form of political decentralization that allows state politicians to 'sell' devolution to the public in this manner. As Bradbury convincingly argues, the decision not to extend the devolution proposals to the English regions during the 1974–9 Labour government was a tactical—even strategic—mistake: '[it] led to the English and constitutional opposition which helped to defeat Scottish and Welsh devolution' (Bradbury, Lynch, et al. 1996: 704). Moreover, since Labour in opposition—particularly New Labour—

---

[9] Labour has never considered devolving power to an English parliament. Apart from the fact that England is too large compared to the other three regions, an English parliament would be almost surely monopolized by the Conservatives, who have overwhelming support there.

centralized much of its criticism of the Conservative period on charges of over-centralization and anti-democratic government, all-round devolution was the only proposal that would give credibility to New Labour's commitment to deepening British democracy, to bringing politics closer to the people.

Supporting devolution and making it relevant in the Labour Party's agenda also made sense as an accompanying strategy to Labour's 'turn to the right'. By 1997 New Labour had moved to the right along the left–right dimension, being very close to the Conservatives in areas such as the economy, defence, education, and law and order (Bradbury, Deacon, et al. 1996; Bradbury, Lynch, et al. 1996). Devolution was the one issue on which the two main state parties were clearly divided and it was to their advantage to exploit this difference.

Labour won the 1997 Westminster election by a landslide majority and the Blair government immediately proceeded to implement its devolution proposals. The 1998 referenda in Scotland and Wales succeeded to pass and paved the way for the first regional elections to the Scottish and Welsh assemblies, which were won by the Labour Party. The need that the Labour Party had to make its devolutionary commitment credible was best reflected in its willingness to accept a proportional electoral system in Scotland and Wales (eventually, the electoral system would be a mixture of proportional and first-past-the-post systems). If the electoral system in these regions were to be a copy of the Westminster elections, Labour would have an in-built majority in the Welsh Assembly and most likely also in the Scottish one and the legitimacy of these institutions would have been at stake (Bradbury, Deacon, et al. 1996).

Devolution to the English regions, however, was postponed for another five years, until May 2002, when the White Paper *Your Region, Your Choice* was published (Jeffery 2006). This is very similar to the way the first devolution reforms in Belgium, Italy, and Spain postponed further decentralization for a number of years.

6.3 CONCLUDING REMARKS

In this chapter, I have shown that state parties' attempts to limit or reverse the electoral growth of peripheral parties by adopting pro-periphery tactics generally failed in the context of unitary centralized states. The reason for this failure is to be found in the lack of credibility of state parties' pro-periphery moves. Devolution is a divisive issue inside any state party because it implies the defence of particularistic regional or cultural interests. The state parties in our sample being *state-wide* parties found it difficult to justify the defence of zero-sum games of interest representation. The divisions inside the parties brought about, as a result, inconsistent centre–periphery moves that rested credibility to the strategy of approximation to the peripheral parties' agendas. State parties could not match the scope and intensity of peripheral parties' positions and this also affected negatively their credibility and left peripheral parties as the exclusive 'owners' of the pro-periphery issues. The attempt to implement periphery-friendly policies that fell short of devolution, such as the Belgian language laws, only made things worse for state parties. These laws increased the relevance of centre–periphery issues in the electoral arena which helped peripheral parties, while simultaneously satisfying no one as they were seen as half-hearted measures which damaged the governing state parties.

Inasmuch as parties remained was state parties and the structure of the state was unitary, they had a difficult time trying to counteract their peripheral competitors with a strategic approximation or incorporation of their pro-periphery agendas.

The solution to this dead-end situation was to change the institutional structure of the state in such a way as to render credible a defence of regional interests by a state party. This is precisely what devolution allows. In the Belgian case, devolution was accompanied by a split of state parties into two linguistically homogeneous organizations, each catering to an exclusively Walloon or exclusively Flemish clientele. State parties devolved political power to regional territorial units in order to save themselves at a time when their electoral strength and power was being weakened by the growth of party challengers with a devolutionist agenda.

What type of devolution reform the threatened state parties engaged in depended, to a great extent, on the country's electoral geography. All-round devolution was preferred to partial devolution when the threatened state parties had concentrated support also in regions in which they did not face a peripheral threat and/or when they were long periods in the opposition. Asymmetrical devolution (more powers devolved to the culturally differentiated regions) was inevitable in all cases. Asymmetry is the result of trying to satisfy the demands coming from the periphery for differential treatment by the state while simultaneously trying to decentralize in a way that will also bring benefits to the devolutionist state party (i.e. all-round devolution). On two occasions, asymmetry and partial devolution came together, in Italy during twenty years (1948–68) and in Britain, where devolved powers were offered to Scotland and Wales to a different degree, with Scotland receiving wider powers than Wales, while England remained, despite the initial intentions, the 'gaping hole in the devolution settlement' (Hazell 2006: 38). In the other three cases asymmetry was chosen together with all-round devolution.

This chapter has further shown that the electoral growth of a peripheral party threat is not always, though it is often, the only possible trigger of a devolution reform. Two remarks need to be made in this respect. First, the fact that under exceptional political circumstances, such as a transition to democracy, peripheral unrest, even if not a direct electoral threat to particular state parties, may represent a threat to the process of political change as a whole, and this is reason enough to convince the democratizing political forces of the need to accommodate the peripheral demands for special treatment by the state. This has been the case of Italy and

Spain, where electoral geography explains the type of reform that was finally adopted but not the decision to devolve in itself. The second remark is that there are 'functional equivalents' to a peripheral party threat. State parties with geographically concentrated support in a few regions and with a devolutionist agenda can play the same role. This is the case of the second devolution reform in Italy, when regional assemblies were extended to the regions of ordinary status, and it is also to be observed in some Latin American cases (O'Neill 2003).

In the next chapter, I will show how the asymmetric nature of the devolution reforms implemented by threatened state parties gave an in-built instability to the decentralized structure of the state. Regions with fewer competences will push to obtain as much as regions with more competences; meanwhile the latter will resist attempts at levelling-up competences that should never be at the same level.

7

State Parties' Electoral Strategies after Devolution

This chapter discusses centre–periphery party competition after devolution. Three main arguments are presented. First, I argue that a pro-periphery convergence strategy by a state party will limit the electoral results of its peripheral party competitor to a larger degree in the recently decentralized state than in the previous unitary centralized one. This expectation is based on the fact that devolution makes pro-periphery strategies more credible for two main reasons. The first one is that devolutionist state parties have already earned a reputation as decentralizers. The second is that state parties in a decentralized state have to respond to sub-state territorial constituencies as well as to the state-wide one. Therefore, state parties develop sub-state institutional interests that make their pro-periphery positions more credible than when they do not have to respond to sub-state constituencies (from now on I will refer to these sub-state territorial constituencies as regions). As a result of this enhanced credibility pro-periphery strategies become more effective (i.e., they stop the growth of peripheral parties) and more widely used.

If pro-periphery convergence is more effective after devolution, does this mean that the peripheral party threat is neutralized? According to my second argument, the answer is: not necessarily. In this chapter, I analyse to what extent peripheral parties are neutralized by the pro-periphery convergence strategies of their state competitors. One of the main theses of this book is that the electoral fortunes of peripheral parties do not only depend on the reaction of state parties to their initial emergence and growth but, more importantly, on their own strategies of competition against state parties. State parties can play the 'peripheral card' more confidently and with enhanced credibility in a decentralized state. However, peripheral parties will also behave strategically and adapt to the new institutional environment, as shown in the following chapter. For this reason, the neutralization of peripheral parties' growth is not taken for granted.

Nevertheless, even in the event of the peripheral party persistence, this chapter will present evidence that belies the alleged costs of devolution for state parties. Against this view, I will show that the establishment of one or more regional strongholds of electoral support and governmental power compensates state parties for the reduction of power of the central government that devolution entails.

Should we expect further decentralization after the first devolution reform? According to the third argument of this chapter, we certainly should. In a decentralized state, electoral competition along the centre–periphery dimension becomes entrenched. Consequently, competing state parties will give saliency to centre–periphery issues in their manifestos irrespective of the presence of threatening peripheral parties if they believe that this will bring them electoral rewards. As Falleti has put it, '[p]olitical decentralisation is likely to produce a policy ratchet effect . . . a group of supporters who will continue to push in the direction of further decentralisation' (2005: 331). Devolution, and more particularly asymmetric devolution, opens the Pandora's box of permanent ongoing decentralization with unforeseen consequences.

7.1 BEYOND OPPORTUNISM: THE EMERGENCE OF 'TRUE' PRO-PERIPHERY PREFERENCES

7.1.1 The regional versus the state level

In a decentralized state, the central leadership of a threatened state party faces a state-wide threat, coming from all the peripheral parties that take voters away from the state party throughout the country. The regional leadership of the threatened state party faces a regional threat, coming from the peripheral party or parties organized in that region in particular. Therefore, the threatened state party's available strategies in response to the peripheral party threat have to be considered for each level. The same state party engages in both state-wide and regional strategies and they need not coincide. Let us start with the regional level.

The centre–periphery strategy most likely to be used by the regional branches of state parties at the regional level is pro-periphery convergence. In regional contests, peripheral parties have a powerful weapon against state parties: the message that they are the best placed to represent regional interests because they are not the 'branch' of a state party. Their 'nationalist' and 'regionalist' labels give credibility to this message. Peripheral parties 'present their independence from state parties as the best guarantee of the defence of the interests of the autonomous community [region], generating their electoral appeal around this idea' (Pallarés and Keating 2006: 100). As Van Biezen and Hopkin have rightly pointed out, 'allowing the ethnoregionalists to claim a "monopoly" of concern for the territory's particular problems can have important electoral costs' (2006: 18). The regional branches of state parties in the devolved regions see a pressing need to defend themselves from these accusations. For this reason, the threatened regional branch of the state party has strong incentives to converge towards the pro-periphery positions of its peripheral competitors. Convergence will convey to the region's voters that the regional branch is not a mere representative of the state party's interests at the state level, that it defends the interests of the region as well as those of the central state. In so doing, however, the regional branch of the state party may collide with the interests of the state party's central leadership.

It is unlikely that the threatened regional branch of a state party will use either a strategy of avoidance or of anti-periphery polarization. These strategies could lead the party to political marginality in the region by confirming the accusations coming from peripheral parties.

Turning now to the state level, pro-periphery convergence has more credibility after devolution for two main reasons. First, the threatened state party that has implemented the devolution reform can now benefit from a reputation as decentralizer. This will make the party a rightful 'owner' of the issue and will give credibility to future pro-periphery moves in a manner that was impossible in a unitary state. It will also provide the party's leadership with a strong argument against accusations of electoral opportunism that may be raised by its state and/or peripheral competitors. After all, they were willing to pay the price for enhancing their credibility. The second reason why pro-periphery strategies are more credible after devolution is the existence of regional constituencies and the presence of multi-level intergovernmental relations. State parties with geographically concentrated electoral support in some particular regions are able to establish regional power strongholds. They develop regional institutional interests and they act to protect them. At the same time, state parties are conditioned by the realities of multi-level governance when it comes to obtaining the necessary parliamentary majorities at the state level. If a state party needs the votes of a peripheral party in order to participate in state government, its pro-periphery promises will have full credibility since everybody knows that, unless the state party satisfies some of the demands of the peripheral party, it will not obtain the parliamentary support it needs. The opportunism behind this type of pro-periphery move will be compensated by the acquired reputation as decentralizer of those state parties which were responsible for the implementation of devolution in the first place. Voters are aware of these regional interests and this is what makes the pro-periphery moves of state parties credible.

To sum up, in a decentralized state, peripheral parties have lost the monopoly of the pro-periphery message, which now may convincingly belong to other parties in the polity. Therefore, I expect to find more pro-periphery moves now than before devolution and I expect that their negative effect on the electoral fortunes of peripheral parties will be stronger.

Turning now to the other available strategies, avoiding centre–periphery issues is hardly a choice for state parties in the post-devolution era. These issues will be on the agenda permanently, under one guise or another. When the economy is in crisis and absorbs all the electoral debates, centre–periphery issues will assume the form of economic inequalities between the regions; when devolution itself is the main issue in the election debates parties can focus more explicitly on the devolution of further competences or on the revision of the region's constitutional status. Either way, state parties will find it difficult to completely ignore centre–periphery issues.

Anti-periphery polarization becomes riskier and less credible than it was before devolution due to the empowerment of the regional level of government that decentralization implies. An anti-periphery polarization strategy would amount to stopping the devolution of power to—or to taking power away from—regional elites that have developed a taste for it. To recentralize power is much more difficult than it is to decentralize power given that the foci of resistance are numerous, powerful, and have autonomous sources of democratic legitimacy. Moreover, the central leadership of a state party that decides to use tactics of anti-periphery polarization may be contradicted at the regional level by its regional branches. A state party will only use an anti-periphery strategy when its main competitor is not a peripheral party but another state party and when there is a large enough pool of voters whose preferences are with the central state. It is in the competition between state parties representing state-wide interests that an anti-periphery strategy pays off. Therefore, I expect to find fewer tactics of anti-periphery polarization after devolution and I expect polarization moves to be more likely among parties in the opposition than among parties in government.

This brings us to the relevance of incumbency as a factor that explains the electoral strategies adopted by state parties. The party in the opposition has incentives to use centre–periphery tactics in order to damage the future electoral chances of the party in government. This is so because the objective of the state party in the opposition is to attract as many voters as possible who had previously voted for the party in government whereas the incumbent's objective is, above all, not to lose voters to the opposition. The opposition is therefore pressed to engage in offensive tactics to take voters away from the incumbent while the incumbent is more predisposed to protect whatever share of the vote it has already achieved. The former will have incentives to be audacious and the latter to be cautious.

Precisely because it has no governmental responsibilities and, therefore, no one will hold it accountable, the party in the opposition can radicalize its stance, by emphasizing either more extreme pro-periphery or more extreme anti-periphery issues than would be the case if it were in government. The party's leaders will engage in such radicalization if they consider that it will bring the party votes. Thus, when facing a governmental party that has arrived in office with a decentralizing agenda or that needs the support of peripheral parties to obtain a functioning parliamentary majority, the opposition party will benefit by emphasizing an anti-periphery programme in order to attract those voters of the incumbent whose preferences are with the centre. Alternatively, if the state party in the opposition has already acquired a reputation as a decentralizer as a result of a previous incumbency period, the opposition party will benefit by emphasizing more extreme pro-periphery positions than those that the government party is willing or is able to entertain.

Until now, I have taken for granted the existence of state parties and, therefore, the relationship between the central leadership of the state party and its regional branches. There is, however, another possible scenario, one in which state parties have ceased to exist (as exemplified by the Belgian case). In the absence of a state party system, the ex-state parties are free from the constraints imposed by the relationship between the central leadership and its regional branches. However, they are not free from the insoluble contradiction of being a state-wide party defending partial regional interests. The incumbent ex-state parties, while in power at the central government and especially if it is the party of the Prime Minister, have to act as state-wide parties, even if they have a pro-periphery agenda. This is why the Flemish Christian Democrats have had difficulties conciliating their pro-periphery preferences with their position as incumbent party of the Belgian state.

7.1.2 The pressure to converge at the regional level

Threatened state parties that implemented the first devolution reform are not the only parties with incentives to assimilate the pro-periphery agenda. The incentives to do so affect all the parties in the polity, including those traditionally opposed to devolution and which have historically preferred a centralized state.

Some examples will serve as an illustration of this. The conservative Partido Popular (PP) in Spain is by history and ideology a Spanish *nationalist* party that believes that the nation in Spain is one and indivisible and that only the Spanish people, as represented by Spanish institutions, are sovereign. Despite its ideological stance, the regional branches of the PP in Valencia and the Balearic Islands defended the position that these regions, where the PP is the largest party and has been the party in office for a long period, be defined as 'historical nationalities' in their respective statutes of autonomy (regional constitutions). At the same time, the PP in Valencia and the Balearic Islands pushed for the highest level of self-government that could be assumed within the Spanish Constitution for these two regions and has succumbed to the rhetoric of peripheral nationalism during the process of elaboration of new—second-generation—statutes of autonomy in the mid-2000s, whose preambles were full of historical and cultural references. To the amazement of some Spanish peripheral parties, the PP of Valencia—with the support of the Socialist Party of Valencia—even demanded the devolution of the Valencian *fueros*, historical institutions of self-government that were abolished by the Spanish monarchy in 1707. This provoked the following sarcastic reaction from a Catalan CIU deputy at the Spanish parliament:

Today we feel comforted to see that also the *Partido Popular* and the *Partido Socialista* are walking on the path of forality [*fueros*]. We welcome you to our approach because today, if you allow me the expression, you are making history by recovering from the past the defence of a historical right . . . and by remembering the

Decret de Nova Planta del País Valenciá from the year 1707. (Xuclà, *Convergència i Unió*, Diario de Sesiones del Congreso de los Diputados, 20 September 2005, p. 5571)

We have other examples outside Spain of state parties flirting with peripheral nationalist rhetoric at the regional level. In September 1984, a harsh political debate was unleashed in Italy after the regional president of Sicily, the Christian Democrat Modesto Sardo, defined himself at a convention in Bari as the representative of the 'Sicilian nation', in opposition to Italy, which he defined as being 'a geographical expression that hopes to become a nation' (*La Repubblica*, 18 September 1984). Again this conversion to the pro-periphery credo happened, as in the examples from Spain, when the state party was in office at the regional level.

In 2007, a political analyst for *The Times* wrote that the British Conservatives, alarmed by the increasing support for Scottish nationalism after devolution, could start escalating their demands that Scottish representation be cut in the English House of Commons or that there be 'English votes for English laws' to the point of mutating into the 'English National Party' (Tim Hames, *The Times*, 10 September 2007). This would be unlikely to happen without the Scottish Conservatives putting up a fight. Their slow electoral recovery in Scotland since the beginning of devolution turned them more pro-Scottish than they ever were before. At the 2004 party conference, the Scottish Conservatives debated two important issues: on the one hand, the need to increase the Scottish Parliament's tax-raising powers; on the other, the need to rid themselves of their anti-devolution image.

The anecdotal evidence just presented indicates that the incentives to assimilate the pro-periphery agenda at the regional level exist irrespective of the incumbency status of the party, although these incentives take different forms depending on whether the party is in office or in the opposition. The incumbent party at the regional level has incentives to adopt pro-periphery issues as a way to remain in office. Keeping its distance from the position defended by the central leadership of the party in state institutions, the regional branch in office shows voters that it is more than a mere branch of the state party and that it has the power to oppose the central party's line, if need be. The state party in opposition at the regional level has incentives to adopt pro-periphery issues as a way to obtain the necessary majority that will place it in regional government, particularly if it has to compete with a peripheral party.

Fortunately, new research applying content-analysis techniques to party manifestos in regional elections is starting to provide us with quantitative empirical evidence of this phenomenon, even if limited to a few countries and elections. The work by Fabre and Martínez-Herrera (2009) on Great Britain sheds new light into the use of 'regionalist' and 'nationalist' rhetoric by state parties in regional manifestos. These authors have shown that in regional elections 'all three state parties make extensive use of references to the region' (Fabre and Martínez-Herrera 2009: 245). In Wales the number of references to the region in state party manifestos exceeded those made by Plaid Cymru. In Scotland, in the 2003 regional elections, the Liberal Democrats and the Conservatives made as many references to the region as the SNP did; whereas Labour made more references to Scotland than the Scottish nationalists. The authors explain this as the way that state parties have to 'compensate a moderately or ambiguously regionalist profile with repeated references to the region. Again, it is much easier to refer to the identity of the region than to make pledges on institutional reform' (Fabre and Martínez-Herrera 2009: 246). Maddens and Libbrecht (2009) have analysed the party manifestos of Spanish parties in regional and state elections for the period between 2000 and 2003. They show that the two main state parties, PP and PSOE, 'shift towards a more regionalist profile' in regional elections as compared to the state ones and that 'this tendency is most evident on the institutional dimension' (Maddens and Libbrecht 2009: 225).

The state parties' true pro-periphery turn at the regional level is nowhere reflected better than in the tensions within state party organizations between the central leadership and the regional organizations. These tensions, on the other hand, may end up in regional splits (Van Biezen and Hopkin 2006) if the stakes are high enough. And the stakes grow with every new step towards further decentralization. The larger the number of competences in the hands of the regional administration the more attractive it becomes to reach and keep office at the regional level.

Italy is a good example of this. As the reforms for further decentralization have proceeded during the Berlusconi's governments of the late 1990s and early 2000s, so have the regional splits from Italian state parties. The Valdotan section of the Partito Popolare Italiano (heir to Democrazia Cristiana), abandoned the mother-party in 1997 and united with the small peripheral party Pour la Vallée d'Aoste to form a new regionalist party, Autonomisti. In Sardinia, the Sardinian section of the Italian party Unione Democratica per la Republicca left the mother-party in 1998 to establish a new peripheral party, Unione Democratica Sarda-Progetto Naziona-litario. In 2008, the new peripheral party Popolari Autonomisti Sardi was created from a split of the Sardinian section of the Italian UDEUR-Popolari. In 1994 in Trentino-Alto Adige, the provincial (Trento) section of the Italian CDU formed a new peripheral party, the Unione Popolare Autonomista. In Sicilia in 2005 the Sicilian section of the Italian party UDC split to form a new peripheral party, Movimento per l'Autonomia. Its leader, Raffaele Lombarda, explained his decision with the following argument: 'too high a price has been paid to the national parties while the interests of our land have not always been defended'. One more case of a split from a state party took place in Sicily. In 2001, the regional branch of the Partito Socialista Italiano left the mother-party and merged with the Partito Siciliano d'Azione to establish a new peripheral party, Nuova Sicilia.

Italy is, of course, a particular case and this abundance of regional splits from state parties could be attributable to the implosion of the state party system in the mid-1990s and its subsequent recomposition. However, politicians in the regions would not take the risk of creating a peripheral party unless they were expecting to reap some political benefits from such a strategy. After the decentralizing reforms of Berlusconi's governments, regional politicians had more incentives to form regional parties than before, since the regional legislatures and executives had increased powers, budgets, and competences.

In Spain, the first relevant victim of the centre–periphery tensions within parties was the eighteen-year-long electoral alliance between the Conservatives (PP) and the peripheral regionalist party Unión del Pueblo Navarro in Navarre. UPN was the electoral brand of the PP in Navarre since 1982. During 2008, a crisis broke out between the UPN leader, Miguel Sanz, and the PP central leadership. UPN was the party of government in Navarre thanks to the external support from the Socialist Party. Without this support, it would lack the necessary parliamentary majority. The interests of UPN in Navarre, however, clashed with those of the PP in Madrid. When the PP ordered UPN MPs in Madrid to vote against the budget presented by the Socialist government, Sanz did not comply. He needed the Socialist support in Navarre and he was willing to pay back by supporting the PSOE at the state parliament. He defended UPN's position in the crisis claiming that 'the home of UPN is in Navarre' (*El País*, 9 September 2008). The crisis ended the long organic relationship between the two parties and forced the leadership of the PP to create from scratch a PP regional branch in Navarre.

In Belgium, the ex-state parties already went fully 'regional' as a result of the party system's territorial split. At the end of the 2000s, the remains of the Belgian peripheral parties signed pre-electoral coalition agreements with the ex-state parties: the FDF with the francophone Liberals, the Volksunie with the Flemish Socialists and Christian Democrats. This is an indication of how far the pro-periphery positions of the traditional state parties in Belgium had gone. In 2007, the electoral alliance of the Flemish Christian Democrats (CD&V) and the ex-Volksunie right-wingers (N-VA) led by Leterme won the federal election with an electoral campaign based on flirting with separatism.

7.2 THE EFFECTIVENESS OF PRO-PERIPHERY CONVERGENCE

While the regional branches of state parties are developing what seem to be 'true' pro-periphery preferences at the regional level, what are the state parties' centre–periphery moves at the state level? In order to compare the state parties' electoral strategies before and after the first devolution reform, I look at three main indicators: the type of moves that were adopted, the evolution of the parties' positions along the centre–periphery dimension, and the absolute and relative saliency of centre–periphery issues in the parties' manifestos. All three indicators are measuring the strategies used by state parties, but they all emphasize different aspects.

As in chapter 6, I classify the electoral moves adopted by state parties according to the saliency of the pro-periphery and anti-periphery issues in their respective manifestos. Table 7.1 summarizes information for a total of 32 state elections in Belgium, Italy, Spain, and the UK.

A number of important differences are evident when comparing this period with the period before the first devolution reform. During the post-devolution period, anti-periphery moves were hardly used by state parties at state elections. We find only four examples: the Flemish Liberals and Christian Democrats at the 1971 election, the Flemish Liberals at the 1978 election and the Popular Party in Spain at the 2004 and 2008 elections. All except the Flemish Christian Democratic Party were in the opposition when adopting their anti-periphery moves. An overwhelming majority of parties adopted pro-periphery moves.

Table 7.2 shows the empirical probability of each of all the possible combinations of electoral moves by the two main state parties before and after the first devolution reforms. The pro-periphery/pro-periphery combination occurs 18 per cent of the times before the first devolution reform in contrast with 69 per cent of the times after it. As expected, pro-periphery moves are considerably likelier in a decentralized context. Also, as expected, state parties find it as difficult to completely avoid the mention of centre–periphery issues as before devolution.

The party systems in all countries except Belgium were more unambiguously pro-periphery after devolution than before it, as reflected by the mean position scores of all state parties in the polity before and after devolution (Table 7.3).

Looking at state parties individually, a majority were also more unambiguously pro-periphery after devolution than before it. Figure 7.1 shows the evolution of centre–periphery moves of the two/three main state parties since the first devolution reform (the UK is not part of the figure since there are only two observations). As in Figure 6.1 of chapter 6, horizontal lines have been included to represent elections.

In the period before devolution the party systems everywhere were polarized along the centre–periphery dimension. There were anti-periphery state parties, such as the Belgian Socialists and Liberals, the Italian Christian Democrats and the MSI post-fascists, the British and Spanish Conservatives, side by side the pro-periphery state parties. After the first devolution reforms, by contrast, the party systems became more homogeneously pro-periphery. The anti-periphery positions were practically abandoned by all the state parties. This is also visible in the electoral strategies being used. There were very few examples of anti-periphery polarization tactics by state parties after devolution. Of course there were still differences among state parties concerning the degree of intensity with which they conveyed pro-periphery positions, but in general parties were not willing to defend a clear unambiguous anti-periphery stance. Some parties made the long—and uncommon—journey of moving from defending anti-periphery

Challenging the State

TABLE 7.1. *State parties' electoral moves and peripheral party growth after the first devolution reform*

Belgium

Parties/Years	1971	1974	1977	1978	1981	1985	1987	1991	1995	1999	2003
Flemish:											
CVP	C	P	P	P	P	P	P	P	P	P	P
SP	P	P	AV	P	P	P	P	P	P	AV	
PLP (later VLD)	C	P	AV	C	AV	P	P	P	P	P	P*
VU	19.4	17	16.2	11.6	16.1	12.9	13.1	9.5	7.3	8.8	–
Walloons:											
PSC	C	P	P	P	P	P	P	P	P	AV	AV
PS	P	P	AV	P	P	P	P	P	P	AV	AV
PLP (later PRL)	C	P	P	P	AV	AV	AV	P	P	AV	AV
RW	19.6	17.6	6.1	6	5	0	0.6	0.2	0	0	
FDF**	28.1	31.9(a)	27.7(b)	28(b)	17.4	8.3	8.2	9	–	–	–

* If I were to derive the classification of the VLD's move in 2003 exclusively from the CMP data, I would classify it as a pro-centre turn. However, this is due to the large space dedicated in the VLD's 2003 manifesto to 'multiculturalism: negative', which is not directed against the internal cultural minority (i.e. the Belgian francophones) but against immigrants. The VLD position at the 2003 elections with respect to the centre–periphery dimension was to move further into the federalization of the Belgian state and therefore the VLD's move has been reclassified as pro-periphery.
**Results in the province of Brabant.
(a) In coalition with PLDP; (b) in coalition with RW.

Italy

Parties/Years	1953	1958	1963	1968	1972	1976	1979	1983	1987	1992	1994	1996	2001
DC (later PPI)	AV	AV	P	P	P	P	P	AV	AV	P	P	P	
PCI (later DS)	AV	AV	P	AV	P	P	P	P	AV	P	P	P	P
PSI	AV	P	P	P	P	P	P	AV	AV	P			
FI					–	–	–	–	–	–	P	P	P
SVP	28	29	28	30	30	32	36	32	33	33	37*		33*
UV		51	50	48	49(a)	49(b)	32(c)	45(c)	39(c)	55(d)			
LN (Lombardy)									3	23	22.1*	25.5*	12.1*

*Results of PR lists.
(a) In coalition with DC, PSDI, and RV; (b) in coalition with DC; (c) in coalition with Dem. P. and PLI; (d) in coalition with CP and PRI.

United Kingdom

Parties/Years	2001	2005
Conservatives	P	P
Labour	P	P
SNP	20.1	17.7
PC	14.3	12.5

Spain

Parties/Years	1982	1986	1989	1993	1996	2000	2004	2008
PP	P	P	P	P	P	P	C*	C
PSOE	P	P	P	P	P	P	P	P
CiU	22.8	32	32.7	31.8	29.6	28.8	20.8	21
ERC	4	2.7	2.7	5.1	4.2	5.6	15.9	7.9
PNV	31.7	27.8	22.8	24.1	25	30.4	33.7	27.1
HB	14.7	17.7	16.9	14.5	12.3	——	——	——

Legend: P – Pro-periphery; AV – Centre–periphery avoidance; C – Pro-centre.
* This is a correction of the CMP-based classification, which would have defined the 2004 PP's move as pro-periphery. However, the pro-periphery references are not about further decentralization to the regional level but to the local one. The 2004 manifesto presents a defence of the decentralized status quo. This is considered as a pro-periphery position. However, the manifesto also includes references to the need to reinforce the competences belonging to the state in order to block the further devolution of power to the regions in the future. The defence of the status quo is thus accompanied by some recentralizing measures, rendering the move an anti-periphery one. The same move, but with greater emphasis, was used in 2008, though for this election the CMP data did capture the pro-centre turn correctly.

TABLE 7.2. *Empirical probability of state parties' electoral strategies*

Combination of Strategies	Probability (Before Devolution)	Probability (After Devolution)
P/P	**0.18** (N = 5)	**0.69** (N = 31)
P/AV	0.26 (N = 7)	0.13 (N = 6)
P/C	0.22 (N = 6)	0.07 (N = 3)
AV/C	0.18 (N = 5)	0 (N = 0)
AV/AV	0.15 (N = 4)	0.11 (N = 5)
C/C	0 (N = 0)	0 (N = 0)
Total # elections	27	45*

* The 11 elections that took place in Belgium are counted twice, since two party systems exist.

TABLE 7.3. *The mean position of state parties along the centre–periphery dimension before and after the first devolution reform*

Country	Position Score Before First Devolution Reform	Position Score After First Devolution Reform
Belgium	1.4	3.1
Italy	1.1	1.8
Spain	2.3	2.7
Great Britain	1.8	3.8

FLANDERS (1971–2003)

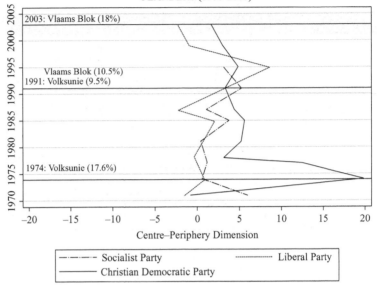

2003: Vlaams Blok (18%)

Vlaams Blok (10.5%)
1991: Volksunie (9.5%)

1974: Volksunie (17.6%)

Centre–Periphery Dimension

— · — · — Socialist Party   ············· Liberal Party
———— Christian Democratic Party

WALLONIA (1971–2003)

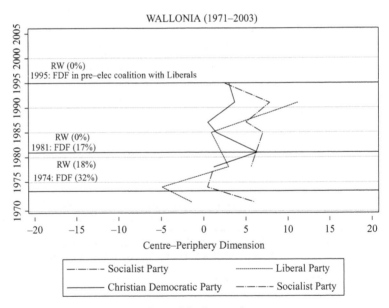

RW (0%)
1995: FDF in pre–elec coalition with Liberals

RW (0%)
1981: FDF (17%)

RW (18%)
1974: FDF (32%)

Centre–Periphery Dimension

— · — · — Socialist Party   ············· Liberal Party
———— Christian Democratic Party   — · — · — Socialist Party

FIGURE 7.1. *Continued*

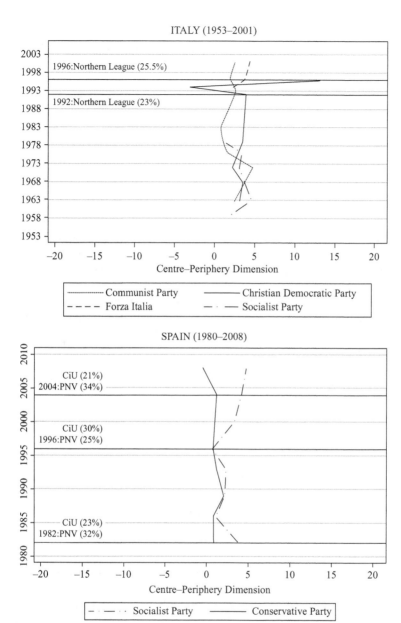

ITALY (1953–2001)

1996:Northern League (25.5%)

1992:Northern League (23%)

Centre–Periphery Dimension

- - - - - - - - Communist Party — Christian Democratic Party
- - - - Forza Italia — · — Socialist Party

SPAIN (1980–2008)

CiU (21%)
2004:PNV (34%)

CiU (30%)
1996:PNV (25%)

CiU (23%)
1982:PNV (32%)

Centre–Periphery Dimension

- · — · · Socialist Party — Conservative Party

Notes: Avoidant positions in the graphs are filled in, for the sake of graph clarity and given that they are already described in Table 7.1. The lines in the graphs go straight from a non-avoidant position (be it pro- or anti-periphery) to another non-avoidant position even if in between there is an avoidant position. When several avoidant positions are placed consecutively (as for example in the Italian Communist and Christian Democratic parties between 1953 and 1958), no line is shown. This empty space is therefore indicative of consecutively ignoring centre–periphery issues.

FIGURE 7.1. *Evolution of state parties' centre–periphery positions in Belgium (Wallonia and Flanders), Italy, and Spain after the first devolution reform*

issues before devolution to defending pro-periphery ones after it. This is the case of the francophone Socialists and the francophone Liberals in Belgium, the post-fascist National Alliance in Italy, and the Conservatives in the United Kingdom.

The Spanish Socialists grew less pro-periphery during the 1980s as a result of incumbency. Their electoral landslide in 1982 took place in a context of economic crisis and of a great need of structural and social reforms. The priority was the economy and the acknowledgement of this reduced the enthusiasm of the Socialist leaders for decentralization, which would only complicate the tasks ahead. Soon they started to have second thoughts about the convenience of the central state losing power to the regions just when this centralized power seemed most necessary. Moreover, the Socialists had an absolute majority in parliament and could pass legislation alone. Between 1982 and 1996 the two main Spanish parties were located at the same very moderate (almost neutral) pro-periphery position. This situation contrasts sharply with the period after 1996, when the Socialists were in the opposition at the state level. There was then a clear pro-periphery turn that contributed to the Socialists' victory in 2004 and that continued throughout their period in office, accompanied by an anti-periphery turn by the Conservatives in opposition. The evolution of state parties' centre–periphery positions in Spain is not so much connected with the peripheral threat, which was permanently there without dramatic upwards or downwards changes, but with the incumbency status of each state party. The Socialists turned pro-periphery while in the opposition and used it as a way to go back to power; the Conservatives turned anti-periphery while in the opposition, using polarization as a way to go back to power.

The francophone Christian Democrats in Belgium grew less intensely pro-periphery after devolution because the pro-periphery position was successfully owned by the francophone Socialists and Liberals. The recent past as sharing the same organization with the sister party, the Flemish Christian Democrats, historically so combative in the defence of Flemish interests, was a heavy weight for the Christian Democrats in Wallonia. The francophone Socialists and Liberals turned openly pro-periphery as a response to the peripheral party threat coming from the Rassemblement Wallon and the Front Démocratique des Francophones. After the split of the Belgian Socialists into two parties, one exclusively francophone and the other exclusively Flemish, the francophone Socialists grew intensely pro-periphery in Wallonia. The Parti Socialiste became unambiguously pro-periphery among the francophone state parties, while the CVP did the same among the Flemish ones. This is not by chance, given that before the split they were the two parties to be most vulnerable to the peripheral party threat in their respective regions. Just as their Socialist competitors, the francophone Liberals increasingly appropriated the pro-periphery agenda, culminating in the pre-electoral coalition with the peripheral party FDF at the 1995 elections. Eventually, the francophone Liberals and the FDF (together with two other minor parties) merged into the Mouvement Réformateur (MR) in 2002.

In Italy, as I have already explained, the Christian Democrats' pro-periphery turn of the late 1960s had to do with the pro-periphery moves initiated by Communists and Socialists. Initially the DC ignored centre–periphery issues. When Communists and Socialists turned pro-periphery, the DC's first reaction was a moderate anti-periphery turn that was then retracted in the following elections. Since the late 1970s the Christian Democrats have, in fact, been more pro-periphery than their left-wing competitors. The successful appearance of the Northern League took the Christian Democrats by surprise. In the years before the party went through a process of transmutation into the Italian Popular Party (PPI) after the 1994 elections, the reaction of the DC towards the success of the Northern League in the electorally relevant regions of the North was a large anti-periphery turn. In the 1992 elections, the ones in which the League increased dramatically its vote shares, the Christian Democrats campaigned with the slogan 'They want to break Italy up'.

The National Alliance (AN) in Italy was also pushed to moderate its openly anti-periphery stance by the political needs of the moment. Until the early 1990s, the National Alliance, which was particularly strong in the southern regions, was strongly anti-periphery. In 1994, the Alleanza Nazionale entered in a coalition government with Forza Italia and the Lega Nord which lasted only a few months, due to deep programmatic disagreements between the coalition partners. When the possibility to repeat the same coalition formula opened up again in 2001 the three coalition partners worked harder to approximate their proposals which resulted in the AN moderating its anti-periphery stance in order to satisfy the demands of the Lega Nord.

In the UK, the Conservatives were the ones to most radically change their centre–periphery positions, moving from the anti-periphery positions of the early 1990s to the intense pro-periphery position of 2005 (7.5), more intense than that of Labour.

Let us look now at the relative saliency of the centre–periphery dimension with respect to the left–right one. This is measured, as we already know, by calculating the left–right/centre–periphery ratio, i.e. the total percentage of sentences that a party manifesto dedicates to centre–periphery issues relative to the total percentage dedicated to left–right issues. This information is shown in Table 7.4, together with the mean saliency scores of pro-periphery issues.

TABLE 7.4. *Mean saliency of pro-periphery issues and mean left–right/centre–periphery ratio in state party manifestos before and after the first devolution reform*

Country:	Before the First Devolution Reform		After the First Devolution Reform	
	Salience Pro-per	LR/CP Ratio	Salience Pro-per	LR/CP Ratio
Belgium	4.3	0.21	4.7	0.23
Italy	1.8	0.10	3.1	0.10
Spain	3	0.08	3.2	0.09
Great Britain	3.3	0.11	4.6	0.10

The mean saliency of pro-periphery issues in state parties' manifestos was higher after devolution than before it in all the countries under analysis, with the increase in Italy being the largest one. This means that state parties were emphasizing pro-periphery issues to a larger extent after the decentralizing reforms had been implemented than when the countries had a unitary structure. Moreover, in Belgium and Spain state parties dedicated more relative space to the centre–periphery dimension compared to the left–right one after decentralization than before it, even if the left–right dimension was always much more relevant than the centre–periphery dimension in all the manifestos of state parties.

So far it has been ascertained that after devolution state parties were more inclined to emphasize pro-periphery issues at state level elections than they had been before the first devolution reforms. According to the hypothesis tested here, this was because pro-periphery strategies were more credible in a decentralized context and, therefore, more effective. The question is whether they really were more effective in putting a stop to the peripheral party growth. Did peripheral parties become redundant and unattractive after devolution?

In order to compare the effectiveness of the pro-periphery convergence strategy to stop the growth of peripheral parties, the number of elections for which the prediction is correct and incorrect has been calculated. It may happen that for the same country and year the state parties' pro-periphery moves produced diverse effects to different peripheral parties. The data are presented in Table 7.5, which compares the empirical probability of each type of prediction (correct, incorrect, and mixed) before the first devolution reform and after. Let us concentrate on the first three columns of the table first.

According to the empirical probabilities shown in columns two and three of Table 7.5, the strategy of pro-periphery convergence is more effective when countries are decentralized than when they have a unitary structure. The strategy was correct 25 per cent of the times before devolution and 35 per cent after it. At the same time, the probability that the strategy was ineffective was reduced by nearly four points after devolution whereas mixed results (i.e., pro-periphery moves that had contradicting effects for different peripheral parties of the same country) more than doubled their probability after devolution.

TABLE 7.5. *Empirical probability that the pro-periphery convergence strategy is effective (i.e. the prediction of stopping peripheral party growth is correct)*

Effective Strategy	Probability (Before Devolution)	Probability (After Devolution)	Probability Without Belgium (After Devolution)
Yes	0.25 (N = 3)	0.35 (N = 16)	0.13 (N = 3)
No	0.58 (N = 7)	0.15 (N = 7)	0.13 (N = 3)
Mixed	0.17 (N = 2)	0.40 (N = 22)	0.82 (N = 18)
# elections in which state parties adopted pro-periphery moves	12	45	23

Two conclusions can be derived from this data. First, the data confirm the hypothesis that an improvement in the effectiveness of the pro-periphery convergence strategy was to be expected after devolution. Second, the large increase in the probability of mixed effects indicates that the effectiveness of the state parties' convergence strategies varied greatly among peripheral parties.

These conclusions, however, are incomplete. If we look at Table 7.5 closely, we see that the effectiveness and ineffectiveness of pro-periphery moves are unequally distributed among countries. In Spain, pro-periphery convergence had in all elections mixed results; in Belgium, pro-periphery convergence was effective 73 per cent of the times. This means that the expected weakening of peripheral parties' electoral growth as a result of the greater effectiveness of the pro-periphery convergence strategy in a decentralized state was strongly mediated by country-specific factors.

Belgium is the only country in which peripheral parties clearly lost in the competition against state parties during the post-devolution period. Their electoral results declined continuously since their highest peak at the 1971 elections, just after the first Belgian devolution reform. At this general election, the Volksunie (VU) gathered 19.4 per cent of the vote in the region of Flanders while Rassemblement Wallon (RW) did the same (19.6 per cent) in Wallonia. A coalition of the FDF and the RW in the province of Brabant reached 24 per cent of the province's vote (see Table 7.2). This was the last time that these parties would see their vote shares increase, with minor exceptions. The VU declined its vote share continuously between 1971 and 1999, falling from 19.4 per cent to 8.8 per cent in 1999, after which election it split into two different parties, the left-wing Spirit and the right-wing N-VA. Only in 1981 and in 1999 did VU manage to reverse the declining tendency, but to no avail. The RW's decline was even more dramatic than that of VU. At the 1977 elections it fell to 6 per cent of the vote in the Walloon region, from nearly 18 per cent reached in 1974. In 1981, the results of the FDF-RW electoral alliance in Wallonia dropped by over 40 per cent and in Brussels by over one-third. The francophone peripheral parties were at this point overtaken by the ecologists. By 1985 RW had disappeared as an electoral force and the FDF continued its rapid decline until 1991, when it obtained a mere 9 per cent of the vote in the Brussels district. The FDF did not disappear completely, as the RW did. It continued to be strong at the local level, although with a very different programmatic agenda, in which the party declared that it wanted to 'contribute to the development of the Brussels region and of its local municipalities' (Deschower 2009: 15), leaving aside its core linguistic programme used at state elections. In 1993, the party's leaders decided to present their candidates on the lists of the francophone Liberals (PRL), an alliance that was maintained ever since, eventually merging into the Mouvement Réformateur (MR) for the 2003 elections. At their height in 1971, the peripheral parties represented 22.3 per cent of the Belgian vote. By 1985, this figure had fallen to 9.3 per cent and, by 1991, to 7.4 per cent. Meanwhile, the ex-state parties continued their climb back towards the levels of dominance that they had had during the 1950s and early 1960s, from 72.5 per cent of the vote in 1971 to 79 per cent of the vote in 1985, the maximum they would ever manage during the post-devolution period.

Apparently, the pro-periphery strategies followed by the Belgian ex-state parties were successful in achieving their aim of making peripheral parties redundant and unattractive to voters. This is the interpretation most widely defended by political scientists. According to Hooghe, 'The nationalist RW became almost completely absorbed by the francophone Socialists (PS) when the PS endorsed a radical federalist program of economic autonomy' (Hooghe 2004: 12). In the same vein, De Winter argues that Belgian ex-state parties 'gradually monopolised most of the issues that the regionalist parties had campaigned upon. Hence, during the first half of the 1980s the traditional parties in Brussels and Wallonia managed to crush the electoral appeal of the FDF and the RW with the latter disappearing from the electoral map completely' (De Winter 2006: 82). Van Haute and Pilet back this interpretation: 'This success urged traditional parties to adapt and reduced regionalist parties' monopoly on the issue. This aspect . . . diminished their specific appeal and influenced their electoral results negatively' (Van Haute and Pilet 2006: 308).

Clearly, there is some sort of 'Belgian effect' influencing the effectiveness of state parties' pro-periphery convergence. In order to get an idea of how large this 'Belgian effect' is, I have recalculated the empirical probabilities of each type of prediction excluding the Belgian elections from the calculation (the fourth column of Table 7.5). Once I exclude the successful Belgian case, I obtain a very different picture about the effectiveness of pro-periphery convergence before and after devolution: after the first devolution reform, pro-periphery moves were accompanied by peripheral party losses a mere 18 per cent of the times. The expected increased effectiveness of pro-periphery convergence after devolution disappears.

Controlling for the 'Belgian effect', on the other hand, uncovers new country-specific factors. For example, a strong 'Spanish effect' is indicated by the large increase of mixed results (a probability of 0.83) compared to the period before devolution. The pro-periphery moves used by Spanish state parties had mixed effects: some peripheral parties saw their vote shares reduced over time while others grew during the same period. Moreover, the number of peripheral parties with a parliamentary presence grew during the post-devolution period.

The disparate consequences of the state parties' pro-periphery strategies in Belgium and Spain require an explanation. Why were the pro-periphery strategies of Belgian state parties so successful in making peripheral parties redundant and unattractive while the pro-periphery strategies of Spanish state parties produced, at best, mixed results? If my hypothesis about the greater effectiveness of pro-periphery convergence in a decentralized context were true, state parties' pro-periphery moves should have been more successful in Spain than they appear to be according to Table 7.5. The degree of decentralization in Spain has been, for most of the period after the first devolution reform, higher than that of Belgium. It was not until 1995 that the Belgians were able to directly elect at the polls their regional representatives for the first time.

7.2.1 Explaining the 'Belgian effect'

The reason for the progressive disappearance of the peripheral parties in Belgium was the territorial split of the party system, by which state parties separated into exclusively francophone and exclusively Flemish organizations. This made the pro-periphery strategy of Belgian state parties credible and effective. More exactly, the pro-periphery programmatic agendas of Belgian ex-state parties became part of these parties' identities. The pro-periphery agenda stopped being 'strategic' and became 'intrinsic'.

The break-up of state parties partially freed the traditional left-wing and right-wing Belgian parties from the contradiction inherent in the defence of regional partial interests by a state-wide party. As Deschower has put it: '[t]he splitting of the parties—in itself also an effect of the success of the regionalist parties—*has transformed all Belgian parties into regional parties*, talking only to one of the two language communities and therefore easily taking over the regionalist attitude' (Deschower 2009: 19, emphasis added). By splitting into homogeneous linguistic organizations, Belgian ex-state parties became convincing 'owners' of the pro-periphery issues. They could freely engage in zero-sum programmatic agendas, avoiding the defence of the Belgian centre, hollowing it out, which they did, particularly after the complete federalization of the state in 1993 (see Table 7.6). This is why the Belgian ex-state parties were much more intensely and homogeneously pro-periphery than Spanish parties ever were even if the peripheral party threat was greater for Spanish parties than for Belgian ones, for

TABLE 7.6. *Mean saliency of anti-periphery issues in Belgian parties' manifestos*

	Before Devolution	After Devolution*	
	(1945–71)	(1971–93)	(1993–2003)
Christian Democrats (CVP-PSC)	2.01		
Flemish CDs (CVP)		0.98	0.79
Francophone CDs (PSC)		0.93	0.23
Socialists (PSB-BSP)	3.55		
Flemish Socialists (SP)		0.26	0.29
Francophone Socialists (PS)		0.48	0.20
Liberals (PL-LP)	4.34		
Flemish Liberals (PVV, VLD)		2.47	0.16
Francophone Liberals I (PRL)		0.42	
Francophone Liberals II (PRL-FDF)			0.43

* Without per608.

whom it had nearly disappeared. Spanish state parties could never freely engage in pro-periphery agendas to the extent that Belgian parties could.

The territorial split of state parties, however, cannot be the whole story. There is a certain degree of determinism implicit in this explanation. After all, the Flemish Vlaams Block, which was originally a split from the Volksunie, managed to thrive in the post-devolution period with its populist extreme right and separatist agenda. Also, the New Flemish Alliance (NV-A), the right-wing split from Volksunie in 2001 defending Flemish separation from Belgium, became the largest party in Flanders at the 2010 federal elections. This means that the fate of peripheral parties does not depend exclusively on the state parties' strategies but also on the peripheral parties' reactions to these pro-periphery strategies, or on the peripheral parties' strategic mistakes and/or successes, something that will be tackled in the following chapter. It also means that, of the two wings that initially lived side by side inside Volksunie, it was the most radical of the two which finally survived and became successful.

7.2.2 Explaining the 'Spanish effect'

Pro-periphery convergence moves did not work as well in Spain, or any other of our countries for that matter, as they did in Belgium. The most obvious difference between the two countries is that in Spain there was no split of the party system along territorial lines. Spanish state parties were not free to pursue a pro-periphery agenda as far as the competition against peripheral parties would have required.

However, the effectiveness of pro-periphery convergence in Spain should not be underestimated. Centre–periphery issues certainly helped the two main Spanish parties, PP and PSOE, in their competition against one another. The concentration of the vote in state elections upon these two parties grew across time, despite the strong presence of peripheral parties in some regions. The peripheral party family as a whole lost electoral weight in Spain at the general elections of 1982, 1996, 2004, and 2008 (see Figure 7.2). Each one of these elections was politically 'special', in the sense that the stakes were very high for the two major state parties in all of them. In 1982 the centre-right party UCD, which had led Spain through the transition to democracy, lost the election to the PSOE and a new period started. In 1996, the Popular Party won the election from the Socialist Party after fourteen years of consecutive Socialist rule, the last of which were full of political and corruption scandals. In 2004, again, there was a change of tendency after two legislatures of PP governments, the last one of them with a parliamentary majority that was systematically used and abused in order to impose decisions that were clearly unpopular, such as the decision to participate in the Iraq war. Finally, the elections in 2008 were special because they legitimized the Socialist victory of 2004, which had been repeatedly questioned by the opposition party (PP) on the basis that it was a spurious victory provoked by the Islamist terrorist attack in Madrid on 12 March 2004.

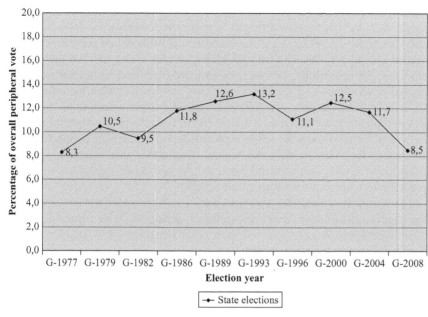

FIGURE 7.2. *Evolution of overall peripheral vote in state elections in Spain (1977–2008)*

During these special junctures, peripheral parties lost voters to one or the other of the two main state parties. This was facilitated by the pro-periphery moves adopted by both parties, and particularly by the PSOE, during the post-devolution era.

The fall of peripheral parties' votes between 2004 and 2008 has to be under-stood, again, within the context of the PSOE–PP confrontation. During this period, the opposition Conservative Party (PP) artificially focused on issues which did not matter significantly to voters but were designed to highlight the Socialists' weak-nesses, and the star issue in this respect was the territorial question. The anti-periphery polarization strategy of the PP was not designed to counteract the growth of peripheral parties, which represented no substantial threat for the PP, since there was little transfer of votes between the largest peripheral parties and the PP, but to damage the electoral prospects of the Socialists by polarizing the territorial debate. The same artificial emphasis, this time on the problem of terrorism, characterized the PP's strategy during the 2008 elections, despite the fact that it ranked penultimate among the personal concerns of Spaniards and fourth among the collective problems (Sampedro and Seoane 2008: 340).

The abundance of mixed effects in Spain, on the other hand, has an easy explanation: the presence of electoral competition within the peripheral party family between two or more peripheral parties active in the same region. The regions of Catalonia and the Basque Country each have at least two peripheral parties competing for votes, one moderate (as defined in chapter 1) and the other radical. We can see in Table 7.1 that the electoral trajectories of the two peripheral parties from the same region diverged. The growth of one was the fall of another, and vice versa. Therefore, a political competition of moderate peripheral parties against radical peripheral parties was clearly at play. Since the first democratic elections, the competition between two or more peripheral parties has not been limited to Catalonia and the Basque Country but has extended to Aragon, the Balearic Islands, Navarre, and Valencia. Spain's exceptionalism turns out to be less exceptional than it seemed initially. The mixed effects of peripheral parties' individual fortunes had to do with the presence of more than one peripheral party competing for votes in the same region. This means that whenever there is competition inside the peripheral party family, we should expect state parties' pro-periphery moves to result in mixed effects.

The competition inside the peripheral party family, however, did not undermine the effectiveness of state parties' pro-periphery strategies. What mattered for this effectiveness was the aggregate vote share of the peripheral party family which, as Figure 7.2 shows, was decreasing.

7.3 THE PAY-OFFS OF DEVOLUTION: STATE PARTIES' REGIONAL POWER

One of the possible consequences of devolution for a state party with geographically concentrated support is the constitution of one or several regional strongholds of electoral and governmental power. This would compensate state parties from the reduction of the power of the state government that devolution entails.

Table 7.7 shows the periods of incumbency of the major state parties at the regional level since the establishment of regional governments and legislatures. It is not meant as an exhaustive enumeration. The intention is merely to illustrate how well or how badly state parties have done in terms of obtaining and preserving regional power. For each region, it shows the longest periods of office have occurred irrespective of whether state parties were in office alone or in coalition with other—state or peripheral—parties.

The figures shown in Table 7.7 speak for themselves. The risk of losing power in the regions after devolution has never quite materialized. Regional power strongholds are clearly visible: Flanders for the CVP; Wallonia for the PS; Andalusia, Extremadura, and Castile-La Mancha for PSOE; Galicia, Castile-Leon, Balearic Islands, and Valencia for PP; Scotland and Wales for Labour; Emilia-Romagna and Tuscany for the PCI; the DC in several Italian regions. The major state parties of each country have been an average of 15 years in office at the regional level. Out of 112 incumbency periods shown in Table 7.7, 36 of them (32 per cent) have been in office 20 years or longer. Let us remember at this

TABLE 7.7. *Duration of state parties in regional government**

Region/Country	Party	Incumbency Periods	Consecutive Years in Office
Belgium ** **(1981–2009)**			
Flanders	CVP (later CD & V)	1981–99	18
		2004–	5
	PVV (later VLD)	1981–92	11
		1999–2009	10
	SP (later SP.A)	1988–	21
Wallonia	PS	1979–85	6
		1988–	21
	PSC (later CDH)	1979–99	20
		2009–	
	PRL-FDF (later MR)	1999–2004	5
Brussels	PS	1989–	20
	CVP (later CD & V)	1989–	20
	SP (later SP.A)	1989–	20
	PRL (later MR)	1995–2004	9
	PVV (later VLD)	2004–	5
	PSC (later CDH)	2004–	5
Italy (1947/70–2009)			
Abruzzi	DC (later PPI)	1970–2000	30
	FI	2000–	9
	AN	2000–	9
Basilicata	DC (later PPI)	1970–	29
	PCI (later PDS, DS)	1995–	14
Calabria	DC	1970–85	15
		1990–5	5
	PSI	1970–92	22
	PCI (later PDS, DS)	1986–90	4
	FI	1995–	14
	AN	1995–	14
Campania	DC (later PPI)	1970–95	25
	FI	1995–9	4
	AN	1995–9	4
	PCI (later PDS, DS)	1999–	10
Emilia-Romagna	PCI (later PDS, DS)	1970–	39
	DC (later PPI)	1995–	14
Friuli-Venezia Giulia	DC (later PPI)	1964–95	31
	PSI	1966–75	9
		1980–95	15
	FI	1998–	11
	AN	1998–	11
Lazio	DC (later PPI)	1970–6	6
	PSI	1970–95	25
	PCI (later PDS, DS)	1976–81	5
		1995–2000	5

(*Continued*)

TABLE 7.7. *Continued*

Region/Country	Party	Incumbency Periods	Consecutive Years in Office
	FI	2000–	9
	AN	2000–	9
Liguria	PSI	1970–95	25
	DC (later PPI)	1970–5	5
		1981–95	14
	PCI (later PDS, DS)	1975–80	5
		1994–2000	6
	FI	2000–	9
	AN	2000–	9
Lombardia	DC	1970–92	22
	PSI	1970–92	22
	FI	1995–	14
	AN	1995–	14
Marche	DC (later PPI)	1970–8	8
	PSI	1970–95	25
	PCI (later PDS, DS)	1995–	14
Molise	DC (later PPI)	1970–98	28
	PCI (later PDS, DS)	1995–	14
Piemonte	PSI	1973–95	22
	DC (later PPI)	1970–5	5
		1985–95	10
	FI	1995–	14
	AN	1995–	14
Puglia	DC (later PPI)	1970–95	25
	PSI	1970–95	25
	FI	1995–	14
	AN	1995	14
Sardegna	DC	1949–99	50
	PSI	1965–70	5
		1973–94	21
	FI	1999–2004	4
Sicilia	DC	1947–59	12
		1961–96	31
Trentino-Alto Adige	DC	1949–99	50
Toscana	PSI	1970–95	25
	PCI (later PDS, DS)	1970–	29
Umbria	PCI (later PDS, DS)	1970–	29
	PSI	1970–95	25
Veneto	DC (later PPI)	1970–95	25
	PSI	1985–94	9
	FI	1995–	14
	AN	1995–	14
Valle d'Aosta	DC	1966–70	4

Spain (1980/83–2009)			
Andalucí	PSOE	1982–	27
Aragón	PP	1987–93	6
	PSOE	1999–	10
Asturias	PSOE	1983–95	12
Baleares	PP	1983–99	16
Canarias	PSOE	1983–7	4
	PP	1995–9	4
Cantabria	PP	1983–2003	20
Castila-León	PP	1987–	22
Castilla-La Mancha	PSOE	1983–	26
Cataluña	PSOE	2003–	6
Communidad of Valenciana	PSOE	1983–95	12
	PP	1995–	14
Extremadura	PSOE	1983–	26
Galicia	PP	1990–2005	15
La Rioja	PSOE	1990–5	5
	PP	1995–	14
Madrid	PSOE	1983–95	12
	PP	1995–	14
Navarra	PSOE	1983–91	8
	PP-UPN	1991–2008	17
País Vasco	PSOE	1984–90	6
		1991–8	6
		2009–	
Región de Murcia	PSOE	1983–95	12
	PP	1995–	14
Great Britain (1998–2009)			
Scotland	Labour	1999–2007	8
Wales	Labour	1999–	10

* Data collection for this table ended on 31 Dec. 2009. Whenever the party is in office after this date, the end-year is left blank. The number of years provided is, therefore, smaller than the real one.

** Between 1981 and 1995 the regional parliaments were not directly elected.

point that regional legislatures have existed only for the last 28 years in Belgium, 39 years in Italy (except the special statute regions, where it varies between 62 years and 45 years), between 29 and 26 years in Spain, and 11 years in Great Britain. The fact that 32 per cent of these incumbency periods have been at least 20 years long, or even longer, is an impressive record.

Moreover, all major state parties have enjoyed a slice of the regional power cake: Liberals, Socialists, and Christian Democrats in Belgium; Communists, Socialists, and Christian Democrats in Italy; Conservatives and Socialists in Spain. The exception is Great Britain, where only Labour (and the smaller Liberal Democrats) has had a taste of regional office. This is due to the partial devolution that was implemented, by which regional assemblies were established only in Scotland and Wales. Nevertheless, the Conservatives would have managed to replicate Labour's feat in England, had there been an English assembly or assemblies at the time. Even in such challenging regions for state parties as Catalonia, the Basque

Country, or Val d'Aosta, where nationalist parties have a very strong presence that has dominated the regional government for most of the period, state parties have managed to scratch some regional power too.

Incumbency, however, can be a misleading indicator of the level of support that a party enjoys. Even if the state parties' incumbency record has been impressive, it is still necessary to confirm whether there has been a corresponding level of voters' support. I do this by looking at state parties' electoral results in regional elections.

If we consider the regional vote shares of the largest state parties as a block, we see a general pattern in all the countries under analysis. The largest state parties get fewer votes in regional elections than in state ones, a clear indication of the presence of differential voting according to the electoral level. The gap is larger in regions where there are peripheral parties because, among other reasons, voters have more choice; but it is to be found everywhere, irrespective of the presence or absence of peripheral parties. Differential voting does not affect all state parties similarly. Some are more vulnerable than others; the most vulnerable being the ones that are in direct competition for votes with peripheral parties.

Figures 7.3 to 7.5 show the evolution of the regional vote shares of the largest state parties calculated as a block.[1] In general, the largest state parties in each country gather an ample majority of the total valid vote in each region. Looking at the mean values, the range goes from a mean vote share of 75.3 per cent gathered by the largest state parties in Italian regional elections, to 64.9 per cent in the UK, with Belgium at 71.6 per cent and Spain at 69.9 per cent in the middle. There is, of course, wide intra-country variation. In Italy, the special statute regions of Valle d'Aosta and Trentino-Alto Adige, with their large peripheral parties, are those in which the largest state parties fail to obtain a majority of the regional vote (45 per cent and 49 per cent respectively) in comparison to the regions of the so-called 'red belt', where the average vote share gathered by the largest Italian state parties in regional elections is higher than 80 per cent. In Spain there is also wide variation. Again, as in Italy, the two regions with the strongest and largest peripheral parties, Catalonia and the Basque Country, are also the ones in which the two largest state parties get the poorest results in regional elections (37 per cent in Catalonia and 33 per cent in the Basque Country respectively). The rest goes to peripheral parties or to smaller state parties. In Belgium, Flanders is the region in which the three traditional parties obtain the poorest results in regional elections, with an average for the three parties together of 63.8 per cent of the valid vote. This contrasts with the situation in Wallonia and Brussels, with 76.8 and 74.2 per cent respectively.

---

[1] Belgium parties in calculation: Christian Democrats, Socialists and Liberal. British parties in calculation: Labour, Conservatives, and Liberal-democrats. Italian parties in calculation: in pre-1994 period, Christian Democrats (DC), Communists (PCI), Socialists (PSI), and post-fascists (MSI); in post-1994 period, PCI Communist splits (PDS-DS and PRC), post-fascists (AN), Conservatives (FI). Spanish parties in calculation: Socialists (PSOE) and Conservatives (PP).

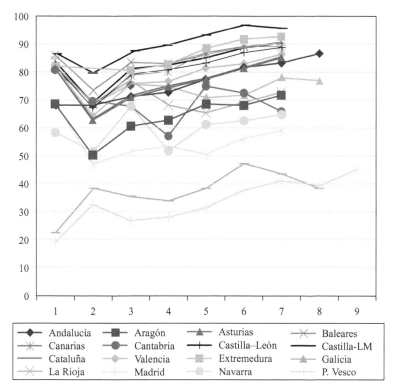

FIGURE 7.3. *Evolution of the state party family's vote shares in regional elections, Spain (% of valid vote)*

In Great Britain, it is in Scotland where state parties find their tightest regional results, with an average of 57.6 per cent of the valid vote in PR lists and 66.7 in first-past-the-post seats, as opposed to 65.2 and 70.1 per cent in Wales.

If we look now at the evolution across time, only in Italy has there been an overturn of votes for the largest state parties at the regional level (Figure 7.4). The decreasing tendency in Italy after 1994 might have been slightly less dramatic than what Figure 7.4 shows, given that the several ex-DC splinter parties have not been included in the calculation, but their contribution to the overall vote shares of state parties was not large. On the other hand, the decreasing vote shares of the state party family in Italy since the late 1970s is not particular to the regional level but has happened more fundamentally in state elections.[2] The final act of this process

---

[2] Thus, between 1970 and 2005, the vote share of the largest state parties in state elections has fallen from 78.7% to 63% in Piedmont, from 83.9% to 63.5% in Liguria, from 81% to 52.9% in Lombardy, from 81% to 67.8% in Campania, from 73.5% to 55.8% in Sicily, etc.

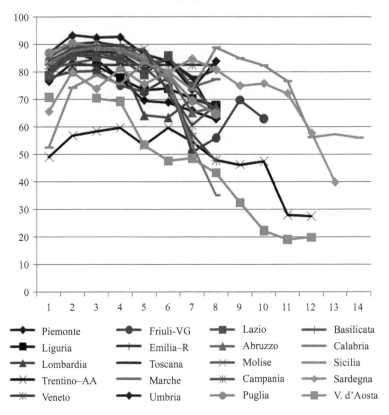

FIGURE 7.4. *Evolution of the state party family's vote shares in regional elections, Italy* (% of valid vote)

was the implosion of the Italian party system in the mid-1990s, when the Christian Democrats and PSI fragmented into various splinter organizations, disappearing as relevant electoral forces, while the Communists split into two different parties, the smaller Rifondazione Comunista and the larger Partito Democratico della Sinistra (PDS), transformed in a short period of time from being an anti-system party, kept away from office by the rest of parties, to becoming a governing party. The largest fall of state parties' vote shares in regional elections took place in the two regions with strongest peripheral parties, Val d'Aosta and South Tyrol, followed by two other special statute regions, Sicily and Sardinia.

In Scotland and Wales, state parties also have had a decreasing tendency, although a minor one compared to the one in Italy. These examples may tempt us to conclude that the presence of peripheral parties is associated with decreasing vote shares for the state party family. The findings from Spain, however, would contradict such conclusion. In the Basque Country and

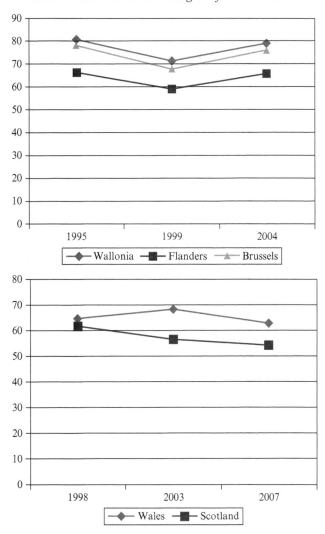

Notes: These are the results for the PR lists.

FIGURE 7.5. *Evolution of the state party family's vote shares in regional elections, Belgium and Great Britain (% of valid vote)*

Catalonia the state party family has been increasing its vote shares across time.[3] Belgium would contradict the conclusion further. The fall of the ex-state party

---

[3] The data for the Basque Country in the last regional election, in 2009, have to be taken with a bit of caution. Around 8.8% of the electors casted null votes, following the directive of the illegalised Batasuna party. If we were to recalculate the vote shares as if Batasuna had participated and had obtained 8.8% of the vote, the total vote share for the state party family would be slightly inferior.

family in 1999 was not due to the growth of peripheral parties—which had all but nearly disappeared, disbanded, or entered into coalitions with the traditional parties—but to the impressive growth of green and extreme-right populist parties in all three regions. The Vlaams Berlang (previously Vlaams Blok) is part of the category of peripheral parties as much as it is part of the extreme-right party family (a characteristic that it shares with the Lega Nord). In fact, as Jagers and Walgrave (2007) have put it, it is the VB's extreme nationalism that explains its extreme-right populism. In this sense, the fall of the ex-state party family in Flanders was in part due to the presence of a peripheral extreme-right populist party. But that would not explain the electoral loss of the francophone Socialists, Christian Democrats, and Liberals to the francophone greens (Écolo) and to the francophone extreme-right (Front National).

The growth of the state parties' vote shares in Spain has not been limited to the Basque Country and Catalonia but has been a general tendency. It is somehow paradoxical that Italy, a country with weak (with the exception of the tiny French- and German-speaking minorities)—albeit growing—peripheral parties has seen the electoral strength of its largest state parties fall whereas Spain, a country with strong peripheral parties and growing new parties, has seen the electoral results of its two largest state parties at the regional level increase. In both countries, on the other hand, state parties have used pro-periphery strategies of similar medium-low intensity (in comparison, for example, with those of Belgium). This is an indication that the presence of peripheral parties does not necessarily lead to a decreasing vote share for the state party family and that other political factors that have to do with the state party system considered as a whole are at play.

In Belgium and Great Britain only three regional elections have taken place at the time of writing this book; therefore, it is difficult to say anything conclusive for these cases. However, some tendencies concerning individual party trajectories are already visible. Labour, the party that implemented devolution, has not been rewarded in regional elections. It has lost votes in both Wales and Scotland while the other two state parties are cashing in. The Liberal Democrats, with a long reputation as supporters of decentralization, have been gaining votes election after election. On the other hand, the Conservative Party has been doing well in Wales, going from 16.5 per cent of the vote in 1998 to 21.4 per cent in 2007 in PR lists and from 15.8 per cent to 22.4 per cent in first-past-the-post seats. Also in Scotland, a Conservative recovery was at play in the second half of the 2000s, after ten years of almost complete wipe-out.[4] The ex-state

---

[4] In 1997 the Conservatives lost all their Scottish seats in the general elections. At the 2001 and 2005 elections they only managed to recover one seat. It has been the establishment of proportional representation in the Scottish regional elections that has saved the Conservatives from oblivion

parties in Belgium have managed to maintain their levels of support similar to those at the state level.

To sum up, it cannot be claimed that state parties are much worse at the regional level than at the state one in terms of political power. Despite the presence of differential voting, state parties in the regions have established power strongholds (even if sometimes shared with other parties) and, in some cases, they have obtained increasing vote shares (albeit lower than their state vote shares). Some state parties have done badly while others have done rather well. This means that devolution cannot be said to have damaged the holding on to power and the electoral fortunes of the state party family as a whole. Devolution is therefore no impediment to the achievement of regional power by state parties. The presence of peripheral parties is an extra challenge but it is not a condition *sine qua non* of state party regional failure. The decision to devolve seems less risky from this perspective.

7.4 PERMANENT DEVOLUTION?

Belgium was the only country in which the pro-periphery convergence strategy was followed by a continuous weakening of the peripheral party vote. Everywhere else, the state parties' pro-periphery moves, though more effective than before devolution, still did not bring about the expected neutralization of the peripheral party threat. Peripheral parties' electoral fortunes took a cyclical form and, every time their vote shares grew, the threatened state parties would respond with pro-periphery strategies to try to reduce the threat. This was due, on the one hand, to the in-built incentives for both peripheral and state parties to demand more competences for the regional level of government. In the race to get more regional competences from the central state, state parties in the regions did not want to be left behind.[5] On the other hand, it was due to the pro-periphery radicalization strategies successfully adopted by peripheral parties in reaction to the state parties' converging moves.

(although inexplicably they opposed the PR system), giving them 18 seats in the first Scottish Assembly.

[5] The Prime Minister of the government of Andalusia, Manuel Chaves, who is a prominent figure in the Spanish Socialist Party (president of the PSOE and general secretary of the Andalusian federation), admitted to the newspaper *El País* in 2008 that he took the initiative to reform the Statute of Autonomy of Andalusia when he considered it irreversible that Basques and Catalans were going to initiate the reform [to upgrade] of their own Statutes. According to him, 'it would have been a *strategic error* to stay outside' (*El País*, 3 March 2008, emphasis added).

For ten years after the first devolution reform of 1970, constitutional issues (i.e., the centre–periphery dimension of competition) dominated electoral campaigns in Belgium. The first reform had left many things open, because no agreement had been possible at the time. For this reason, the following ten years were a period of 'acrimonious debate' (Falter 1998: 183). The 1978 election was called as a result of disputes within the government over institutional reforms to implement the Pacte Communautaire. The new government established after the elections, which included the Flemish and francophone Christian Democrats, the Flemish and francophone Socialists and the francophone peripheral party from Brussels (FDF) faced the same disagreements with the added element of a deteriorating economy (MacMullen 1982: 193). Finally, an opportunity for getting out of the gridlock emerged in 1980, after the withdrawal of the FDF from government. For a few months, the Flemish (PVV) and francophone (PRL) Liberals joined the Christian Democrats and Socialists in government under the premiership of the Flemish Christian Democrat Wilfried Martens. Martens managed to solve part of the disagreements that had led to the gridlock over constitutional issues, although he did so by 'circumventing' the main problem, that of Brussels, as his predecessor Eyskens had done ten years earlier (MacMullen 1982; Falter 1998: 183).

The 'grand coalition' government passed a reform package in the summer of 1980. The reform established institutions for the Flemish and French communities, and the regions of Flanders and Wallonia, making them finally operational. However, the regional parliaments would not be directly elected but would be composed of the state MPs elected in each region. The regional governments, by contrast, were completely independent from the state government and were made responsible before their regional assemblies. The following election, in 1981, was the first in a long time to revolve, for a change, around economic issues. Still, even within a context of economic priorities the centre–periphery dimension managed to be present due to the prominent regional dimension of Belgian economic policy. As MacMullen explains, '[t]he 1980 institutional reforms gave a convenient focus for regional economic discontents based on calculations of relative advantage or disadvantage' (MacMullen 1982: 196). Thus, while the Walloons focused their protests on their relative poverty with respect to Flanders and demanded more aid to be poured into the region, the Flemish insisted that Wallonia was already a net beneficiary, through the fiscal system, of a sizeable redistribution from the Flemish region.

The 1987 election was again precipitated by centre–periphery conflict over the status of a village in Flanders that was populated mainly by French speakers. The dispute was particularly acute between the Flemish (CVP) and the francophone (PSC) Christian Democrats. According to Leonard's analysis of this election, 'the CVP was especially nervous of being outflanked on any issue concerning language problems by the Flemish Nationalist party, the Volksunie, which was a strong rival for its votes throughout Flanders' (Leonard 1989: 159). '[A]fter the longest government crisis in Belgian history' (Falter 1998: 187), a new government presided over by the Flemish Christian Democrat Jean-Luc Dehaene and participated in by the Christian Democrats of both communities, the Socialists of both communities, and the Flemish Volksunie, negotiated yet another constitutional agreement, this time tackling the conflictual Brussels issue. Finally, the third Belgian region would exist de facto, with its own government and a directly elected parliament.

By the early 1990s, despite the continuous electoral losses of the peripheral party family, centre–periphery conflicts had far from disappeared. On the contrary. In Wallonia and Brussels, the defence of federalism had been assumed by the francophone Socialists (PS) while the Liberals on both sides opposed too extreme federalism, arguing instead in favour of keeping a minimum Belgian identity (Fitzmaurice 1992). The position of the Liberals, however, would evolve across time towards a greater emphasis on more extreme forms of federalism, particularly after the political crisis of 1991. What was originally an ideological dispute turned into 'a conflict of nationalities' (Falter 1998: 189). In the aftermath of the crisis, a window of opportunity opened for a new constitutional reform, the one to federalize the Belgian state, finally establishing direct elections to the regional parliaments. At the 1995 elections, the VLD supported 'independent Flanders in a federal Belgium and a federal Europe' (Downs 1996: 339) while its sister party, the francophone Liberals (PRL) merged with the peripheral party from Brussels FDF.

The insatiable desire for more decentralization did not stop with the major 1993 reform. At the 2003 elections, the next step towards increased devolution was again on the agenda.[6] The Flemish parties were in favour of more decentralization while their francophone sisters wanted no further institutional reform (Fitzmaurice 2004: 152). For this election, the Flemish Christian Democrats changed the party's name to Christian Democratic and Flemish (CD & V), 'underlining its radicalization with regard to Flemish issues' (Swyngedouw 2004: 567). A process of outbidding the adversary seemed to have established itself in Belgium.

In Spain and Italy, decentralization opened a window of opportunity for the formation of new peripheral parties, to the extent that some authors see the emergence and/or strengthening of peripheral parties in these countries as institutionally induced (Pallarés and Keating 2006; Tronconi 2006; Brancati 2007). In neither country were pro-periphery convergence strategies by state parties able to prevent this emergence. Rather, it was the entrenched pro-periphery preference for decentralization that provided the appropriate incentives for this emergence to take place. In both Italy and Spain, this continuous presence of the peripheral party threat led to new rounds of decentralizing reforms.

The establishment of regional legislatures and executives offered incentives for regional politicians to create new peripheral parties from scratch. Many of the

---

[6] Market research showed a public particularly concerned about employment, public health insurance, and pensions (Swyngedouw 2004: 568).

regions that exist today in Italy and Spain as a result of the devolution reforms had no relevant peripheral mobilization prior to the establishment of regional legislatures. Peripheral parties were non-existent or, when they existed, were very weak and marginal.

In Spain, new peripheral parties from the Canary Islands, Aragon, Cantabria, Galicia, and Navarre were quite successful during the 1990s and the first years of 2000. Chunta Aragonesista, from Aragon, increased its vote share by more than 10 points since 1990. This growth was rewarded with a seat in the Spanish parliament during the last two legislatures (2000–8). Similarly, PSM-Entesa Nacionalista, from the Balearic Islands, increased its vote share throughout the 1990s reaching its best results ever in a state election at the 2004 elections, with 8.5 per cent of the vote in the region (though it was not enough to get a seat in parliament). The formation of the party Coalición Canaria in 1993, a coalition of several dispersed peripheral parties in the Canary Islands, boosted the electoral results of the Canarian peripheral party family in state elections. From an average of 10 per cent of the vote share in the region between 1979 and 1989 it went up to 25 per cent and four seats in the Spanish parliament. The Partido Regionalista de Cantabria was another success story at the regional level, since it does not present lists at the state one. Between 1986 and 2007 it went from 6 per cent to 28 per cent of the regional vote. In Galicia, the Bloque Nacionalista Galego also did very well. During the last 20 years it increased its electoral vote share by 15 points in state elections. It has had representation in the Spanish parliament since 1996. In Catalonia, Esquerra Republicana de Catalunya, a radical left peripheral party, continuously increased its vote share throughout the 1990s until reaching a peak at the 2004 state elections, with 16 per cent of the vote in Catalonia and eight seats in the state parliament, nearly as many as those from the main Catalan peripheral party, Covergència i Unió (ten seats).

These electoral results gave peripheral parties valuable parliamentary seats for state parties to achieve governing majorities (except during the years 2000–4, when the Popular Party enjoyed a majority government). There are several previous examples of this phenomenon. Between 1993 and 1995 the strategic importance of CiU for the governability of Spain was seen when, initially, it supported the Socialist Party in order to keep Felipe González in power but, later, it withdrew its support thereby forcing an early election. At the 1996 general elections, the Popular Party came out short of a parliamentary majority despite expectations to the contrary. It was the PP's first victory over the PSOE since the re-establishment of democracy and it was the first election since 1977 in which the two main state parties have gathered the largest percentage of the vote, 76 per cent. Paradoxically, 'this advance for the main "Spanish" parties formed part of an overall equation that points to the further enhancement of Catalonia's role in Spanish politics' (Gillespie 1996: 430). The PP needed the support of peripheral parties, above all that of CiU, if it was to govern. Its prospects for collaboration with the Basque and Catalan peripheral parties were not very promising, given its express opposition to further devolution during the election campaign and the party's alliances with strongly anti-Catalan peripheral parties in Aragon and Valencia. The support from Basque and Catalan peripheral parties came only after major policy concessions to the regions. It was precisely in regions with strong peripheral party support where the PP did worse, in Catalonia and the Basque Country, causing the insufficient victory in 1996. At the 2000 general elections, the peripheral parties taken together increased their electoral support by rather more than two percentage points compared to the 1996 election. The total number of regional parties with representation in the Spanish parliament increased from seven to nine and their total number of seats went from 29 to 33. At the 2004 elections the PP suffered its heaviest losses in those regions in which the party's anti-periphery strategy had led to the greatest tension regarding territorial issues: Andalusia, Catalonia, Galicia, and the Basque Country. The PP had been hostile to the idea of revising, to upgrade, the statutes of autonomy of these regions. Even after the last state elections in March 2008, when the vote had concentrated more than ever around the two main state parties, comprising 84 per cent of the total vote, the wining PSOE needed seven seats to achieve a working parliamentary majority. These seats came mainly from peripheral parties.

The Spanish Socialists won the 2004 general elections with a pro-periphery agenda. During the campaign, the Socialist leader, José Luis Rodríguez Zapatero, promised that his party would agree to initiate a revision of the statute of autonomy of all those regions that had the will to do so. This initiated a legislature (2004–8) that was heavily dominated by centre–periphery issues. The new –second generation– statutes of autonomy of several Spanish regions were elaborated and approved by the regional branches of the two main state parties or, at least, with their participation. The Popular Party participated actively in the formulation of the second generation statutes of autonomy of Valencia and the Balearic Islands which were, in turn, rejected by the peripheral parties in their respective parliaments for not taking self-government far enough. The Socialists were the initiators of the reform in Andalusia, Aragon, the Canary Islands, and Catalonia, in the last two cases in coalition with the peripheral parties in each region.

The Popular Party showed a very inconsistent policy towards the process of reform of the statutes of autonomy. It supported in Valencia policies it rejected in Catalonia; it rejected in the Andalusian parliament policies it supported in the Spanish one. This was the consequence of the internal tension that the party experienced between the interests of its central leadership and those of its regional branches. The Socialist Party was not free from this tension either, as was evident by the different approaches that the party in Catalonia and the party in Madrid maintained with respect to the reform of the Catalan statute of autonomy (Roller and Van Houten 2003).

The second Italian decentralizing reform in 1970 was not initiated as a defence against the peripheral party threat. As has already been discussed, it was the result of electoral competition between the main state parties. However, subsequent decentralizing reforms were the result of the electoral threat coming from a new peripheral party, the Northern League.[7] The Northern League was the result of merger of various regionally based 'leagues' that emerged in different Northern regions at the end of the 1970s. Initially the strongest one seemed to be the Liga Veneto, which gathered 4.2 per cent of the vote in Veneto at the 1983 state elections and was able to send a senator to Rome. After a few years, however, the Lombard League took the lead and became a great success story. Under the leadership of Umberto Bossi, the Lombard League gained ground year after year. In the 1987 state elections the Lombard League made impressive inroads into several regions of the Italian North. In Piedmont, it gathered 16 per cent of the region's vote; in Lombardy, 23 per cent; in Friuli-Venezia Giulia, 17 per cent; in Liguria, 11 per cent. In 1989, several of these 'leagues', with the Lombard League as the main organization, merged into the Lega Nord.

At the 1992 state elections, the Northern League consolidated its gains at a time when the main state parties were losing heavily. The Christian Democrats suffered severe losses in the Northern regions. Most of the votes the DC lost in the North 'seemed to go to the League whose appeal is largely based on its campaign against southern corruption and clientelism' (Hine 1992: 364), thus undermining the hegemony of the Christian Democrats in their northern bastions of Lombardy and Veneto. The Italian Communists also lost voters to the Northern League in the North, although to a smaller degree (Hine 1992: 365). The immediate response of the state parties that were most vulnerable to the Northern League growth, i.e., those of the centre-right, was to adapt 'their position by increasing the pledges for a deeper decentralization of power. On the contrary, the left—whose electorates were less susceptible to the Lega's right-wing rhetoric—did not respond strongly' (Mazzoleni 2009: 213).

The 1992 state elections were the last to take place with the old party system and the old electoral system. Between 1992 and 1994 the Christian Democrats broke into several smaller parties, the largest among which was the Partito Popolare Italiano (PPI), and the Communists split into the moderate and larger Partito Democratico di Sinistra (PDS) and the radical and smaller Partito della Rifondazione Comunista (PRC). The new electoral system was a mixed member-majoritarian system introduced for the 1994 state elections. Seventy-five per cent of the seats were selected through first-past-the-post single-member districts and 25 per cent were selected through proportional party lists. The new electoral system, therefore, had a largely majoritarian character with 'a weakly proportional

---

[7] Strictly speaking, the Northern League presents its lists wide across the Italian geography. In practice, however, it displays all the characteristics of a peripheral party, since it has a peripheral agenda of decentralization and it receives votes exclusively in those regions whose autonomy it demands and defends (Wilson 2009; Tambini 2001; Amoretti 2002). According to Warner and Varese, 'Bossi does not position himself primarily on the traditional left–right axis, but rather on the unity–secession axis' (Warner and Varese 1996: 569).

corrective' (Warner and Varese 1996: 567). As I already argued in detail in chapter 5, this system makes the peripheral party threat larger than under a proportional system. At the same time, it stimulates the formation of pre-electoral coalitions if parties are to win the majoritarian contests. These pre-electoral coalitions proceed directly to forming governing coalitions (Wilson 2009: 58).

In the 1994 state elections, the Northern League was part of the centre-right pre-electoral coalition Polo della Libertà, together with Forza Italia, founded a few months earlier by the Italian tycoon Silvio Berlusconi, the post-fascist Alleanza Nazionale (previously called Movimento Sociale Italiano), and other minor parties. This coalition was improvised just before the elections and had little internal congruence in terms of coordinated political agenda. Alleanza Nazionale was strongly pro-centralist while the Northern League was strongly pro-periphery. The centre-right coalition won the elections. The Northern League had continued its dramatic growth and became the second party in number of seats, after the new centre-right party Forza Italia. The disagreements inside the 1994 Berlusconi's government with respect to the territorial question led the Northern League to withdraw from the government, making it fall. The rapid replacement of Berlusconi's first executive by a government of technicians 'emphasised the novelty of a regionalist party setting the Italian political agenda' (Levy 1996: 2).

In 1995, a new electoral law for regional elections was introduced. It was characterized as 'PR with a majoritarian bonus' (Wilson 2009: 59). Between 80 and 90 per cent of the seats were selected through party lists in provincial constituencies. The remaining seats were selected through regional lists tied to competing candidates for regional president and allocated exclusively to the presidential candidate who obtains a plurality of the regional votes. The electoral system gave the regional presidents a new democratic legitimacy that they lacked before. In interviews realized to regional actors after the 1995 reform, Loughlin and Bolgherini show that regional actors unanimously identified the 1995 reforms as the turning point in prompting the rise in significance of regional issues: 'All interviewees agreed that territorial issues are also likely to increase in importance in future years' (Loughlin and Bolgherini 2006: 150). And so they did.

At the 1996 state elections the Northern League decided to go it alone, outside the centre-right coalition. This undermined significantly the Polo coalition in the Northern regions. The parties of the Polo received more votes than those of L'Ulivo in the PR seats although the Ulivo won the election in terms of seats. Meanwhile, the Northern League obtained fewer parliamentary seats than in 1994 even if its share of the vote increased. The victory of the centre-left coalition was precisely due to the failure of the Northern League and Berlusconi's Polo della Libertà to maintain the electoral pact in Northern Italy (Parker and Natale 2002: 665). Forza Italia lost votes both to the Northern League and the AN more than to the parties of L'Ulivo (Warner and Varese 1996: 567).

The success of the Lega in the 1996 state elections was that, finally, federalism became one of the main items on the political agenda of most parties. The elections brought to power a centre-left 'Olive-tree' coalition with Romano Prodi as Prime Minister. Under the pressure of the Lega, and also of the new directly elected regional presidents, the centre-left government initiated institutional reforms that changed radically the distribution of power between the Italian state and the regions. The reforms introduced the subsidiary principle in the exercise of administrative functions, with some exceptions in matters reserved to the state. Moreover, in the run-up to the 2001 state elections, the government also approved a reform of the Constitution which gave formal constitutional legitimacy to many of the reforms passed in the 1990s. By this time, federalism had been accepted by all main actors. Even if the centre-right placed more emphasis on pro-periphery issues than the centre-left during the 2001 campaign, the centre-left parties had already earned credibility as decentralizers. The fact that the Northern League threatened above all the parties from the centre-right and, particularly, Forza Italia, did not protect the centre-left government coalition presided over by Romano Prodi against pressure from the Italian periphery to decentralize. According to Mazzoleni, 'pressurized by the separatist Lega in the North and the lobby of the newly empowered regional presidents, the Prodi government introduced radical reforms' (Mazzoleni 2009: 209).

After its success in the 2000 regional elections, in which the Lega continued with a strongly pro-periphery discourse (although this time combined with an increased emphasis on anti-immigration issues), the party negotiated a coalitional deal in which Berlusconi's centre-right coalition agreed to deepen the process of federal reform if elected to state government (Wilson 2009).

At the 2001 state elections, the Lega entered again a new electoral coalition with Forza Italia and Alleanza Nazionale and other smaller Catholic parties. This time, however, 'the coalition was based not only on electoral pragmatism, which proved insufficient to keep the 1994 governing coalition in power for no longer than seven months, but also on a greater ideological convergence around issues such as immigration, law and order, *devolution*, tax cuts, and social security' (Parker and Natale 2002: 665, emphasis added). The centre-right coalition won the elections and Berlusconi established its second government after the 1994 fiasco. The leader of the Northern League, Umberto Bossi, was appointed Minister for Devolution and Institutional Reform and new decentralizing reforms took place. Very importantly, these reforms ended the central government's power to suspend regional legislation (Hooghe, Schakel, and Marks 2008: 190). The reforms strengthened the political, administrative, and financial autonomy for the regional authorities. All the new constitutional provisions, including those initiated by the previous Prodi government though later revised, were adopted by referendum in October 2001. Each region was required to draw up and approve its own regional constitution, something that they have been doing at different paces since the end of 2003.

The Labour Party had arrived in government in 1997 with an agenda of devolution for Scotland, Wales, and the English regions. However, while devolution for

Scotland and Wales was initiated immediately upon taking office, devolution for the English regions advanced only reluctantly during New Labour's years in office.

The Labour government's unambitious proposal offered the English regions 'indirect levers of power and modest financial capacities' (Jeffery 2006: 15). The opponents of English devolution had an easy task criticizing the proposal for unnecessarily creating just another layer of administration and bureaucracy without much substance. On the other hand, Labour's proposal insisted that elected English assemblies would only be established according to demand from below. There was a good reason behind this, since this condition would favour only Labour and not the Conservatives. The calculation was that only the northern regions, in which Labour was dominant, would ask for devolution (North-East, North-West, and Yorkshire & Humber) while Conservative-dominated southern England would not press for it. As Jeffery has put it, 'political alienation, economic disadvantage and a sense of territorial difference' of the northern English regions 'would appear to be fertile soil for regional government' (2006: 23). The regional administrations that would result from this reform would be controlled by Labour.

When doubts emerged about the degree of support that a referendum over elected regional assemblies in the North-West and Yorkshire & Humber regions would gather the Labour Party, unwilling to take the risk, only called a referendum for the North-East region (Jeffery 2006) which was electorally the least relevant of the three. The 2004 referendum in North-East England failed to pass. It was difficult to defend, given the very few powers that were to be devolved to the region. Also, the argument of the democratic deficit that was so effectively used in Scotland and Wales was unavailable in this case, since Labour was the incumbent party in Whitehall, with many ministers and MPs original from the North-East region.

A long period of Conservative government with little support in North-East England may again be the trigger that precipitates Labour into a wholehearted defence of an elected assembly with wide devolved powers in the region, as happened with Scotland and Wales. Meanwhile, the defeat of the North-East region's referendum makes 'a revival of the policy... scarcely conceivable in the foreseeable future' (Jeffery 2006: 8).

The Conservatives' opposition to devolved assemblies in the south of England, where they have overwhelming support, seems to go against my model's predictions. However, the Conservatives' strategy is fully rational. The party supports 'English votes for English laws' (only English Westminster MPs can vote on legislation that affects exclusively or mainly England). For the Conservative Party, this is the best solution to the English question since it would harm Labour while leaving intact the Conservatives' credibility as defenders of the Union. Since the Conservative Party has a large majority of its MPs elected in English constituencies, the policy of English votes for English laws would always benefit this party while Labour would have great difficulties in passing legislation in England, even if it controlled the government.

Since the first devolution reform was implemented, several new rounds of decentralization have taken place in the countries under analysis. Nothing indicates that they will be the final ones. These new rounds have been, in all cases, the result of competition between parties along centre–periphery issues and, as I keep claiming, the centre–periphery dimension is now part of everyday politics in these countries.

7.5 CONCLUDING REMARKS

I have shown in this chapter that, as hypothesized, pro-periphery moves were more widely adopted during the post-devolution period. State parties in a decentralized state were freer to defend pro-periphery positions without risking their reputations as state-wide parties and without being looked at as sheer opportunist parties by their voters. However, the wider use of pro-periphery convergence did not always result in lower electoral returns for peripheral parties. Moreover, new peripheral parties such as the Northern League, the Vlaams Blok, and the New Flemish Alliance emerged and grew dramatically in short periods of time. These parties were all characterized by radical pro-periphery agendas of a kind impossible for state parties to match. Only in Belgium could ex-state parties, those that had become de facto regional parties, attempt to match these radical agendas. Still, even in Belgium this attempt was not without difficulties—particularly for the party of the Prime Minister in the federal government. In Italy, Spain, and the UK state parties were divided between a central leadership, which defined its electoral strategies according to state-wide lines of conflict, and a set of regional branches that had incentives to adapt to the strategic context of competition in their respective regions even at the expense of the party's state-wide interests.

The persistence of the peripheral party threat, combined with the institutional incentives that state parties found to compete along territorial issues, produced new rounds of decentralizing reforms. This was facilitated and even encouraged by the asymmetric nature of the first devolution reform. This asymmetry gave regional governments with less devolved powers incentives to press for levelling-up with the regions of widest autonomy while, at the same time, making regional governments with the largest self-government powers very jealous and defensive of their differential status.

The next chapter analyses the reasons why peripheral parties persisted and some even grew despite the state parties' pro-periphery moves.

8

Peripheral Parties' Electoral Strategies
after Devolution

Despite the pro-periphery strategies used by state parties, the peripheral party threat was not neutralized all the time. This still holds true after devolution, when state parties' pro-periphery strategies were more credible than at the time when the states were unitary.

Until now, I have offered a one-sided view of the strategic game played between peripheral and state parties. I have discussed the defensive strategies developed by state parties to counteract the peripheral party threat. And yet peripheral parties are as rationally—and strategically—oriented as state parties are. As such, they respond to the pro-periphery strategies of state parties and to the new reality of decentralized multi-level politics. It is in this response, and its interaction with the wider political context, where we shall find an explanation to the endurance of the peripheral party threat.

8.1 THE COSTS OF DEVOLUTION FOR PERIPHERAL PARTIES

With the establishment of self-governing regions, peripheral parties lost the monopoly of representation of the distinctive territories and the distinctive cultural communities that they claimed to represent. After the implementation of the pro-periphery strategies initiated by state parties, whose credibility was enhanced by the devolution reforms, state parties also could—and did—claim to represent regional interests and communities. The programmatic agenda of peripheral parties was thus partially assimilated by their competitors. This left peripheral parties with a restricted space for new policy proposals and with fewer policy proposals that were distinctive of their programmatic agenda.

Besides eroding their programmatic distinctiveness, devolution increased factionalism and splits among peripheral parties for two main reasons. The first reason is that the preferences over strategy and aims were altered with the new institutional framework. Peripheral parties after devolution had increased chances to become government parties at the regional level. Incumbency was seen by some as a disadvantage, in the sense that office could come at the price of renouncing the party's core ideology and losing the party's core supporters. In such scenario, factionalism and splits would be the price to pay for losing office (Newman 1994; De Winter 1998). The second reason why decentralization increased peripheral party divisions was that the costs of party splits were reduced in the presence of regional legislatures, particularly in proportional electoral systems. Before regional legislatures existed, the cohesion of the peripheral movement was important since peripheral parties had to rely, exclusively, on regional, as opposed to state, electoral support while the game of politics took place at the state-wide level. Thus, representation in state institutions would be achieved only if peripheral parties managed to gather a large number of votes. Fragmentation of the peripheral movement into several small parties was an obstacle to parliamentary representation, thereby condemning the peripheral parties to electoral and political marginality. Once regional legislatures were established, however, the incentives changed. The likelihood of finding 'a place under the sun', even if one was just a small peripheral party, increased now that the scale was regional. Therefore, the costs of party splits were reduced. Moreover, there could be some advantages to splitting, such as acquiring blackmail potential with which to extract concessions from the larger parties in the region.

The empirical evidence from the four countries under analysis seems to confirm the effects of devolution on internal party factionalism and splits. Between 1900 and 2008 there have been a total of 64 peripheral party splits, of which 84 per cent (54) occurred after 1970. Indeed, party splits were one of the main mechanisms through which new peripheral parties were established and, as expected, they occurred considerably more often after the first devolution reforms.

At the time when the states were still centralized, the pro-periphery agenda was monopolized by one main party in each peripheral territory. This is not to deny that a majority of the European peripheral movements at an early stage were subject to internal tensions and to splits over final goals and political strategy, but more often than not there was one party coming out victorious from these disputes and maintaining the lion's share of the peripheral support. By contrast, after the establishment of regional legislatures, the number of new peripheral parties changed the landscape of party competition, making party systems more fragmented, by comparison with the previous decades. Looking at each country individually, we see that this pattern of evolution is to be found almost everywhere.

The relatively cohesive picture of peripheral parties until the first devolution reform changed afterwards to one of moderate to high fragmentation almost everywhere, as the figures for party splits showed. Between 1967 and 2007 the party of the French-speaking minority in Valle d'Aosta, Union Valdôtaine, suffered four splits: Rassemblement Valdôtaine (1967), Union Valdôtaine Progressiste (1973), Vallée d'Aoste Vive (2005), and Renouveau Valdôtaine (2006). The two major peripheral parties in Trentino-Alto Adige, the Südtiroler Volkspartei and the Partito Autonomista Trentino Tirolese, have also seen splits within their organizations. In 1989 the Union für Südtirol was formed after a split from the Südtiroler Volkspartei. In 2002, the party Trentino Autonomisti emerged after separating from Partito

Autonomista Trentino Tirolese. In Flanders, the majority peripheral party after the Second World War, Volksunie, saw its supremacy erode with time after the first split, in 1978, of a group of dissidents that formed the Vlaams Blok (today Vlaams Belang). In 2001, Volksunie split again, this time disappearing into two new parties, the New Flemish Alliance (Nieuw Vlaamse Alliantie), right-wing, and Spirit (today Vlaams Progressivien), left-wing. Also in Belgium, the main—and only—peripheral party of Wallonia during the 1960s and 1970s, Rassemblement Wallon, suffered a split in 1981, from which a new peripheral party was created, the Rassemblement Populaire Wallon, of ephemeral existence, since in 1984 it integrated into the Parti Socialiste. Splits have also been present in Northern Ireland among Irish Nationalists and Unionists. Official Sinn Féin split from Sinn Féin in 1970. The Ulster Unionist Party went through three splits between 1973 and 1974. In Wales, the main peripheral party, Plaid Cymru, suffered a split in 2000, from which a new Welsh peripheral party was established, Cymru Annibynnol. The new party, however, is quite marginal and represents no challenge for its mother-party yet. In Scotland, the peripheral and left-wing Scottish Socialist Party has very recently experienced the split of a group of dissidents that have established the new party Solidarity. In Spain the most relevant split was that suffered by the Basque Nationalist Party in 1986, which resulted in the creation of a new Basque peripheral party, Eusko Alkartasuna, more to the left and more radically pro-periphery than its mother-party.

However, it is the presence of state parties with pro-periphery agendas that posed the major challenge for the capacity of peripheral parties to continue to win votes. Peripheral parties that wanted to maximize their vote shares had necessarily to react to this challenge.

8.2 PERIPHERAL PARTIES' MOVES IN RESPONSE TO THE STATE PARTIES' PRO-PERIPHERY TACTICS

Threatened state parties that engage in pro-periphery strategies give way to threatened peripheral parties. When faced with a state party that is increasing the emphasis of pro-periphery issues in its agenda, the peripheral party will develop electoral strategies that minimize or reverse the electoral losses to the state competitor.

As I explained in chapter 2, peripheral parties will use two main centre–periphery moves to respond to the state party threat. In order to avoid losing the peripheral party's programmatic distinctiveness, peripheral parties will radicalize their pro-periphery position, moving towards the periphery extreme of the dimension. Although state parties may eventually level up with the peripheral party's new position, the risks involved in this sort of reaction will be high and, therefore, it will happen seldom. Radicalization, however, is not the most convenient response under all circumstances. For this reason, peripheral parties will enhance their repertoire with electoral strategies outside the centre–periphery dimension in the

TABLE 8.1. *Peripheral parties' electoral tactics and their measurement*

Electoral Moves	Empirical Indicator Based on CMP Data
Pro-periphery radicalization	Change of position* towards the periphery extreme of the centre–periphery dimension between elections at time t-1 and t.
Pro-periphery moderation	Change of position towards the centre extreme of the centre–periphery dimension between elections at time t-1 and t.
Issue diversification	Increase of the manifesto's issue diversity between elections at time t-1 and t.
Issue concentration	Decrease of the manifesto's issue diversity between elections at time t-1 and t.
Left–right intensification	Increase in the saliency of the left–right dimension between elections at time t-1 and t.
Left–right weakening	Decrease in the saliency of the left–right dimension between elections at time t-1 and t.

* Let us remember that the position scores of the Comparative Manifesto Project combine saliency and position.

form of issue diversification and reorientation. Issue diversification entails emphasizing an increasing number of issues that are not part of the core identity of the peripheral party in an attempt to extend its appeal beyond the voters with strong pro-periphery preferences. Table 8.1 summarizes these electoral moves and the empirical indicators that I use to measure them.

Peripheral parties use these electoral moves in combination. Each peripheral party decides what combination of centre–periphery saliency, left–right saliency, and new issues saliency is appropriate for each election. There are five possible combinations. The first, which I call the *pure centre–periphery combination*, concentrates the attention of the manifesto in fewer issues, emphasizes pro-periphery issues, and dedicates less space to left–right ones. With this combination the party signals that the defence of territorial and cultural issues is its major concern. The second, called the *pure left–right combination*, increases the attention dedicated to left–right issues in detriment to the centre–periphery ones while the diversity of the manifesto is reduced. This means that the party is not moving into new issues but is refocusing its attention from the centre–periphery dimension to the left–right one. The third combination, *the pure new issues combination*, is characterized by a reduced emphasis on both centre–periphery and left–right issues simultaneous to a diversification of the manifesto's contents. Through this combination, peripheral parties exploit a new electoral niche or make use of valence issues given that their previous monopoly of the territorial/cultural conflict has been lost. Finally, there are two *mixed strategies*. On the one hand, there is the combination of issue diversification and pro-periphery radicalization to the detriment of left–right issues. This implies that the party is reducing left–right saliency in favour of other issues while at the same time increasing the emphasis of its pro-periphery agenda. It is, therefore, a mixed strategy aimed at reinforcing the pro-periphery profile while simultaneously making an incursion into new issues. This will strengthen the image of the party as an alternative to mainstream parties. On the other hand, issue diversification may be combined with pro-periphery moderation and increased left–right saliency. It is, therefore, a mixed strategy aimed at changing the image of the party as a single-issue party exclusively concerned with narrow territorial and cultural interests to one of a party with a diversified issue portfolio and governing aspirations.

Devolution offers the peripheral party the possibility of using economic issues to increase the relevance of its pro-periphery stance. State–region relations are at the core of some economic aces of electoral competition. The distribution of financial resources among the self-governing regions and their unequal levels of development are a fundamental source of conflict in multi-level governance. Despite Meguid's affirmation that peripheral parties' issues are more susceptible to being left off the agenda 'because they are not the core economic aces around which the political system is built and on which most mainstream parties are founded' (Meguid 2008: 26), peripheral parties have excelled at using the *economic comparative grievance* as a core argument to defend the devolution of more financial resources—and more powers—to the regional level. The idea that other regions in the country—or the state itself—have more financial resources and more economic power and that this is what keeps the region behind the rest in terms of development and well-being is a powerful one among voters. The reverse idea according to which other territories in the country—or the state itself—are lagging behind and, as a result, the more advanced region is paying for the underdevelopment of the others is also an appealing idea among voters and has been widely used by peripheral parties in Catalonia, the Basque Country, Northern Italy, and Flanders.

What factors explain the choice of strategy by a peripheral party? That will depend on three main factors. First, it will depend on the centre–periphery strategies used by the two main state parties; second, on the peripheral party's past trajectory and main issue profile; and third, on the structure of party competition in the region where the peripheral party organizes itself.

It is a constant factor for all the peripheral parties under analysis that their state competitors are using a strategy of pro-periphery convergence (see chapters 6 and 7). We know, however, that there are always at least two main state parties at the state level and that they do not always use the same centre–periphery tactics. One of the state parties may decide to make an anti-periphery turn as a way to harm electorally the pro-periphery state competitor. This will render the peripheral party's strategy of radicalization more effective. The defence of anti-periphery issues by one of the two main state parties makes the 'centralist danger' of the peripheral party rhetoric a reality and, therefore, contributes to make the centre–periphery dimension the most salient one in the eyes of the voters. By contrast, when all state parties adopt pro-periphery moves the defence of the periphery becomes common to all parties in the system and the rhetoric warning of 'the centralist danger' loses credibility and appeal. The peripheral parties' need to radicalize their agenda is more difficult to justify (other than by admitting that it is a pure electoral calculation).

There is a caveat to this, however. The presence of a radical–moderate split in the peripheral party family may alter the calculations of peripheral parties. If a peripheral party competes with another peripheral party as well as with state parties the incentives to radicalize in the two scenarios just mentioned will be different. In the presence of an anti-periphery state party, both competing peripheral parties will have incentives to radicalize and even to outbid each other. In the event of a generalized defence of pro-periphery issues the moderate peripheral party will have more difficulties than the radical party to justify the need for radicalization. Only the moderate peripheral party will look opportunistic—even irresponsible—in the eyes of voters.

The peripheral party's past profile will also condition its choice of future strategy. For a peripheral party whose programmatic agenda is highly diversified and in which left–right issues occupy a large space the use of issue diversification will play a less relevant role than for a single-issue peripheral party. For these highly diversified peripheral parties, issue diversification will be more tactical and contingent on other factors at play in a particular election than a long-term strategic development. Therefore, the diversification of issues is to be expected the more the peripheral party has a single-issue profile which limits its appeal when competing with a left-wing or right-wing state party. On the other hand, the effectiveness of the diversification strategy will be enhanced by the absence of niche parties such as the greens or the anti-immigrant extreme right which can credibly claim ownership of these issues.

Finally, the structure of the party system will define the limits beyond which state parties cannot venture. When these limits disappear, state parties may follow peripheral parties in their radicalization strategy. This is what happened in Belgium after 1978, the year in which the territorial and linguistic split of the Belgian state parties was completed. At this point, as Deschower has pointed out, 'this party system context gives no incentives to parties to defend moderate positions ... *[T]hese other parties can easily follow the regionalist route and copy or even outbid the regionalists*' (Deschower 2009: 5, emphasis added). In this context, peripheral parties are more likely to attempt alternative routes to reach the electorate, such as the incorporation of new issues in their programmatic agendas.

8.3 PERIPHERAL PARTIES' RADICALIZATION AND DIVERSIFICATION STRATEGIES

The saliency and position of peripheral parties along the centre–periphery and the left–right dimensions changed across time in Belgium, Italy, and Spain,[1] an

---

[1] I have no cross-time observations for the British peripheral parties SNP, SF, UUP, DUP. The CMP data-set contains only the observations of the 2001 general election.

TABLE 8.2. *Peripheral parties' electoral moves*

Belgium (1961–95):

	1961	1965	1968	1971	1974	1977	1978	1981	1985	1987	1991	1995
RASSEMBLEMENT WALLON												
Radicalization/ Moderation					MOD	RAD	MOD	MOD				
Diversification/ Concentration					DIV	CON	CON	DIV				
LR intensification/ weakening					WEAK	WEAK	WEAK	INT				
FRONT DÉMOCRATIQUE DES FRANCOPHONES												
Radicalization/ Moderation			MOD	MOD	RAD		MOD	MOD	MOD	MOD	MOD	
Diversification/ Concentration			DIV	DIV	=		CON	DIV	CON	=	DIV	
LR intensification/ weakening			INT	INT	WEAK		WEAK	=	WEAK	INT	INT	
VOLKSUNIE												
Radicalization/ Moderation	MOD	RAD	RAD	RAD	RAD		RAD	MOD	RAD	MOD	RAD	RAD
Diversification/ Concentration	DIV	DIV	CON	DIV	CON		CON	=	CON	DIV	DIV	CON
LR intensification/ weakening	WEAK	INT	INT	WEAK	WEAK		WEAK	INT	INT	WEAK	INT	INT
VLAAMS BLOK												
Radicalization/ Moderation												RAD
Diversification/ Concentration												CON
LR intensification/ weakening												INT

Spain (1977–2008):[*]

	1977	1979	1982	1986	1989	1993	1996	2000	2004	2008
CONVERGÈNCIA I UNIÓ										
Radicalization/ Moderation				MOD	RAD	RAD	RAD	RAD	MOD	RAD
Diversification/ Concentration				CON	DIV	CON	DIV	CON	CON	CON
LR intensification/ weakening				INT	WEAK	WEAK	WEAK	INT	INT	INT

(*Continued*)

TABLE 8.2. Continued

	1977	1979	1982	1986	1989	1993	1996	2000	2004	2008
ESQUERRA REPUBLICANA DE CATALUNYA										
Radicalization/Moderation	RAD	MOD	MOD	RAD	RAD	—		RAD	RAD	MOD
Diversification/Concentration	CON	=	DIV	CON	DIV	—		CON	CON	DIV
LR intensification/weakening	WEAK	INT	INT	WEAK	WEAK	—		WEAK	WEAK	WEAK
PARTIDO NACIONALISTA VASCO										
Radicalization/Moderation	MOD	MOD	RAD	RAD	MOD	RAD		RAD	RAD	MOD
Diversification/Concentration	DIV	DIV	DIV	DIV	DIV	CON		DIV	CON	DIV
LR intensification/weakening	WEAK	WEAK	INT	INT	WEAK	INT		WEAK	INT	WEAK
EUSKO ALKARTASUNA										
Radicalization/Moderation					RAD	MOD		—	MOD	MOD
Diversification/Concentration					CON	CON		—	DIV	CON
LR intensification/weakening					WEAK	INT		—	WEAK	INT
BLOQUE NACIONALISTA GALEGO										
Radicalization/Moderation									RAD	RAD
Diversification/Concentration									CON	CON
LR intensification/weakening									WEAK	WEAK
COALICIÓN CANARIA										
Radicalization/Moderation								MOD	RAD	MOD
Diversification/Concentration								DIV	CON	DIV
LR intensification/weakening								INT	WEAK	INT
CHUNTA ARAGONESISTA										
Radicalization/Moderation										MOD
Diversification/Concentration										DIV
LR intensification/weakening										WEAK
PARTIDO ANDALUCISTA										
Radicalization/Moderation									RAD	
Diversification/Concentration									DIV	
LR intensification/weakening									WEAK	

Italy (1994–2001):**

	1994	1996	2001
LEGA NORD			
Radicalization/Moderation		RAD	MOD
Diversification/Concentration		CON	CON
LR intensification/weakening		WEAK	WEAK

* For some parties the Comparative Manifestos data-set only has a few observations.
** The Comparative Manifestos data-set only has these observations for this party.

indication that peripheral parties used saliency and position strategically when competing for votes (see Table 8.2).

Some trends are particularly salient: In Belgium, the relevance of left–right issues in the peripheral parties' manifestos increased over the years quite substantially, from a mean score of 12 per cent in the 1960s to 41 per cent in the 1990s; meanwhile the saliency of centre–periphery issues decreased, from a mean score of 15 per cent in the 1960s to a mean score of 8 per cent during the 1990s. Belgian peripheral parties reacted to the state parties' converging moves by resorting to the emphasis of issues other than the exclusively pro-periphery ones (Newman 1994; Van Haute and Pilet 2006; Deschower 2009). After the first devolution reform in 1970, the three Belgian peripheral parties moved their attention to left–right issues. Rassemblement Wallon's rhetoric turned increasingly leftist, Volksunie turned to the conservatives within its ranks and the Front Démocratique des Francophones 'split into several different factions that appealed to former Catholic, Socialist and Liberal voters independently' (Newman 1994: 47). Rassemblement Wallon was stressing its socialist origins; Volksunie was approximating the right-wing position of its immediate competitor, the Flemish Christian Democrats; the FDF was harvesting the limits of its previous catch-all strategy.

In Spain, the saliency of the centre–periphery and the left–right issues in peripheral parties' manifestos went through different phases, although the maximum levels of centre–periphery relevance took place during the period of transition to democracy, in the late 1970s. The mean saliency score of the centre–periphery dimension in peripheral parties' manifestos was 25 per cent during those years, compared to 16 per cent in the 1980s and 18 per cent and 19 per cent in the 1990s and 2000s respectively. During the 1980s, the saliency of the centre–periphery dimension decreased with respect to the years of transition. This coincided with the end of the first phase of development of the Estado de las Autonomías, since by 1983 all regional assemblies had been constituted and all the legislative framework was in place. Moreover, the 1980s was the decade of the first Socialist (majority) governments in post-Franco Spain, engaged in the establishment of a modern welfare state, and a decade of deep economic crisis and social unrest. The

Challenging the State

centre–periphery conflict was not at the top of the agenda and peripheral parties had no instrument with which to force state parties to hear their demands at the state level.

During the 1990s, centre–periphery issues became more relevant again while the saliency of left–right issues in peripheral parties' manifestos dropped from 37 per cent in the 1980s to 27 per cent during the 1990s, an indication of pro-periphery radicalization as well as of diversification into new issues such as the environment and valence issues such as government efficiency. The saliency levels reached during the 1990s remained mainly constant well into the 2000s, with a slight decrease of the left–right issues to 26 per cent and a slight increase of the centre–periphery issues to 19 per cent. This period of increased centre–periphery saliency and more intense pro-periphery positions coincides with the years of minority government in Spain. State parties needed the support of peripheral parties to pass state legislation and, in exchange for this support, peripheral parties demanded more regional autonomy (Heller 2002).

In Italy, the Lega Nord dedicated less space to both centre–periphery and left–right issues in 2001 than it did in 1994, an indicator of issue diversification into new niche issues. This is congruent with the increasingly extreme-right anti-immigrant ideology that this party has shown since 1996.

In Great Britain, the Scottish National Party and Plaid Cymru changed their tactics after the referendum defeat of the late 1970s. The SNP downplayed its support for independence and moved to the left, emphasizing working-class concerns. This strategy made sense during the long period of anti-devolutionist and neoliberal policies of Thatcher's governments. Between 1983 and 2003 the SNP received on average 23 per cent of the working-class vote, therefore representing a highly significant rival to the Labour Party (Alonso and Richards 2006). Plaid Cymru also moved to the left, increasing the emphasis on traditional left and 'new left' issues (Fowler 2003). Despite its historically low working-class vote, since the beginning of the 1980s it increased from 4.5 per cent, its lowest level in the period 1974–2001, to 12.2 per cent in 2001 (Alonso and Richards 2006). This is very likely the result of an intentional strategy on the part of Plaid Cymru to mobilize explicitly the working-class vote in order to compete with Labour. The strategy worked well. In a 2001 survey,[2] 71 per cent of those who had an opinion said that Plaid Cymru looked after the working class very closely or fairly closely. In contrast, only half of Welsh respondents considered New Labour to be looking after working-class interests. Moreover, the position of Plaid Cymru on the ideological scale moved to the left according to the views of the surveys' respondents. In 1983 its position on a scale from 1 to 10 (1 being the extreme left and 10 being the extreme right) was 5.2; by 1997 this had moved to 4.5; finally, according to the data from the 2005 British Election Study, Plaid Cymru was placed by

---

[2] 'Devolution and Constitutional Change', no. 4766.

respondents at 4.3. Simultaneously, Welsh respondents placed the Labour Party increasingly to the right: from value 3.3 in 1983 to value 4.1 in 1997 to value 5.1 in 2005 (Alonso and Richards 2006). Plaid Cymru's left turn, however, brought divisions within the party, since traditionally it had included 'a diversity of members with the whole axis of left/right opinion reflected in its membership' (McAllister 2001: 182).

Comparing the levels of fluctuation of the left–right and the centre–periphery positions in peripheral parties' manifestos, it is possible to identify two types of parties (see Table 8.3). On the one hand, there are those peripheral parties whose left–right position across time fluctuated to a larger extent than their centre–periphery stance. Among them were Volksunie and the Front Démocratique des Francophones in Belgium and the Basque and Catalan peripheral parties together with Partido Andalucista and Chunta Aragonesista in Spain.[3] These parties used tactics of left–right repositioning to a greater extent than they developed electoral

TABLE 8.3. *Fluctuation of left–right and centre–periphery position scores in peripheral parties' manifestos*

Country	Party	Left–Right Positional Fluctuation[*]		Centre–Periphery Positional Fluctuation
Belgium	Volksunie	3.87	>	0.58
(1946–2003)	Vlaams Blok	0.01	<	1.47
	Front Démocratique des Franc.	1.48	>	0.62
	Rassemblement Wallon	0.32	<	0.76
Spain	Convergència i Unió	18.1	>	0.20
(1977–2008)	Esquerra Republicana de Cat.	0.33	>	0.23
	Partido Nacionalista Vasco	0.89	>	0.18
	Eusko Alkartasuna	0.35	>	0.25
	Coalición Canaria	0.07	<	0.23
	Bloque Nacionalista Galego	0.10	< =	0.11
	Partido Andalucista	0.28	>	0.11
	Chunta Aragonesista	0.25	>	0.22
Italy	Lega Nord	0.41	<	9.6
(1946–2001)				

[*] The levels of fluctuation of the position scores are the coefficient of variation of the centre–periphery and the left–right position scores of a party's manifestos across time.

[3] Coalición Canaria and Bloque Nacionalista Galego show very low positional fluctuation in both dimensions, in clear contrast with the other parties. This means that they have not moved their left–right and centre–periphery positions in any relevant degree across time. For this reason, I have excluded these parties from either of the two groups identified.

212

tactics in the centre–periphery dimension of competition, where they had a con-solidated reputation and credibility that they cherished and protected. This is particularly the case among the Spanish peripheral parties, which showed a low coefficient of variation of their centre–periphery positions. The implication is that these parties were more consistent on the centre–periphery dimension which is their primary dimension of competition and the one where strategic behaviour took precedence over tactics. On the left–right dimension, by contrast, tactical decisions dominated over long-term strategies.

The second group of peripheral parties is constituted by Vlaams Blok, Rassem-blement Wallon, and Lega Nord. The parties in this group have in common that the fluctuation of the centre–periphery position scores was larger than that of the left–right ones, an indication that the parties' centre–periphery profile had been subject to important changes with the passage of time and had been used tactically more often than their left–right positions. This result raises a question: what did these parties share that can explain this comparatively more uncommon behaviour?

Two out of three, Vlaams Blok and Lega Nord, shared an extreme-right anti-immigrant ideology and, particularly in the case of the Vlaams Blok, an anti-system attitude. This profile was used strategically by these parties once the pro-periphery agenda was incorporated into the state parties' manifestos. Following the state parties' strategies of convergence, Vlaams Blok and Lega Nord moved to empha-size new niche issues that at times took precedence over the separatist stance.

This precedence is confirmed if we look at the profile of these parties' elector-ate. According to the 1995 General Election Study of Belgium, 25 per cent of those respondents who voted for Vlaams Blok did so due to its anti-immigrant stance while another 11 per cent declared it was as a revenge or protest against politics and the political class. Only 1 per cent gave their vote to VB because of its defence of Flanders and the Flemish and a negligible 0.6 per cent did so because of VB's Flemish nationalist values.[4] According to Deschower, '[t]he breakthrough was not due to its regionalist or separatist programme, but to its ability to combine national (regional) pride with themes related to immigration and security' (Deschower 2009: 17). The anti-immigrant attitudes of the Lega Nord voters were also stark. According to the 2001 Italian post-electoral survey, 68 per cent of LN's voters completely agreed with the statement that 'in case of job scarcity Italians should be preferred to immigrants' and 19 per cent completely agreed that 'immigrants are a threat to [Italian] culture and identity'. The respective figures for those who fairly agreed were 18 per cent and 36 per cent. At the same time, regional identity was not particularly strong among LN voters in 2001: 30 per cent of respondents who had voted for the Lega Nord felt that they belonged to their region more than anywhere else, while an equivalent 31 per cent felt that they belonged to Italy.

---

[4] Unfortunately, the 2003 General Election Study did not include this question so it is not possible to see the evolution across time.

TABLE 8.4. *Peripheral parties' electoral moves: frequencies*

Combination of Electoral Tactics	All Countries		BELGIUM		SPAIN	
	%	Frequency	%	Frequency	%	Frequency
Pure Centre–Periphery	26.3	15	18.2	4	30.3	10
Pure Left–Right	22.8	13	22.7	5	24.2	8
Pure New Issues	28.1	16	36.4	8	21.1	7
New Issues + CP	10.5	6	4.5	1	15.1	5
New Issues + LR	12.3	7	18.2	4	9.1	3
Total	100	57	100	22	100	33

Compared to the Lega Nord and Vlaams Blok, the positions of Rassemblement Wallon along the centre–periphery dimension fluctuated much less across time, though this fluctuation was double the party's fluctuation along the left–right divide. In contrast to its Belgian counterparts, Rassemblement Wallon had a strong leftist profile (Van Haute and Pilet 2006: 309) that anchored its left–right positions across time to a greater extent than the more ideologically catch-all Volksunie and Front Démocratique des Francophones. These parties, by contrast, moved from an initially plural ideological profile, facilitated by a heavy emphasis on pro-periphery issues that these parties framed as cutting across class divisions, to a more left-leaning or right-leaning repositioning.

Let us turn to discuss the combination of electoral moves that were used by peripheral parties (shown in Table 8.2) and their diverse degrees of success in terms of electoral results. Table 8.4 shows the relative frequencies of the combined moves of peripheral parties in Belgium and Spain (I have not enough observations for Italy and only one for the UK). The most used combination reflects the dominant strategy of peripheral parties in each country.

In the three countries as a whole, the dominant strategy was the emphasis on new issues to the detriment of pro-periphery and left–right issues (28 per cent of observations), followed very closely by the pure centre–periphery combination (26 per cent of combinations) and by the pure left–right combination (23 per cent of observations). Thus we can see that radicalization was not always peripheral parties' preferred option. These parties did make extensive use of issue diversification and left–right repositioning as well. There are, however, important country differences. Thus, while peripheral parties in Belgium tended to adopt tactics of diversification emphasizing new issues untouched by mainstream parties, peripheral parties in Spain concentrated their strategic response mainly in emphasizing and intensifying their centre–periphery profile.

This confirms the hypothesis that issue diversification will be more used by parties with a strong single-issue profile. We know from chapter 3 that Spanish peripheral parties had much more diversified manifestos since the beginning of their trajectories than Belgian peripheral parties. Therefore, the diversification of issues in parties' manifestos was a more urgent matter for peripheral parties in the Belgian context, where sticking to a single-issue profile was limiting these parties' electoral growth. For example, in a party congress in 1969, the Volksunie repre-sentatives took the explicit decision to propose a global project to the electorate instead of restricting the party's agenda to the Flemish peripheral cause (Wauters 2005; Van Haute and Pilet 2006). They did so with the clear intention of extending their electoral appeal and maximizing their vote. Years later, in 1985, the electoral defeat at the elections was attributed to the outsized dispersion of the party's programmatic profile and the Volksunie's president, Vand der Elst, proposed to refocus the party's agenda on pro-periphery issues rather than socio-economic ones (Van Haute and Pilet 2006).

Diversification into other issues was also extensively used by the Lega Nord in 1994 and 2001, and in the UK by Plaid Cymru and the SNP, as we have already seen. In the UK, issue diversification was used in particular after the referendum defeat of the late 1970s, during Thatcher's years in government. However, after devolution in 1997, we see a return to the emphasis of centre–periphery issues in state elections. During the 2001 election, the SNP campaign 'focused tightly on three connected issues', two of them related to the improvement and funding of public services and one concerned with 'the prospect of full fiscal autonomy for the Scottish Parliament' (Lynch 2002: 197). Plaid Cymru, by contrast, ignored centre–periphery issues and concentrated on conveying an image to the left of the Labour Party (Trystan 2002), a strategy that had worked so well in the 1999 Welsh parliamentary elections. In the 2003 Welsh elections, Plaid repeated the strategy, but this time the results were not as good as expected. Welsh Labour had had time to move to the left since the 1999 elections and had radicalized its left-wing message, following Plaid's re-positioning strategy (Jones and Scully 2003). On this occasion, it worked better for Welsh Labour.

The aim of peripheral parties' electoral moves was to win votes at election time or, at a minimum, to stop losing them. Table 8.5 shows the relationship between the combinations of tactics used and electoral performance.

There is a common pattern in Belgium and Spain. The dominant strategies in each country were not the most successful ones. Other factors, already advanced in the previous section, influenced the degree of effectiveness of the peripheral parties' electoral moves.

Table 8.6 shows the relationship between the tactics of issue diversification and electoral performance, taking into account the presence or absence of other niche parties. In Spain there were no relevant niche parties. Therefore, in Spain, we cannot compare the strategy of diversification in the presence and absence of niche parties. However, Belgium is a good case for such test. In Belgium, green parties began to gather relevant electoral records in the 1980s and the main extreme-right anti-immigrant party, Vlaams Blok (also a peripheral party), was not created until 1978. For this reason, we have used Belgium before and after 1980 as a measure of the presence or absence of niche parties.

TABLE 8.5. *Peripheral parties' electoral moves and electoral performance*

Electoral moves	All Countries			BELGIUM			SPAIN		
	Party Gains Votes %	Party Loses Votes %	N	Party Gains Votes %	Party Loses Votes %	N	Party Gains Votes %	Party Loses Votes %	N
Pure Centre–Periphery	33	67	15	0	100	4	40	60	10
Pure Left–Right	46	54	13	40	60	5	50	50	8
Pure New Issues	37	62	16	50	50	8	29	71	7
New Issues + CP	50	50	6	0	100	1	60	40	5
New Issues + LR	43	57	7	75	25	4	0	100	3
All combinations	40	60	57	41	59	22	39	61	33

TABLE 8.6. *Green Party presence and the effectiveness of issue diversification in Belgium*

Electoral Tactics	Presence of Niche Parties	Party Loses Votes at Election %	Party Gains Votes at Election %	N
Issue diversification	Niche parties	50	50	6
	No niche parties	33	67	6
Issue concentration	Niche parties	60	40	5
	No niche parties	86	14	7

According to the data in Table 8.6, the use of issue diversification tactics in Belgium was only effective while niche parties were absent from the electoral game. It was then that peripheral parties could widen their appeal by introducing new issues that no other parties were emphasizing yet. The environment was one such issue. The environment was strongly emphasized by Volksunie during the 1970s, being a pioneer in this respect (Deschower 2009: 7). The emergence of the Flemish green party Agalev changed the political scenario because voters attracted by the ecological and anti-militarist stance of Agalev moved their vote to it.

The emergence of a relatively strong green party in the UK at the end of the 1980s was also a blow to the electoral prospects of Plaid Cymru and the SNP. The incursion of Plaid Cymru into environmental issues had been taking place since the mid-1980s. At the 1989 European elections, the Green Party emerged as the third political force in some Welsh constituencies, with Plaid Cymru pushed to fourth position (Fowler and Jones 2006) and left with fewer prospects of extracting electoral benefit from its emphasis on environmentalist policies. Plaid's reaction was to enter into an electoral alliance with the Greens in 1991–5, which contributed to strengthen its reputation as a party with environmentalist worries. Although the alliance was short-lived, the electoral success it experienced would subsequently benefit Plaid, which emerged as a strong political force within the

National Assembly of Wales, while the Greens never repeated the electoral success that they managed in coalition with Plaid (Fowler and Jones 2006: 328). In Scotland, the Scottish Green Party made relevant breakthroughs in the 2003 Scottish elections. The Greens' strategy of convergence towards Scottish separatism (the Scottish Green Party assumed the SNP's agenda of independence) may be part of the explanation for this growth (Fowler and Jones 2006: 329).

Anti-immigration was another such niche issue that peripheral parties could exploit to their benefit. The anti-immigration card was played in Belgium by Vlaams Blok and in Italy by Lega Nord as part of their strategy of issue diversification, but not until the late 1980s. It worked very well for both parties in electoral terms. The Vlaams Blok has been the only peripheral party to survive intact in the Belgian political arena. In contrast to the Volksunie and the Flemish Green Party, Vlaams Blok benefited from the fact that no other anti-immigration niche party emerged for a long time, meaning that it had no competition as the 'owner' of the issue. In the case of the Lega Nord, the strategic use of anti-immigration issues grew particularly after the Lega had won the 2001 state elections in coalition with Forza Italia and Alleanza Nazionale. The implementation by state parties of the Lega's devolutionary agenda put an end to the Lega's monopoly of the pro-periphery issues and, therefore, the Lega Nord moved into issue diversification. The choice of anti-immigration as the new issue to emphasize placed the Lega Nord in an advantageous situation with respect to the state parties, given that it had a long tradition in anti-immigration statements and, therefore, an already built credibility as owner of the issue.

The reader may wonder why it seemed so easy, even 'natural', for these peripheral parties to move into the anti-immigration niche issue. The answer is that, being peripheral parties, (minority) ethnic nationalism was a strong component of their ideology and *nativism* (i.e. ethnic nationalism) is typical of extreme-right parties with a strong anti-immigrant agenda (Mudde 2007).

Between the 1994 and the 2001 elections, however, the Lega Nord made use of pro-periphery radicalization with very good results. As we have already seen in chapter 6, during Berlusconi's first coalition government in 1994 the Lega did not see any policy advances on its pro-periphery proposal during the campaign and eventually removed its support, leading to the government's fall after only seven months in office. After the 1994 fiasco, which caused much internal divisions within the party, the Lega's leader returned 'to the only strategy he knew that would bring him to heel, and galvanise it into further action: Northern nationalism' (Tambini 2001: 130). In the aftermath of the government's fall, the Lega intensified its identity discourse. The party's newspaper was renamed *La Padania* and a 'Parliament of the North' was symbolically established in Mantova in May 1995. At a meeting of the 'Parliament of the North' a year later, Bossi claimed that 'federalism is no use anymore' (Tambini 2001: 130). According to Tambini, the reason for this rejection of federalism is to be found in the fact that federalism 'had been taken up by the other parties, such as Forza Italia' (Tambini 2001: 131).

During the 1970s, Belgian parties used pro-periphery radicalization even if it did not bring about good electoral results. This was a period of particularly acrimonious debate in Belgium over the centre–periphery conflict. Centre–periphery issues, in the form of proposals for constitutional reform, dominated electoral campaigns. It was not only the Belgian peripheral parties that were concentrating their focus on pro-periphery issues in their manifestos; as a matter of fact, they did so in response to the concentration followed by the state parties' manifestos. It took some years for peripheral parties to see that the territorial and cultural split of state parties unfolding before their eyes was rendering the radicalization strategies ineffective. Only then did peripheral parties change their dominant strategies. Consequent tactics moved to issue diversification and focused more efforts on competing with the ex-state parties in the left–right dimension. This sometimes led Belgian peripheral parties to pursue simultaneous centre–periphery and left–right radicalization, as did the Volksunie during the 1990s with disastrous consequences (Wauters 2005).

Spanish peripheral parties returned to radicalization strategies during the 1990s and 2000s, a period characterized by the emergence of minority governments at the state level for which the support of peripheral parties was necessary in order to achieve parliamentary majorities and pass legislation. Spanish peripheral parties always declined invitations by state parties to participate in government coalitions. They preferred to offer external support instead, a strategic decision that with time proved right, if we think of the disastrous results that the participation in state coalition governments had for Belgian peripheral parties. The first such minority government emerged out of the 1993 state elections, when the Spanish Socialists won without a majority and had to rely on the external support of the Catalan Convergència i Unió and the Basque Nationalist Party to approve legislation. It was precisely the Catalan party which forced the government to call for new elections in 1996 when it decided to withdraw its support (Vallés 1994: 90). During the minority government of the Popular Party, between 1996 and 2000, the Catalan party Convergència i Unió, the peripheral party from the Canary Islands Coalición Canaria, and the Basque Nationalist Party concentrated their efforts on extracting centre–periphery concessions in exchange for parliamentary support (Heller 2002). The same can be said about Zapatero's minority government of 2004–8. During this period, Spain engaged in a territorial debate of unseen intensity and polarization since the late 1970s and early 1980s, when the first statutes of autonomy were negotiated and approved. Between 2005 and 2007, new—second generation— statutes of autonomy for Aragon, Andalusia, Balearic Islands, Catalonia, Valencia, and Castile-Leon were discussed and approved by the Spanish parliament.[5] The

---

[5] The draft statute for the Basque Country proposed by the Basque parliament in 2005 was rejected by the Spanish legislature for its radicalism. The declared reasons for rejecting the draft proposal from the Basque parliament were that the draft statute did not have majoritarian support in the Basque Country (it was backed by 39 out of 74 seats, enough to be legal, but not to be legitimate) and that it went beyond the Spanish Constitution (in other words, it was believed to be unconstitutional). On the

negotiation of new statutes of autonomy had been the way chosen by Spanish peripheral parties to obtain what had been impossible in the early 1980s.

The pro-periphery radicalization strategy reflected in the demand for recognition of the regions as nations.[6] This demand was rhetorical and symbolic more than anything else. Whether the statute of autonomy defines the territory and its inhabitants as a nation, as a historical nationality, or as a region, has no de iure effect on the scope of self-government that it can incorporate (Aja 2003: 200). It has, however, political consequences. It is a way of 'strengthening the symbols of identity' of the different peoples (Puigcercós, ERC, Diario de Sesiones del Congreso de los Diputados, 23 May 2006, p. 8950). The governing Socialist Party rejected that the new statutes of autonomy explicitly defined their regional parliaments as nations. Simultaneously, however, the use of the term 'nation' was accepted through the back door. It was accepted, after harsh negotiations, in the preamble of the new statute of autonomy of Catalonia. And it was accepted, albeit in a convoluted formulation, in the statute of autonomy of Andalusia, where it was called 'national reality'.

Table 8.7 shows the relationship between the strategy of pro-periphery radicalization and electoral performance in the presence and absence of a state party with an anti-periphery polarization agenda. I have already shown in the previous chapter that state parties engaging in anti-periphery moves were very few after the first devolution reform. For reasons beyond my control, the CMP data for peripheral parties are majoritarily concentrated in the period after 1970, with only a few observations for Belgium in the 1960s. This is the reason why the number of observations of anti-periphery state parties is so small.

According to the data in Table 8.7, the hypothesis saying that the presence of anti-periphery state parties renders the strategy of radicalization more effective seems to find some confirmation. However, there is a need to be cautious given the few observations that fall into the table's cell 'radicalization strategy plus vote

---

other hand, the draft statute for the Canary Islands was retrieved by the representatives of the regional parliament in the middle of the process of discussion at the Spanish parliament.

[6] For example, the question of how to define the people of Andalusia, whether as a 'nation', a 'nationality', or a 'national reality', occupied a sizeable part of the debate to negotiate a new statute of autonomy for Andalusia among all the parties represented at the Andalusian parliament. Against the position maintained by the Partido Popular, for which Spain is one nation-state, the peripheral party Partido Andalucista and part of the Andalusian left claimed that Andalusia was a nation and resented the accusations of banality by the Spanish right (Diario de Sesiones del Parlamento de Andalucía, 2 May 2006). The issue of the definition of Andalusia as a nation was so important for the representatives of the peripheral party Partido Andalucista that they did not give their support to the new statute of autonomy on the basis of it. The mere fact that these discussions were taking place was already a victory for peripheral parties. This victory was implicitly celebrated by one parliamentarian from the Catalan peripheral party Esquerra Republicana de Catalunya who, during the debate in the Spanish parliament, declared: 'Who would have said twenty years ago that the Statute of Autonomy of Andalusia would contain the concept of national reality!' (Puigcercós, Diario de Sesiones del Congreso de los Diputados, 23 May 2006, p. 8951).

TABLE 8.7. *Peripheral parties' radicalization and electoral performance*

Pro-periphery Radicalization	Presence of Anti-Periphery State Party	Party Loses Votes at Election %	Party Gains Votes at Election %	N
Yes	Yes	0	100	4
	No	64	36	28
No	Yes	83	17	6
	No	61	39	23

gain'. Five out of the six cases in which there was a state party's anti-periphery move although no radicalization was used by peripheral parties correspond to Spanish peripheral parties in the 2008 elections. Why did peripheral parties abstain from further emphasizing pro-periphery issues given that a state party with an openly anti-periphery agenda was present, the Popular Party?

In the Spanish general election of 2008, peripheral parties dedicated more space in their manifestos to valence issues such as governmental efficiency, technology and infrastructure, and welfare state expansion, or to niche issues such as the environment and minority groups (immigrants, handicapped, homosexuals, etc.) than they did in 2004. The result was a diminished presence of pro-periphery issues. The reason may be the following. The 2004–8 legislature years, as we have already seen, were characterized by relevant advances in the territorial question, with second generation statutes of autonomy approved that gave more power to the regions. This fact would have made the insistence on pro-periphery demands on the part of peripheral parties redundant and, in a way, harmful to their reputations. Insisting on pro-periphery radicalization in the face of a strongly adversarial Popular Party would have benefited the pro-periphery PSOE more than it would have benefited the peripheral parties. The 2008 campaign was characterized by a high polarization between the PSOE and the PP (Barreiro 2008; Maravall 2008; Sampedro and Seoane 2008). The Popular Party made abundant use of the argument that the PSOE's pro-periphery policies were contributing to the break-up of Spain while the Socialists' counter-argument claimed that the PP was artificially exacerbating territorial conflicts. An anti-periphery strategy such as the one initiated by the Popular Party was so aggressive that it had the effect of grouping all voters afraid of the PP's extremism—pro-periphery, left and centre-left voters alike—around the Socialist Party. This has been sufficiently demonstrated by Maravall in his detailed account of these elections and of the PP's electoral strategy. Peripheral parties suffered severe electoral losses in the 2008 general elections because the fear of the PP led many pro-periphery voters to vote for the Socialists (Maravall 2008: 119). If peripheral parties had emphasized centre–periphery issues during the campaign after their demands had in great part been met in the period between 2004 and 2008 by the Socialist government they might have lost even more votes.

Belgian peripheral parties were not less rational in their strategies than Spanish, Italian, or British parties. Most analysts attribute the electoral weakening, and eventual disappearance, of peripheral parties in Belgium to the loss of distinctiveness of their pro-periphery agenda in a context of generalized defence of decentralization by state parties (Wauters 2005; De Winter 2006; Van Haute and Pilet 2006; Deschower 2009). Belgian peripheral parties met the majority of their objectives and, as a result, these parties lost their 'unique selling point' and their appeal among voters (Wauters 2005: 348).

Having the agenda fulfilled, however, was never the real problem. Also in Spain, Italy, and the UK, peripheral parties had been progressively meeting their objectives—at least their short- and medium-term ones. When peripheral parties see their pro-periphery policy preferences met, they can always use strategies of radicalization in order to recover their lost distinctiveness and the political initiative. Peripheral parties in Belgium used radicalization strategies, as did peripheral parties everywhere else. This radicalization 'could be interpreted as the construction of new goals to produce new reasons to exist, and as a desperate quest to get back a withdrawing electorate' (Van Haute and Pilet 2006: 309). The problem in Belgium was that radicalization was not effective after the territorial and linguistic split of the state parties and eventually peripheral parties gave up on it. Belgian state parties were free to push their pro-periphery agendas as far as the peripheral parties were willing to take them and even beyond. Therefore, if peripheral parties were to survive, they had to find a new niche with which to combine their extreme pro-periphery positions. Only the parties that found this niche (Vlaams Berlang and the NV-A) survived and thrived. In Italy, Spain, and Great Britain, by contrast, state parties were limited by their being state-wide parties. They could not follow peripheral parties everywhere, and this left space for peripheral parties along the centre–periphery dimension to continue to grow, and to push their agendas further.

8.4 THE BATTLE FOR ISSUE OWNERSHIP

Winning votes is not the same as winning elections. We explain the former attending to what factors influence the vote of a person; we explain the latter attending to what factors influence the formation of electoral majorities (Maravall 2008). Large mainstream state parties worry above all about winning the election; smaller peripheral parties worry mainly about winning more votes, votes that will give them political influence.[7] Obviously, the formation of electoral majorities requires winning votes. Before political parties can be large enough to win elections, they need to win votes

---

[7] In regional elections, large peripheral parties also care about winning the election.

and build themselves an electoral constituency. However, winning elections and winning votes do not necessarily require the same electoral strategies. Winning elections is sometimes a question of trading votes, of forming alternative electoral majorities. Winning more votes is about adding up, not about trading.

In order to build an electoral constituency, peripheral parties need to be the preferred choice among voters with intense pro-periphery preferences. To maximize their vote shares, however, peripheral parties need to be the preferred party also among moderate centre–periphery voters. The central position of the centre–periphery dimension is where the largest number of voters concentrates in the countries under analysis in this book[8] (see chapter 4). The problem is that dominating the centrist space and the pro-periphery extreme simultaneously implies a trade-off. The more the party wins at the centre the more it loses at the extreme. A vote-maximizing strategy always comes with a dilemma. This dilemma was best discussed by Przeworski and Sprague in their analysis of socialist parties in Europe:

> Whether parties deliberately restrict their appeal to specific groups or attempt to conquer the entire electorate, their opportunities are limited by the heterogeneity of developed capitalist societies. In a heterogeneous society, no party can win the support of everyone without losing the support of someone, because some other party will put in the wedge. (Przeworski and Sprague 1986: 183)

Thus, when socialist parties moved their appeal from the workers to the masses, they found it increasingly difficult to recruit and maintain the support of workers (Przeworski and Sprague 1986). Peripheral parties face similar trade-offs. Vote-maximizing peripheral parties need to appeal to voters beyond their cultural and territorial identities, particularly if they face competition coming from other peripheral parties and if the minority is not demographically large. However, when the peripheral parties' appeal is so extended, they will face competition from state parties willing to 'put in the wedge'.

Smaller peripheral parties with a more radical agenda and a very ideological base of support will tend to consolidate their domination of the pro-periphery extreme. Large peripheral parties with a more moderate agenda will try to dominate the centrist space without losing their grip of the intense pro-periphery voters, although if pushed to choose between one and the other the choice will be contingent upon the circumstances particular to each case. In the Basque Country, for example, the outlawing of the separatist party Batasuna, which would no longer participate in state elections after 1998, gave the Basque Nationalist Party a unique opportunity to become the majority party among extreme pro-periphery voters as long as the party opted for a radicalization strategy, which it did.

---

[8] The pro-centre extreme in Belgium and the pro-periphery extreme in Spain host more voters than the opposite extremes, although the voters in these relatively more populous extremes are always considerably less numerous than the number of voters that place themselves in the centre of the scale.

Besides declarations and rhetoric, peripheral parties will use office to change the distribution of centre–periphery preferences in society. This will be done through the implementation of *nation-building* public policies that will move the electoral majority into a preference for pro-periphery positions. Peripheral parties are well aware that 'policies produce politics' (Schattschneider 1935).[9] Thus, if they manage to increase the number of voters with intense pro-periphery preferences, the strategies of radicalization will bring them better electoral results.

This section is an exploration of the effects that political parties' strategies had on their electoral weight among the different constituencies along the centre–periphery dimension. I want to know in the first place to what extent the anti-periphery and pro-periphery moves of state parties had an impact on anti-periphery and pro-periphery voters. In other words, I want to know to what extent state parties that used strategies of pro-periphery convergence displaced peripheral parties as the 'owners' of the pro-periphery agenda while state parties that used anti-periphery polarization became the 'owners' of the anti-periphery agenda. Second, I want to find out whether peripheral parties managed to be the largest party among pro-periphery voters and how much of the centrist space of the centre–periphery dimension they managed to get hold of.

The data in this section come from electoral surveys in Belgium, Spain, and the UK. Unfortunately, as we already know, Italian electoral surveys do not ask the respondents' self-placement along a centre–periphery dimension of competition and therefore they cannot be used for our purposes.

I do not have survey data for the period of the 1970s in Belgium (see Table 8.8). The earliest data are from 1991. By then, the francophone Rassemblement Wallon (RW) had already disappeared as an electoral force and the Front Démocratique des Francophones (FDF) was about to enter into a coalition with the francophone liberals. Therefore, I am unable to say anything about the electoral weight of francophone peripheral parties among pro-periphery voters other than to ascertain the negligible influence that both had in the 1990s among the electorate as a whole. Survey data from Wallonia show that the francophone Socialists, Christian Democrats, and Liberals (former state parties) dominated the space occupied by the extreme pro-periphery respondents between 1991 and 2003, although the weight of each of them varied through time. The francophone Socialist Party always had a larger support among pro-periphery than among anti-periphery respondents, being always the largest party among extreme pro-periphery respondents. Nevertheless, in 1991 the Socialists' electoral majority in Wallonia was so large that the party dominated most sections of the electorate. The francophone Liberals, on the other hand, found increasingly larger support among anti-periphery respondents through

[9] The application of *policy feedback* to the political behaviour of citizens is still an under-explored area in political science, with some relevant exceptions (Ingram and Smith 1993; Schneider and Ingram 1993, 1997, 2005). As Mettler and Soss have put it, 'policy-feedback scholarship still pays insufficient attention to citizens as political actors' (Mettler and Soss 2004: 60).

the years. By 2003, the francophone Liberals had overtaken the Socialists as the majoritarian party among extreme anti-periphery respondents, even if their growth was also visible in all other sections of the electorate (in parallel to the increase of their vote share). The francophone Christian Democratic Party, in contrast to its Flemish sister, always had weak support among Walloon extreme pro-periphery respondents but its hold of anti-periphery respondents decreased with time in favour of the Liberals.

In Flanders, peripheral parties found the largest support among extreme pro-periphery respondents, although their electoral weight in the pro-periphery extreme is considerably smaller than that of peripheral parties elsewhere, as we will see below. Flemish peripheral parties taken together did not gather the majority of the votes among extreme pro-periphery respondents; ex-state parties did. In 1991, Volksunie had 20 per cent of the vote among extreme pro-periphery respondents and this made it the majoritarian party in this section of the electorate. However, ex-state parties followed very closely (let us remember that the Flemish party system was highly fragmented into several parties of similar size). The Flemish Christian Democrats had 18 per cent of the extreme pro-periphery respondents and the Liberals and Socialists followed with 15 per cent and 14 per cent respectively. Another 18 per cent of extreme pro-periphery respondents supported the other peripheral party, the Vlaams Blok. Therefore, the space occupied by extreme pro-periphery respondents did not belong to any party in particular, peripheral or not, but was evenly distributed among all parties in the electoral arena. Flemish peripheral parties did not 'own' the pro-periphery space in the early 1990s. The data at hand do not tell us whether they lost credibility as the 'owners' of pro-periphery issues or whether they never had such credibility. However, given their impressive electoral performance in the 1970s, it is more likely that they had earned this credibility but, eventually, they lost it.

The centrist space of the centre–periphery dimension in Flanders was dominated in 1991 by the Flemish Christian Democrats, with the support of 30 per cent of the centrist respondents. By 2003, however, the Christian Democrats had lost their hold of the centrist vote in favour of the Flemish Socialists (in coalition with the Volksunie's left-wing split, Spirit). At the same time, Vlaams Blok had displaced Volksunie as the majoritarian party among extreme pro-periphery respondents, growing from 18 per cent in 1991 to 33 per cent in 2003. The interesting aspect of this openly separatist party is that between 1991 and 2003 it received increasing support from the extreme anti-periphery respondents too, from 7 per cent in 1991 to 11 per cent in 2003. This means that VB was getting electoral support for reasons other than its separatism, a support based on issues outside the centre–periphery dimension of competition, confirming what the manifesto data show.

In Spain, the Socialist Party has been a consistent follower of pro-periphery convergence, particularly since the early 2000s. The results of this strategy are clearly visible across regions (see Table 8.9). The percentage of anti-periphery respondents that voted for the PSOE diminished with time in almost all regions, though more dramatically in Catalonia, the Canary Islands, and Andalusia. The Popular Party

TABLE 8.8–8.10. *The evolution of respondents' past vote according to centre–periphery positions in Belgium, Spain, and Great Britain*
(The vote percentages are calculated over the total number of respondents who voted in state elections, excluding 'don't know/cannot answer')
Table 8.8. Belgium

Vote Nat. Elections	[Region] must decide everything (1...)				...2...				...3...				...4...				Belgium must decide everything (...5)			
	1991	1995	1999	2003	1991	1995	1999	2003	1991	1995	1999	2003	1991	1995	1999	2003	1991	1995	1999	2003
FLANDERS																				
CVP	18	22	14	—	27	31	24	—	30	33	28	—	32	31	28	—	25	30	23	—
VLD	15	19	19	20	17	20	27	29	20	19	26	26	23	21	22	26	20	22	24	31
SP	14	14	8	—	12	17	9	—	15	19	13	—	14	23	19	—	21	26	19	—
SP.A-SPI.	—	—	—	11	—	—	—	23	—	—	—	28	—	—	—	31	—	—	—	32
VB	18	23	26	33	8	8	11	11	7	7	8	9	7	5	7	8	7	7	11	10
VU	20	14	23	—	15	14	14	—	5	7	7	—	3	6	5	—	3	2	5	—
CD&V	—	—	—	20	—	—	—	23	—	—	—	23	—	—	—	27	—	—	—	19
N-VA	—	—	—	13	—	—	—	10	—	—	—	5	—	—	—	1	—	—	—	1
Others	15	8	10	3	21	10	15	4	23	15	18	3	21	14	19	7	24	13	18	7
N	100 (362)	100 (194)	100 (154)	100 (102)	100 (416)	100 (307)	100 (295)	100 (142)	100 (637)	100 (652)	100 (614)	100 (335)	100 (489)	100 (380)	100 (448)	100 (257)	100 (627)	100 (383)	100 (383)	100 (173)
WALLONIA																				
PS	46	47	37	100	43	36	37	25	33	32	30	26	24	24	26	23	31	34	28	24
PSC	10	11	10	0	17	18	17	12	26	25	15	18	31	26	19	18	25	25	16	8
PRL	17	28	—	—	12	20	—	—	13	19	—	—	18	30	—	—	19	22	—	—
FDF	1	—	—	—	0.5	—	—	—	0.8	—	—	—	0	—	—	—	0.7	—	—	—
PRL-FDF	—	—	23	—	—	—	29	—	—	—	26	—	—	—	26	—	—	—	30	—
MR	—	—	—	0	—	—	—	12	—	—	—	36	—	—	—	36	—	—	—	32
RW	0	—	—	—	0	—	—	—	0	—	—	—	0.5	—	—	—	0.4	—	—	—
Others	26	14	30	0	27.5	26	17	51	27.2	24	29	20	26.5	20	25	20	24.3	19	26	36
N	100 (105)	100 (36)	100 (30)	100 (2)	100 (209)	100 (73)	100 (80)	100 (8)	100 (488)	100 (372)	100 (421)	100 (39)	100 (218)	100 (211)	100 (238)	100 (26)	100 (271)	100 (287)	100 (216)	100 (25)

BRUSSELS

	(1) 1991	1995	1999	2003	(2) 1991	1995	1999	2003	(3) 1991	1995	1999	2003	(4) 1991	1995	1999	2003	(5) 1991	1995	1999	2003
CVP	3	10	18	—	4	4	4	—	4	2	5	—	3	6	8	—	10	4	6	—
VLD	0	0	12	—	4	0	13	2	7	4	3	0	1	0	8	0	4	5	9	0
SP	3	0	6	—	0	0	0	—	4	4	2	—	1	6	2	—	2	3	5	—
SP.A-SPL	—	—	—	—	—	—	—	—	—	—	—	—	—	—	—	—	—	—	—	—
VB	21	10	29	—	2	11	0	0	3	3	3	0	1	4	1	0	0	7	4	1
VU	7	20	12	—	4	0	11	—	1	2	3	—	1	0	1	—	1	0	0	—
CD&V	—	—	—	0	—	—	—	0	—	—	—	0	—	—	—	0	—	—	—	1
PS	21	30	0	35	4	31	4	47	18	13	12	33	9	18	5	32	14	9	7	41
PSC	3	0	0	19	11	15	7	23	8	14	8	19	16	18	8	18	10	9	9	20
PRL	10	—	—	—	18	—	—	—	20	—	—	—	21	—	—	—	24	—	—	—
FDF	3	—	—	—	13	—	—	—	6	—	—	—	18	—	—	—	4	—	—	—
PRL-FDF	—	0	18	—	—	27	18	—	—	15	21	—	—	35	30	—	—	39	33	—
MR	—	—	—	23	—	—	—	17	—	—	—	26	—	—	—	38	—	—	—	30
Others	29	30	5	23	37	1	43	11	29	43	43	22	29	13	37	12	37	24	27	7
N	100 (29)	100 (10)	100 (17)	100 (26)	100 (45)	100 (26)	100 (45)	100 (57)	100 (110)	100 (92)	100 (154)	100 (252)	100 (68)	100 (53)	100 (128)	100 (167)	100 (110)	100 (70)	100 (103)	100 (158)

Notes: The question on territorial preferences was originally a 0–10 point scale. It went from 0 '[Region] must decide everything' to 10 'Belgium must decide everything'. For the sake of comparability with the survey results of the other two countries and for the sake of simplicity, the question was recoded into a 5-point scale.

Sources: General Election Studies Belgium 1991, 1995, 1999, 2003.

Table 8.9. Spain

CATALONIA

Vote Nat. Elections	I feel only Spanish			I feel more Spanish than [Region]			I feel as Spanish as [Region]			I feel more [Region than Spanish]			I feel only [Region]		
	1992	1998	2005	1992	1998	2005	1992	1998	2005	1992	1998	2005	1992	1998	2005
PP	6	33	38	20	32	30	8	21	9.6	3	2	1.2	3	1.3	0.8
PSOE	80	60	59	60	60	59	55	53	66	25	27	44	14	16	24
CiU	3.4	1.4	0	13	4	3.7	26	16	13	59	53	28	61	53	15
ERC	0	0	0	1	0	1.8	1.8	1	2	4.8	6.3	19.4	13.4	27	56
Others	10.6	5.6	3	6	4	5.5	9.2	9	9.4	8.2	11.7	7.4	8.6	2.7	4.2
N	100 (236)	100 (70)	100 (42)	100 (92)	100 (50)	100 (54)	100 (491)	100 (260)	100 (302)	100 (351)	100 (142)	100 (165)	100 (291)	100 (75)	100 (114)

BASQUE COUNTRY

	I feel only Spanish			I feel more Spanish than [Region]			I feel as Spanish as [Region]			I feel more [Region than Spanish]			I feel only [Region]		
	1992	1998	2005	1992	1998	2005	1992	1998	2005	1992	1998	2005	1992	1998	2005
PP	14	33	48	19	40	13	3	13	14	1.2	2	0	0	0	0
PSOE	56	33	52	55	50	61	40	42	51	4.2	7.8	6.2	3.4	3.7	3
PNV	0	0	0	9.5	10	13	30	31	19	60	63	72	25	40	63
EA	0	0	0	1.2	0	0	5.7	3.6	1.2	9	16	14	13	22.5	13
HB	0	0	0	0	0	0	3	2.4	0	4.2	2	0	55	32.5	0
Others	30	34	0	15.3	0	13	18.3	8	14.8	21.4	9.2	7.8	3.6	1.3	21
N	100 (69)	100 (15)	100 (23)	100 (84)	100 (10)	100 (23)	100 (262)	100 (84)	100 (86)	100 (167)	100 (51)	100 (64)	100 (175)	100 (80)	100 (68)

GALICIA

	I feel only Spanish			I feel more Spanish than [Region]			I feel as Spanish as [Region]			I feel more [Region than Spanish]			I feel only [Region]		
	1992	1998	2005	1992	1998	2005	1992	1998	2005	1992	1998	2005	1992	1998	2005
PP	43	54	53	48	72	37	44	57	43	30	56	13	23	30	8.3
PSOE	42	36	47	44	16	50	48	29	49	47	20	57	43	18.5	33
BNG	0	4.5	0	0	12	10.5	2.2	12.6	5.8	8.5	22	28	22	48.	58
Others	15	5.5	0	8	0	2.5	5.8	1.4	2.2	14.5	2	2	12	3.5	0.7
N	100 (69)	100 (22)	100 (19)	100 (63)	100 (25)	100 (38)	100 (600)	100 (182)	100 (225)	100 (270)	100 (128)	100 (97)	100 (86)	100 (27)	100 (12)

CANARY ISLANDS

	1992	1998	2005	1992	1998	2005	1992	1998	2005	1992	1998	2005	1992	1998	2005
PP	32	67	67	20	75	44	16	43	37	11	40	24	12	35	28
PSOE	58	17	17	60	25	44	64	35	49	63	32	52	71	43	55
CC	0	8.3	0	5	0	11	0	17	11.6	1.5	20.5	19	0	20.4	17
Others	10	7.7	16	15	0	1	20	5	2.4	24.5	7.5	5	17	1.6	0
N	100 (41)	100 (12)	100 (6)	100 (20)	100 (4)	100 (9)	100 (279)	100 (176)	100 (198)	100 (196)	100 (112)	100 (94)	100 (34)	100 (49)	100 (18)

ANDALUSIA

	1992	1998	2005	1992	1998	2005	1992	1998	2005	1992	1998	2005	1992	1998	2005
PP	29	45	80	28	50	52	12	29	27	4.5	22	15	2	30	20
PSOE	64	41	20	60	30	46	74	58	66	68	57	73	70	60	80
PA	2	2	0	2	5	0	3.5	2.7	1	8.4	6	6	6	0	0
Others	5	12	0	10	15	2	10.5	10.3	6	19.1	5	6	22	10	0
N	100% (217)	100 (49)	100 (15)	100 (222)	100 (40)	100 (67)	100 (1849)	100 (405)	100 (434)	100 (309)	100 (101)	100 (85)	100 (50)	100 (20)	100 (5)

ARAGON

	1992	1998	2005	1992	1998	2005	1992	1998	2005	1992	1998	2005	1992	1998	2005
PP	29	50	21	30	64	50	27	62	35	26	44	27	17	0	0
PSOE	55	44	58	46	32	45	56	32	52	48	37	52	56	60	100
CHA		0	10.5		0	0		0	7		6.8	12.5		0	0
Others	16	6	10.5	24	4	5	17	6	6	26	12.2	8.5	27	40	0
N	100 (128)	100 (16)	100 (19)	100 (82)	100 (31)	100 (22)	100 (592)	100 (185)	100 (229)	100 (100)	100 (59)	100 (40)	100 (18)	100 (5)	100 (3)

Sources: CIS 2025–2041 (1992); CIS 2286 (1998); CIS 2610 (2005).

replaced the Socialists as the defender of Spanish anti-periphary voters, with large growing percentages precisely in those regions where the Socialists had lost grip among this type of voters: Catalonia, the Canary Islands, and Andalusia. At the same time, the Socialists consolidated through time their dominion of the centrist space in Catalonia and the Basque Country, to the detriment of the largest peripheral parties in each region, Convergència i Unió and the Basque Nationalist Party respectively.

This centrist space, on the other hand, was very sensitive to contingent state parties' tactics. The year 1998 represents the mid-term of a legislature in which the Popular Party, under the leadership of José María Aznar, was leading a minority government which was sensitive to peripheral parties' demands because it needed these parties' parliamentary support to pass legislation. Thus, in this year, the PP's reputation as being pro-periphery grew, which was reflected in the dramatic growth of its electoral weight among centrist respondents in all regions with relevant peripheral parties. In some regions, it even grew among respondents with extreme pro-periphery preferences, as in Galicia, the Canary Islands, and Andalusia. Once the PP was out of government and its anti-periphery strategy began, it lost its pro-periphery reputation together with its weight among centrist and pro-periphery voters. In 2005, in contrast to 1998, the PP had come to dominate the space of anti-periphery voters, displacing the Socialists.

The PSOE's strategy of convergence served the party not just to dominate the centrist space in all regions but, most importantly, to increase its presence among moderate pro-periphery and extreme pro-periphery respondents. In Catalonia, for example, the Socialists in 1992 had received the vote of 25 per cent of moderate pro-periphery respondents and 14 per cent of the extreme pro-periphery respondents; the same figures in 2005 had grown to 44 per cent and 24 per cent respectively. The only exception to this trend is in the Basque Country, where the PSOE had historically kept its position between the anti-periphery extreme and the centre of the dimension and never attempted to make incursions into extreme pro-periphery respondents as it did in Catalonia.

If we turn now to Spanish peripheral parties, we see that their fortunes varied enormously across regions and within regions across parties. In Catalonia, peripheral parties experienced opposed trajectories, in parallel to their divergent electoral fortunes. In 1992, the more moderate Convergència i Unió (CiU) dominated the space of pro-periphery respondents: 61 per cent of extreme pro-periphery respondents and 59 per cent of moderate pro-periphery respondents voted for CiU. Moreover, it was the second party among centrist respondents after the PSOE. Therefore, CiU had managed the difficult feat of attending, simultaneously, the extreme pro-periphery voters and the centrist ones. On the other hand, the radical Esquerra Republicana de Catalunya (ERC) was voted for mainly by extreme pro-periphery voters, but even here it lay behind CiU. In 2005, by contrast, ERC had evolved to be the preferred party among extreme pro-periphery respondents, with 56 per cent of their vote, whereas CiU was relegated to a third far away position, with 15 per cent of the extreme pro-periphery respondents' support. The Socialists were ahead of CiU with 24 per cent! CiU also lost among centrist respondents, who moved their preferences to the PSOE. CiU was the largest peripheral party in Catalonia for a long period, which shows in its long occupation of office at the regional level. With time, however, the increasingly pro-periphery moves of the Socialists[10] and the radicalization of the pro-periphery message by ERC started to inflict electoral losses to the moderate and pragmatic approach of CiU, to the extent that CiU was displaced among the centrist and moderate pro-periphery respondents by the PSOE and among the extreme pro-periphery respondents by ERC. In order to recover part of the lost terrain, CiU will likely engage in strategies of radicalization.

In the Basque Country, the evolution of peripheral parties was a quite different story. In 1992 the radical party Herri Batasuna (HB) dominated the space of extreme pro-periphery respondents: 55 per cent of them voted for HB, followed by the Basque Nationalist Party (PNV), with 25 per cent and the PNV's 1986 split Eusko Alkartasuna, with 13 per cent. State parties had a negligible presence among extreme pro-periphery respondents. The centrist space, on the other hand, was shared between the moderate PNV and the Socialists. The PNV was the undisputed dominant party among moderate pro-periphery respondents, with 60 per cent of their vote. Thus, in 1992 each party was dominant among a section of the Basque electorate: the PSOE was majoritarian among Spanish anti-periphery voters and among centrist voters; the PNV was majoritarian among moderate pro-periphery respondents; and HB was majoritarian among extreme Basque pro-periphery voters. By 2005, things had changed considerably. The PNV, after years of radicalization and helped by the declaration of HB as an illegal party (and therefore excluded from electoral participation), managed to become the dominant party among both moderate and radical pro-periphery respondents. The party had lost considerable ground among centrist respondents. Therefore, all the pro-periphery space constituted its privileged hunting ground. Meanwhile, the Socialists increased their presence among the centrist respondents while maintaining mainly unchanged at a very low level their electoral weight among moderate and extreme pro-periphery respondents.

In Galicia, the Popular Party has been the largest party in the region for a long time, even among pro-periphery respondents and despite the Popular Party's Spanish nationalism. In 1992, the PP was the dominant party among anti-periphery respondents and among centrist respondents, while the PSOE was the largest party among the moderate and radical pro-periphery respondents. Nevertheless, the presence of the PP was not negligible among pro-periphery respondents: 30

---

[10] The radicalization of the PSOE in Catalonia and its incursion into the 'hunting grounds' of the extreme pro-periphery voters was possible due to the fact that the Socialist Party of Catalonia (PSC), the electoral brand of PSOE in the region, is an autonomous political party, federated to the PSOE but retaining a great deal of autonomy as a differentiated party. The assumption that the PSC-PSOE is a state party in Catalonia is, in this respect, disputable.

per cent of moderate pro-periphery respondents and 23 per cent of extreme pro-periphery respondents had voted for the PP in 1992. This has two alternative explanations. Either the PP managed to be a credible defender of Galician's interests in Madrid, or Galician voters were voting according to left–right ideology to a greater extent than according to their centre–periphery preferences. In fact, both are true to some extent. The PP in Galicia had always defended a *regionalist* position along the centre–periphery dimension of competition, a position that assumed the compatibility between being Spanish and being Galician. For years since the transition to democracy, Galician peripheral parties were a weak force whose electoral breakthrough did not take place until the mid-1990s when they managed to obtain parliamentary seats in Madrid for the first time. In 1992, the Galician Nationalist Bloc (BNG) concentrated its support among extreme pro-periphery respondents, where it gathered 22 per cent of the votes, as much as the PP. Its presence among centrist and moderate pro-periphery respondents was negligible. By 2005, however, the PP had lost influence among centrist respondents and gained it among Spanish anti-periphery voters. Meanwhile, the PSOE was growing among pro-periphery respondents, moderate and extreme alike, and the BNG consolidated its position as the uncontested dominant party among extreme pro-periphery respondents. The PP lost its weight dramatically among this section of the electorate. Its presence dropped from 23 per cent in 1992 to 8 per cent in 2005.

In the Canary Islands during the 1990s the PSOE dominated all the sections of the Canarian electorate. It was the largest party among anti-periphery voters, among centrist voters, and among moderate and extreme pro-periphery voters. However, it was among the extreme pro-periphery respondents where the PSOE enjoyed its strongest grip, gaining 71 per cent of their vote. This is an indication that, in the Canary Islands, the centre–periphery dimension was not relevant for voters when casting their votes. With time, however, the landscape changed. In 2005, the PP had already become the largest party among extreme anti-periphery respondents, a section of the electorate where the PSOE lost its weight dramatically. Meanwhile, the peripheral party Coalición Canaria (CC) had grown relevantly among moderate and extreme pro-periphery respondents. In 1992 it was still a very small party but by 1998 20 per cent of pro-periphery respondents, moderates and radicals were voting for CC, a figure that remained nearly unchanged in 2005. The Socialists were still the majoritarian party among centrist respondents and among pro-periphery respondents in 2005, although the PP had been clearly extending its support among these categories. This was particularly the case during the periphery-friendly PP minority government of 1996–2000. At the time, the PP dramatically increased its electoral weight among moderate and extreme pro-periphery respondents. Of this, at least half was lost in 2005 when the PP's anti-periphery strategy had already been initiated. This means that Canarian voters were very receptive to the strategies of convergence of the PP. Were the party to pursue a convergence strategy more consistently it may replace the PSOE as the

TABLE 8.10. *Great Britain*

Vote Nat. Elections	I feel only British				I feel more British than [Region]				I feel as British as [Region]				I feel more [Region] than British				I feel only [Region]			
	1979	1997	2001	2005	1979	1997	2001	2005	1979	1997	2001	2005	1979	1997	2001	2005	1979	1997	2001	2005
SCOTLAND																				
Conservative	31	34	20	38			37	42		22	15	20			8	11	26	7	7	11
Labour	34	45	32	23			34	33		54	55	47			57	49	35	60	53	37
Liberal	14	16	32	27			14	21		11	18	20			16	21	4	3	9	16
SNP	21	5	6	8			11	3		13	9	13			17	17	31	30	26	32
Others	0	0	10	4			4	1		0	3	0			2	2	4	0	5	4
N	100 (123)	100 (38)	100 (34)	100 (26)			100 (35)	100 (33)		100 (285)	100 (265)	100 (199)			100 (329)	100 (222)	100 (254)	100 (259)	100 (351)	100 (210)
WALES																				
Conservative	40	33	36	29			26	32		19	19	20			12	19	18	8	8	10
Labour	38	59	27	37			51	37		62	56	44			60	46	51	67	51	43
Liberal	8	6	27	27			13	25		8	16	19			13	19	6	4	12	14
Plaid Cymru	1.8	0.8	7	3			6	4		9	9	11			15	10	9	20	27	28
Others	12.2	1.2	3	4			4	2		2	0	6			0	6	16	1	2	5
N	100 (274)	100 (122)	100 (67)	100 (86)			100 (82)	100 (68)		100 (288)	100 (227)	100 (187)			100 (161)	100 (106)	100 (479)	100 (166)	100 (171)	100 (99)
ENGLAND																				
Conservative			27	36			25	34			27	35			32	38			38	46
Labour			56	37			54	37			50	39			44	37			39	31
Liberal			17	21			18	25			21	23			20	21			20	18
Others			0	6			3	4			2	3			4	4			3	5
N			100 (199)	100 (184)			100 (180)	100 (132)			100 (727)	100 (752)			100 (246)	100 (234)			100 (312)	100 (261)

Notes: The election survey of 1979 only asked respondents whether they felt British or Scottish/Welsh, without giving other options. Therefore, I have placed the answers in the categories 'I feel only British' and 'I feel only [Region]'. The election survey of 1997 asked respondents whether they felt British or Scottish/Welsh and gave them the option to answer 'both British and Scottish/Welsh'. Therefore, I have placed the answers in the extreme categories and the middle one.

Sources: BES 1591 (1979); BES 1604 (1979); Scottish Referendum Study 3952s (1997); Welsh Referendum Study 3952w (1997); Devolution and Constitutional Change 4766 (2001); BES 2448 (2005).

majoritarian party among pro-periphery voters. The PP's anti-periphery strategy allowed the PSOE to recover its influence among pro-periphery Canarian voters, which it had lost during the PP's minority government.

The Andalusian Party (PA) was not a credible 'owner' of the pro-periphery cause. In Andalusia, the PSOE dominated the space of moderate pro-periphery and centrist respondents increasingly through time while the PP became with the passage of years the undisputed majoritarian party among anti-periphery voters. In Aragón, the peripheral party Chunta Aragonesista (CHA) increased its presence among pro-periphery respondents across time, although it is still far from being the dominant party in this position. If we add to this the fact that extreme pro-periphery respondents are a tiny minority in Aragón then we have to conclude that the centre–periphery dimension is not relevant for the electorate when deciding what party to vote for. CHA still has a long way to go before consolidating its position among respondents with pro-periphery preferences and before managing to make the centre–periphery issues relevant for party choice.

The Labour Party dominated the centrist space of the centre–periphery dimension in both Scotland and Wales at least since 1997, the first year for which we have data on the centrist position of respondents (see Table 8.10). Although this domination declined with time in favour of the Liberal Democrats and the peripheral parties, this was more the result of a general downward trend of Labour's vote shares in Great Britain as a whole than the result of Labour's loss of the centrist space. In fact, if we compare how much Labour lost between 1997 and 2005 among extreme pro-periphery respondents (23 per cent in Scotland and 24 per cent in Wales) and among extreme anti-periphery respondents (22 per cent in Scotland and 22 per cent in Wales), then we have to conclude that the centrist space was the only one in which Labour minimized its generalized losses. And it is this position as the majoritarian party among centrist respondents that allowed Labour to remain the largest party in both regions.

As in Spain, the implementation of decentralizing reforms gave state parties a boost in credibility as decentralizers and this is visible in survey data. In 1997, when Labour won the elections and initiated a process of devolution to Scotland and Wales, its weight among extreme pro-periphery respondents was at the maximum level for the period under analysis. In 1997, 60 per cent of extreme pro-periphery respondents in Scotland and 67 per cent in Wales voted for Labour. By the next general election, the figures had dropped to 53 per cent and 51 per cent respectively. By 2005, Labour's weight among extreme pro-periphery respondents had dropped to the levels of 1979, when the centre–periphery dimension was irrelevant to explain party choice.

In 1979, 35 per cent of extreme pro-periphery respondents in Scotland and 51 per cent in Wales voted for Labour. These are undoubtedly significant figures. That year, however, the elections were highly focused on the left–right polarization between the Conservatives and Labour, with the Labour Party in disarray, and with its reputation as decentralizer touched by the failed devolution attempt of the previous legislature (see chapter 7). The Conservative Party also had a relatively large weight among extreme pro-periphery respondents in 1979, despite its mostly anti-periphery stance during the previous years: 26 per cent of respondents that felt only Scottish and 18 per cent of respondents that felt only Welsh voted for the Conservative Party. Therefore, these high figures indicate that the centre–periphery dimension was not relevant to pro-periphery respondents when they cast their vote. By 1997 the Conservative Party's vote share among extreme pro-periphery respondents was nearly negligible. The years between 1979 and 1997 were years of Conservative majority governments opposed to the project of devolution. They were also the years of Labour's warming up to the project of devolution, particularly by Scottish Labour. This explains the respective figures of the Labour and Conservative parties for 1997 among extreme pro-periphery respondents. It was not until 2005 that the Conservatives started to regain electoral weight among extreme pro-periphery respondents in both Scotland and Wales.

At the same time, if we look at England, we can see that between 2001 and 2005 the Conservative Party became the preferred party among those respondents that felt exclusively English. In England, the Conservative's electoral weight was larger among the respondents who felt only English than among the respondents who felt only British. This is symptomatic of the emergence of a reactive regionalism in England that is being capitalized by the Conservative Party, which has much to gain by defending the extension of devolution to the English regions, since it is in England where its electoral support is concentrated. It is still early for this, since there is not yet popular support for the idea of establishing directly elected assemblies in the English regions, but there is some evidence that public opinion is growing in that direction (Bond and McCrone 2004).

Turning now to British peripheral parties, we observe diverse trajectories in Scotland and Wales. In 1979 the Scottish National Party (SNP) had a larger electoral presence among respondents who felt exclusively Scottish than among those who felt exclusively British. However, the difference was smaller than one would have expected had the SNP been the 'owner' of the pro-periphery agenda: 31 per cent of respondents who felt only Scottish voted for the SNP while 21 per cent of respondents who felt only British also voted for the SNP. The contrast with the Welsh Plaid Cymru (PC) is stark. Although the figures for PC are considerably smaller, because in 1979 Plaid was still a small party with little support among the electorate in general, it received the bulk of its support among the respondents who felt only Welsh. Since 1979, Plaid grew its support base dramatically among extreme pro-periphery voters (i.e. those respondents who felt only Welsh): from 9 per cent in 1979 to 28 per cent in 2005. These were voters that Plaid had taken away from Labour. Meanwhile, its command of the centrist voters was small during this period (here the Labour Party was the absolute winner) and relatively stable across time. After the years of anti-devolution Conservative governments, the SNP emerged in the 1997 national elections as a party with the bulk of its support concentrated among moderate and extreme pro-periphery voters, although its growth among this section of the electorate had been limited by Labour and its electoral manifesto in favour of devolution. In 2005 the SNP still had more or less the same distribution of support as it had in 1997: larger among moderate and extreme pro-periphery voters, small among centrist voters, negligible among anti-periphery voters. As we already know, between 1997 and 2005 Labour lost dramatically its electoral support among the extreme pro-periphery voters, which went not to the SNP but to the Liberal Democrats instead. The SNP is now in office at the regional level. It remains to be seen how this fact will strengthen its hold of the pro-periphery and of the centrist voters, if it does.

To sum up, state parties tended to dominate the space of voters in the centre and the anti-periphery side of the centre–periphery dimension of competition, whereas peripheral parties dominated the space of pro-periphery voters. In Belgium, however, ex-state parties dominated all the sections along the centre–periphery dimension, including the pro-periphery one. By the early 1990s all Belgian peripheral parties except the Vlaams Blok had lost the monopoly of the pro-periphery agenda and voters with strong pro-periphery preferences could cast a pro-periphery vote by choosing any one of the parties in competition.

The dominion of the centrist space by state parties played to their advantage, given that it was here where the bulk of the electorate concentrated and it was here where the strategies of pro-periphery convergence of state parties helped them win more votes and compensated for their losses somewhere else. The relevance of the centrist space is further indicated by the fact that the largest peripheral parties were those which had also a relevant weight among centrist voters, such as CiU and PNV in Spain.

On the other hand, the data show that being relevant in the centrist and the extreme pro-periphery spaces simultaneously was nearly an impossible task. Peripheral parties had to choose whether they would concentrate their efforts among centrist voters or among extreme pro-periphery voters and in the presence of state parties' pro-periphery strategies a majority opted for growing among pro-periphery voters. Finally, in the years of decentralizing reforms or (partial) implementation of peripheral parties' demands all state parties benefited by increasing their credibility among the pro-periphery voters, even the state parties with a most centralist trajectory, as in the case of the PP.

8.5 CONCLUDING REMARKS

When state parties emphasize pro-periphery issues to respond to the challenge of peripheral party growth, peripheral parties' response will be twofold. On the one hand, peripheral parties will radicalize their pro-periphery positions. On the other hand, peripheral parties will combine these strategies of radicalization with issue diversification and left–right repositioning contingent upon political circumstances and past choices.

Radicalization strategies are facilitated by the establishment of elected regional assemblies and governments. First, because this makes it easier for peripheral parties to reach office at the regional level, allowing them to change the distribution of preferences in society through regional policies of *nation-building*. Second, because in a decentralized state with state parties that have a *state-wide* agenda, there is always a market for peripheral parties to exploit. Peripheral parties can always resort to the comparative grievance among the different regions and to zero-sum games. Irrespective of the type of decentralization that state parties defend, either symmetric (in Spain referred to as the 'coffee for all' doctrine) or asymmetric, it will always give fuel to one or another peripheral party attack, depending on the gains and losses that each type of decentralization brings to the different regions. Moreover, peripheral parties can trade state policy for regional authority every time the political context to do so emerges. Only full independence can completely remove the give-and-take politics of decentralized states. Anything short of independence leaves space for the pro-periphery grievance.

State parties face a dilemma. Anti-periphery polarization strategies may make sense contingently to fight a particular election or for a short period of time. It may give the anti-periphery state party many votes because it mobilizes the anti-peripheral vote while it may create problems for the pro-periphery state party competitor. However, it facilitates radicalization on the part of peripheral parties, something that has political consequences if the state party in government has no majority to govern. In order to pass legislation, the party that leads the minority government will turn to the peripheral parties for support and peripheral parties will put a price to it. The anti-periphery polarization strategies of one of the two main state parties fuels the credibility and distinctiveness of the pro-periphery agenda of peripheral parties, giving no incentives to these parties to stop pushing this agenda ever further. We have seen that pro-periphery voters are sensitive to the state parties' pro-periphery convergence and reward them with votes. In this sense, I would expect that with time all state parties will strengthen their pro-periphery profile. However, there will always be elections in which the incentives to harm the competitor are larger than the incentives to take votes away from peripheral parties. In such elections, polarized state party competition will lead to peripheral party loss and to subsequent peripheral party radicalization, setting the stage for future peripheral party gains, one step closer to the maximalist peripheral programmatic agenda.

9

Conclusions

This book is neither an explanation of the emergence and breakthrough of peripheral parties nor a search for all the causes of a devolution reform. The study had two interconnected objectives. The first objective was to understand the *strategic behaviour* of parties competing for votes along a centre–periphery conflict dimension in two different institutional settings, a centralized and a decentralized state; the second was to understand the *political decision* to devolve political power in a centralized state with culturally distinct peripheries.

These two objectives are often discussed by scholarly analyses in terms of a double paradox: the paradox of policy success and the paradox of devolution. According to the paradox of policy success, the more peripheral parties see their policy agendas implemented the more they suffer electoral stagnation and/or decline. As the peripheral agenda is increasingly incorporated into mainstream politics by strategizing state parties peripheral parties' exclusive focus on centre–periphery issues becomes redundant. Policy success leads to political irrelevance and, in the worst-case scenario, to complete disappearance. The paradox of devolution states that the institutional measures that are taken to respond to the separatist threat (in turn the result of peripheral parties' electoral success) provide peripheral parties with the institutional incentives and opportunities necessary to push separatism ahead. In other words, the defence mechanism par excellence against separatism, i.e., political devolution, helps to keep separatism alive. These alleged paradoxes arrive at opposite conclusions. According to the paradox of policy success, at the end of the day peripheral parties are made redundant and become electorally irrelevant forces. According to the paradox of devolution, not only do peripheral parties remain and endure despite the policies of decentralization but they even thrive in a decentralized state.

The findings of this book show that these paradoxes are not so paradoxical after all. They are based on the wrong assumptions about the nature of the centre–periphery conflict and of centre–periphery party competition. The paradox of peripheral parties' policy success makes two assumptions that are contested by the findings of this book: first, that peripheral parties are niche parties that cannot and do not strategize outside the centre–periphery dimension even when their survival is at stake; second, that political devolution is the direct result of peripheral parties' demands for territorial self-government. The paradox of devolution assumes that the decision to decentralize is taken in order to neutralize the separatist threat and secure the territorial integrity of the state, an interpretation that this book proves wrong for the countries here compared. The contribution of the book lies precisely in presenting findings that contradict these assumptions, offering a different explanation of why state parties devolve centralized power and why peripheral parties endure in a decentralized state.

9.1 PERIPHERAL PARTIES AND CENTRE–PERIPHERY PARTY COMPETITION

This book abandons the assumption, either explicit or implicit in many scholarly analyses, that only mainstream parties are vote-maximizers and, therefore, have a wider and more effective range of strategies to use against their smaller non-mainstream adversaries (Meguid 2008). Peripheral parties address a minority group inside the state that is geographically concentrated in some areas of the state territory. Even inside the peripheral territory, peripheral parties are seldom voted for by the largest number of people. The reason is that the peripheral territory's electorate is a plural one, with diverse interests and preferences formed along different lines of conflict. At the individual level, this means that voters have several identities to choose from when they decide their ballot; at the aggregate level it implies that social cleavages cross-cut one another.

In this context, a peripheral party knows that voters do not decide their vote exclusively according to their territorial identity. Such an expectation would condemn the party to be permanently on the side of the minority.[1] Since peripheral parties do care about votes and office they want to extend their appeal to a majority of voters in the peripheral territory. In order to do so peripheral parties have to move beyond the centre–periphery dimension and strategically diversify their issue profile. For the same reasons, peripheral parties that see their programmatic agendas being defended in the rhetoric and manifestos of state parties will react with electoral strategies that aim at stopping the defection of voters with peripheral identities to the state adversaries. In other words, as has been shown here, the electoral fortunes of peripheral parties do not automatically suffer whenever state parties assume pro-periphery positions or whenever the centre–periphery dimension is less salient at election time.

---

[1] True enough, there are some peripheral parties that only care about their programme and that address only their electoral niche. One can find this type of party in other dimensions of competition as well (for example, some communist, green and extreme-right parties are of this type). However, the fact that such type of party exists in no way implies that some dimensions of competition are exclusively populated by it.

The findings of this work have demonstrated that in a country where the policy space is made up of at least two relevant dimensions of competition that cross-cut each other—the centre–periphery and the left–right dimensions—parties will appeal to voters by using saliency and position in both dimensions simultaneously. The ideology of the party (in its wider Downsian sense of 'a conception of the good society') will determine which of the two relevant conflict lines is the party's primary dimension and which the secondary one. The party can use tactically and/ or strategically the secondary dimension of competition in order to avoid talking about the party's failures, or to hide its true intentions, in the primary dimension. The book has discussed many examples of peripheral and state parties that use their respective secondary dimensions—the left–right for peripheral parties and the centre–periphery for state parties—for tactical and strategic purposes that have to do with their interests in the primary dimension.

A way to radicalize a party's position along a dimension of competition is by transforming a positional issue into a valence issue. This means that the party *primes* and *frames* the issue in such a way that the large majority of voters support the party's position. For example, an anti-periphery state party can convey its preference for a centralized state (a clearly positional issue: centralization versus decentralization) in terms of the need to defend the territorial integrity of the state from the separatist threat (a valence issue: only a small minority would support separatist movements and agendas; most people agree that the territorial integrity of the state must be preserved). In turn, a peripheral party may convey its preference for further decentralization (again, clearly a positional issue: centralization versus decentralization) by referring to the need to defend the peripheral territory from 'occupation' by the central state or from 'near extinction' by the abuses of the central state. Interestingly enough, the feasibility of these strategies is not limited by the structure of preferences in society. Voters will follow parties in their moves if the parties' pledges are credible.

We have seen that parties' electoral tactics and strategies change before and after devolution. Peripheral parties go from being minority parties at the state level— always filling the benches of the opposition and protected from the punishment of voters for incumbency failures—to being large parties with government responsi- bilities at the regional level. Peripheral parties' constituencies, however, do not change; they continue to be regionally based, as before devolution. By contrast, state parties go from being state-wide parties catering to a state-wide constituency to being simultaneously state-wide parties in state elections and regional parties in regional elections. This is both an organizational and a political challenge for state parties. The party's unity and its territorial cohesion are at stake in a decentralized state. The multi-level institutional structure of electoral competition introduces centrifugal pressures within the structure of state parties. Despite the scarcity of data that measure state parties' policy preferences and centre–periphery positions at the regional level, I have presented and discussed some new evidence confirming a tendency towards the programmatic centrifugation of state parties at different elec- toral levels.

I have also shown that state parties engage more intensely and consistently in pro-periphery tactics after devolution. This is an indication that the use of pro-periphery tactics is less constrained in a decentralized context and that it is easier for state parties to define and carry out a pro-periphery converging strategy to compete against peripheral parties. In this respect, the survey findings that have been presented show that voters with pro-periphery preferences are sensitive to the state parties' pro-periphery moves and reward them with votes. Therefore, pro-periphery moves by state parties in a decentralized context are more effective than in a centralized one.

These findings lead me to expect that with time all state parties will strengthen their pro-periphery profile, particularly in regional elections. However, there will always be state elections in which a strategy of anti-periphery polarization will bring one or another state party short-term electoral benefits. In such elections, polarized competition between the two main state parties will lead to peripheral party loss and to subsequent peripheral party radicalization, as has happened in Spain.

9.2 CREDIBILITY CONSTRAINTS AND DEVOLUTION

The findings presented here have shown that a centralized state is an institutional environment that sets insurmountable credibility constraints for threatened state parties that want to converge towards pro-periphery positions. Pro-periphery convergence by threatened state parties was in general an ineffective electoral strategy and did not put a stop to the growth of peripheral parties in the countries under analysis. This was due to the credibility constraints attached to these electoral moves in a centralized state. State parties have a *state-wide* constituency. These parties represent all the territories of the state equally and not some territories over others. Voters with anti-periphery preferences punish the state party's pro-periphery turn and the defence of particular—as opposed to general—territorial interests. Voters with pro-periphery preferences do not believe that a state party can or wants to deliver pro-periphery policies. Peripheral parties contribute to extend this belief among pro-periphery voters through their rhetoric about the opportunism of state parties' pro-periphery positions and through their criticisms of state governments' failure to deliver pro-periphery policies. To be credible the pro-periphery move has to be intense and consistent across time, something difficult for a state party whose primary issue dimension is the left–right one. But even in those countries where the state parties were comparatively intense and consistent the growth of peripheral parties did not stop, as the case of the Belgian Christian Democrats has shown.

The failure of the pro-periphery convergence strategy, incapable of stopping the electoral growth of peripheral parties, convinced state parties that they could not defend pro-periphery issues with credibility as long as their constituencies were *only* state-wide. Political decentralization was a solution. Devolution would establish democratic representatives to be elected by regional constituencies. In the presence of regional electoral arenas, the state party's leaders reckoned, it would be easier for a state party to convince voters that its leaders really care about what happens in the region. The reason is that state parties in a decentralized polity are made accountable at the regional level as well as at the state level. In regional elections, state parties can compete against peripheral parties emphasizing exclusively regional issues and defending regional particular interests vis-à-vis the state.

I have not presented evidence showing whether state parties' leaders also reckoned the impact that devolution would have on their internal organization and their inter-territorial programmatic consistency. What I have shown, however, is that after devolution the regional branches of state parties had incentives to assimilate the pro-periphery agenda and to make it part of their programmatic identity and not just the result of a tactical move. In the race to get more regional competences from the central state, the regional branches of state parties did not want to fall behind. And the race was always fed by peripheral parties' demands.

After devolution, peripheral parties lost the monopoly of the pro-periphery agenda but gained, instead, direct influence over policy. Peripheral parties were more likely to be elected for office at the regional level, which meant that they could rebuild and strengthen their pro-periphery reputation through policy-making.

Political devolution, therefore, was not without costs. This is why it is wrong to understand a devolution reform as the direct result of peripheral pressure and growth or, in other words, as the policy success *of* peripheral parties and *by* peripheral parties. The decision to devolve power to sub-state territories was a cost–benefit political calculation inside state parties. As I have demonstrated, the leaders of state parties supported devolution only when they expected the benefits to outweigh the costs.

9.3 THE COST–BENEFIT CALCULATION LEADING TO DEVOLUTION

I have defended in this book the argument that devolution is a political decision and in order to understand it we must explain *the timing* of the decision, *the actors* that decide and the form that the decision assumes (*scope* and *depth*). Devolution entails two major costs for state parties: first, a weakening of the central party leadership vis-à-vis its regional branches; second, encouraging peripheral parties to radicalize their demands and push until the end their separatist agenda. State break-up and more generally the intensification of separatist demands were considered by state parties' leaders to be possible effects of devolution. Despite these costs, however, most threatened state parties eventually supported and/or implemented devolution. Behind this decision was the calculation about the distribution of costs and benefits attached to each of the two alternatives—devolution or no devolution—between the threatened state party and its state competitors.

The two main costs of devolution would be shared by all state parties in the polity. They would all be subject to the same organizational and political pressures in favour of ever greater decentralization so it would be up to each state party to solve this problem as best it could when in state office. Sharing the costs among all electoral competitors meant that the threatened state party initiating the devolution reform was not placed in a disadvantaged position with respect to its competitors in a decen-tralized context. In contrast, the costs of the decision not to decentralize would be assumed mainly by the state party that was being threatened by the growth of one or several peripheral parties. The electoral benefits of not decentralizing would be distributed among the peripheral parties and the state parties that were not threatened by the peripheral party threat. The electoral benefits of devolution, however, would be divided between the state and the regional levels and, in both, the state party that decided to decentralize power would benefit the most for reasons that have to do with the country's electoral geography, as I discuss in the following section.

The loss of central government's power is not a cost for state parties but for the governing party alone and only for as long as it remains the party of government. Political power does not disappear from the polity (as would be the case if the power were to be transferred to a supra-national entity); it merely gets dispersed down the ladder of state administration. The same amount of power is now divided among a larger number of institutional actors. Power is de-concentrated to the benefit of the largest parties in the polity because sooner or later it will happen that they go into the opposition at the state level. When this happens, it is no small consolation if the state party that is elected out of central government is still in office in several self-governing regions of the country. In a centralized state, the stakes for a state party are starkly simple: either in office or out of it; either benefiting from the perks of office or suffering in the ranks of the opposition; either deciding on policy or monitoring policy from outside. The stakes in a decentralized state are diversified. It is not a question of 'all the power or no power at all' but a question of 'no power here but some or all the power there'.

9.4 THE RELEVANCE OF ELECTORAL GEOGRAPHY

The literature on the partisan incentives to decentralize is divided between those who claim that devolution is worth its risks because of the electoral benefits for the devolutionist state party at the state level (Meguid 2009) and those who defend that it is because of its benefits at the sub-state level (O'Neill 2003; Mazzoleni 2009). The findings presented here confirm the hypothesis that state parties opt for devolution when it brings political benefits at the state and the regional levels simultaneously. It would not be rational for a state party to yield power voluntarily to an inferior level of administration unless it was quite certain that its future chances of winning elections at the sub-state level were at least as good as its chances at state elections. These chances, in turn, were in large part determined by the combined effects of the country's electoral geography and its electoral system.

I understand by electoral geography the number and electoral relevance of a country's constituencies and the distribution of parties' votes among them. In this analysis I have treated electoral geography as external to the first devolution reform. I have shown that a peripheral party is an electoral threat to a state party when voters defect to the peripheral party in regions that are electorally relevant, particularly if the state party has a high concentration of its total state-wide vote there. The number of electoral constituencies that make up a peripheral region will vary depending on the electoral system, but this is not so relevant for the argument defended here. What matters is the number of seats that are elected in the region as a whole, i.e., taking all its component constituencies together. The larger this number the more relevant the region is for the party that wants to obtain and retain office. This is why the size of the peripheral regions is so important for state parties that are losing votes to peripheral parties. If this loss is taking place in a region that is electorally very relevant and if it so happens that, for historical reasons, the state party has concentrated support precisely in this region, the peripheral threat is then at its maximum level and the state party cannot simply ignore centre–periphery issues, contrary to the prediction of the saliency theory of party competition.

The number of regions, not only their relative sizes, is also very important. The more regions exist in the country the more opportunities state parties have to attempt to compensate losses in some of them with gains in others. This is part of the political calculation behind the decision to devolve. A country with many regions, only some of which represent a peripheral challenge, offers the threatened state party incentives to support all-round devolution. By extending devolution to all regions in the country, the state party can compensate its losses in the peripheral region or regions with its positive electoral prospects in those regions where there are no strong peripheral parties and where the state party benefits from a high concentration of support. The way the preferences of the Italian Christian Democrats turned from supporting all-round devolution to retreating towards partial devolution was precisely due to the election results of 1948 that changed the party's perception of the electoral benefits to be extracted from the existing electoral geography in Italy at the time.

The likelihood of establishment of regional power strongholds that could make devolution worth its costs depended, to a large extent, on the number and size of the countries' culturally distinct regions. Where the cultural majority occupied a very large territory, as is the case in Italy, Spain, and the UK, this territory was divided into administrative regions that served as a basis for the future devolved units. In Italy and Spain the borders of the regions were renegotiated during the constitutional process with a view to the consequences of these borders for the establishment of regional pockets of support. In the United Kingdom, the three peripheral territories (Scotland, Wales, and Northern Ireland) were relatively similar in terms of size and very different in turn to the size of England, a much larger region than the other three. Moreover, a large portion of England, with the exception of the northern constituencies, was the dominion of the Conservative Party. For this reason, Labour always opposed devolution to England as a whole but preferred to divide it into several regions. Even so, Labour was still ambivalent about the benefits of all-round devolution. The reason is Labour's fear that all-round devolution would benefit the Conservatives more than it would benefit Labour, given that the regions in which the Conservatives were hegemonic were larger than the northern regions where Labour dominated.

A country divided into just two distinct regions generates insurmountable centrifugal pressures to the threatened state parties, as the Belgian case has shown. For Belgium the incentives worked differently compared to the other three countries. Here there were two opposing linguistic groups, each roughly concentrated in its territory, of relatively equal size (though Flanders is larger than Wallonia) and then there was Brussels, the capital of the country and an island of French speakers situated in the 'wrong' territory. The structure of incentives was therefore centrifugal: three regions and three state parties, each one dominant in one of the three regions. Each state party was threatened by a peripheral party in its respective regional stronghold. As a consequence, the state parties had little hope of compensating their losses in one territory by growing electorally in another. Besides, the contradiction inherent in the defence of regional and/or cultural interests by a state party in a centralized state was particularly acute among Belgian parties precisely due to this particular electoral geography. Since there were only two communities, each one opposing the other, the defence of regional and cultural interests took a blunt inescapable zero-sum form. In order to credibly pursue the defence of regional and cultural particularistic interests, Belgian state parties were progressively pressed to abandon their state-wide—that is to say, cross-communitarian—structure. Splitting a party into two is less costly than splitting it into seventeen or into twenty, as would have been the case in Spain and Italy respectively.

Partial or asymmetrical devolution is hardly an option when the country is divided into two relatively equal regions. In contrast, countries with multiple regions of which only a few are culturally distinct are open to different arrangements. All-round devolution can be combined with asymmetrical competences, as the Spanish, British, and Italian cases have shown. This combination is a middle point between the preferences of state parties and those of peripheral parties. For state parties *symmetrical all-round devolution* is the best option, easier to 'sell' to their electorates than asymmetrical and/or partial institutional arrangements. They can justify symmetrical all-round devolution with appeals to the enhanced quality of a decentralized polity that brings politics closer to the people and that benefits the country as a whole and all its citizens and regions equally. For peripheral parties, the defence of their historical and cultural particularities with respect to the rest of state regions is their main *raison d'être*. This is why they want *asymmetrical partial devolution*: devolved powers only to the peripheral territories inside the state. An *asymmetrical all-round devolution* offers something to each of the electoral adversaries. State parties obtain all-round devolution while they can justify the asymmetries to their voters with pledges that in the future regional competences will be levelled up. Peripheral parties obtain asymmetrical devolution and can, in turn, justify all-round devolution to their constituencies by framing it as a first step towards a much more ambitious final settlement (that may or may not be the separation from the state).

To sum up, the finding that the type of electoral geography determines in large part the preferences and decisions of state parties concerning the form that devolution will assume follows the same line as other findings in the literature according to which devolution is more stable with multiple regions rather than two or three large ones or a single dominant one (Brancati 2009; Erk and Anderson 2009).

Finally, I would like to conclude this section emphasizing one more relevant finding. In Spain and Italy peripheral parties have emerged and grown in non-peripheral regions. These countries are, therefore, clear cases of institutionally induced regionalism (Levi and Hechter 1985), where there is no presence of established peripheral parties prior to the implementation of political decentralization. In this respect, the institutional induction of regionalism in the United Kingdom is also to be expected once all-round devolution is implemented.

9.5 DEVOLUTION AND THE SECESSIONIST THREAT

The assumption that peripheral parties are vote-maximizers has two main implications. The first implication is that vote-maximization has an ambivalent effect. On the one hand, vote-maximization means that peripheral parties are willing to achieve majorities at the expense of ideological purity. Therefore, peripheral parties will strategically moderate their maximalist objectives in exchange for larger vote shares. On the other hand, since state parties are also moved by vote maximization, they will eventually adopt pro-periphery agendas in order to maximize their vote shares vis-à-vis the peripheral adversaries. As peripheral parties see their policy preferences implemented by state parties in government, they have incentives to move up the ladder to the next policy objective, which is always more ambitious than the previously achieved one. To put it differently, the pro-periphery strategic turn of threatened state parties pushes peripheral parties to radicalize their programmatic agenda. Radicalization serves to differentiate the threatened peripheral party's programme from that of its state competitor and thus to recover the ownership of this issue dimension. Radicalization also serves to artificially create a climate of emergency for the peripheral cause, contributing to make the centre–periphery dimension the most salient in voters' minds when they cast their vote. To sum up, vote-maximization has two opposite effects on the programmatic agenda of peripheral parties: moderation and radicalization. Which of the two effects will be the strongest one will depend on the behaviour of their state competitors.

The more programmatic concessions peripheral parties receive the more they can present these concessions as achievements to their constituencies and get rewarded with votes in return. This is when the second implication of peripheral parties' vote-maximization comes into play. Contrary to the belief that the pro-periphery programmatic agenda can exhaust itself once it has been implemented, peripheral parties always find new policies and new institutional changes to demand of the central government in order not to become electorally irrelevant parties. Pro-periphery concessions will not leave peripheral parties without agenda and without constituency. On the contrary, anything that is short of full independence can be profitably used by peripheral parties to adapt their policy packages to the structure of political competition at any particular time.

If peripheral parties do not manage to successfully differentiate their centre–periphery agenda from that of the other parties, they risk becoming irrelevant, as was the case of Volksunie, the Front Démocratique des Francophones, and Rassemblement Wallon. In order to avoid it, the best peripheral parties can do is to diversify their programmatic agenda, either emphasizing left–right issues, in order to compete with state parties in their issue dimension, as peripheral parties in Spain and the UK have done, or emphasizing new issues still untouched by other parties, as parties in Italy (Lega Nord) and Belgium (Vlaams Blok) have done. According to my findings, issue diversification and pro-periphery radicalization is the combination of strategies that most likely leads to the political survival of peripheral parties. Of the two wings that initially lived side by side inside Volksunie, it was the more radical of the two, both in the left–right dimension (i.e., the extreme- ight wing) and in the centre–periphery dimension (i.e., the separatist wing), the one which after splitting twice from Volksunie finally survived and became very successful: the Vlaams Blok in the 1980s and Nieuw-Vlaamse Alliantie in the 2000s.

The recurrence of the strategy of radicalization that I have found precisely after devolution contradicts the thesis according to which political decentralization appeases peripheral parties in their quest for regional power. According to my findings, devolution encourages peripheral parties further in their demands. The question then is not how much decentralization is enough to make peripheral parties redundant or irrelevant but whether the spiral of radicalization can be stopped. And the answer is that only full independence can completely remove the give-and-take politics of decentralized states. Anything short of independence leaves space for the pro-periphery grievance. The pro-periphery grievance will always be voiced by peripheral parties with the regional branches of state parties following closely. The continuous presence of the peripheral party threat, combined with the institutional incentives that state parties find to compete along territorial issues, will inevitably produce new rounds of decentralizing reforms in the countries analysed. The only limit to this spiral of decentralization is in the preferences of the electorate and, in this respect, there is still a huge research agenda ahead of us before we are able to establish any causal relationships.

Probably, the most enduring and deep effect of political devolution is that it changes the distribution of centre–periphery preferences in the electorate, although testing this hypothesis exceeded the objectives of this book. A policy of decentralization may have the unanticipated side-effect of making the electorate in general more receptive to pro-periphery issue positions. Whether this makes secession more likely, however, is open to discussion. Peripheral parties with openly short-term secessionist agendas must convince voters that the secessionist agenda is more important than any other problem that exists in the polity or than any other problem that they have in their lives; they must convince voters that independence will contribute to improve their welfare and the welfare of the society as a whole. This is not an easy task although it is by no means an impossible one. It seems plausible that the more the rights of peripheral minorities are recognized and guaranteed by the democratic state and the more the regional authorities increase their powers to the detriment of those of the state, the less the people see it as necessary—or even legitimate—to break up the state. However, the logic of partisan competition at the state level may push one or another state party to try to stop further devolution or even to reverse the level of devolution achieved if the party believes that doing so will put the party back in office or will keep the party there. If this happens, the preferences of the peripheral electorates may turn towards secession as the only viable way to see their aspirations fulfilled.

The fact that this scenario is a plausible one (since 2010 it has began to unfold in Spain with respect to Catalonia) is the clearest indication that state parties did not devolve power in order to neutralize the peripheral party threat. If this were true, state parties would not use anti-periphery radicalization or pro-periphery outbidding as electoral tactics and/or strategies to maximize their state-wide vote shares. The neutralization of the peripheral party threat requires a degree of consensus among state parties that the dynamic of electoral competition disincentives. There will always be electoral benefits to reap from manipulating the centre–periphery conflict in one or another state party's benefit.

However, I would not like to finish with gloomy thoughts about states that break up against the alleged best intentions of the politicians in charge. Rather, I would like to finish with a positive thought. The prospect of ongoing decentralization gives incentives to all players, at the centre and in the peripheries, to keep playing the game within the established democratic rules. This is the best we can aspire to after we have seen that other attempted responses during the nineteenth and twentieth centuries to the peripheral challenge, that were based on systematically ignoring the grievances from the periphery or on imposing a centralized homogeneous state, have guaranteed neither the territorial integrity of the state nor the survival of democracy.

Bibliography

Adams, J., M. Clarke, et al. (2006). 'Are Niche Parties Fundamentally Different from Mainstream Parties? The Causes and Electoral Consequences of Western European Parties' Policy Shifts, 1976–1998'. *American Journal of Political Science* 50(3): 513–29.

Agasoster, B. (2001). 'A Framework for Analyzing Local Party Policy Emphases in Scotland'. In *Estimating the Policy Positions of Political Actors*, ed. M. Laver. London: Routledge, 76–89.

Aja, E. (2003). *El estado autonómico: Federalismo y hechos diferenciales*. Madrid: Alianza Editorial.

Alonso, S. (2008). 'Enduring Ethnicity: The Political Survival of Incumbent Ethnic Parties in Western Democracies'. In *Controlling Governments: Voters, Institutions and Accountability*, ed. J. M. Maravall and I. Sánchez-Cuenca. Cambridge: Cambridge University Press, 82–104.

—— and B. Gómez Fortes (2011). 'Partidos nacionales en elecciones regionales: ¿Coherencia territorial o programas a la carta?' *Revista de Estudios Políticos* 152: 183–209.

—— and A. Richards (2006). 'Competition between Socialist and Nationalist Parties in Established Democracies: The Cases of Britain and Spain'. Paper presented at the 16th ISA World Congress of Sociology, Durban (South Africa).

Amoretti, U. (2002). 'Italy Decentralizes'. *Journal of Democracy* 13(2): 126–40.

—— and N. G. Bermeo (2004). *Federalism and Territorial Cleavages*. Baltimore, Md., and London: Johns Hopkins University Press.

Balsom, D. (1983). 'The Red and the Green: Patterns of Partisan Choice in Wales'. *British Journal of Political Science* 13: 299–325.

Barreiro, B. (2008). 'El centro en las elecciones del 9-M'. *El País*. 11 March.

Benoit, K., and M. Laver (2006). *Party Policy in Modern Democracies*. London and New York: Routledge.

Beramendi, J. (1995). 'Identity, Ethnicity and State in Spain: The 19th and 20th Centuries'. *Nationalism and Ethnic Politics* 5(3–4): 79–100.

Bird, R. (1993). *Fiscal Decentralization in Developing Countries*. Cambridge: Cambridge University Press.

Blas Guerrero, A. (1988). 'La Lzquierda española y el nacionalismo. El caso de la transición'. *Leviatán* 31: 71–85.

Bond, R., and D. McCrone (2004). 'The Growth of English Regionalism? Institutions and Identity'. *Regional and Federal Studies* 14(1): 1–25.

Bradbury, J. P., R. Deacon, et al. (1996). 'Policy Review Section'. *Regional Studies* 30(7): 689–712.

—— P. Lynch, et al. (1996). 'Policy Review Section'. *Regional Studies* 30(6): 601–18.

Brancati, D. (2007). 'The Origins and Strengths of Regional Parties'. *British Journal of Political Science* 38: 135–59.

—— (2009). *Peace by Design*. Oxford and New York: Oxford University Press.

Budge, I., and D. Farlie (1983). 'Party Competition: Selective Emphasis or Direct Confrontation? An Alternative View with Data'. In *Western European Party Systems*, ed.
H. Daalder and P. Mair. London: Sage, 267–71.

—— H.-D. Klingemann, et al. (2001). *Mapping Policy Preferences: Estimates for Parties,
Electors, and Governments, 1945–1998*. Oxford: Oxford University Press.

—— Robertson, et al. (1987). *Ideology, Strategy, and Party Change: Spatial Analyses of
Post-War Election Programmes in 19 Democracies*. Cambridge: Cambridge University
Press.

Butler, D., and M. Pinto-Duschinsky (1971). *The British General Election of 1970*. London:
Macmillan.

Castles, F., and P. Mair (1984). 'Left–Right Political Scales: Some Expert Judgements'.
European Journal of Political Research 12: 73–88.

Coakley, J. (ed.) (1992). *The Social Origins of Nationalist Movements: The Contemporary
West European Experience*. London: Sage.

Cook, C. (1978). 'The Challengers to the Two-Party System'. In *Trends in British Politics
Since 1945*, ed. C. Cook and J. Ramsden. Basingstoke: Macmillan, 132–57.

Coombes, R., and R. Norton-Taylor (1968). 'Renewal in Belgian Politics: The Elections of
March 1968'. *Parliamentary Affairs* 22: 62–72.

Cozens, P., and K. Swaddle (1987). 'The British General Election of 1987'. *Electoral
Studies* 6(3): 263–88.

De Winter, L. (1998). 'Conclusion: A Comparative Analysis of Electoral Office and Policy
Success of Ethnoregionalist Parties'. In *Regionalist Parties in Western Europe*, ed. L. De
Winter and H. Türsan. London: Routledge, 204–43.

—— (2006a). 'In Memoriam, the Volksunie 1954–2001: Death by Overdose of Success'. In
*Autonomist Parties in Europe: Identity Politics and the Revival of the Territorial
Cleavage*, ed. L. De Winter, M. Gómez-Reino, and P. Lynch. Barcelona: Institut de
Ciènces Polítiques i Socials (ICPS), 11–46.

—— (2006b). 'Multilevel Party Competition and Coordination in Belgium'. In *Devolution
and Electoral Politics*, ed. D. Hough and C. Jeffery. Manchester and New York:
Manchester University Press, 76–96.

—— M. Gómez-Reino, and P. Lynch (eds) (2006). *Autonomist Parties in Europe: Identity
Politics and the Revival of the Territorial Cleavage*. Barcelona: Institut de Ciènces
Polítiques i Socials (ICPS).

Deschower, K. (2003). 'Political Parties in Multi-Layered Systems'. *European Urban and
Regional Studies* 10(3): 213–26.

—— (2009). 'The Rise and Fall of the Belgian Regionalist Parties'. *Regional and Federal
Studies* 19(4–5): 559–78.

Downs, A. (1957). *An Economic Theory of Democracy*. New York: Harper & Row.

Downs, W. (1996). 'The Belgian General Election of 1995'. *Electoral Studies* 14(3):
336–41.

Dunn, J. (1974). 'The Revision of the Constitution in Belgium: A Study in the Institution-
alization of Ethnic Conflict'. *The Western Political Quarterly* 27(1): 143–63.

Edwards, A. (2007). 'Social Democracy and Partition: The British Labour Party and
Northern Ireland, 1951–1964'. *Journal of Contemporary History* 42(4): 595–612.

Elias, A. (2009). 'From Protest to Power: Mapping the Ideological Evolution of *Plaid Cymru* and the *Bloque Nacionalista Galego*'. *Regional and Federal Studies* 19(4–5): 533–57.

Erk, J. (2005). 'Sub-State Nationalism and the Left–Right Divide: Critical Junctures in the Formation of Nationalist Labour Movements in Belgium'. *Nations and Nationalism* 11 (4): 551–70.

—— and L. Anderson (2009). 'The Paradox of Federalism: Does Self-Rule Accommodate or Exacerbate Ethnic Divisions?' *Regional and Federal Studies* 19(2): 191–202.

Esman, M. (1977). *Ethnic Conflict in the Western World*. Ithaca: Cornell University Press.

Fabre, E., and E. Martínez-Herrera (2009). 'Statewide Parties and Regional Party Competition: An Analysis of Party Manifestos in the United Kingdom'. In *Territorial Party Politics in Western Europe*, ed. W. Swenden and B. Maddens. New York: Palgrave Macmillan, 229–49.

Falleti, T. (2005). 'A Sequential Theory of Decentralization: Latin American Cases in Comparative Perspective'. *American Political Science Review* 99(3): 327–46.

Falter, R. (1998). 'Belgium's Peculiar Way to Federalism'. In *Nationalism in Belgium: Shifting Identities, 1780–1995*, ed. K. Deprez and L. Vos. London: Macmillan Press, 177–97.

Field, B. (2009a). 'Minority Government and Legislative Politics in a Multilevel State: Spain under Zapatero'. *South European Society & Politics* 14(4): 417–34.

—— (2009b). 'Minority Government and Legislative Politics in Spain, 2004–2008'. Paper presented at the 2009 APSA Annual Meeting, Toronto.

Finlay, R. (2004). 'The Labour Party in Scotland 1888–1945: Pragmatism and Principle'. In *The Scottish Labour Party: History, Institutions and Ideas*, ed. G. Hassan. Edinburgh: Edinburgh University Press, 21–34.

Fitzmaurice, J. (1992). 'The Belgian Election of 1991'. *Electoral Studies* 11(2): 162–5.

—— (2004). 'Belgium Stays "Purple": The 2003 Federal Election'. *West European Politics* 27(1): 146–56.

Fowler, C. (2003). 'Nationalism and the Labour Party in Wales'. *Llafur (Journal of the Welsh People's History Society)* 8(4): 97–105.

—— and R. Jones (2006). 'Can Environmentalism and Nationalism be Reconciled? The Plaid Cymru/Green Party Alliance, 1991–1995'. *Regional and Federal Studies* 16(3): 315–31.

Gerard, E. (1998). 'The Christian Workers' Movement as a Mass Foundation of the Flemish Movement'. In *Nationalism in Belgium: Shifting Identities, 1780–1995*, ed. K. Deprez and L. Vos. London: Macmillan Press, 127–38.

Gillespie, R. (1996). 'The Spanish General Election of 1996'. *Electoral Studies* 15(3): 425–43.

Green-Pedersen, C., and J. Krogstrup (2008). 'Immigration as a Political Issue in Denmark and Sweden'. *European Journal of Political Research* 47: 610–34.

Groppi, T. (2007). 'L'evoluzione della forma di stato in Italia: Uno stato regionale senz' anima?' *Federalismi.it* 4: 1–23.

Harmel, R., and L. Svasand (1997). 'The Influence of New Parties on Old Parties' Platforms'. *Party Politics* 3(3): 315–40.

Hazell, R. (ed.) (2006). *The English Question*. Manchester and New York: Manchester University Press.

Hebbert, M. (1987). 'Regionalism: A Reform Concept and its Application to Spain'. *Environment and Planning C: Government and Policy* 5: 239–50.

Heller, W. (2002). 'Regional Parties and National Politics in Europe: Spain's Estado de las Autonomías, 1993 to 2002'. *Comparative Political Studies* 35(6): 657–85.

Hepburn, E. (2009). 'Introduction: Re-Conceptualizing Sub-State Mobilization'. *Regional and Federal Studies* 19(4–5): 477–99.

Hine, D. (1992). 'The Italian General Election of 1992'. *Electoral Studies* 11(4): 362–7.

Hinich, M., and M. Munger (1997). *Analytical Politics*. Cambridge: Cambridge University Press.

Hooghe, L. (2004). 'Belgium: Hollowing out the Center'. In *Federalism and Territorial Cleavages*, ed. U. Amoretti and N. Bermeo. Baltimore, Md., and London: Johns Hopkins University Press, 55–93.

—— A. Schakel, and G. Marks (2008). 'Appendix A: Profiles of Regional Reform in 42 Countries (1950–2006)'. *Regional and Federal Studies* 18(2–3): 183–258.

Hopkin, J., and P. Van Houten (eds) (2009). 'Decentralization and State-Wide Parties'. *Party Politics*, Special Issue 15(2): 131–253.

Hough, D., and C. Jeffery (2006). 'An Introduction to Multilevel Electoral Competition'. In *Devolution and Electoral Politics*, ed. D. Hough and C. Jeffery. Manchester and New York: Manchester University Press, 2–14.

—— —— (eds) (2006). *Devolution and Electoral Politics*. Manchester and New York: Manchester University Press.

Huber, J. (1989). 'Values and Partisanship in Left–Right Orientations: Measuring Ideology'. *European Journal of Political Research* 17: 599–621.

—— and R. Inglehart (1995). 'Expert Interpretations of Party Space and Party Locations in 42 Societies'. *Party Politics* 1(1): 73–111.

Inglehart, R., and H.-D. Klingemann (1976). 'Party Identification, Ideological Preference and the Left–Right Dimension among Western Mass Publics'. In *Party Identification and Beyond: Representations of Voting and Party Competition*, ed. I. Budge, I. Crewe, and D. Farlie. London and New York: Wiley, 243–76.

Ingram, H. M., and S. R. Smith (1993). *Public Policy for Democracy*. Washington, D.C.: Brookings Institution.

Iversen, T. (1994). 'The Logics of Electoral Politics: Spatial, Directional and Mobilizational Effects'. *Comparative Political Studies* 27(2): 155–89.

Jackson, A. (2003). *Home Rule: An Irish History, 1800–2000*. London: Weidenfeld & Nicolson.

Jagers, J., and S. Walgrave (2007). 'Populism as a Political Communication Style: An Empirical Study of Political Parties' Discourse in Belgium'. *European Journal of Political Research* 46(3): 319–45.

Jeffery, C. (2006). 'Elected Regional Assemblies in England: An Anatomy of Policy Failure'. In *The Northern Veto*, ed. M. Sandford. Manchester and New York: Manchester University Press, 8–25.

Jones, R. W., and R. Scully (2003). '"Coming Home to Labour"? The 2003 Welsh Assembly Election'. *Regional and Federal Studies* 13(3): 125–32.

Kalyvas, S. (1996). *The Rise of Christian Democracy in Europe*. Ithaca and London: Cornell University Press.

Keating, M., and D. Bleiman (1979). *Labour and Scottish Nationalism*. London: Macmillan.

—— and J. Loughlin (1997). *The Political Economy of Regionalism.* London and Portland, Oreg.: Frank Cass.

Kelly, G. (1969). 'Belgium: New Nationalism in an Old World'. *Comparative Politics* 1(3): 343–65.

Kesteloot, C. (1998). 'Growth of the Walloon Movement'. In *Nationalism in Belgium: Shifting Identities, 1780–1995*, ed. K. Deprez and L. Vos. London: Macmillan, 139–52.

Kim, J.-O., and M.-G. Ohn (1992). 'A Theory of Minor-Party Persistence: Election Rules, Social Cleavage, and the Number of Political Parties'. *Social Forces* 70(3): 575–99.

Klingemann, H.-D., R. I. Hofferbert, et al. (1994). *Parties, Policies, and Democracy.* Boulder, Colo.: Westview Press.

—— A. Volkens, et al. (2006). *Mapping Policy Preferences II: Estimates for Parties, Electors and Governments in Eastern Europe, the European Union and the OECD, 1990–2003.* Oxford: Oxford University Press.

Kogan, N. (1975). 'Impact of the New Italian Regional Governments on the Structure of Power within the Parties'. *Comparative Politics* 7(3): 383–406.

Kymlicka, W. (1998). 'Is Federalism an Alternative to Secession?' In *Theories of Secession*, ed. P. Lehning. London: Routledge, 109–48.

Laver, M., K. Benoit, et al. (2003). 'Extracting Policy Positions from Political Texts Using Words as Data'. *American Political Science Review* 97(2): 311–31.

—— and I. Budge (1992). *Party Policy and Coalition Government.* New York: St. Martin's Press.

—— and J. Garry (2000). 'Estimating Policy Positions from Political Texts'. *American Journal of Political Science* 44(3): 619–34.

—— and W. Hunt (1992). *Policy and Party Competition.* New York: Routledge.

León, S. (2006). *The Political Economy of Fiscal Decentralization: Bringing Politics to the Study of Intergovernmental Transfers.* Madrid: Centro de Estudios Avanzados en Ciencias Sociales.

Leonard, D. (1989). 'The Belgian General Election of 13 December 1987'. *Electoral Studies* 8(2): 157–62.

Levi, M., and M. Hechter (1985). 'A Rational Choice Approach to the Rise and Decline of Ethnoregional Political Parties'. In *New Nationalisms of the Developed West*, ed. E. Tiryakian and R. Rogowski. Boston: Allen & Unwin, 128–46.

Levy, C. (ed.) (1996). *Italian Regionalism: History, Identity and Politics.* Oxford and Washington, D.C.: Berg.

Libbrecht, L., B. Maddens, et al. (2009). 'Issue Salience in Regional Party Manifestos in Spain'. *European Journal of Political Research* 48: 58–79.

Lipset, S., and S. Rokkan (1967). 'Cleavage Structures, Party Systems and Voters' Alignments: An Introduction'. In *Party Systems and Voter Alignments: A Cross-National Perspective*, ed. S. Lipset and S. Rokkan. New York: Free Press, 1–64.

Loosemore, J., and V. Hanby (1971). 'The Theoretical Limits of Maximum Distortion: Some Analytic Expressions for Electoral Systems'. *British Journal of Political Science* 1(4): 467–77.

Loughlin, J., and S. Bolgherini (2006). 'Regional Elections in Italy: National Tests or Regional Affirmation?' In *Devolution and Electoral Politics*, ed. D. Hough and C. Jeffery. Manchester and New York: Manchester University Press, 140–57.

Lustick, I. S., D. Miodownik, et al. (2004). 'Secessionism in Multicultural States: Does Sharing Power Prevent or Encourage It?' *American Political Science Review* 98(2): 209–29.

Lynch, P. (2002). 'UK General Election 2001: Scotland'. *Regional and Federal Studies* 12 (1): 193–200.

—— (2009). 'From Social Democracy Back to No Ideology? The Scottish National Party and Ideological Change in a Multi-level Electoral Setting'. *Regional and Federal Studies* 19(4–5): 619–37.

MacMullen, A. (1982). 'The Belgian Election of November 1981: Economic Polarisation in a Multi-party System'. *West European Politics* 25(2): 193–200.

Maddens, B., and L. Libbrecht (2009). 'How Statewide Parties Cope with the Regionalist Issue: The Case of Spain—A Directional Approach'. In *Territorial Party Politics in Western Europe*, ed. W. Swenden and B. Maddens. New York: Palgrave Macmillan, 204–29.

Mair, P. (1990). *The West European Party System*. Oxford and New York: Oxford University Press.

—— and C. Mudde (1998). 'The Party Family and its Study'. *Annual Review of Political Science* 8(1): 211–29.

Maravall, J. M. (1981). *La política de la transición 1975–1980*. Madrid: Taurus.

—— (2008). *La confrontación política*. Madrid: Taurus.

Marks, G., L. Hooghe, et al. (2008). 'Regional Authority in 42 Countries, 1950–2006: A Measure and Five Hypotheses'. *Regional and Federal Studies* 18 (Special Issue: 2–3): 1–307.

Martínez-Herrera, E. (2002). 'From Nation-Building to Building Identification with Political Communities: Consequences of Political Decentralization in Spain, the Basque Country, Catalonia and Galicia, 1978–2001'. *European Journal of Political Research* 41: 421–53.

Massetti, E. (2009). 'Explaining Regionalist Party Positioning in a Multi-Dimensional Ideological Space: A Framework for Analysis'. *Regional and Federal Studies* 19(4–5): 501–31.

Mazzoleni, M. (2009). 'The Saliency of Regionalization in Party Systems'. *Party Politics* 15(2): 199–218.

McAllister, I. (1981). 'Party Organization and Minority Nationalism: A Comparative Study in the United Kingdom'. *European Journal of Political Research* 9: 237–55.

McAllister, L. (2001). *Plaid Cymru: The Emergence of a Political Party*. Bridgend: Seren.

McLean, B. (2004). 'Labour in Scotland since 1945: Myth and Reality'. In *The Scottish Labour Party*, ed. G. Hassan. Edinburgh: Edinburgh University Press, 34–51.

McLean, I. (2001). *Rational Choice and British Politics*. Oxford: Oxford University Press.

—— (2004). 'Scottish Labour and British Politics'. In *The Scottish Labour Party: History, Institutions and Ideas*, ed. G. Hassan. Edinburgh: Edinburgh University Press, 146–60.

Meadwell, H. (2009). 'The Political Dynamics of Secession and Institutional Accommodation'. *Regional and Federal Studies* 19(2): 221–35.

Meguid, B. (2008). *Party Competition between Unequals*. Cambridge: Cambridge University Press.

—— (2009). 'Institutional Change as Strategy: The Role of Decentralization in Party Competition'. Paper presented to the APSA 2009 Toronto Meeting.

Melucci, A., and M. Diani (1992). *Nazioni senza stato: I movimenti etnico-nazionali in Occidente*. Milan: Feltrinelli.

Mettler, S., and J. Soss (2004). 'The Consequences of Public Policy for Democratic Citizenship: Bridging Policy Studies and Mass Politics'. *Perspectives on Politics* 2(1): 55–73.

Mudde, C. (2007). *Populist Radical Right Parties in Europe*. Cambridge: Cambridge University Press.

Müller-Rommel, F. (1994). 'Ethno-Regionalist Parties in Western Europe: Empirical Evidence and Theoretical Considerations'. In *Non-State Wide Parties in Western Europe*, ed. L. De Winter. Barcelona: Institut de Ciencies Politiques i Socials.

—— and G. Pridham (eds) (1991). *Small Parties in Western Europe*. London: Sage.

Newman, S. (1994). 'Ethnoregional Parties: A Comparative Perspective'. *Regional Politics & Policy* 4(2): 28–66.

—— (1996). *Ethnoregional Conflict in Democracies: Mostly Ballots, Rarely Bullets*. Westport, Conn., and London: Greenwood Press.

—— (2000). 'Nationalism in Postindustrial Societies: Why States Still Matter'. *Comparative Politics* 33(1): 21–41.

Núñez-Seixas, X. (2005). 'De la región a la nacionalidad: Los neo-regionalismos en la España de la transición y consolidación democrática'. In *Transiciones de la dictadura a la democracia: Los casos de España y América Latina*, ed. C. H. Waisman. Bilbao: Universidad del País Vasco, 101–40.

Olivesi, C. (1998). 'The Failure of Regionalist Party Formation in Corsica'. In *Regionalist Parties in Western Europe*, ed. L. D. Winter and H. Türsan. London and New York: Routledge, 186–209.

O'Neill, K. (2003). 'Decentralization as an Electoral Strategy'. *Comparative Political Studies* 36(9): 1068–91.

Pallarés, F., and M. Keating (2006). 'Multilevel Electoral Competition: Sub-State Elections and Party Systems in Spain'. In *Devolution and Electoral Politics*, ed. D. Hough and C. Jeffery. Manchester and New York: Manchester University Press, 96–119.

—— J. R. Montero, et al. (1997). 'Non State-Wide Parties in Spain: An Attitudinal Study of Nationalism and Regionalism'. *Publius: The Journal of Federalism* 27(4): 135–69.

Parker, S., and P. Natale (2002). 'Parliamentary Elections in Italy, May 2002'. *Electoral Studies* 21: 649–80.

Petrocik, J. R. (1996). 'Issue Ownership in Presidential Elections, with a 1980 Case Study'. *American Journal of Political Science* 40(3): 825–50.

Pogorelis, R., B. Maddens, et al. (2005). 'Issue Salience in Regional and National Party Manifestos in the UK'. *West European Politics* 28(5): 992–1014.

Preston, P. (ed.) (1984). *Revolution and War in Spain, 1931–1939*. London: Routledge.

Przeworski, A., and J. Sprague (1986). *Paper Stones: A History of Electoral Socialism*. Chicago and London: University of Chicago Press.

Pulzer, P. (1988). 'When Parties Fail: Ethnic Protest in Britain in the 1970s'. In *When Parties Fail: Emerging Alternative Organizations*, ed. K. Lawson and P. Merkl. Princeton: Princeton University Press, 338–64.

Rabinowitz, G., and S. Macdonald (1989). 'A Directional Theory of Issue Voting'. *American Political Science Review* 83: 93–121.

Rae, D. (1971). *The Political Consequences of Electoral Laws*. New Haven and London: Yale University Press.

Rodden, J. (2004). 'Comparative Federalism and Decentralization: On Meaning and Measurement'. *Comparative Politics* 36(4): 481–500.

Roeder, P. (2009). 'Ethnofederalism and the Mismanagement of Conflicting Nationalisms'. *Regional and Federal Studies* 19(2): 191–202.

Rokkan, S., and D. Urwin (1983). *Economy, Territory, Identity*. London and Beverly Hills: Sage.

Roller, E., and P. Van Houten (2003). 'A National Party in a Regional Party System: The PSC-PSOE in Catalonia'. *Regional and Federal Studies* 13: 1–22.

Rudolf, J. (1977). 'Ethnic Sub-States and the Emergent Politics of Tri-Level Interaction in Western Europe'. *The Western Political Quarterly* 30(4): 537–57.

—— and R. Thompson (1985). 'Ethnoterritorial Movements and the Policy Process: Accommodating Nationalist Demands in the Developed World'. *Comparative Politics* 17(3): 291–311.

Ruiz-Rufino, R. (2007). 'Aggregated Threshold Functions or How to Measure the Performance of an Electoral System'. *Electoral Studies* 26: 492–502.

Saey, P., C. Kesteloot, et al. (1998). 'Unequal Economic Development at the Origin of the Federalization Process'. In *Nationalism in Belgium: Shifting Identities, 1780–1995*, ed. K. Deprez and L. Vos. Basingstoke: Macmillan.

Sampedro, V., and F. Seoane (2008). 'The 2008 Spanish General Elections: "Antagonistic Bipolarization" Geared by Presidential Debates, Partisanship, and Media Interests'. *The International Journal of Press/Politics* 13(3): 336–44.

Sartori, G. (1976). *Parties and Party Systems*. London and New York: Cambridge University Press.

Schattschneider, E. E. (1935). *Politics, Pressures and the Tariff: A Study of Free Private Enterprise in Pressure Politics, as Shown in the 1929–1930 Revision of the Tariff*. New York: Prentice-Hall.

Schneider, A. L., and H. M. Ingram (1993). 'Social Construction of Target Populations: Implications for Politics and Policy'. *American Political Science Review* 87(2): 334–47.

—— —— (1997). *Policy Design for Democracy*. Lawrence: University Press of Kansas.

—— —— (2005). *Deserving and Entitled: Social Constructions and Public Policy*. Albany: State University of New York Press.

Sharpe, L. J. (1993). *The Rise of Meso Government in Europe*. London: Sage.

Slapin, J. B., and S.-O. Proksch (2008). 'A Scaling Model for Estimating Time-Series Party Positions from Texts'. *American Journal of Political Science* 52(3): 705–22.

Smith, G. (1991). 'In Search of Small Parties: Problems of Definition, Classification and Significance'. In *Small Parties in Western Europe*, ed. F. Müller-Rommel and G. Pridham. London: Sage, 23–40.

Smith, J. (2006). '"Ever Reliable Friends?" The Conservative Party and Ulster Unionism in the Twentieth Century'. *English Historical Review* 121(490): 70–103.

Sorens, J. (2009). 'The Partisan Logic of Decentralization in Europe'. *Regional and Federal Studies* 19(2): 255–72.

Spotts, F., and T. Wieser (1986). *Italy: A Difficult Democracy. A Survey of Italian Politics*. Cambridge: Cambridge University Press.

Stepan, A. (1999). 'Federalism and Democracy: Beyond the US Model'. *Journal of Democracy* 10(4): 19–34.

Stokes, D. (1963). 'Spatial Models of Party Competition'. *The American Political Science Review* 57(2): 368–77.

Swyngedouw, M. (2004). 'The General Election in Belgium, May 2003'. *Electoral Studies* 23: 545–71.

Taagepera, R., and M. Shugart (1989). *Seats and Votes: The Effects and Determinants of Electoral Systems*. New Haven and London: Yale University Press.

Tambini, D. (2001). *Nationalism in Italian Politics: The Stories of the Northern League, 1980–2000*. London and New York: Routledge.

Tarrow, S. (1974). 'Local Constraints on Regional Reform: A Comparison of Italy and France'. *Comparative Politics* 7(1): 1–36.

Thorlakson, L. (2006). 'Party Systems in Multilevel Contexts'. In *Devolution and Electoral Politics*, ed. D. Hough and C. Jeffery. Manchester and New York: Manchester University Press, 37–54.

Tiryakian, E. (1994). 'Nationalist Movements in Advanced Societies: Some Methodological Reflections'. In *Nationalism in Europe: Past and Present*, ed. J. Beramendi, R. Maíz, and X. Núñez. Santiago de Compostela: Universidad de Santiago de Compostela, 325–51.

Tronconi, F. (2006). 'Ethnic Identity and Party Competition: An Analysis of the Electoral Performance of Ethnoregionalist Parties in Western Europe'. *World Political Science Review* 2(2): 137–63.

Trystan, D. (2002). 'UK General Election 2001: Wales'. *Regional and Federal Studies* 12 (1): 201–6.

Türsan, H. (1998). 'Ethnoregionalist Parties as Ethnic Entrepreneurs'. In *Regionalist Parties in Western Europe*, ed. L. De Winter and H. Türsan. London and New York: Routledge, 17–27.

Tussell, J. (1982). *Las constituyentes de 1931: Unas elecciones de transición*. Madrid: Centro de Investigaciones Sociológicas.

Urwin, D. (1983). 'Harbinger, Fossil or Fleabite? "Regionalism" and the West European Party Mosaic'. In *Western European Party Systems*, ed. H. Daalder and P. Mair. London: Sage, 221–56.

Vallés, J. (1994). 'The Spanish General Election of 1993'. *Electoral Studies* 13(1): 87–91.

Van Atta, S. (2003). 'Regional Nationalist Parties and "New Politics": The Bloque Nacionalista Galego and Plaid Cymru'. *Regional and Federal Studies* 13(2): 30–56.

Van Biezen, I., and J. Hopkin (2006). 'Party Organization in Multi-level Contexts'. In *Devolution and Electoral Politics*, ed. D. Hough and C. Jeffery. Manchester and New York: Manchester University Press, 14–37.

Van der Bruggen, C. (1950). 'Belgium: A Survey of Recent Events'. *International Affairs* 26(3): 339–48.

Van Haute, E., and J. B. Pilet (2006). 'Regionalist Parties in Belgium (VU, RW, FDF): Victims of their Own Success?' *Regional and Federal Studies* 16(3): 297–314.

Van Houten, P. (2000). 'Regional Assertiveness in Western Europe: Political Constraints and the Role of Party Competition'. D.Phil. dissertation, Department of Political Science, University of Chicago.

Verge, T., and O. Barberà (2009). 'Devolution and Party Organization Strategies: The Special Relationships between Statewide Parties and Non Statewide Parties in Spain'. Paper presented at the 5th ECPR General Conference, Postdam.

Verleden, F. (2009). 'Splitting the Difference: The Radical Approach of the Belgian Parties'. In *Territorial Party Politics in Western Europe*, ed. W. Swenden and B. Maddens. New York: Palgrave Macmillan, 145–66.

Volkens, A. (2001). 'Manifesto Coding Instructions'. WZB Discussion Papers FS III(02-201): 1–41.

—— M. McDonald, et al. (eds) (2007). *Mapping Policy Preferences II: Estimates for Parties, Electors and Governments in Central and Eastern Europe, European Union and OECD, 1990–2003*. Oxford: Oxford University Press.

Warner, S., and F. Varese (1996). 'The Italian General Election of 1996'. *Electoral Studies* 15(4): 562–9.

Warwick, P. V. (2002). 'Toward a Common Dimensionality in West European Policy Spaces'. *Party Politics* 8(1): 101–22.

Wauters, B. (2005). 'Divisions within an Ethno-Regional Party: The *Volksunie* in Belgium'. *Regional and Federal Studies* 15(3): 329–52.

Wilson, A. (2009). 'Coalition Formation and Party Systems in the Italian Regions'. *Regional and Federal Studies* 19(1): 57–72.

Index